ENGLISH-PUNJABI DICTIONARY

(In Roman Script)

T. Grahame Bailey

(OVER 7,500 ENGLISH WORDS & PHRASES TRANSLATED INTO PUNJABI IN ROMAN SCRIPT)

ENGLISH-PUNJABI DICTIONARY

(In Roman Script)

T. Grahame Bailey

ISBN : 81-7650-004-6

Edition : 2008

Published by
Star Publications (Pvt.) Ltd.
4/5B Asaf Ali Road,
New Delhi-110002

Printed at : Star Print-o-Bind, New Delhi

PREFACE

Punjabi is the spoken language of a very large population in India and Pakistan. In India, the script used for Punjabi is Gurmukhi, while in Pakistan it is written in Persian script. There are millions of people settled all over the world who speak Punjabi but may not be knowing either of the scripts.

This dictionary is compiled for those who find it more convenient to read and write Punjabi in Roman script. It will be equally helpful to foreigners who are doing studies on Punjabi, but are not acquainted with Gurmukhi or Persian scripts to read the Punjabi language.

June, 1989 Publishers

INTRODUCTION.

THIS book has been issued primarily to meet the need of those Europeans who use Panjabi in their intercourse with the people of the country, and secondarily to enable Panjabis, schoolboys and others, to ascertain the meanings of the commoner English words which they daily come across. No English-Panjabi dictionary at present exists. It did not, however, seem desirable to compile an exhaustive dictionary; that would have been both bulky and expensive. What appeared to be required was a volume, which, while containing a large selection of words likely to be useful, would be small enough to be easily handled, and cheap enough to be within the reach of all. The price has been increased by the war, but it has been kept as low as possible, and no attempt has been made to do more than cover expenses.

The number of English words translated is about 5800, a number sufficiently large for most purposes. The idea of this work was suggested by Col. D. C. Phillott's excellent "English-Hindustani Vocabulary."

Panjabi may be divided into two main dialects, the northern or western, and southern or eastern. The former is spoken west and north of Amritsar and is used throughout in this Vocabulary. It is commonly called northern Panjabi to distinguish it from the southern dialect.

Special Features:—(i) As most of those who use this book will possess the "Panjabi Manual and Grammar" written some years ago by Dr. T. F. Cummings and myself, I have made frequent references to it. In this way it has been possible to refer the student to fuller explanations of words and phrases.

(ii) Nouns: The gender of every noun is given. It is indicated in most cases by m. or f., but when the infinitive or the sign of the genitive (*dā*) is given along with a noun the letters m. and f. are omitted. The endings of the infin. *-ā*, *-ī*, *-e*, *-īā* or the variations of the genitive sign *dā*, *dī*, *de*, *dīā* show the gender. When both m. and f. are used the word may be either masc. or fem., the commoner gender being given first. The addition of "pl." means that the word is nearly always plural.

In Appendix I several pages have been added containing notes on the grammatical portion of the "Panjabi Manual" including a complete conjugation of the verb with pronominal suffixes.

(iii) Verbs: Both trans. and intr. forms are frequently given the latter often correspond to the English passive. Occasionally the causal is added. Irregular past participles are generally mentioned. With one or two exceptions intensive compound verbs (such as *mukā chaḍḍṇā, wēkh laiṇā*) have not been used in the Vocabulary. There are not more than one or two verbs of which it can be asserted that the compound form is always necessary. Another reason is that in most cases several different compound forms are possible; and finally Europeans when they learn a compound form generally employ it to excess. See Compound Verbs, p. 150. See also (iv).

(iv) Construction: A special effort has been made to show the construction of verbs, what prepositions they use, and how the object is expressed. This is a matter of importance as foreigners are often in difficulties about these points. It should be noted that when there is no indication of how to express the object, it is usually the direct accusative with *nū̃*, or it may be without *nū̃*, in which case it is the same as the nominative.

(v) Idioms: Special pains have been taken to include as many idioms as possible. They will be found throughout the Vocabulary.

(vi) Cross references: By means of these much space has been saved. The student should always look up the references even though the connection may not be obvious. A great deal of additional information will in this way be obtained.

(vii) It often happens that words used by Hindus are not used by Muhammadans and vice versâ. Hindu and Muhammadan words have been distinguished. Christians employ the one or the other according to the majority of the people by whom they are surrounded. There are also specifically Christian words, which will be found in their proper places. See also the letters K. and U. in the list of abbreviations.

(viii) Word jingle: This is so usual a feature of Panjabi speech that it has been thought advisable to include the commonest examples: such are *kūnā saihṇā*, speak: *gohā gaṭṭā*, cowdung.

(ix) At the end of Appendix I are notes on the agreement of adjectives, the uses of *calṇā* and *paiṇā*, the formation of the past part. and causal verbs, on verbal roots in *g* and *kh*, and a few hints on common mistakes.

(x) In Appendix II are additions to the Vocabulary.

(xi) Special lists: Names of birds are given under "bird" in the Vocabulary; names of stars under "stars" in Appendix II; weights and measures under "Weights and Measures" in Appendix II.

SPELLING.—The chief difficulties in spelling are due to the existence of different pronunciations and, in the case of words common to Urdu and Panjabi, to doubt as to how far removed from literary Urdu the normal pronunciation of a word is. Some educated speakers, not realising that Panjabi is a language distinct from Urdu, endeavour to assimilate words to their Urdu forms, and thus spoil the pronunciation. The best rule is to follow the pronunciation of those who have a little, but not too much, education. Lest anyone should think that some of the forms in this book are vulgar it may be mentioned that the proofs have been shown to three educated Indian gentlemen whose names are given at the end of this introduction. Two are Hindus and one a Muhammadan. The Muhammadan is a graduate of the Panjab University and a teacher of Panjabi. Of the Hindus one has, for many years, been a school-teacher and has wide experience of teaching Panjabi; the other has taught in school for some years and this year is going up for his B.A. It is not likely that these gentlemen would pass vulgar forms. They did not try to Urduise the spelling, on the contrary in some cases they suggested that my spelling too closely resembled Urdu and advised a change.

An unaccented vowel in Panjabi always tends to become the short neutral vowel heard in the first syllable of the English words "along", "announce", "America", hence *milkiyat*, *shikāyat*, etc. generally become *malkiat*, *shakait* and so on. Frequently this neutral vowel is omitted as in *zindgī*, *bandgī* where we might anticipate *zindagī*, *bandagī*.

Further difficulties arise in connection with the length of vowels, the doubling of consonants at the end of accented syllables (e.g. *ghatnā* or *ghattnā*, *Panjābī* or *Panjābbī*), the omission or insertion of *y* (*dhyān* or *dhiān*) and in a number of other cases. It should also be borne in mind that words with the low tone may often be written in at least two ways without affecting the pronunciation. Thus it is immaterial whether we write *dhigāṇe* or *tighāṇe*, uselessly: *kandhāṛe* or *ghandāṛe*, on one's shoulders: *culhāṇī* or *jhulāṇī*, village kitchen: *panjhāḷ* or *bhanjāḷ*, partner: again *hanerā*, *nherā* and *anherā* are pronounced practically alike. The high tone is not constant and depends partly upon the accent. Thus the word for sahib is pronounced *sāhb* when the accent falls upon it, but when in a compound word it follows the syllable with the accent, it is simply *sāb*, as *lāṭ sāb, miss sāb, mem sāb*. In such cases it is not certain which is the better way to write the word. Occasionally a word is here spelt in two different ways. It will be found that both may be defended. See also next heading.

Pronunciation.—Differences of pronunciation are due to (i) individual idiosyncracy: (ii) difference of degree of education: (iii) difference of district. In a few words *ḷ* or *l* and *n* or *ṇ* are both correct. The commonest are—

melā, meḷā, fair.	*aglā, agḷā*, former.
dil, diḷ, heart.	*pauli, pauḷi*, four-anna bit.
din, diṇ, day.	*hanekeā jāṇā, haṇekeā jāṇā*, get out of order.
waḷgan, walgaṇ, courtyard.	
naṇān, nanāṇ, husband's sister.	*kalpā, kaḷpā*, goatherd's crook.

City dwellers are often unable to distinguish between *ḷ* and *l*.

Explanation of Contractions.—A list of abbreviations is given after the table of contents. Further points are now mentioned: (i) When a word has occurred as a heading, it is referred to within the limits of that one entry by its first letter: e.g. "acquit, *chaḍḍṇā, barī k.*: be a. etc.;" here "be a." means "be acquitted."

(ii) There is a difference between "or" and a comma: thus *zore laiṇā* or *ugrāhṇā* would mean that one may say *zore laiṇā* or *zore ugrāhṇā*, but "*zore laiṇā, ugrāhṇā*" means either *ugrāhṇā* or *zore laiṇā*, but not *zore ugrāhṇā*. The very few cases where to save space this rule has been departed from will not cause confusion.

(iii) A hyphen has sometimes been employed with *k* and *h*. This is to show that the whole is regarded as one verb: e.g. *natthī-k* means that *natthī karnā* is all one verb, and one might have *natthī kītā* or *natthī kīte* or *natthī kītīā* according to the gender of the word with which the past part. agrees. But when we have *pakkī karnī* or *jhī karnī* the past part. must remain fem. and we should have *ohnū pakkī kītī* or *jhī kītī* (not *kītā*).

Students must be prepared to find in use words, genders and constructions differing from those in this work. Only in a few words will difference be observable as regards gender. It is due sometimes to local variations but not infrequently to mistakes on the part of men who have learnt Urdu and use Urdu genders. Certain words common in one district are rare in another, or if used, assume a different form. Only after much inquiry can one venture to say that any particular word is wrong. One must remember that village speech is the real standard in Panjabi.

In conclusion I desire to express my grateful thanks to three Indian gentlemen whose assistance throughout has been of much value to me. They are Lālā Sundar Dās, teacher in the Church of Scotland High School, Gujrāt; Qāzī Muhammad Zafr Alī, B.A., holder of the Govt. Oriental Language Teachership Certificate in Panjabi; and Lālā Dēw Datt, teacher in the Church of Scotland High School, Wazīrābād. I have been fortunate in enlisting the interest of gentlemen so competent and so willing to help.

T Grahame Bailey.

Wazirabad:
March 22, 1919.

TABLE OF CONTENTS

ABBREVIATIONS

A , App. refers to Appendix II, Additions to Vocabulary.
acc., accus., accusative.
adj., adjective.
adv., adverb.
aux. v., auxiliary verb.
bet., between.
caus., causal.
d., *dēṇā*.
educ., used in schools.
f., fem., feminine : f. pl., feminine plural : f. m., feminine or masculine.
fr., from.
G., refers to the last or Grammar section of the "Panjabi Manual and Grammar."
gen., in general, generally.
H., word used by Hindus.
h., *hōṇā* : *-h.*, e.g., *jārī-h.*, see Introduction, Explanation of Contractions, p. vi.
inf., infin., infinitive.
infl., inflec., inflected.
interj., interjection.
int., intransitive.
k , *karnā* : *-k.*, e.g., *natthī-k.*, see Introduction, Explanation of Contractions, p. vi.
K., khansama's language.
leg., legal language.
loc., locative case.
M. (alone), word used by Muhammadans.
M. followed by number refers to the earlier parts of the "Panjabi Manual and Grammar."
m., masculine : m. pl., masculine plural : m. f., masculine or feminine.
metaph., metaphorical.
neg., negative.
obj., object.
obl., oblique.
occ., occasionally.
pa. p., past participle.
pl., plur., plural.
prep., preposition
pres., present.
pron., pronoun.
pronom. suff., pronominal suffix.
rel., relig., religious.
Rom. Cath., Roman Catholic.
sthg., something.
tr., transitive.
U., word or expression borrowed or altered from Urdu, Urduised Panjabi.
v., verb.
verb subst., verb substantive, the same as auxiliary verb.
W., see Weights and Measures in Appendix.

PRONUNCIATION.

CONSONANTS.

b, *g*, *j*, *m*, *n*, *s*, *z* are nearly as in English.

d, *t* are made with the tongue covering the inner side of all the upper teeth, both front and side teeth.

c, *j* are approximately as in English, but the tongue is further forward, and *c* is unaspirated.

The cerebral letters *ḍ*, *ṭ*, *ḷ*, *ṇ*, *ṛ* the tongue strikes or touches the hard palate rather far back.

kh is approximately the *gh* in Irish "lough" or the *ch* in Scotch "loch": *g* is the same sound voiced.

l is nearly as in English "willing."

ñ is like *ñ* in Spanish "señor" or *gn* in Italian and French words, practically the same as *ni* in English "lenient."

ṅ is like *ng* in "singing."

r is made with a single tap of the tongue, like the so-called trilled *r* in Scotland. In genuine Panjabi words it is never found doubled.

w has hitherto been described by all writers (including myself) as a bilabial letter made by the lips without the use of the teeth. It is not bilabial; it is made by the contact of the upper teeth with some part of the lower lip, either where it is visible or lower down, but the contact is so faint that the acoustic effect is quite different from that of English *v*. *f* is the same letter unvoiced.

y is like English *y*, but when doubled tends towards an attenuated *zh*, written phonetically *J*.

h:—(i) *h* is like English *h* when it occurs in *ch*, *kh*, *ph*, *th*, *ṭh*; in the word *āho*, yes; and occasionally in *āhā̃*, no; *oe hoe*, alas or oh; *āe hāe*, alas or oh; *īho*, this very one; *ūho*, that very one; and possibly two or three more words.

(ii) *h* coming after, even though not immediately after, the vowel of an accented syllable is not pronounced, but gives the high-falling tone to the syllable.

(iii) *h* coming before, even though not immediately before, the vowel of an accented syllable, is not pronounced, except when it stands alone, but gives to the syllable the low-rising tone. When the *h* is alone, i.e. without another consonant, it is faintly pronounced as a sonant *h*, and the syllable has the low-rising tone.

Tones.—Panjabi is a tone language like Chinese, but the tones do not play so important a part in speaking. There are four tones :—

(i) level tone found in about 75% of the words. It might also be described as absence of tone.

(ii) high-falling. The syllable is begun about six or seven semitones above the lowest note that the speaker can reach, and falls about two semitones. If no pause follows, the fall is in the following syllable.

(iii) low-rising. The syllable is begun about a tone above the lowest note that the speaker can reach, and rises one or two semitones. If no pause follows, the rise is in the following syllable.

(iv) A combination of low-rising and high-falling, the former always coming first. See "Panjabi Manual," pp. xvii–xix.

The following points connected with consonants are worth remembering :—

(1) The surd letters *c*, *k*, *p*, *t*, *ṭ* must be kept unaspirated (unlike the corresponding English letters which always have slight aspiration). *ch*, *kh*, *ph*, *th*, *ṭh*, are strongly aspirated.

(2) Some letters when occurring undoubled after a vowel are frequently, but not always, changed to certain others. Thus *g* becomes *g̣*; *tag̣ṛā* strong, not *tagṛā*: *kh* becomes *kh̲*, as *ākh̲dā* saying for *ākhdā*: *nj* becomes *ñ*, as *aiñ*, thus, rather than *ainj*: *s* becomes English *h*, as *maĩ tenū̃ dahnā̃ dah paihe ditte hāhū*, I tell you he gave ten pice. This is extremely common in rapid conversation, but Panjabis have not, as a rule, observed it themselves and most of them will not admit that they pronounce in this way. A little careful listening will convince the student that they do.

(3) Foreigners have a strong tendency to allow the letters *r*, *ṛ*, *ḍ*, *ṭ*, *ṇ*, *ḷ* to alter the sound of vowels immediately preceding or following. This must be avoided. They have no effect upon vowels.

Vowels.

ă, *a* are like *u* in "mutton" when stressed, and like *a* in "along" when unstressed.

ā, ī, ū are like Italian *a*, *i*, *u*, and approximately like English *a* in "calm," *ee* in "seen" and *u* in "rule."

ē is between French *é* and *è*, not unlike the Scotch vowel in "lane."

e, **ĕ** are the same but shorter.

ō is approximately like *o* in Scotch "mote," not like the English diphthongal sound. *o* is the same but shorter.

i is like English *i* in "linen."

u is like *u* in pull. Scotch and North Irish speakers should note that it is quite different from *ū* which is like *u* in "rule" or *oo* in "pool."

ai is almost identical with *a* in English "man," i.e. it is longer than the same vowel in "mat." It is far removed from the vowel in "height," "like," "side," etc.

au is not far from *aw* in "shawl." More exactly it begins with the vowel of "shawl" and goes on with the "*o*" in "O'Neill," the two being combined into a diphthong. It is utterly unlike the English diphthong in "how," "mound," "shout," etc. The *au* in *maulwī* is practically the same as that in English "maul."

Nasal vowels are as in French except that nasalisation does not change the vowels.

I have gone more fully into the question of pronunciation in my "Panjabi Phonetic Reader." (See back of Title-page).

ERRATA.

jamhā (*karnā*), add, collect, is preferably *jamhā*, not *jamā*.

likhṇā, write, is *likhṇā*, not *likhṇā* or *likkhṇā*.

To express the idea of drawing or painting (pictures, maps, etc.) the Panjabi tendency is to use *banāṇā*, make, and to reserve *khiccṇā* for photographs, a distinction being made between what is done by hand and what is mechanical.

The short *a* usually written in the following words is better omitted: *barkhlāf*, contrary: *kīmtī*, costly: *banāuṭī*, counterfeit, etc.: *nazāktā*, *nazāktī*, see delicacy, delicate: *dadēhs* and *patēhs*, see father: *saltnat*, kingdom.

p. 153, *wajjṇā*, strike, be struck, normally has past part. *wajjeā* or *wajjā*, but when it means "o'clock" it is *wajeā*: *ikk wajeā e*, it is one o'clock: *trai waje*, at three o'clock.

augur: *for* augur *read* auger.
bean: ,, *bin* ,, *bīn*.
p. 15, quail: ,, *baṭērā* ,, *baṭērā*.
shrike: ,, *laṭōr* ,, *laṭōr*.
bit: ,, *kaṛe āḷā* ,, *kaṛeāḷā*.
bitterly: ,, *rōṇā* ,, *rōṇā*.
blow (1): add *dhapphā*, m., slap.
brain: *omit* "2nd and."
calm: for *kaṛnā* read *karnā*.
careless: add "*see* thoughtless."
conspire: for *pākāṇī* read *pakāṇī*.
coronation: ,, *gaddī* ,, *gaddī*.
cotton: *waṇēwā*, add "or *waṛēwā*, m."
cultivator: *for* leg, *read* lēg.
cupola: ,, *gumbaz* ,, *gumbaz*.
dark, of colour, add "*kālī bhai mārdā e*: see somewhat."
depth: for *ḍuṅghiāī* read *duṅghiāī*.
dislocated: after *talṇā* insert comma.
district: *taihsīl*, add "or *tasīl*."
door: for *bhītt* read *bhitt*.
entrust: for *de peṭe*, *de pāṇā* read *de peṭe pāṇā*.
excitement: for *macnā* read *macnī*.
family: ,, *munde* ,, *munḍe*.
grand-daughter; add "*see* grand-son."
grand-mother: ,, "*see* grand-father."
grave (1): for *khāngāh* read *khāngāh*.

hollow: after *khoḷā* insert comma.
house: for *baṅgḷā* read *baṅglā*.
impress upon: add *jhī karnī* (*nū̃*).
instrument: for *ṛacch* read *racch*.
invite: „ rotī „ roṭī.
kitchen: „ He's „ H.'s.
layer: after *raddā* add " or *radā*."
marry: *duhājū*: I have heard a fem. *duhājaṇ*.
milk: for *bauhlā* read *bauhḷā*.
moustache: „ *daṛhī* „ *dāṛhī*.
passenger: note that *suārī* is fem.
rainbow; for *piṅgh* read *pīṅgh*.
sailor: after *beṛīwāḷā* insert comma.
sauce: for *grēbbī* read *grēbbī*.
shoe: *tehrī*, *cauhdī jutī*: they also say *tehrā*, *cauhdā*, *pair*.
signal: for *hōṇā ḍauṇ h. hatth*, read *hōṇā*, *ḍauṇ h.*: *hatth*.
sponge: for spane read *spanc*.
stair: „ paurī „ *pauṛī*.
stick (1): „ *dāṅg* „ *ḍāṅg*.
tattoo: after *ukkhaṇṇā* insert comma.
test: for *ṭēst* read *ṭēsṭ*.
thread: omit comma after *paṛkatteā*.
tune: for *thīk* read *ṭhīk*.
vaccinate: add *ṭikā ukkhaṇṇā*, see inoculate. tattoo.

English—Panjabi Dictionary

A

a, an, omit or use *ikk*, one : *koī*, some.
abandon, *chaḍḍṇā* : (an idea) *dilō kaḍḍhṇā*, or *bhulāṇā*.
abate, *see* lessen.
ability, *liākat*, f. : *jinnī pujj e*, up to one's : *jinnā sare*, as far as one can financially.
(1) **able,** *laik*, *tagṛā* : able for, *de jogā*, or *jogā* w. inflec. infin., G. 95.
(2) **able, to be,** *saknā*, *kolō* w. tr. passive or int. or inflec. inf., G. 66, 96, 97. 112.
ablution, perform (relig.) *wuzū karnā* (M.), *ashnān karnā* (H.) : *see* wash.
abnormal, *see* strange, wonderful.
abolish, *maukūf k.* : *band k.* : *band karāṇā*.
abominable, *burā*, *ghinaoṇā*, *makrūh*.
abound, *bauht hōṇā* : *see* much.
(1) **about,** *eddhar oddhar* (here and there) : *see* round, approximately, concerning.
(2) **about to do,** verb w. *wāḷā*, *diggaṇwāḷā*, a. to fall : G. 44, 45, 98, 99 : sometimes w. *caleā*, G. 67 : a. to go, come, *ṭureā*, *āyā cāhndā e*, G. 112 : *see* ready.
above, prep., *de utte*, *de te*, *te* : *see* upon : adv., *utte* : *see* up : from a., *uttō* : by way of a., *uttō dī*.
above-mentioned, use *jihdā utte zikar hoeā* or *āyā e*.
abroad, *pardēs*, m., foreign country : *wilait*, f., Europe, America.
abrogate, *see* abolish, cancel, repeal.
abscond, *nass jāṇā*, *bhajj jāṇā*.
absence, *gair-hāzrī*, f. : in my a., *mere picche*, *merī gair hāzrī wicc* : *see* back.
absent, adj., *gair-hāzar*.
absolute, *jihnū sārā ikhtyār e*.
absolutely, *ukkā*, *atte*, *aslō*, *mūḷō*, *bilkul*. A.
abstain (from forbidden food), *thō parhēz* (m.f.) *k.* : (from defiled food), *thō choh karnī* : (give up doing sthg.), *muṛnā*, *chaḍḍṇā*.
abundant, *see* much.
abuse, n , v., *gāḷ* (plur. *gāhḷā*) *kaḍḍhnī* (gen. indecent) ; be abused, *gāḷ lainī*, *khāṇī* ; *gāḷ painī* (*nū*), M. 125. 9 : (very bad) *phakkaṛ tōlṇā* : (very mild) *phiṭak dēṇī* ; be a., *phiṭak lainī*, *khāṇī* : use badly, *see* injure, spoil.
abusive, *gandī zabān-wāḷā*, *baṛīā gāhḷā kaḍḍhaṇwāḷā*, *trakkī hoī zabān-wāḷā*.
acacia (various kinds), *kikkar*, m. : *kikkrī*, f. : *phulāh*, f. : *sharīh* (siris), m.

accent (in language), *laihjā*, m.: (stress), *zōr*, m. (*d*).
accept, *manzūr k.*, *kabūlnā*, *kabūl k.*: *see* agree, assent.
acceptable, use like.
acceptance, *manzūrī*, f.
accident, *hādsā*, m. (U.): use injury.
accidental, *takdīrī*, *itfākī*, *itfāk dā*.
accidentally, *sbabb nāḷ*, *aīwē*, *ēwē*, *takdīr nāḷ*, *itfāk nāḷ*.
accommodation, *gunjaish*, f.: place, *thā̃*, m. f.: *jaghā*, f.
accompany, *de nāḷ jāṇā* or *calnā*.
accomplice, *bhētī*, m., *nāḷ raḷeā hoeā*.
accomplish, *mukānā* (int. *mukknā*): *kar laiṇā*, *kar chaḍḍnā*: *see* finish, complete.
accomplished, *see* learned, able.
accomplishment, *hunar*, m.: *ilm*, m. (knowledge).
according to, *de mūjab*.
accordingly, *so*, *bas pher*.
account (money, etc.), *lēkhā*, m.: *hisāb*, m.: settle a., *hisāb k.* or *mukānā*: to his account, *ohde pete pāṇā*: *see* responsibility: (narration), *bĕān* (m.) *k.*: on no a., *kadī nehī*, *kise tarhā̃ nehī*: on a. of, *see* because of.
account-book (village) *behī*, f.: *wehī*, f.: (gen.) *hisāb dī kitāb*, *f.*, or *pōthī*, f.
accountable, *see* responsible.
accountant, village, *paṭwārī*: his business, *paṭwār*, f.: head a., *gardaur*, *kānū̃go*: his business, *gardaurī*, f.
accumulate, *katthā k.*, *jamā k.*
accurate, *thīk*, *durust*.
accuse, **accusation**, *ilzām lāṇā* (*utte*): *cugḷī khāṇī* or *k.* (*dī*): *bhanḍī karnī* (*dī*): *nindyā karnī* (*dī*): *bhanḍnā* (*nū̃*): *shikait karnī* (*dī*, lit. complaint): *see* slander.
accused, *mulzam*.
accuser, *ilzām lāṇwāḷā*: (in court) *nālish karnwāḷā*.
accustom, v. tr., *haḷāṇā*, *gijhāṇā*.
accustomed, become, *gijjhṇā* (pa. p. *giddhā*, *gijjheā*), *hiḷnā*, both w. inflec. inf. as *ittā ḍhōṇ hiḷeā hoeā e*, or *gijjhā e*, he is a. to transporting bricks: state of being a., *gējh*, f., *hiḷtar*, f.: *see* habit.
ache, *see* pain, hurt.
acid, sour, *khaṭṭā*.
acidity, *khaṭeāī*, f.
acknowledge (saint, prophet, ruler, error, sin) *mannṇā*.
acquaintance (person), *jāṇū̃*, m.f.: *see* information, knowledge.
acquire, *see* obtain.
acquit, *chaḍḍṇā*, *barī k.*: be a., *chaḍḍeā jāṇā*, *barī h.*, *khalāsī hōṇī* (*dī*).
acquittal, *khalāsī*, f.
acre, *ghumā*, m.: *ēkaṛ*, m.: *see* App. weights and meas.
acrobat, *see* tumbler.
across, *-ō pār*, *de pār*, *de parle pāse*: *see* crosswise.
(1) **act**, v., drama, *see* imitate.
(2) **act**, n. (law), *kanūn*, m.: of God, *Khudā dā kamm*.
action, *fēhl*, m.: *kamm*, m: *amal*, m.: *karam*, m.: *see* deed.
active, *kamm karnwāḷā*, *tagṛā*, *cust*.
actual, *aslī*.
actually, *asl wicc*; *saccī muccī* (truly).

acute (severe) *sakht* : (clever) *siānā*, *aklwālā*.
Adam's apple, *ghaṇḍī*, f.
add, *jōṛnā*, *jamā k.*
(1) **address** (residence), *patā*, m. : on letter, *patā*, m. : *sarnāmā*, m. : short, relig. a., *nasīhat*, f. (*k.*) : *see* sermon, lecture, speech. [nī.
(2) **address,** v., *kise nāḷ gall kar-*
adhere (of stamp, etc.) *laggṇā* ; to opinion, *apṇī gall nā chaḍḍṇī* : to someone, *camba-ṛnā* (*nū*).
adherent, *see* follower.
adhesive, *lēslā*.
adieu, *see* farewell.
adjacent, *nāḷ dā*.
adjoin, *see* adjacent.
adjourn, *chaḍḍṇā* (for two days, *dūh diṇā wāste*, etc.) : *see* postpone : (legal), *pher tarīk pai geī e*, another date fixed.
adjure, *see* conjure.
administer, *bandobast karnā* (*dā*), *intizām karnā* (*dā*) : *see* arrange, settle, oath.
admire, *wēkhke khush hōṇā*, *acchā* or *sohṇā laggṇā* (*nū*) : *see* praise.
admit (acknowledge), *mannṇā* : (person) *wāṛnā*, *andar aun d.* : not be admitted, *ḍhoī nā hōnī* or *miḷnī* (women's talk).
admittance, *ḍhoī*, *f.* (*miḷnī*).
admonish, *samjhāṇā*, *nasīhat dēnī* (*nū*) : *see* reprimand.
adopt (boy) *putrēla banāṇā* : (girl) *dhī karke rakkhṇī*.
adopted son, *putrēlā* : daughter, *dhī karke rakkhī hoī* or *pāḷī hoī*. [ship.
adore, no good word, use wor-
adorn, *sajāṇā* (int. *sajjṇā*) : *sajāwat karnī* (*dī*).
adorned, *sajjeā hoeā*.
adult (man) *gabbhrū*, *juān* : (woman) *muṭeār*, *juān* : *see* young.
adulterate, *ohde wicc pāṇī*, *trāmma*, etc., *raḷāṇā* or *pāṇā*, a. w. water, copper, etc. A.
adulterated, *raḷā milā*, *nakhā-khrā nehī*.
adulterer, fornicator, *zanāhī*, *harāmkār*.
adultery, fornication, *zanāh karnā* (*nāḷ*), *burāī karnī* (*nāḷ*), *harāmkārī karnī* (*nāḷ*).
advance, *trakkī karnī*, *agā waddhṇā* : (money) *pēshgī dēṇī* (int. *miḷnī*) : *see* earnest.
advantage, *fāidā*, m. (*uthāṇā*) : *nafā*, m. (*uthāṇā*) : *see* profit, good : a. and disadvantage, *nafā nuksān*, m.
advantageous, *mufīd*, *fāidewālā* : *see* useful.
adversary, *see* enemy : man of other side, *dujjī dhir dā*, *dujje pāse* or *dhaṛe dā*.
adversity, *see* misfortune, poverty. [(*dā*).
advertise-, -ment, *ishtihār dēnā*
advice, advise, *matt*, f. : *salāh*, f. : *nasīhat*, f. : *hidait*, f. : (all w. *dēnī* and *nū*) : *see* consult.
advisable, *cāhīdā* w. inf., G. 67, 96 : *see* necessary, duty, require, have to.
adze, *tēsā*, m.
aeroplane, *jahāz*, m. : *hawāī jahāz*, m.
aesophagus, *shāh rag*, f.
affair, *gall*, f. : *bāt*, f. : *kamm*, m. : *muāmlā*, m.
affection, *see* love, friendship.
affix, *lāṇā* (int. *laggṇā*).
affliction, *see* grief, pain, misfortune.

afford, *dē saknā*, *sarnā* (*nū̃*), M. 248. 6.

affray, *fasād*, m. : *daṅgā fasād*, m.

aforesaid, *see* above-mentioned.

afraid, *see* fear.

afresh, *nawī̃ suannī*, *nawē̃ sireõ* : *see* beginning.

after, *de picche*, *de magar* : from a., *de picchõ*, *de magarõ* : after all, *aksar* : *see* behind, finally.

afterwards, *magarõ*, *picche*, *picche nū̃*, *picchõ*.

afternoon, *pishlā paihr*, m : divisions w. approximate times (which vary with the season) are :—*kaccī pēshī*, 1-0 P.M. ; *pēshī*, 2-0 ; *nikkī dīgar*, 3-0 ; *dīgar* 4 or 5 ; *laudhewelā*, 5 or 6 : in the a., *pishle paihr*, *dīgarī*, *pēshī*, *laudhewēle*, etc. : *see* morning, evening, A.M.

again, *mur*, *phēr*, *watt* ; a second time, *dujje phēre*, *dujjī wārī* : *see* repeatedly.

against, *de khalāf*, *de barkhlāf*.

age, *umar*, f. : present a., *hāl dā zamānā* : past a., *purāṇā z.* : old age, *see* old : of same a., *see* equal : *see* hair.

aged, *buḍḍhā*, *buḍhrā* : *see* old.

agent (advocate, lawyer) *wakīl*, *mukhteār*, *mukhtār* : (land -a., etc.) *gumāshtā* : a. in gen., verb w. ending *-wāḷā*, G. 44, 45, 98, 99, or *-ū*, G. 45.

agitation, be in state of, *taṛapṇā*, *dil taṛapṇā* (or *taṛafṇā*).

agitate, *see* excite, incite, shake.

agitator, *lokā̃ nū̃ bhaṛkāṇwāḷā* or *cukkaṇwāḷā*.

ago, five years ago ; *panjā̃ warheā̃ dī gall e paī*, *panj warhe hoe ne paī* : *see* since.

agree, *mannṇā*. *manzūr k.*, *rāzī h.* : a. w., *itfāk k.* (*nāl*), *see* assent : a. to take, pay money, *karnā*, M. 119. 38 : G. 118.

agreeable, *dil nū̃ caṅgā laggṇā* ; *suādḷā* (tasty).

agreement, *itfāk*, m. : *mēḷ*, m. : written a., *karārnāmā* : written reconciliation, *rāzīnāmā*, m. : *see* settle, covenant.

agriculture, *wāhī*, f. : *khētī*, f. : *khētī bāṛī*, f. : *see* plough.

agriculturist, *zamīndār* : *wāhī karnwāḷā* : (legal) *kāshtkār*.

ague, *kāmbū*, m. : *kāmbū tāp*, m. (both *caṛhnā*, *nū̃*).

ahead, *see* front.

aim, *irādā*, m : *matlab*, m. : *manshā*, f. : a. at target, etc., *nishānā*, m. (*mārnā*) : *see* intention, object, interest.

(1) **air**, *wā*, f. : *hawā*, f. : in the open a., *waule* : airs, give oneself, *nakhre karne* : *nazākatā̃ karnīā̃* : *shēkhī mārnī* : *ākaṛnā* : *see* conceit, show, tune. [*sukṇe pāṇā*.

(2) **air** (clothes, etc.) *sukāṇā*,

airing, go for, *wā bhakhnī*.

alarm, *see* fear, start, startle.

alarming, *ḍaraoṇā*, *ḍarnwāḷā*, *ḍarāṇwāḷā*.

alas ! *hāe hāe*, *āe hāe*, *hoe hoe*, *oe hoe*.

alert, *hushyār*, *cukannā*, *khabardār*.

alight, *laihṇā* (pa. p. *latthā*), *utrnā*.

alike, *ikse kism de*, *ikkojehe*, *āpe icc raḷde ne*.

alienate (person) *apṇe wallõ dil khattā k.* (*kise dā*).

alive, *jiūndā*, *jiūndā jāgdā*.

all, *sabbh*, *sāre*, *sārā*, *sāre de*

sāre: not at all, *ukkā nā*, *atte nā*: nothing at all, *kujjh wī nehī*.
allay, *see* lessen, quench.
alliance, *aihd*, m.: *dōstī*, f.
alligator, *saṅsār*, m.: *magarmacch*, m. (U).
allow, *dēṇā* w. inflec. inf., G. 66: *ijāzat dēṇī* (*dī*).
allowance (food) *rāsan*, m.: *rasad*, m.: food a. in travelling, *bhattā*, m.: travelling a. (money). *safar kharc*, m.: famine a., *mahṅgāī*, f. (pron. *maṅghāī*): *see* famine.
allude, *ishārā kaṛnā* (*ohde wall*, to him): hit at someone, *nōk lāṇī* (*nū*), *see* hit.
almanac, *jantrī*, f.
almond, *badām*, m.; w. thin shell, *kāgzī badām*, m.: colour, *badāmī*.
almost, *karīb*: *see* approximately: a. falling, *ḍigg caleā e*, G. 67.
alms, give alms, *khair*, m. (*pāṇā*, M.), *khairāt*, f. or *kharait*, f. (*d.*, M.), *luṭāṇā*, G. 109: *dāt*, f. (*dēṇī*, M.), *dān*, m. (*d.*, H.): *dānpun*, or *pundān* m. (*d.* or *k.* H.)
aloe, *keoṛā*, m.: soft kind, *kuār gandal*, f.
alone, *kallā*, *chaṛā*, *kall mukallā*, *chaṛā muṛā*, *chaṛā chāṇḍ*, *dam dā dam*: *see* unmarried.
along (road, bank, etc.), locative case repeated; a. bank, *dande dande* or *kaṇḍhe kaṇḍhe*: a. road, *sarke sarke*: a. side, *nāḷ*, *nāḷo nāḷ*
aloud, *uccī*: *see* loudly: ideas hardly distinguished.
alphabet, *allaf bē*, f.
also, *wī*, *bī*: *see* moreover.
alter, *see* change.
altercation, *see* quarrel.
alternate, on a. days, *dujje dujje dihāṛe*, *ikk ikk din chaḍḍke*.
alternately, *wārī wārī*, *wāro waṭṭī*.
alternative, *koī hōr tajwīz* (f.) or *gall* (f.)
although, *bhāwē*, *bhāwē jīkar*, *hālā̃*: conjunct. part. of verb, as *sārī gall wekhke wī nehī muṛeā*, he did not desist a. he had seen the whole thing.
altitude, *see* height.
altogether, *kull*, *sārā*, *sāre dā sārā*: *see* absolutely.
alum, *phaṭkaṛī*. f.
always, *hamēshā*, *hamēsh*, *sadā*, *nitt*: *see* continuously.
amass, *see* collect.
A.M., P.M., use *rāt de*, *shām de*; *din de do waje*, 2 P.M.; M. 61.
amazed, *harān*, *hakkā bakkā*: *see* astonished.
amazement, *harānī*, f.: *see* astonishment.
ambassador, *wakīl*: *ēlcī* (U.).
ambiguous, *shakkī*, *dūh maihneā̃ wāḷī gall*, *gōḷ mōḷ*: *see* obscure.
ambition, no word: use *waḍḍe waḍḍe khyāl karne*, have high thoughts: *waddhaṇ dī baṛī kōshish karnī*, try to increase.
amble (of horse), *rawhāḷ calṇā*.
amend, *see* improve.
amiable, *khushmizāj*, *khushtabīat*.
amicable, *see* friendly.
amidst, *de wicc*, *de wishkār*, *de darmiān*: *see* between.
amiss, take, *burā mannṇā* (*gall nū̃*).
amnesty, *muāfī*, f.: general a., *ām muāfī*.

among, *see* amidst.
amount, n., *rakam*, f.: a. to, *baṇṇā*, *h.*
amputate, *waḍḍhṇā*.
amulet, *tawīt*, m.: *tāwīz*, m. (U.).
amuse, *dil parcāṇā* (int. *parcṇā*): *dil bhulāṇā* (int. *bhullṇā*): *khush k.* (int. *h.*): *mauj karnī*: *bullhe luṭṭne*: *lillī luṭṭṇīā*: *noshe luṭṭne*: *see* delight, charm.
amusement, *tamāshā*, m. (often suggests dancing girls): *mauj mēlā*, m.
amusing, *hasāṇwālī gall*: *see* amuse.
anarchy, *mulkh wicc gaṛbaṛī* (*paiṇī*), *hanēr* (*macṇā*).
ancestors, *pyōdādde*, *waḍḍe*, *waḍēre*, m. pl.
anchor, *laṅgar*, m.: weigh a., *cukkṇā*: let down, *saṭṭṇā*.
ancient, *kadīm*, *muṇḍh kadīm dā*, *purāne zamāne dā*.
and, *te*, *nāḷe*: both this and that, *nāḷe eh te nāḷe oh*, *eh wī te oh wī*.
anecdote, *see* story.
angel, *farishtā*, m.
angle, corner, *nukkar*, f.: *guṭṭh*, f.
anger, *gussā* (*k.* and *h.*): *tā*, m. (heat, *auṇā*): *lāl h.*, *lālo lāl h.*: God's wrath, *kahr*, m.: swallow down one's a., *gussā pī laiṇā*: *see* angry, flare, rage.
angry, *gussā auṇā* or *caṛhnā* (*nū*) M. 117. 3: G. 117: *gusse h.*, *saṛnā*, *balṇā*, *lūsṇā*: *see* annoy, displease, frown. A.
animal, *hawān*, m.: *jānwar* or *janaur*, m. (gen. means bird).
animosity, *see* enmity, envy.
aniseed, *saũf*, f.
ankle, *giṭṭā*, m.
anklet, *kaṛī*, f.: *toṛā*, m. A
anna, *ānnā*, m.: two a., *duānnī*, f.: four a., *paulī*, *paulī*, f., *cuānnī*, f.: eight a., *dhēllī*, f., *athiānnī*, f.: half a., *ṭaga*, m., *adhiānnī*, f.
annihilate, *fanā k.*: *see* exterminate.
announce, *khabar dēṇī*: *itlāh dēṇī*: *see* proclaim, inform.
annoy, *satāṇā*, or *satā mārnā*, *dikk k.*, *ḍicc k.*, *taṅg k.*, *akāṇā*, *chēṛnā*: int. *satnā*, *dikk h.*, *ḍicc h.*, *akkṇā*, also *wiṭarnā*, *kiṛnā*, *ciṛhṇā*: *see* tease, displeased, angry, bore.
annual, *see* year, yearly.
anoint, *lēp karnā* (*tē*): *copaṛnā*, put on oil, *ghi*, butter, etc.: *see* ointment, apply, rub.
anonymous, *gumnām*.
another, *ikk hōr*, *dujjā*.
answer, *juāb*, m. (*d.*): flat refusal, *sukkā juāb*: know the a., *juāb auṇā*, (*nū*), M. 117. 2, G. 117. *see* refusal.
ant, *kīṛī*, f.: whiteants, *syõk*, f. or *simak*, f. (used collectively in sing.).
antagonist, *see* enemy, adversary.
antagonism, *mukhālfat*, f. (*k*): *wair*, m. (*k.*): *dushmanī* (*k.*), 2nd and 3rd mean enmity: *see* enmity, envy.
antelope, *harn*, fem. *harnī*.
antecedents, *paihlā hāl* or *cāl caln*.
antimony, *surmā*, m., *kajjal*, m.
anvil, *airan*, f., *aihran*, f.
anxiety, *waswās*, m.: *fikr*, m.: *andēshā*, m.: *sōc*, f. (thought)

any, anyone, *koī*. [*tarhā*.
anyhow, *ēwē*, *aīwē*, *kiwē*, *kise*
anything, *kujjh*.
anywhere, *kitale*, *kite*.
apart, adv., *nawēklā*, *pasittā*, *alagg*, *ikk pase*, *alaihdā* : *see* separate.
aperient, *see* purgative.
apologise, *muāfī mangnī*. A.
apostle, *rasūl*, m.
apostleship, *rasālat*, f.
apparatus, *samān*, m.
apparent, *zāhr* ; *see* appear, seem, visible.
apparently, *wēkkhan wicc* : of person's professions, *uttō-wālī*, *uttōdī*.
appeal (legal), *apīl*, f. (*k*.) : as interj., *duhāī* : *duhāī Rabb dī*, I a. to God : *see* ask, beseech.
appear, *see* seem, visible.
appearance, *sūrat*, f. : *shakl*, f.: *rang rūp*, m. : *see* form.
appease, *manānā*, *rāzī k*. A.
appetite, no word, use *bhukkh*, f., hunger : *shauk*, m., desire, liking.
apple, *syō*, m. : crab-a., *cōtā*, m. : custard a., *sharīfā*.
applicant, *umēdwār*, *jihdī dar-khāst e*, etc. : *see* beggar.
apply (ointment, varnish, etc.), *lānā* (int. *laggnā*) : *see* anoint, ointment : apply to, use ask, speak to, write to.
appoint (servant) *rakkhnā* : sometimes *lānā*, M. 196. 18 : (*see* servant) : (day) *din mitthnā* : (date) *tarīk* or *tārīkh pānī* (int. *painī*) or *rakkhnī*.
appointment, *naukrī*, f.
apprentice, *shagird*, m.
approach, *nēṛe aunā* : *ḍhukknā* (esp. of marriage procession, or ox to yoke).
approximately, *nēṛe trēṛe*, *nēṛe*, *aṭā saṭā*, *atkal paccū*, *duāle* : *koī*, *ko* and *ku*. as *koī trai*, *trai ku*, about three, G. 87.
apricot, *khurmānnī*, f.
April, *aprail*, m. : *ēpril*, m. : *wasākh*, m. (about Apr. 13 to Mar. 12).
apt to, *see* prone.
arbiter, *tarfain*, m. : *see* mediator.
arch, n., *dāṭ*, f.
arena, *akhāṛā*, m. : *piṛ*, m.
argue, *baihsnā*, *baihs karnī*, *dalīlā chāṇnīā*, *dalīlī laggṇā*, M. 131. 8.
argument, *dalīl*, f. : quibble, *hujjat*, f., *see* quibble.
argumentative, *hujtī*, *baih-sanwālā*, etc. : *see* argue.
arid, *sukkā*, *jitthe pāṇī nehī*.
arise, *utthṇā* : *see* stand, happen, rise.
arithmetic, *hisāb*, m. : (educ.) *riāzī*, f., (mathematics).
arm (whole), *bāh*, f. : fore-a., *wīnī*, f. : upper, *daulā*, m. : *see* biceps ; a. of river, *shākh*, f. : in arms (of child) *kucchaṛ* (m.) *wicc*. : *see* arms, tie. A.
armpit, *kacch*, f.
arms, *hathyār*, m.
army, *fauj*, f. : *lashkar*, m.
around, *see* round.
arouse, *see* wake, incite, excite.
arrange, arrangement, *thīk thāk k*. : *sajānā* (adorn), *sāmbhnā* or *sambhālnā* (look after) : a. about, *āhr karnā*, *āhr pāhr karnā* (*dā*) : *intizām karnā* (*dā*) : *bandobast karnā* (*dā*) : *tajwīz karnī* (*dī*) : make some arrangement or other, *koī bhantrik karnā* : *see* settle : a. to pay, take money, *see* agree.

arrears, *bakāyā*, m.
arrest, *pharnā*.
arrival, *aunā* (come): news of a., *awāī*, f.
arrive, *appaṛnā*, *aunā*, *paũhcṇā*, *ḍhukkṇā* (esp. of marriage procession).
arrow, *tīr*, m.
artery, *nāṛ*, f.: (also vein, sinew).
artful, *calāk*, *hīlebāz*, and words for deceitful.
artifice, *see* trick, deceit.
artificer, *kārīgar*, m.
artificial, *baṇāwṭī* (also of made-up story or excuse).
artillery, *tōpkhānā*, m.
as, adj., *jehā*, *jaisā*: adv. *jīkaṇ*, *jīkar*, *jīkarā*, *jiwẽ*, *jis tarhā̃*, *jiñ* (rare): as if, *jiwẽ*, *goyā*, *jāttā*, *jāno*.
ascend, *caṛhṇā*, *uṭṭā jāṇā* (tr. *cāṛhnā*, *caṛhāṇā*).
ascent, *caṛhāī*, f.
ascertain, *see* discover, investigation.
ashamed, *sharmindā*, *lāzam* (both gen. of actual shame, not shyness): *see* shame, shy.
ashes (from fire) *sāh*, f., *suāh*, f.: (still hot) *bhubbal*, f.: (from decomposition), *see* dust.
aside, *see* apart, aside.
ask (question), *p u c c h ṇ ā*, *pucchṇā gicchṇā*: *suāl karnā* (also make petition): ask for, *mańgṇā*, (*see* beg); ask after health, *see* inquire: *see* beg, beseech.
aslant, *see* slanting.
asleep, *suttā hoeā*; while people are a., *suttī bandī*, G. 78: half a., *jāggo mīṭī*: a. (of limb) *suttā hoeā*, *sunn*: *see* numb, sleepy.
aspire, *see* ambition, desire.
ass, *khōtā*, fem. *khōtī*: *waihtar* m. (any beast of burden): *see* horse, mule.
assafoetida, *hiṅg*, *f*.
assault (leg.), *mār piṭṭ*, f.: *see* attack.
assemble, *katthā k.* (int. *h.*): *jamā k.* (int. *h.*).
assembly, *majlis*, f.: *jalsā*, m. (of large a.): *mandlī*, f. (company): *see* company, meeting.
assent, *hā̃ karnī*, *huṅgārā bharnā*, *mannṇā*.
assert, *zōr nāḷ ākhṇā*, *takīd nāḷ ākhṇā*.
assess (of land), *muāmlā lāṇā*: *see* settlement, tax.
assessment, *muāmlā*, m.
assist, *see* help.
assistant, *madadgār*, m.: Asst. Commissioner, *Ashtant Sāhb*.
associate, n., *see* companion: v., *milṇā julṇā* (*nāḷ*), *wartnā* (*nāḷ*), *wāh paiṇā* (*nāḷ*).
assure, *tsallī duāṇī*, *yakīn duāṇā*: *see* insure.
astonish, *harān k.*: *hakkā bakkā k.*: astonished, be, *harān h.*, *hakkā bakkā h.*: *tajjab k.*, *h.* and *acarj h.* (mildly): *see* wonderful.
astonishment (mild), *tajjab*, m.: (great) *harānī*, f.: interj. of a., *balle balle*, *bāī bāī*.
astray, go, (*rāhõ*) *khunjhṇā* or *ghussṇā*, *kurāhe* or *kurāh paiṇā*: *see* way, seduce.
astrologer, *ramlī*, m.; *naiūmī*, m.: *jōtshī*, m.
asylum (lunatic), *pāgalkhānā*, m.
at, *wicc*: at well, shop, tank, railway station, etc., *te*: for at often use loc., G. 9, 10,

77: at of time, loc. G. 10, 34, 78.
atheist, *daihrīā*.
athlete, *see* wrestler, tumbler.
atone, atonement, *kafārā*, m. (*d.*, *h.*)
attach, *lāṇā* (int. *laggṇā*): *see* file (papers), tie, apply.
attachment, *see* love.
attack, *hamlā*. m. (*k.*, *utte*): of dog, *paiṇā* (*nū̃*), G. 120, M. 125. 8.
attain, *see* obtain, reach.
attempt, *see* try.
attend (to someone), *dhiān karnā* (*de wall*): a. upon, serve, *taihl karnī* (*dī*), *khidmat karnī* (*dī*): *see* serve: a. sick person (of doctor), *ilāj karnā* (*dā*).
attendance (being present), *hāzrī*, f. (*lāṇī*, to enter attendance in book, int. *laggṇī*): *see* call.
attendant, *see* servant.
attention, *dhiān*, m. (also meditation).
attentive, use *dhiān nāḷ*, *dil nāḷ*, *dilō wajhō hōke*.
attribute, *see* quality.
auction, n., *lalāmī*, f.: v., *lalām-k.* (*nū̃*)
audience (people present), *hāzrīn*, m. pl. (U.): *jehṛe hāzir* or *baithe ne*: *jamāt*, f.: *see* congregation, spectator.
audit, *paṛtāḷ k.* (*dī*, rarely *nū̃*).
augur, *warmā*, m.
August, *agast*, m.: *bhādrō*, m. (about 13th Aug. to 12th Sep.).
aunt, father's sister, *phupphī*, *bhūā*: mother's sister, *māssī*: father's elder brother's wife, *tāī*: father's younger brother's wife, *cāccī*: mother's brother's wife, *māmmī*: wife's or husband's aunt, *see* father.
auspicious, *nēk* (M.), *mubārak* (M.): *shubh* (H.), *mahūrat caṅgā* (H.): *see* fortunate.
author, (*kitābā̃*) *likkhaṇwāḷā*.
authorise, *ikhtiār dēṇā*, *mukhtār rakkhṇā* or *baṇāṇā* (*see* advocate): *hukam dēṇā* (order): *ijāzat dēṇī* (permit).
authority, *ikhtiār*, m.: *ijāzat*, f. (permission): *hukam*, m. (order): *hakk*, m. (right): *kadr*, m. f. (value, i.e. who was he to do so and so?): *tākat*, f. (power).
avarice, avaricious, *see* covetous, covetousness.
avenge, *see* revenge.
average, n., *ausat*, *aust*, f.: adj., *wishkārle mēḷ dā*; strike an a., *aust kaḍḍhṇī*: *see* approximately, mediocre.
avert, *ṭāḷṇā*, *rōkṇā*, *rafā dafā k.* (int. *ṭaḷṇā*, *rukkṇā*, *rafā dafā h.*).
avidity, *see* desire, wish, long.
avoid (food, actions), *parhēz* (f. m.) *k.* (*-ō̃*, *te*): avoid meeting someone, *matthe nā laggṇā* (*de*), *neṛe nā jāṇā* (*de*): *see* escape.
avow, *see* admit, confess.
await, *see* wait. [wake.
awake, adj., *jāgdā*: v., *see*
aware, *patā h.* or *laggṇā*, *khabar hōṇī*, *mālūm h.* (all *nū̃*).
away (from home on visit) *wāhndā*: begone! *jā parā̃*, *parā̃ hō*, *dūr hō*, *radd hō*, *dafā hō*; *jā*, *ṭur jā*: (*see* rise): (to dog) *dŭr dŭr*, *dŭre*: (to cat) *chir chir*, *chire*.
awe (person's influence), *rohb*, m.: *see* fear.

awkward, *bhaddā, kōjhā, kuḍhabbā.*

awning (over shop), *chappar*, m. (strictly thatch) : (kind of large tent), *shāmiānā*, m.

axe (large) *kuhāṛā*, m. : (small) *kuhāṛī*, f.

axle, *dhurā*, m.

azure, *asmānī* (*rang*, m.).

B

baby, *baccā*, m. (*kucchaṛ wicc*. in arms).

bachelor, *kuārā* : *chaṛā* (alone).

(1) back, *piṭṭh*, f. : upper b. *kanḍ*, f. : lower, *lakk*, m. (… waist) : b. of shoulders *maur*, m. : *see* spine : b. … book, paper, *pusht*, f. : … hind one's back, … *ō* *kanḍī*, *piṭṭh picche* : *see* absence : (carry) on one's b., *kandhāṛe*, shoulders : at the b. of, *see* behind, after. A.

(2) back, adv. (as send b., go b.), *pa. tāke, partke* : *see* return.

(3) back out of, *phirnā, thiṛnā, pasrnā.*

backbite, *see* tale, slander, accuse.

bad, *burā*, *kharāb*, *mandā*, *bhaiṛā*, *raddī* : rotten, *trakkā hoeā* ; slightly, *musseā hoeā* : go bad, *trakknā*, *see* rot ; slightly, *mussnā* : (of milk) *see* sour : *see* worthless, useless : a bad business, *matthī gall, burī gall, mandī gall* : (of land) *niras, raddī, karlāṭhī* : *see* coin, evil, soil, sin.

badness, *burāī*, *bureāī*, f. : *kharābī*, f. : *see* sin.

badge, *nishān*, m. : (for *caprasi*) *capṛās*, f.

baffle, *see* bewilder.

bag (large) *thailā* : (small) *thailī*, f. : for schoolbooks, *bastā*, m. : *jhōḷī*, chudder or front of shirt used as b. : *see* purse, sack : b. and baggage, *gonḍh gaṭṭhṛī*, *grām gaṭṭhṛī*, f. : *bistrā bōrīā*, m. : *bhānḍā ṭinḍar*, m. : *bā̃ bistar*, m. : (all w. *bannhṇā*, tie up).

baggage, *samān*, m. : *asbāb*, m. : *see* bag and baggage.

bail, *zamānat*, f. (security) : release on b. *zamānat te chaḍḍṇā* ; person going b., *zāman*, m.

bake, *pakāṇā*, *bēk k.* (K).

baker, *roṭīāwāḷā*, or as U *roṭīwāḷā* : village b., *māchī*, fem. *māchan* : *nānwāī*, no fem.

balance, *see* scales : (financial) *bakāyā*, m.

bald, (head b. and face bare) *rōḍḍā* : b. through disease (favus), *ganjā* : *see* hairless.

ball (for play), *khehnū*, m. : *gēnd*, m. : *bāl*, m. : *khiddo*, m. (made of cloth) : bullet, *gōḷī*, f. : cannon-b., *gōḷā*, m.

bamboo, *wanjh*, m. : *bā̃s*, m.

banana, *kēlā*, m. : more often *phaḷī* or *kēle dī phaḷī*, f.

band (music) *wājewāḷe*, m. pl. : *see* company.

bandsman, *wājewāḷā*, m.

bandage, *paṭṭī* f. : (v., *paṭṭī bannhṇī*) : over ointment, etc., *phāh*, m. (*lāṇā*).

bangle, *see* bracelet.

banish, *mulkhō* or *watnō bāhr kaḍḍhṇā.*

banjo, *see* guitar.

bank (of river, lake, etc.) *kanḍhā*, m. : *danḍā*, m. : (for money), *bank*, m. : (actual building) *bank-ghar*, m.

banker (Hindu) *shāh, shāhūkār*: (European) *bankwālā*.
banknote, *nōṭ*, m.
bankrupt, become, *duālā nikḷnā*: he has become b., *ohdā duālā nikḷeā e*: he claims to be b., *oh duālā kaḍḍh baiṭhā e*.
banner, *see* flag.
banquet, *khāṇā*, m.: invite to, *dāwat karnī*: *see* invite.
banyan tree, *bōṛh*. f.
baptise, *baptismā* (m.) *d.* (*nū̃*): be b., *baptismā h.* (*dā*) or *laiṇā*.
bar (for door), *hohṛkā*, m.: *hohṛā*, m.: *arl*, m.: *see* rod.
barbarian, *waihshī, jāṅglī*: original inhabitants of canal districts called *jāṅglī*.
barber, *nāī*, fem. *naiṇ*.
bare, *naṅgā*: barefooted, *naṅgī pairī* (G. 10. 78), *pairā̃ tō̃ wāhṇā*: bareheaded, *naṅge sir*: lay bare, *naṅgā k.*: lay bare thoughts, *thullṇā*: matter, *phōlṇā*.
barely, *see* scarcely.
bargain, *saudā*, m.: good b., *caṅgā saudā*: a b. *i.e.* cheap, *sastā*.
(1) **bark**, v., *bhauṅkṇā*.
(2) **bark**, n., *see* tree.
barley, *jaū*, m.: barley and wheat, *gojī*, f.
barracks, *bārak*, f.
barrel (of gun) *nāḷī*, f.: (cask) *pīpā*, m.
barren (land), *kallar, banjar*: (of tree) *apphal*: (woman) no good word, say *baccī baccā* or *dhī puttar koī nehī*, etc.: *autrī nakhattrī* means either barren or children dead: often as abuse.
barrow, *reṛhī*, f.: *see* cart.
barter, exchange, *waṭāṇā*.
(1) **base**, adj., (low family or ideals) *kamīnā*: (evil) *see* bad, wicked.
(2) **base**, n. (plinth) *kursī*. f.: *see* foundation.
bashful, *see* shy, shyness.
basin, *cilamcī*, f.
bask (in sun) *siyā sēkṇā*: *siye* or *dhuppe baihṇā*: *dhupp sēkṇī*.
basket, *ṭōkrā*, m.: *ṭōkrī*, f.: *caṅer*, f.: for winnowing, *chajj*, m.: for fruit, vegetables, sweets, *chābṛī*, f.: of fruit, vegetables, presented to superior, *ḍāhḷī*. f.: in scales, *chābbā*, m.
bastard, *harām dā*.
bastion, *burj*, m.
(1) **bat** (animal) *cāmcṛikk-* or *-ī*, f.: *cāmciṭṭh*, f.
(2) **bat**, for playing, *ballā*, m.: *baiṭ*, m.: village bat and ball, *khehnū̃ ṭallā*.
bath, n. (the article) *ṭapp*, m.: *see* cistern: Turkish b., *hamām*, m.: *see* boiler, bathe: bathroom, *guslkhānā*, m.
bathe, *nhauṇā* (pa. p. *nhātā*), *gusl karnā*: b. someone else, *nalwhāṇā*, *nuhāṇā*, *gusl dēṇā* (*nū̃*): *see* wash, ablution.
battalion, *baṭālyan*, f.
bawl, *see* scream, shout.
battle, *laṛāī*, f.: *see* war.
bay (of horse) *kumaid, kumait*.
bayonet, n. and v., *saṅgīn mārnī* (*nū̃*).
bazar, *bazār*, m.
be, to, verb subst., am, was, etc., only pres. and past: G. 50, 55, 56: become, *hōṇā*: let it be, *raihṇ dē*: *see* mind.
bead, *maṇkā*, m.
beadle, *caprāsī*, m.

beak, *cunjh*, f. : *cinjh*, f. : *see* peck.

beam, large, *shatīr*, m. : small, *shatīrī*, f. : *ballā*, m. : small cross bit in ceiling, *karī*, f. : *see* log.

bean, *sēm*, f., French, *frās* [*bin*, f.

(1) bear, n., *ricch*, m : fem. *ricchṇī* : sometimes *bhālū*, m.

(2) bear, *see* endure : b. children, *jammṇā* : b. young (cattle) *sūṇā* (int.) : in gen. *baccā dēṇā* : *see* born.

beard, *dāṛhī*, f.

bearded, *dāṛhīwāḷā*, m.

beardless (because too young), *alū̃* : (older person) *khōddā* : gen., *andāṛhīā* : *see* bald, hairless.

bearer (servant), *baihrā*, m.

beast, *hawān*, m. (not much used, if possible name animal) : *jānwar*, *janaur*, m. (nearly always means bird).

beat, *mārnā*, *kuṭṭṇā*, *phaṇḍṇā*, b. w. shoe, stick, blows of fist, etc., *mārnā* w. word for shoe, stick, etc., and *nū̃* of person struck : *see* blow, strike : rush at to strike, *tuṭike paiṇā* (*nū̃*), G. 120, M. 125. 14, *mārn paiṇā* (*nū̃*), G. 120, M. 125. 13 : drum, *wajāṇā* : carpets, *phaṇḍṇā*, *phaṇḍākā mārnā* : whisk eggs, *phēṇṭṇā*.

be beaten, *mār khāṇī*, or passive of *mārnā* or *phaṇḍṇā* ; *khāṇā* w. word for shoe, stick, etc., or these words w. *paiṇā* and *nū̃* of person beaten. [(U.).

beautiful, *sohṇā* : *k͟hūbsūrat*

beauty, *suṇh-ippaṇ*, *-appaṇ*, m.

because, *kyū̃ jo*, *ēs wāste pai*, *ēs karke pai*, *ēs lai pai*, *kyū̃ pai* : *jo* as enclitic, M. 221. 12.

because of, on account of, *de sadkā* : G. 37, 38 : *de sbabb*, *de sbabbō̃* : *dā mārā*, *de mārēā* (last two of intellectual condition), G. 37, 38.

beckon, *hatth nāḷ saddṇā*, *sainat karnī* (*nū̃*) : *see* wink.

become, *hōṇā*, *ho jāṇā* : *see* suit, suitable. [able.

becoming, *see* beautiful, suit-

(1) bed, *manjī*, f. : (large) *palangh*, m. : side-piece, *hī*, f. : end-piece, *sērū*, m. : head, *sarhāndī*, f. : foot, *puāndī*, f. : make b., *wachaunā* or *bistrā wachāṇī* : sometimes *bistrā k.* : bedding, *sōt*, f., *wachauṇā*, m., *bistrā*, m : bedroom, *sauṇā kamrā*, m

(2) bed *see* flower-bed.

bee, *māk͟hyō̃ dī makkhī*, f.

beef, any word for meat w. *waḍḍā*, big, or *gōkā*, cow's, or *gā̃ dā*, cow's, prefixed : also *bīf*, m. (K.).

beer, *bīr sharāb*, m. (K.).

beetle for levelling road, *durmaṭ*, m. : *damūsā*, m.

beetroot, *cakundar*, m.

before, adv. of time (both previously and in future), *agge*, *agge nū̃* : (previously only), *paihlā̃*, *paihle*, *paihlū̃*, *paihle nū̃*, *agētre*, *agdū̃* : adv. of place, *agge*, *sāhmṇe* : forward, *agā̃* : from before, from in front of, *aggō̃*, *sāhmṇeō̃* : by way of in front, *aggō̃ dī*, *sāhmṇeō̃ dī*.

prep., *de agge*, *de sāhmṇe* : one in front of the other, *agge picche*, *aggaṛ picchaṛ* : *see* front, face :

conj., inflec. inf. w. *tō̃* or *thō̃* or *thī* or *-ō̃* followed by *agdū̃* or *paihlū̃* : G. 95.

befriend, *see* help.
beg, ***mangnā***, ***suāl karnā*** : *see* ask, beseech.
beggar, *manganwālā*, ***suālī***, ***mangtā***, *fakīr*, fem. *fakīrnī*.
beggary, *see* poverty.
begin, *laggnā* (pa. p. *lagā*, when unemphatic, and *laggā* when stressed) w. inflect. inf. : *shurū k.* (w. inf. agreeing w object) : to begin w., *paund satte*. [*lagā*.
beginner, *aje hune sikkhan*
beginning, *shurū*, m. : from the b., *mundhō* : from b. to end, *alfō laike yē tōṛī* : *mundhō laike akhīr tōṛī*.
begone, *see* away.
behalf, on my, etc., ***mēre wallō*** from me : ***mērī khātar***, for my sake : ***mēre laī***, ***mēre wāste***, for me : *see* for.
behaviour, *see* character.
behead, *sir waddhnā* (*dā*).
behind, adv., *picche*, *pichēre*, *pishēre* : *see* afterwards : towards behind, *pishā* : from b., *picchō*, *pichēreō*, *pishēreō*, prep., *de picche*, *de magar* : sheltered b. or hidden b., *de ohle* : pass b., *picchō dī* or *magarō dī langhnā* : *see* after, before.
belie, *jhūṭhā k.* or *banānā*.
believe (a fact) ***mannnā***, ***yakīn k.*** or *h.* or *aunā* (M. 153. 30, 31) : b. in (God, Christ, etc.) *imān leaunā* (*utte*), M. 154. 33-6, 155 : *see* faith, trust, confide, reliance.
bell, large, *ghaintā*, m., *tall*, m. : gong, *ghaṛeāl*, m. : iron bar, *ghaintī*, f. : bicycle, dinner bell, *tallī*, f. : tongue of b., *dur*, m. : ring b., strike gong, *wajāṇā* : (*tallī*) *chankāṇī*, *wajāṇī*, int. *chaṇakṇī*, *wajjṇī* : tiny bells on hands, feet, neck of horses, etc., *ghunghrū*, m. (*chaṇakṇā*).
belly, *see* stomach.
beloved, *pyārā* : *see* lover.
below, adv., *hēṭh*, *hēṭhā*, *thalle*, *hēṭhle pāse* : downwards, same words : from b., *hēṭhō*, *thalleō* : prep. *de hēṭh*, etc. same words : pass b., *hēṭhō dī*. *hēṭh dū*, *thalleō dī*, all w. *langhnā*.
belt, *pēṭī*, f. : *bilṭ*, m. (*k*) : *see* badge.
bench, *banc*, f. : *see* seat, chair.
bend, *lafāṇā* : be bent, *lifṇā* : b. head, *sir jhukāṇā* : *see* crooked, stoop.
beneath, *see* below.
benediction, *barkat dā kalmā* (pronounce, *suṇāṇā*) : *see* blessing. [(kind).
benefactor, *murabbī*, *mehrbān*
beneficial, *see* advantageous.
(1) **benefit**, v. tr., *fāidā*, m. (*karnā*): int. *fāidā h.* (*dā*) : arrogantly claim to have benefited someone, *ahsān* (pron. *as-hān*) or *ṭhāhrā cāṛhnā* (*utte*) : admit being benefited, *ahsān* or *ṭhāhrā mannṇā* (*dā*) : *see* obligation.
(2) **benefit**, n., *fāidā*, m. : *ahsān* m. (kindness) : *see* profit.
benumbed, *see* numb.
bequeath, *wasīat karke d.* : *wasīatnāme wicc d.*
beseech, *tarle karne*, *tarlā karnā*, *minṭā karnīā*, *minṭ tarlā k.*, *minṭ mājrā karnā* (all w. gen.) ; *hatth bannhke arz karnī* (*de agge*) : *see* ask.
(1) **beside**, *see* near.
(2) **besides**, *ehnū chaḍḍke*, *ehde suā* : *see* without.

besiege, *ghernā*, *muhāsrā karnā* (*dā*). [*laggṇī*.
bet, *shart*, f.: v., *lāṇī*: int.
best, *sārēā tō* or *sārēā wiccō caṅgā*: best man, *sarbāhlā*, m.
betel-leaf, *pān*, m.:—nut, *sipārī*, f.
between, *wishkār*, *de darmiān*: *see* through: go-between, *see* mediator.
bewilder, v. tr., *ghabrāṇā*: be b. *ghābbarnā*.
bewitch, *see* charm.
beyond, adv., *pare*, *parle pāse*, *pār*: towards b., *parā*: prep., *de pare*, *de parle pāse*, *de pār*.
Bible, *baibal*, f.: ***Khudā dī*** (*dā*) *kalām*, or ***dī kitāb***, f.: *see* Testament.
bhang, *bhaṅg*, f.: *cars*, f. (a preparation of b.): man who uses b., *bhaṅgī*.
bias, *see* partiality.
biceps, triceps, *ḍauḷe dā paṭṭhā*, m.
bicycle, *baiskal*, m.: among children, *aṅgrēzī ghōṛā*, m.
bid (at auction), *bōlī dēṇī*.
big (age, size) *waḍḍā*, G. 34: *see* great; so b., *ēḍḍā*, *ōḍḍā*: how b., *kēḍḍā*: as b., *jēḍḍā*: as b as I, *mēre jēḍḍā*: G. 91, 92.
bigoted, *tassabī*.
bigotry, *tassab*, m.
bill (of exchange), *hunḍī*, f.: *see* cheque, beak.
bind, *see* tie: b. books, *jild bannhṇī* (int. *bajjhṇī*).
binoculars, *dūrbīn*, f.
bird, *jānwar*, m.: *janaur*, m.: *painchī*, f.: *pakhērū*. m.: small, *ciṛī*, masc. *ciṛā* (esp. sparrow): *see* fledgling.

LIST OF COMMON BIRDS.

Great confusion exists in the nomenclature, and Panjabis are certain of none but the best-known.

babbler (seven sisters) *sehṛ*, f.
bee-eater, *harī ciṛī*, f.
bulbul, *bulbul*, f.
cock, *kukkaṛ*, m.
crane, *kūnj*, f.
crow, *kā*, m.
crow, jungle, Indian corby, *pahāṛī kā*.
cuckoo, pied crested, *bambīyā*, m.
dabchick, *ḍubkū*, m.; *jalkukkaṛ*, m.
dove, ring-, *ghuggī*, f.
dove, little brown and red turtle, *totrū*, m.
duck, *batakh*, f., masc. *batkhī*.
duck, wild, *mugrāī*, *murgābī*, f.
duck, Brahminy, *nikkā maggh* or *maṅgh*, m.
eagle, *bāz*, *ukāb*, m.: often *ill*, f.
falcon (lugger), *lagaṛ* (often used for tawny eagle)
flamingo, *lamḍhīng*, f.
goose, *batakh*, f.: rare, *hans*, m.: wild g., *maggh*, *maṅgh*.
goshawk, *bāz*, f.
grebe, *see* dabchick.
grouse, *bhaṭittar*.
hen, *kukkṛī*, f.
heron, pond, *baglā*, m.
heron, grey, *waḍḍā baglā*, *naṛī*, f.
hoopoe, *cakkī rāh*, m.
ibis, black, *bōjā*, m.
jay, *see* roller
kestrel, *cūhe mār*, m.
king-crow, *lāṭ*, f.: *kāḷ kṛiccī*, f.: *kāḷ kḷiccī*, f.

king-fisher, ***macchī mār***, m.
kite, *ill*, f.
koel, *koēl*, f.: ***kōl***, f.
lapwing, ***ṭaṭauḷī***, f.
lark, ***candōl***, m.
merlin, ***turmtī***, f.: ***turmcī***, f.
minivet, ***lāl***, m.: ***surkh***, m.
myna, common, ***lāllī***, f.: ***lālṛī***, f.
myna, bank, ***shārk***, f.
nightjar, ***cabākhī***, f.
owl, ***ullū***. [f.
owlet, ***bilbatauṛī***, f.: ***cabākhī***,
paddy bird, *see* pond heron.
parrot (rose-ringed paroquet), ***tōttā***, m.
parrot (large Indian paroquet), ***rā tōttā***, m.
partridge, ***tittar***, m.: ***bhaṭittar***, m.
peacock, ***mōr***, fem. ***mornī***.
pigeon, ***kabūt-ar***, m., fem. ***-rī***.
pigeon, hybrid (tame), ***khumrī***, f.: ***kumrī***, f.
pipit, same as lark.
quail, ***batērā***, m.
raven, ***ḍhoḍḍar kā***, m., ***ḍhoḍdrī***, f.
redstart, same as robin.
robin, and any bird like it, ***piddī***.
roller, ***lalāran***, f.: ***garaṛ pōpō***, m., ***garaṛ***, m.
sandpiper, ***kakauā***, m.
shikra, ***shikrā***, m.
shrike, bay-backed and rufous-backed, ***syōṇ ciṛī***, f. ***sōṇ ciṛī***.
shrike, grey, ***latōr***, f.
sparrow, ***ciṛī ghar dī ciṛī***, f.: masc., ***ciṛā***.
starling, common Indian, ***tilyar***, m.
starling, rose-coloured, ***gulābī tilyar***.
stork, ***lamḍhīṅg***, f.
swallow, ***abābīl*** f.
swift, ***abābīl***, f.
tern, ***jhiūrī***, f.: wrongly ***taṭauḷī***, f.
tree-pie, often ***bambīyā***, m.
turkey, ***pērū***, m.
vulture, any large v., ***girjh***, f.
vulture, Egyptian (larger white scavenger), ***ganjā***, m.: sometimes ***baggī ill***, f.: or simply ***nikkī girjh***, f.
wagtail, ***mamōlā***, m.
warbler, particularly ashy wren w., ***camūṇā***, m.: ***timmā***, m.
woodpecker, golden backed, or any large w. ***ṭōkkā***, m.: ***tarkhāṇ***, m.
woodpecker, pied, ***nikkā ṭōkkā***; ***nikkā tarkhāṇ***.

birth, *jamm*, m.: ***paidāish***, f.: when was she (he) born, ***oh kadō dī (dā) jamm e?***: *see* bear, born.
birthday, ***janam din***, m.
biscuit, ***biskuṭ***, m.: very thin, ***tunkī***, f.: Indian, ***khatāī***, f.
bit, *see* piece, mouthful: horse's, ***kaṛe ālā***, m: *see* bridle.
bite, ***waḍḍhṇā***, ***waḍḍh khāṇā***: ***danḍiā waḍḍhṇā***: of horse, ***cak mārnā*** (all ***nū***): of rats, mice, ***ṭukkṇā***, ***kutarnā***: *see* gnaw, attack (dog).
bitter, ***kauṛā***: of person, ***kauṛā***, ***saṛeā baḷeā***: *see* annoy: of mind, ***khaṭṭā***: *see* embitter.
bitterly, ***saṛke***: weep b., ***uccī uccī***, loudly, or ***bauht***, very much, &c., ***rōṇā***.
black, ***kālā***: *see* jet-black.
blackness, ***kālakh***, f. (especially from soot, smoke).
blackguard, ***badmāsh***, ***sharīr***, immoral, ***luccā***.

blacking, for boots, *syāhī*, f. *see* polish.
blacksmith, *luhār*, fem. *luhārī*.
blade, of knife, etc., *phal*, m.
bladder, *bhakānnā*, m.
blame, *ilzām lāṇā*, (*utte*): *pēṭe gall pāṇī* (*de*): *see* reprimand, accuse, sit upon.
blameless, *bēkasūr*, *bēgunāh*: *see* sinless, innocent.
blank (paper), *kōrā*: *see* unused.
blanket, *kambal*, m.: *jhull*, f.: *loī*, f. (fine): *bhūrā*, m. (esp. for horses, cattle): *see* quilt, sheet, shawl.
blaspheme, blasphemy, *kufar*, m.: (*bakṇā*, *bōlṇā*).
blasphemer, *kāfar*, M.: *kufr bakaṇwālā*: *see* atheist, unbeliever.
blaze up, *bhakhṇā*, *bhakh paiṇā*: *see* burn, heat.
bleat, of sheep, goats, *maīkṇā*.
blemish, *nuks*, m.: *dāg*, m. (spot, stain): *aib*, m.
bless, blessing, God to man *barkat dēṇī*: *asīs dēṇī* (H.): man God, *see* praise: man man, *duā dēṇī*: see benediction, curse.
blessed, *mubārak*, *dhann*.
blind, *annhā*: (title by courtesy), *hāfaj* (for *hāfiz*,: *see* Quran): of one eye, *kāṇā*: *see* see.
blindly, *annhe wā* or *wāh*.
blindness, at night, *artānnā*, m. *andhrātā*, m.
blister, *chāllā*, m. (*paiṇā*): *see* water.
blood, *ratt*, f.: *khūn*, m.: *lahū*, m.
bloody, *ratt nāl bhareā hoeā*.
blossom, n., *kalī*, f.: *phull*, m. v.: *see* flower.
blot, *dāg*, m.: moral, *dhabbā* m.: *see* disgrace, delete.
blotting paper, *syāhīcaṭ*, m., *blāṭiṅ*, f.
(1) **blow**, n., *saṭṭ* (*laggṇī*, *wajjṇī*: tr., *lāṇī*, *mārnī*): *see* wound: b. w. fist, *hūrā*, m., *ghasunn*, m., *gubbh*, f.: slap, *capēṛ*, f.: w. stick, *hujj*, f. (*see* prod), or *sōṭī* f.: w. shoe, *chittar*, m., *juttī*, f.: verb for all, *wajjṇā*. *khāṇā*, *paiṇā*; tr. *mārnā*: *see* beat: come to blows, *hatthī paiṇā*: struggled w. me, tried to strike me, *mērī hatthī peā*: G. 120, M. 125. 7.
(2) **blow**, v., *phūk mārnī*: trumpet, bugle, &c., *wajāṇā*: of wind, *wagṇā*: b away (of wind), *udāṇā*.
blue, light, *asmānī* (*raṅg*): darker, *līllā*, *nīllā*: very dark, *kālā*.
blunt, *khuṇḍhā*.
boar, same as pig: wild, *bēlle dā*.
board, large, *phaṭṭā*, m.: *takhtā*, m.: small, *phaṭṭī*, f., *takhtī*, f.
boast, *phaṛā mārnīā*: *baṛīā gallā karnīā*: *shēkhī mārnī*.
boat, *kishtī*, f., *bēṛī*, f.: *bēṛā*, m. (esp. raft).
boatman, *mallāh*, m.: *mānjhī* (Hindu caste).
body, *piṇḍā*, m.: *jussā*, m.: *wujūd*, m.: *jism*, m.: *badan*, m.: *sarīr*, *sharīr*, m.: one's form, outline, *but*, m.: *see* corpse, carcase.
(1) **boil**, n., *phōṛā*, m.: small. *phimhṇī*, f.: *gaṛ*, m.: in armpit, *kachrāḷī*, f.
(2) **boil**, v. tr, *kāṛhnā*, *khulāṇā*, *ubālṇā* (make bubble): (int. *kaṛhnā*. *khaulṇā*, *ubbalṇā*):

cook, *rinnhṇā* (pa. p. *riddhā*) (also stew : int. *rijjhṇā*).
(3) boiled, *kaṛheā hoeā*, *riddhā hoeā*.
(4) boiler, for heating water, *hamām*, m.
(5) boiling, *khauldā*.
bold, *see* brave, forward.
boldness, including forwardness, *jurat*, f. : *dalēri*, f.
bolt, n., *ciṭkhanī*, f. : screw-b., *kāblā*, m. : v., *ciṭkhanī mārnī* or *lāṇī* (int. *wajjṇī*, *laggṇī*).
bomb, *bamb*, m.
bond, *karār*, m. : *likhat paṛht*, f. : *see* agreement, covenant.
bondage, *see* slavery, imprison.
bone, *haḍḍī*, f.
(1) book, *kitāb*, f. : *pōthī*, f. (esp. relig. H.) : note-b., copy-b., *kāpī*, f. : b.-language, *kitābī bōlī* : *see* account [f.
bookcase, (*kitābā̃ wālī*) *almārī*,
bookseller, *kitābā̃ wēccaṇwālā*, *kutub-farōsh* (U.).
(2) book, v., ticket, *ṭikaṭ laiṇā* : seat, *thā̃ rakhāṇā* : b.-ing office, *ṭikṭā̃ dā daftar* : b.-ing clerk, *ṭikṭā̃ wālā bābū* : b. luggage, *asbāb tulāṇā* (have weighed), *buk karāṇā*
boot, *see* shoe.
booty, *luṭṭ dā māl*, m.
border, *see* boundary, edge, skirt.
bore, *mōrī kaḍḍhṇī* or *karnī* : *chēk kaḍḍhṇā* : (worry) *akāṇā*, (int. *akkṇā*) ; *sir khapāṇā* : *see* annoy.
borer, *see* auger.
born, be, *jammṇā*, *paidā h.* : b. (blind), *jamāhndrū* (*annhā*).
borrow, *udhār laiṇā* (money) *karz cukkṇā* (money) : *mang leauṇā* (gen.).
borrowed, *udhār*, *udhārā* (money) : *māngwā̃* (gen.).
both, *dowē̃* : *see* also.
bottle, *bōtal*, f. : small, *shīshī*, f.
bottom, of vessel, box, almirah, *thallā*, m. : *see* foot.
boundary, *hadd*, f. : narrow, bet. fields, *bannā*, m., *bannī*, f., *waṭṭ*, f., *see* path : b. pillar, *buttī*, f. ; bet. three villages, *tarhaḍḍā*.
boundless, *bēant*, *bēbahā*.
(1) bow, for arrows, *kamān*, f. : b. and arrow, *tīr kamān*, f. : for pellets, *gulēl*, f. : *see* sling, pellet.
(2) bow, v., *matthā ṭēkṇā* (esp. relig.), *see* salute, stoop.
bowels, *āndrā̃*, f. pl.
(1) bowl, n., *pyālā*, m. : *bōl*, m. (K.).
(2) bowl, v., (cricket) *bāl dēṇā*.
box, *sandūk*, m. : *sandūkṛī*, f. : *bakas*, m. : *pēṭī*, f. (esp. wooden) : rough wooden, *khōkhā*, m. : steel, *ṭarank*, m. : very small, *ḍabbī*, f. : for measuring *kankar*, lime, etc., large, *sandūkṛī*, f. : small, *ḍaggā*, m.
boy, *munḍā*, *kākkā*, *jātak* : *see* child, son.
boyishness, *munḍpuṇā*, m. : *munḍeā̃-* or *añāṇeā̃-wālī tabīat*, f.
bracelet, *cūṛī*, f. : *cūṛā*, m. : *waṅṅ*, f. : *gajrā*, m. : *kaṅṅan*, m. : *gokhṛū*, m. : *parībaṅ*, m. : *paunci*, f., *juṭ*, m. A.
braces, *gālas*, f.
brackish, *kauṛā*, *khārā*.
brain, *bhējā*, m. : *magz*, m. : *damāg*, m. : (2nd and 3rd gen. of conceit) : *see* sense, intelligence, conceit, pride.
brake-van, *birk*, m. *brēk*, m.

bran, *cōkar*, m. (wheat and gram): *chāṇ*, m.: *see* straw.
branch, large, *ḍāhn*, m.: *ḍāhl*, m.: smaller, *ṭāhṇī*, f.: *ḍāhlī*, f.: small switch, broken off, *chamak*, f.: shoot, *gullā*, m.: thorn b., *mōṛhā*, m.: *mōṛhī*, f.: *ḍhīnghṛī*, f.
brand, *dāg*, (*lāṇā*): morally *dhabbā*, (*lāṇā*): int. *laggṇā*.
brandy, *brāndī*, f.
brass, *pittal*, m.: b. worker, *ṭhaṭhyār*. [age.
brave, *bahādar*, *dalēr*: *see* cour-
bravo! *sadke*, *balle balle*, *shābāse*, *shāhbā*, *bāī bāī*.
bray, of ass, *hīṅgṇā*.
bread, *rōṭī*, f.: made of maize, millet, *ḍhōḍḍā*, m.: *see* loaf, food.
breadth, *pēṭ*, m.: *cuṛāī*, f.
break, *bhannṇā* (int. *bhajjṇā*): *tōṛnā*, *trōṛnā* (int. *ṭuṭṭṇā*): b. into bits, *ṭōṭe ṭōṭe k.*: b. against, *see* knock: b. open (box, etc.), *jandrā trōṛnā*: b. down (become ill) of well, cart, man, animal (not woman), *hanēkeā jāṇā*, M. 118. 32: into house, *sannh mārnī*: b. fast, at right time, *rōzā kholhṇā*: at wrong time, *see* fast: b. in for ploughing, *hālī kaḍḍhṇā* (*nū*): for burdens, *lādū kaḍḍhṇā* (*nū*) (int. of both *nikḷṇā*): b. off habit, *ādat chaḍḍṇī* (for someone else, *chuḍāṇī*).
breakfast, *hāzrī*, f.: early b., *chōṭī hāzrī*.
breast, *hikk*, f.: *chāṭī*, f. (U.):
breath, breathe, *sāh*, m. (*laiṇā*, also stop talking): *dam laiṇā*: *see* rest: out of b. become, *haff jāṇā*, *sāh caṛhṇā* (*nū*).
bribe, *waḍḍhī*, f.: take b., *laiṇī*, *khāṇī*: give b., *dēṇī*: *rishwat*, f.: taker of b's *waḍḍhīkhōr*, *rishwatkhōr* (U.).
brick, *iṭṭ*, f.: well-baked, *pakkī*: half-baked, *pillī*: sun-dried, *kaccī*: broken bit, *rōṛā*, m.; small, *rōṛī*, f.: b-powder, *surkhī*, f.: b-maker, *pathērā*, m.: b-making, *pathēr*, f.: b-layer, *rāj*, m.: *see* layer.
bride, use *kuṛī*, girl. A. [man.
bridegroom, *lāṛā*, m.: *see* best
bridge, *pul*, m.: make b., *pul bannhṇā*: (int. *bajjhṇā*).
bridle, *lagām*, f. (*cāṛhnī*).
brief, *mukhtsar*, *thoṛeā lafzā wicc*.
bright, *baṛī lō*, *baṛā cānan* or *cānnā*, *baṛī rōshnī*: *see* shine: colour, *gūṛhā*, *shōkh*, *tēz*.
brim, *kandhā*, m.: of hat, *kannī*, f.: *see* edge.
bring, *leauṇā*, *laiāuṇā*: pa. p. *le-*, *lai-āndā* or *-āyā*: take w. one, *khaṛnā*: b. near of cattle to yoke, *ḍhōṇā* (int. *ḍhukkṇā*): cause to be brought, *anwāṇā*.
brinjal, *see* egg-plant.
brink, *see* edge.
brittle, *ṭuṭṭanwāḷā*: *see* crisp.
broad, *cauṛā*, *caiṛā*: broadways, across, *cauṛe dā*.
broad-cloth, *banāt*, f.
broker, *dalāl*.
bronze, *kaīh*, f. [*nadī*, f.
brook, *nāḷā*, m. (wet or dry):
broom, *jhāṛū*, m.: *bauhkar*, f.: *bahārī*, f.: *kharkṇā*, m.: *mānjā*, m.: *see* sweep.
broth, *shurūā*, m.
brother, *bhrā*, *bhāī*: full b., *sakkā bhrā*: step b., *matrēā bhrā*: wife's b., *sāḷā*: *sāḷā's*

wife, *sāḷihār*, *sāḷihāj*: sister's husband, *bhanūjā*: husband's elder b., *jēṭh* (*jēṭh's* wife, *jaṭhāṇī*): husband's younger b., *deōr* (*deōr's* wife, *darāṇī*): *jēṭh's* son, *jaṭhuttar*: husbands of two sisters are *sāṇḍhū* to each other: *see* sister.

brotherhood, *bilādrī*, f.

brown, *bhūsḷā*, *bhūrā*: *badāmī*, almond colour: *khākī*, dust-colour: *naswārī rang*, snuff colour.

brush, n., v., *burs*, *bursh* (*karnā*, *nū*): *see* sweep, broom.

bubble, *bulbulā*, m.

bubo, *phōṛā*, m.: *giḷṭī*, f.: *phimhṇī*, f.

bucket, *bāḷṭī*, f. (pail): leather b., *bōkkā*, m.: iron, *ḍōl*, m.

buckle, *bagsūā*, m.

bud (flower) *kalī*, f.: tiny shoot, *kōpal*, f.: *see* sprout, branch.

buffalo, *sanḍhā*, m.: *majjh*, *maīh*, f.: gen. *mehrū*, m.: b. calf, *jhōṭṭā*: smaller, *kaṭṭā*: adj., *mājhā*.

bug, *khaṭmal*, m., *caṛ*, f.

bugle, *bigal*, m. (*wajāṇā*, *wajjṇā*).

build, *banāṇā*: raise walls, *usārnā*, (int. *usrnā*).

building, *makān*, m.: large, *hawēlī*, f.: *amārat*, f. (U.).

bull, *ḍhaggā*, *bald*: for breeding, *sāhn*: *see* calf, ox.

bullet, *gōḷī*, f.

bullock, *see* bull, calf.

bundle, *ganḍhṛī*, f.: of corn, etc., *pūḷī*, f., *thabbā*, m., *bharī*, f., *panḍ*, f.

bunch, of flowers, grapes, keys, *gucchā*, m.

burden, *see* load, weight.

burdened, *bhār hēṭh dabbeā hoeā*.

burn (as fuel), *bāḷṇā*, int. *baḷṇā*: b. up, *sāṛnā*, int. *saṛnā*: *phūkṇā*: *see* firewood.

burning, n., *sāṛā*, m. (fire, also feeling mental or physical).

burrow, *see* hole.

burst, *pāṭṇā* (tr. *pāṛnā*): by crushing, squeezing, *phissṇā* (tr. *phehṇā*).

bury, *dabbṇā*: *dafn k.* (U.).

bush *jhāṛī*, f.

busy, be, *rujjhṇā* (pa. p. *ruddhā*, *rujjhā*): being b., n., *rujjh*, f: b., adj., *ruddhā hoeā*, *laggā hoeā*.

butcher, *kasāī*, fem. *kasaiṇ*.

but, conj. *par*: *see* only, except.

butt, v., *mārnā*, *sing mārnā*.

butter, *makkhan*, m.: *see* ghee.

butter-dish, *makkhandān*, m.

butterfly, *bāhman baccā*, m. A.

buttermilk, *lassī*, f. A.

button, *bīṛā*, m.: *baṭan*, m. (*mēḷṇā*, *mārnā*, rarely *band k.*) unbutton, *bīṛā kholhṇā*: put on b., *bīṛā lāṇā*: *see* stud: b.-hole, *kāj*, m.

buy, *mull laiṇā*: *khariḍṇā* (U.): *see* purchases.

buyer, *gāhk*, *laiṇwāḷā*.

buzz, of bees, mosquitoes, etc., *ghankūr*, f., *shukāṭ*, f.

by (agent), use agent case, G. 8, 74: *koḷō*, G. 66, 90, 112: by himself, *see* alone: of himself, *see* spontaneously; one by one, *ikk ikk karke*: ten by ten, *das das karke*.

by and by, *see* afterwards.

byre, *kuṛh*, f.

C

cabbage, *gobhī*, f.: *band gobhī*: *ganḍh gobhī*.

cactus, flat, *chittar thōhr*, m.: round, *thōhr ḍaṇḍā*, m.
cage, *pinjrā*, m. [*gāci*, f.
cake, *kēk*, m. (K.): of soap,
calamity, *balā*, f.: *āfat*, f.: *biptā*, f.: *musībat*, f.: *ākhar (auṇī)*.
calculate, *lēkhā lāṇā*: *hisāb karnā*: *kiās karn-ī*, *-ā*: *see* guess, approximately, count, estimate.
calf, *wacchā*, m.: bigger, *waihṛā*: *see* buffalo: calf of leg, *pinnī*, f.: *pinnī dī machlī*, f.
caligraphy, *khatt*, m.: *khush-khattī*, f.: -ist, *khush nawīs*.
call, *saddṇā*, *kuāṇā*, *bulāṇā*: *wāz*, or *awāz mārnī (nū)*: *see* name, remember: c. out, *see* shout, scream, proclaim: pay a call, *miḷṇ jāṇā*: *mulākāt wāste jāṇā*: c. attendance, *hāzrī laiṇī* or *lāṇī*.
(1) calm, adj., of water, *khlōtā hoeā*: of person, neg of excited, or use calmly: *see* still, quiet.
(2) calm, v. tr., *phēr rāzī k.*, *thanḍā k.*, *gussā thanḍā* or *maṭṭhā karnā*: *see* peace, quiet, appease.
calmly, *hausle nāḷ*, *saihe nāḷ*, *saihj nāḷ*, *amn nāḷ*.
calumniate, *see* slander.
camel, *ūth*, fem. *uthṇī*, *ḍācī*, *sāhnnī*: young c., *bōttā*, m.
camp, *kampū*, m.: *see* tent.
camping ground, *paṛā*, m.
camphor, *kāfūr*, m.
can, *see* tin.
canal, *naihr*, f.: branch c., *sūā*, m.: channel made by farmers, *mohgā*, m.. *khāḷ*, m.: to make such, *khāḷṇā*: c. bank, *paṭṛī*, f.

cancel, order, *hukm band karnā*: name, *nā kaṭṭṇā*.
candidate, *umēdwār*, m.: in exam., *imtihān deṇwāḷā*.
candle, *mōmbattī*, f.
candle-stick, *battīdān*, m.
candour, *safāī*, *sāfdilī*, *sāf sāf ākhṇā*.
cane, *baint*, m. (*mārnā*, *nū*): *see* sugar-cane: be caned, *baint khāṇā*, *paiṇā*.
canister, *see* tin.
cannibal, *ādamkhōr* (U.): *bandeā dā gōsht khāṇwāḷā*.
cannon, *tōp*, f. (*calāṇī*, int. *calṇī*).
canopy, *see* awning.
canter, (horse) *poīā calṇā*.
cantonment, *chāoṇī*, f.
cap, *ṭōpī*, f.
capable, *laik*: *see* able.
capacious, *mōkḷā*.
capacity, *gunjaish*, f.: *samāī*, f.: *see* ability.
capital, *pūñī*, f., *sarmāyā*, m., *rās*, m., *rupayye*, m. pl.: chief town, *dār ul khalāfa*, m. (U.).
captive, in war, *asīr*: prisoner, *kaidī*: take c., *phaṛnā*, *kaid k.*
captivity, *kaid*, f.: *asīrī*, f. (U.).
caravan, *kāflā*, m., *kārawān*, m., *ṭōllā* m., *ṭōllī*, f.
carcase, *murdār*, m. (collective term): *lōth*, f.: *see* corpse.
(1) card, v., cotton, etc., *piññā*, *jhambhṇā*. A.
(2) card, n., post-c., *kāṭ*, m.: *khatt*, m.
cards, *tāsh*, m. (*khēḍṇā*).
cardamum, *lācī*, f.
care, *see* anxiety, look after, protect, like: take c., interj., *backe*, *khabardār*, *sambhaḷke*. I don't care, *menū koī parwāh nehī*.

caretaker, *rakhwālā*, *rakhwāl*, *caukīdār*.
careless, *lāparwāh*, *bēparwāh*.
carelessness, *lā-* or *bē-parwāhī*, *gaflat*, f.
caress, *pyār dēṇā*; *see* fondle, kiss.
carpenter, *tarkhāṇ* : fem. *tarkhāṇī*.
carpet, *darī*, f. : rug, *galīcā*, m.
carriage, driving, *bagghī*, f. : *ṭamṭam*, f. : (tonga) *ṭāṅgā*, m. : phaeton, *fiṭṇ*, f. : (railway) *gaḍḍī*, f. (also train) : *see* class : ladies only, women only, *zanānī gaḍḍī* : servants, *sarwanṭī*, f. : act or price of carrying, *see* cartage.
carrion, *murdār*, m. (including animal dead, not killed).
carrot, *gājar*, f.
carry, *cukkke* or *uṭhāke kharnā* or *laijāṇā* : c. bricks, earth, *ḍhōṇā* : be carried, *hūṇte* or *kūhṇte laiṇe* (M. 122. 34 : tr. *dēṇe*), *see* ride, swing, back : c. on work, *kamm ṭōrnā* or *calāṇā* (int. *ṭurnā*, *calnā*).
cart, for two bullocks, *gaḍḍā*, m. : for one bullock, handcart, wheel-barrow, *reṛhī*, f.
cartage, act or price, *ḍhuāī*, f.
cartridge, *kārtūs*, m.
carve, *ghaṛnā*.
case, *see* cover : lawcase, *mukadmā*, m. : bring c. ag., *kise te arzī pāṇī* or *dāhwā karnā* or *nālish karnī* : in this c., *es hālat* or *sūrat wicc* : in no c., *cāre banne* w. neg., or *kise sūrat wicc* and neg. : *see* lose.
cash, *nakad*, m. : v., *ṭōṛnā*. A.
cask, *pīpā*, m.
cast, *see* throw, lots.
caste, *zāt*, f. : *gōt*, f. (division of c.) : low, *nīwī* : high, *uccī* : put out of c., *chēknā*, *hukkā pāṇī band k.* (*dā*).
castor-oil plant, *harnōḷā*, m.
cat, *billā*, fem. *billī*.
cataract (in eye) *mōtīā*, m. A.
catarrh, *sardī*, f. : *zukām*, m.
catastrophe, *see* calamity, accident.
catch, *phaṛnā*, *phagaṛnā* : ball, etc., *jhōpṇā*, *jhaṛapṇā* : *see* seize : allow oneself to be caught, *phaṛā dēṇā*, *phaṛāī dēṇī* : G. 74, 75. A.
catch, n., in door, window, *hudhkā*, m., *billī*, f.
catechumen, *mutlāshī*, m.
caterpillar, *sunḍī*, f. : *bhaṅgū kuttā*, m., *bhaggū kuttā*.
cattle (horned), *māl*, m. : *ḍaṅgar*, m. : *caukhar*, m.
cauliflower, *phull gobhī*, f.
(1) cause, n., *wajhā*, f. (reason) : *sbabb*, m. : *see* reason, purpose : causeless, *see* reason, useless.
(2) cause, v., use causal vv. w. direct acc. or *kolō* of agent : G. 41-3, 109, 110 : *see* force.
caution, *hōsh*, f., *hushyārī*, f. *khabardārī*, f.
cautiously, words for caution w. *nāḷ* : *samjhke*.
cavalry, *risālā*, m.
cave, *khundhar*, f. : *gār*, f. (U.).
ceaselessly, *see* continuously.
cedar, *diār*, m. : *biāṛ*, m.
ceiling, *chatt*, m. : thin planks, *pakkhar*, m.
celebrated, *see* famous : be c., of fair, festival, *laggṇā*, *manneā jāṇā*.
cement, *see* mortar, glue.
cemetery, *see* graveyard.

centre, *markaz*, m. (U.): adj., *wiclā*, *wishkārlā* : *see* middle.
ceremony, *rīt*, f. : *rasm*, f.
certain, *pakkā*, *yakīnī* : a. c. man, *fulāṇā*.
certainly, *bĕshakk*, *nishang*, *zarūr*, *lājarūr* ; *hōr kī* ? *te hōr* ? *hā̃ te*.
certainty, *yakīn*, m.
certificate, *sāṭifkaṭ*, m. ; *sanad*, f.
certify, *zimewār* or *zimmewār h.*, *guāhī dēṇī*, *tsallī dēṇī*.
chafe, *see* rub, annoy, grief: be chafed (of skin, etc.) *ucchṇā*, *ambṇā*.
chaff, of rice, barley, etc., *phakk*, f. : *see* bran : chopped straw from wheat, *tūṛī*, f., *ciṭṭā bhoh* : from gram, etc., *bhoh*, m., *missā bhoh*. A.
chain, *saṅgal*, m. : smaller, *saṅglī*, f. : very small, *zanjīrī*, f., *e.g.* watch-c. A.
chair, *kursī*, *khursī*, f. : low, all wood, *caukī*, f. : of reeds, *mūṛhā*, m. : easy c., *arām kursī*, f. : *see* stool, seat.
chalk, *cāk*, m., *khaṛīā miṭṭī*, f.
chamber, *see* room : c. pot, *pāṭ*, m.
champ (horse) *cabakṇā*.
chance, *sbabb*, m. : by c., *sbabb nāl*, *ĕwē̃*. *aĩwē̃*, *kār e kazā*.
(1) change, *tabdīlī*, f. : *see* difference: for rupee, etc., *bhanghaṛ*, m., *bhān*, m., but *see* rupee : whole unchanged rupee, *baddhā rupayyā*.
(2) change, v., *badalnā* : c. person, animal, regiment for other, *badlī karnī* (int. *hōṇī*) : *see* exchange: c. several things, *adal badal k.* : c. notes, rupees, *tōṛnā* : get them changed *tuṛāṇā* (int. *ṭuṭṭṇā*) : give back, *partāṇā* : c. opinions, *phir jāṇā*, *dalīl badalnī*.
changeable, *kacce khyāl dā*, *dudilā* : *see* vacillate.
channel, *nāḷā*, m. : small, *nālī*, f. : *see* stream, drain, brook.
chap, (hands, feet) *biāī pāṭnī* [(*dī*).
chapter, *bāb*, m.
character, no good word, use adj. describing person, or word for disposition, temperament: of good moral c., *nēkcalan* : of bad, *badcalan* : *see* good : life and actions. *cāl calan*, m.
characteristic, *sift*, f.
charcoal, *koḷā*, m. : *koḷe*, m. pl. : *lakkaṛ de koḷe*, m. pl. : *see* coal: small broken bits, *kērī*, f.
charge, give into c., *de hawāle k.* : *de pēṭe pāṇā* : give over c., *cāraj d.* : take over c., *cāraj laiṇā* : c. price, *lāṇā* (int. *laggṇā*) : M. 122. 27 : *see* cost.
charity, *see* alms.
charm, please, *baṛā khush k.* : bewitch, *jādū k.* or *pāṇā* (*utte*), *mantar paṛhnā* (*utte*) : *see* amuse, delight.
charmer, *see* magician, snake.
chase, *see* pursue, hunt.
chaste, *pāk*.
chatter, foolishly, *yabbhā̃ mārnīā̃*, *yabbhṇā*, *bakṇā*, *cilkṇā* : of birds, *cī cī karnī* : of teeth, *dandoṛikke wajjṇe* (*de*) : *see* talkative.
cheap, *sastā*, *suwallā*.
cheat, *rupayye* or *paise mārne*, M. 123, 46 : *see* deceit, deceive.
check, *see* hinder, stop, compare, examine.

cheek, *gallh*, f.
(1) cheer, *see* amuse, comfort.
(2) cheers, applause, *cirs dēṇe*: *see* clap.
cheerful, *khush*.
cheese, *panīr*, m.
cheque, *cikk*, m.: *see* bill.
cherish, *see* support.
chess, *shatranj*, m. (*khēḍṇā*).
chest, (body), *hikk*, f.: *chātī*, f. (U.): of drawers, *almārī*, f.: *see* drawer, box.
chew, grain, etc., *cabbṇā*: suck, *cūpṇā*.
chick, *see* chikk.
chicken, *cūccā*, m.: for table, *see* fowl.
chief, chieftain, *sardār*, fem *sardārnī*.
chikk, hanging screen, *cikk*, f.: *cikh*, f.
child, *baccā*, m., *bāl*, m.: *añāṇā*, m.: *bacṛā*, m.: European, *bāwā*, fem. *bāwī*: plur., *dhī puttar*, m.: *dhīā puttar*, m. pl.: *munḍe kuṛīā*, m. pl.: *see* descendants.
childish *munḍeāwālā*, *añāṇeāwālā*.
childishness, *see* boyishness.
childless, *dhī puttar nehī*: *autrā* or *autrā nikhattrā* is mild abuse or self pity.
chimney, of lamp, *cimṇī*, f.: for fire, *dhūkash*, m.: for sugarcane furnace, *lūhmbā*, m.: *see* funnel.
chimneypiece, *paṛchattī*, f.
chin, *ṭhōḍḍī*, f.
china (ware), *cīnī*, f. (*de bhānḍe* or *bartan*). [m.
chip, of wood, *sakk*, m. *sakṛā*,
chocolate, *caklēṭ*, f.: *see* cocoa.
choice, use *marzī*, f. (will): *see* select.
choke (food going wrong way), *athrū auṇā* (*nū*): from disease, *galghōṭū hōṇā*: v. tr., *see* smother, strangle, hang: by pressure, *saṅgh ghuṭṭṇā*.
cholera, *haizā*, m. (gen. merely severe vomiting).
choose, *see* select.
(1) chop, n., (meat) *cāp*. f. (K.).
(2) chop, v. tr., wood, *lakkaṛ dalṇi*: cut long piece into thick bits, *mōche pāṇe*: into long thin bits, *phāṅgā karnīā*.
chopper, farmer's, *ṭōkkā*, m.: kitchen, *cāpaṛ*. m. (K.).
Christ, *Masīh*.
Christian, *Isāī*, *As-hāī*, fem. *Isain*, *As-hain*.
Christmas Day, *waḍḍā din*.
chudder, *see* veil.
church; building, *girjā*. m.: congregation, *jamāt*, f.: many congregations, *kalīsyā*, f.
chutney, *catnī*, f.
cinnamon, *dālcīnī*, f.
circle, *ghērā*, m., *dāirā*, m. (educ.) [round.
circuit, *cakkar*, m.: *see* tour,
circuitous, use *walā paiṇā*: *see* round.
circular, *gōl*: *see* roundness.
circumcise, *suntī bahāṇā* (*nū*): be c., *suntī baihṇā*.
circulate, (money), *calṇā* (tr. *calāṇā*): *see* pass: (story) *dhummṇā* (tr. *dhumāṇā*).
circumstance, *gall*, f.: *wākiā*, m.: *hāl*, m.: *hāl hakīkat*, f.: in no c.: *see* case.
cistern, *hauz*, m.: *hauzī*, f.: (also place for bath in bathroom).
citizen, *shaihrīā*, *shaihrī*, *shaihrdār* (all city-dweller): *see* subject.

citron, *khattā*, m.
city, *shaihr*, m.
civil, not military, *mulkhī*: not criminal, *duānī*: see polite.
civilised *muhazzab* (U.).
claim, *dāhwā*, m. (*k*.).
claimant, *mudaī*, m. (leg.).
clandestine, *see* secret.
clap hands, *māhṅgā mārnā* (approval, applause): *tauṛī mārnī* (derision).
class, in school, *jamāt*, f.: of people, railway, *darjā*, m: first c., *paihlā darjā*, *fast klās* (*see* excellent); second c., *dujjā darjā*, *sikanḍ klās*, *sĕkanḍ klās*, m.: intermediate, *ḍeoḍhā darjā*, *inṭar*, m.: third c., *trījjā* or *tīsrā darjā*, *thaḍḍ klās*, m.
claw, *naūh*, m.: whole foot, *panjā*, m.
clay, *miṭṭī*, f.: *see* mud.
clean, *sāf*, *suthrā*: ceremonially, *see* holy: *see* scrub, wash, pure.
cleanliness, *safāī*, f.: *see* purity.
clear (water, sentence, meaning) *sāf*: (water) *nitreā hoeā*: v., water, meaning, etc., *natārnā* (int. *nitrnā*): *see* evident, acquit: c. up (weather), *see* weather; (difficulty, *see* solve: c. away table), *see* table.
clerk, *munshī*, *bābū*, *klārak*.
clever, *see* able, intelligent: *hushyār*, *kārīgar*, *ustād*, *siāṇā*: (bad sense) *calāk*, *hikmatī*, *catur*.
cleverness, *hushyārī*, f.: *hikmat*, f.: *kārīgarī*, f.: *ustādī*, f.: bad sense, *calākī*, f., *catrāī*, f.: *see* intelligence, ability.
climate, *hawā*, f.: *āb hawā*, f.
climb, *caṛhnā* (*utte*): climbing plant, *wĕl*, f.: *walī*, f.
cling to, *cambaṛnā* (*nū̃*).
clip (w. scissors) *katrnā* *see* prune.
clique, *dharā*, m.: *see* party.
cloak, *cogā*, m.: *see* coat: v., *paṛdā pānā* (*utte*): *see* screen.
clock, *ghaṛī*, f.: *see* o'clock.
clockmaker, *ghaṛīsāz*, m.
clod, *dhehm*, f., *ḍhīhm*, f.
clogged, dirty, *jaḍḍā*.
(1) **close**, v. tr., door, window: *phērnā*, *ḍhoṇā*, *bhīṛnā*: *see* shut: w. closed doors, *wajjī būhī*, G. 78: *see* shut.
(2) **close**, adj., *see* near.
cloth, *kapṛā*, m.: *see* sheet, skirt, shawl, etc.: c.-merchant, *bazāz*: trade of selling c., *bazāzī*, f.
clothe, oneself, *kapṛe pāṇe*: another, *kapṛe pāṇe* (*nū̃*): make him put on clothes, *kapṛe puāṇe*: in gen. clothe, *kapṛe dēṇe*.
clothes, *kapṛe*, m. pl.
cloud, *baddal*, m.: clouds all over, *jhaṛ*, m., *baddal ghuleā hoeā e*: c-less, *see* weather.
clove, *lauṅg*, f.
clown, *see* jester.
club (building) *kalafghar*, m.: wooden, *see* stick.
clue, *patā*, m.: *see* discover.
clumsy, *see* awkward.
cluster, *see* bunch.
coach-house, *bagghī-khānā*, m.
coagulate, *jammnā* (tr. *jamāṇā*).
coal, *patthar dā kōlā*: *see* charcoal: live coal, *bhakheā hoeā kolā*, m.: small broken bits, *kērī*, f.
coarse, not fine, *mōṭā*.
coast, *samundar dā kaṇḍhā* or *ḍanḍā*, m.

coat, *kōṭ*, m. : servant's double breasted, *aṅgā*, m. : *see* overcoat, waterproof. [*cāṇā*.
coax, *khush karke manāṇā* : *par-*
cob of maize, *challī*, f. : without grain, *tukkā*, m.
cobbler, *mōcī*, fem. *mōcaṇ*.
cobweb, *jāḷā*, m.: single thread. *tār*, f., *cinākh*, m.
cock (bird) *kukkaṛ*, m. : of gun, *ghōṛā*, m.
cocoa, *kōkō*, f. : *see* chocolate.
cocoanut, whole, *nanyēr*, m. : half of kernel, *thūthī*, f. : *khōppā*, m. : kernel in gen., *garī*, f. (cf. *girī*, f., kernel of other fruit, pith).
coffee, *kāfī*, f. : -pot, *kāfīdān*, m.
coffin, *sandūk*, m. : *see* shroud.
coin, no word, use rupee, pice, etc., good, *kharā* : bad, *khōṭā*.
coincide, *raḷṇā*, *miḷṇā*.
cold, n., *pāḷā*, m. : *sardī*, f. : *sīt*, f. : *ṭhaṇḍ*, f. : feel cold, *pāḷā*, etc., w. *laggṇā*, G. 108 : hands, feet feel c., *hatth, pair ṭharne* : air get c., *pāḷā uttō paiṇā* : catch c., *sardī laggṇī*, *zukām hōṇā* or *laggṇā*.
colic (*ḍhiḍḍh wicc*) *waṭṭ*, m.
collar, *kālar*, m.
collect, *kaṭṭhā k.*, *jamā k.* : money, *ugrāhṇā* (int. *ugghaṛnā*).
college, *kālij*, m.
coll-ide, -ision, *ṭakkar khāṇī*, *mērī ṭakkar wajjī* (*nāḷ*) ; tr. *mērī ṭakkar mārī* (*nāḷ*) : *see* knock.
colloquial, *ām bōl cāl dī*.
colonel, *karnail*.
colonise, *see* people (2).
colony (canal), simply *naihr*, f. : in the c., *naihr te*.

colour, *raṅg*, m. : dark, *see* dark in A. : *see* light, fast, bright : faint, *maddham*.
coloured, *raṅgdār*, *raṅgwāḷā* : many-c., *raṅg baraṅgī*.
colt, *wachērā*, m.
comb, *kaṅghī*, f. : of cock, *kalgī*, f., *pagg*, f.
come, *auṇā* (pa. p. *āeā*) : c. in, *see* enter : c. out, *nikḷ auṇā* ; of sun fr. clouds, *dhupp nikḷṇī* ; of stain, *see* delete.
comet, *bōdī āḷā tārā*, m.
comfort, *tsall-ī* or *-ā dēṇī nū* : be c.-ed., *tsallī hōṇī* (*nū*) : *see* ease, condole, soothe.
Comforter (Holy Spirit), *Tsallī Dēṇwāḷā*.
command, *hukm* m. (*d.*) ; unwarrantably, *hukm cāṛhnā*.
commander-in-chief, *jaṅgī lāṭ*.
commemoration, *yādgārī*, f.
commence-, -ment, *see* beginning.
commend, *see* recommend, praise.
commentary, *tafsīr*, f.
commerce, *see* trade, intercourse.
commercial, *tajārtī* : c. usage, *sudāgrī* or *bazār dā dastūr*.
commission (discount, percentage) *dastūrī*, f. : (written authority), *sanad*, f. ; *see* order : seller on c., *āhṛtī*, *āhṛtaḷī* : his c. is *āhṛtaḷ*, f. : (a committee) *kamēṭī*, f.
committee (of all kinds, relig. and secular) *kamēṭī*, f. : c-meeting, *kamēṭī*, f.
common, *ām*, *mamūlī* ; *see* much : shared by others, *sānjhā* : c. village land, *shāmlāt*, f. : c. people, *ām lōk*, *kamīne lōk* (low), *see* everyone, people.

commonly, *aksar.*
commotion, *see* disturbance.
communication, *see* intercourse, information.
communion, *see* intercourse: Holy C., *Ashā Rabānī*, f.: celebrate H. C., *karnī*. take, *lainī*.
companion, *sāthī*, *jōṛīdār*, *mēre nāḷ dā*: bet. men, *yār*: bet. women, *sahēlī*, f.: *see* partner, equal.
company, of people, *katth*, m.: *ṭōllā*, m., *ṭōllī*, f.: *jatthā*, m.: *taraṇḍī*, f.: *taraṇḍā*, m.: *see* assembly, congregation: business c., *kaumpaṇī*, f.: good or bad c., *baihṇī*, f.: M. 127. 3: G. 121.
compare, *raḷāṇā*, *miḷāṇā*, *mukāblā karnā*: c. weights, size, etc., *hāṛnā*: comparison of size, cost. etc., *see* time, G. 23: compared w., *ohde mukāble wicc.*
compass, *kutabnumā*, m.
compassion, *see* pity.
compassionate *raihm-dil*, *tars karnwāḷā*: God, *rahīm*.
compatriot, *see* fellow-countryman.
compel, *see* force, cause.
compensation, *harjānnā*, m.: *iwzānnā*, m.: in c. for, *ohde*, *badle*: *see* loss, damage in A.
compet-e, -ition, *see* emulate.
competent, *laik*, *samajhdār*, *khabardār*: *see* able, clever.
complain-, -t, *shikait*, f. (*k.*, *dī*): *faryād*, f. (*k.*, *dī*): leg. *nālish*, f. (*k.*, *utte*).
complainant, *see* plaintiff.
complete, *pūrā*, *mukammal*: *see* finish.
complex: *see* intricate.
complexion, *rang*, m.
complication, *see* intricate, entangle.
compliment, *see* praise: present my compliments, *mēre wallō salām ākhṇā* or *hatth bannhṇā*.
comply, *see* agree, assent.
composed of, *dā baṇeā hoeā*.
compromise, leg., *rāzīnāmā*, m.
compulsion, *see* force.
compulsory, subject in exam., *lāzmī*.
comput-ation, -e, *see* calculate, count
comrade, *see* companion, friend.
conceal, *see* hide.
conceit, *baṛī mizāj*, f.: *baṛā damāg*, m.: *see* pride, sense.
concentrate, *see* attend.
concerning, *dī bābat*, *de bāre wicc.*
concession, *riait*, f.: adj. *riaitī*.
conciliate, *razī k.*, *manāṇā*.
concise, *see* brief.
conclude, draw conclusion, *natījā kaḍḍhṇā* *see* settle, finish.
concussion, *ṭakkar*, f.: *see* collide.
condemn, *mujrim k.*, *baṇānā*: be c, *mujrim h.*, *jurm sābit hōṇā*: *see* guilt.
condemnation, *sazā dā hukm*, m.
condition, *hāl*, m.: *hālat*, f.: *hāl hakīkat*, f.: *hawāl* m. (often story): make c., *eh shart e*: on c. that, *es shart te pai*.
conditional, *shartī*.
condole, (go to), *mukāṇī jāṇā*: *see* comfort, mourn-, -ers, -ing, sympathise.
conduct, *see* character, lead.
confectioner, *halwāī*, fem. *halwaiṇ*: *miṭhāī-wāḷā*.

confederate, *see* partner.
conference (meeting) *kamēṭī*, f.: (consultation) *salāh mashwarā*, m.
confess, *mannnā*: c. under torture, *bakṇā* (tr. *bakāṇā*): force to c., without torture, *dhakke nal* or *zōre manāṇā*.
confidant, *bhēṭī*, m., fem. *bhēṭan*.
confide, *wasāh karnā* (*dā*): *wasāh hōṇā* (*menū̃ ohdā*): *see* trust.
confidence, *wasāh*, m.: lack of c., *bēwasāhī*, f.
confidently (speak), *dāhwe nāl*.
confirm, *pakkā k.*: *see* ratify.
confiscate, *ghar kurk* (*k.*, *h.*), house confiscated: *ghar dī kurkī* (*k.*, *h.*), furniture, etc., c-ed.
conflicting, *āpe wicc nehī̃ ralde*.
confront, *mū̃h te ākhṇā*: *see* face.
confuse, things, *rauḷā mārnā*: *garbaṛī pāṇī*: persons, *ghabrāṇā*, *ghabrā chaḍḍṇā* (int. *ghābbarnā*, *ṭhiṭhambarnā*): *see* perplex.
confusion, *gaṛbaṛī* f.: mistake, *ṭapḷā*, m.: *see* disorder.
confute, *jhūṭhā sābit k.*
congeal, int. *jammṇā*: tr. *jamāṇā*.
congratulate, *mubārakbādī dēṇī*: *see* bravo.
congregation, *jamāt*, f. (either audience or settled c.).
conjecture, *see* guess, calculate, estimate, approximately.
conjectural, *kiāsī*.
conjure, adjure, *saũh duāṇī* (*nū̃*).
conjurer, *madārī*, fem. *madāran*.
connection, *tallak*, m.: *wāstā*, m. (both *menū̃ ohde nāl*): *see* relative, relationship.
conquer, *jittṇā*, *fatā-karnā* (*fatā* used alone is fem.): *see* possess, defeat.
conscience, *dil*, m.
conscious, *hōsh wicc*: *see* aware, remember.
consciousness, *hōsh*, f. (also sense).
consecrate, *Khudā de hawāle k.*, *makhsūs k.* (U.) *bilkull Khudā dā samjhṇā*: give in charity, *Khudā de nā dēṇā*.
consecutive, *suāhrā*, or use *nā chaḍḍṇā*. [assent.
(1) consent, v., *see* agree,
(2) consent, n., *razāmandī*, f.: *manzūrī*, f.: *marzī*, f.: *razā* f.: w. c. of all, *sāreā̃ dī razā* or *marzī nāl*.
consequence *natījā*, m.: of no c., *koī gall nehī̃*, *see* matter: *see* useless, worthless.
consider, *sōcṇā*, *gaur karnā*.
consideration, *sōc*, f.: *gaur*, m.: *dhiān*, m.: out of c. for, *ohdā lihāz karke*: *see* concession, esteem, partiality, deference.
considering, conj., *see* since.
consist, *see* composed.
console, *see* comfort, condole.
conspicuous, *jehṛā sāf disse*, etc.: *see* visible.
conspire, *de khalāf gall pākāṇī* (int. *pakkṇī*).
constant, *see* faithful, resolute, continuous, repeatedly.
consternation, *harānī*, f.: *see* astonish-, -ishment.
constipation, *kabzī*, f.: the pain and straining, *marōṛā*, m.
consult, *salāh karnī* (*nāl*): *mashwarā karnā* (*nāl*): *rā pucchṇī* (*dī*).

consum-e, -ption, *kharc karnā* (int. *h.*) : *see* waste, phthisis.
contagious disease, *lagganwāḷī bimārī*, f.
contain, be contained, *auṇā* (come) : *see* room.
contaminate, *see* defile, unclean. [sider.
contemplate, *see* think, con-
contemplation (relig.) *dhiān*, m.
contempt, *hikārat*, f. : *see* despise, scorn.
contemptible, *kamīnā, burā*.
contend, *see* argue, fight.
content, *rāzī, khush*.
contentious, *see* argumentative, quarrelsome.
contents, *jehṛā wicc e* : (of letter, book) *mazmūn*, m.
continual-, -ly, *see* always, repeatedly, daily.
continue, *raihṇā* : c. throwing, *saṭṭdā rehā, saṭṭī geā* : G. 68.
continuously, *barābar* : *see* continual. [*see* settle.
(1) **contract,** *ṭhēkā*, m.(*d., laiṇā*) :
(2) **contract, v.,** *see* shrink.
contractor, *ṭhēkedār-*, fem. *-nī*.
contradict, *jhūṭheā k.* : *gall mōṛnī*.
contrary, *de khalāf, de barkhalāf, de ulṭ* : *see* opposite : on the c., *sagō̃, sagō̃*.
contrast, *fark*, m. : *see* compare.
contribution, *madad, madat*, f. : *rupayye*, m. pl. : *candā*, m.
contriv-e, -ance, *see* arrange : c. w. difficulty : *taradad*, or *taraddad*, m. (*k.*), *taragas*, m. (*k.*).
control, *kābū*, m. : *ikhtiār*, m. : *wass*, m. : *hatth*, m (all w. *wicc rakkhṇā* or *h.*) : self-c., *hauslā* : *see* patience.
controversy, *see* argu-e, -mentative, quarrel-, -some.
convalescent, *kujjh wall, wall hōṇ lagā e*.
convene, *karāṇā, jamā k.* (both w. word for meeting as object).
convenien-ce -t, -tly, *see* ease, inconvenience: use *je taklīf nā hōwe, lokā̃ wāste eh welā ṭhīk e*, etc., *see* inconvenience.
conversational, *bōl cāl dā*.
convers-e, -ation, *gall katth*, f. : *gallā̃ katthā̃*, f. pl. (*k.*) : *carcā* f m. (*k.*) : *bāt cīt*, f. (*k.*) : *gallā̃*, f. pl. (*k.*).
conversion (rel.) *dil dā badalnā, nawē̃ sireō̃ jammṇā, dil dī tabdīlī*.
(1) **convert, v.** (make) *banāṇā* : to Christianity, etc., *Isāī k.* (often used of baptism) : be converted, *see* conversion.
(2) **convert, n.,** *Isāī, Musalmān, Āryā*, etc., *ho geā*.
convey, *see* carry.
conveyance, *see* carriage, car[t].
(1) **convict,** *kusūr*, m. : *galtī*, f. (etc. all w. *sābit k.*) : *see* condemn, convince.
(2) **convict, n.,** *kaid-ī*, fem. *-an*.
convince, *kail k., manāṇā, yakīn karāṇā*. [*lāngrī*.
(1) **cook, n.,** *khānsāmā̃, bāorcī*,
(2) **cook, v.,** *pakāṇā* (int. *pakkṇā*) : roast, *bhunnṇā* (int. *bhujjṇā*) : bread, *pakāṇā, lāṇā*, M. 121. 10 (int. *laggṇā*.) A. : c. in pot, *rinnhṇā* (pa. p. *riddhā*, int. *rijjhṇā*) : put on pot, put on to c., *cāṛhṇā* (int. *caṛhṇā*) : M. 118. 23, 26 : ready cooked, *pakkā pakāeā*.
cool, *see* cold : nice and cool (wind, water, etc.) *ṭhaṇḍā ṭhaṇḍā*.
coolie, *kulī, mazdūr*.

co-operate, *nāḷ raḷke kamm k.*
copper, *trāmmā*, m.
coppersmith, *ṭhaṭhiār*.
copse, few trees, *jhaṅghī*, f.
copy, n., *nakl*, f. : sample, *namūnā*, m. : (book), *kāpī*, f. : v., *nakl k.* : boy at school *nakl mārnī* : *see* imitate.
copyist, *kātib*, *naklnawīs*.
cord, of leather, *waddhrī*, f. : *see* string, rope.
cordial-, -ity, use love, friendship.
coriander, *dhaniā*, m.
cork, *ḍaṭṭ*, m. (any stopper, plug) : *kāg*, f. : of maize-cob, *ṭukkā*, m.
corkscrew, *pēckass*, m.
(1) corn, on toe, etc., *caṇḍī*, f : on sole, *bhaurī*, f. [wheat.
(2) corn, *see* grain, maize, oats,
corner, of room, box (outside or in), *nukkar*, f. : *guṭṭh*. f. : four -ed, *caunukrā*, *cauguṭṭhā* : c.-dish, *ḍōṅghā*, m.
coronation, *tājpōshī*, f. : of raja, *gaddī te bahāṇā* (int. *baihṇā*).
corpse, *lōth* f. : *murdā* (dead person) : *see* carcase.
corpulent, *mōṭā* jocular, *ḍhiḍḍhū*, *ḍhiḍḍhal*.
correct, *ṭhīk* (*k.*) : *durust* (*k.*) : c. character, *sudhārnā* : *see* rebuke, reprimand, improve.
correspond, *raḷṇā*, *miḷṇā* : (write letters) *ikk dujje nū ciṭṭhīā likhṇīā* : *khaṭṭ kitābat karnī* (U.).
corrupt, v. tr., *wigāṛnā*, *kharāb k.* (int. *wigaṛnā*, *kharāb h.*) : adj., *wigṛeā hoeā* : *see* bad, bribe.
cost, n., *mull*, m. : *kīmat*, f. : costs (leg.) *kharcā*, m., *kharc*, m. ; v., how much c. ? *kinnā mull e*, *kinnā laggā*, *kinne tō āeā* : *see* spend, expense.
costly, *baṛe mull dā*, *kīmatī* ; *maihṅgā* (dear). [hut.
cottage, *nikkī kōṭhī*, f : *see*
cotton, growing, *kapāh*, f., *phuṭṭī*, f : wool, *rū*, m. : c.-seeding machine, *welṇī*, f. : c.- seed, *waṇēwā*, m.
couch, *see* sofa.
cough, n., *khaṅgh*, f. : v., *khanghṇā*, *khaṅgh auṇī* (*nū*) : severe c. and sneezing, *dhrāṅṇā*, *dhrāsṇā*.
council, *kamēṭī*, f. : *kaunsal*, f.
count, *giṇṇā*, *gintrī karnī* : *see* calculate.
countenance, *see* face.
counteract, *see* hinder.
counterfeit, *banāwaṭī*, *naklī* : forged, *jāhlī* : (coin) *khōṭā*.
countermand, *see* cancel.
countless, *see* innumerable.
country, *mulkh*, *muḷkh*, m. : *dēs*, m. : native c., *waṭan*, m. : in c. (not town) *piṇḍā wicc* : adj., not foreign, *dēsī*.
countryman (fellow), *mērā waṭnī*, *mēre dēs* or *mulkh dā*.
couple, *jōṛā*, m. : *jōṛī*, f.
courage, *bahādrī*, f. : *dalērī*, f., *see* boldness : patient c., *himmat*, f., *hauslā*, m.
courageous, *see* brave : patiently c., *himmatwāḷā*, *hauslewāḷā*.
course, *see* method, arrangement, way, path : of c., *hōr kī*, *bēshakk*, *nishaṅg*, *hā te*, G. 94 : of c. (concessive), *hā*.
court, of law, *kacaihrī*, f. : official, royal, raja's darbar, *darbār* m. : person w. right to sit in darbar, *darbārī* : court dress, *darbārī kapṛe*.

courteous, no real word, use *ashrāf*, or kind, good: *see* polite.
courtesy, *see* favour, kindness.
courtier, *see* court.
courtyard, *walgan*, m.: *walgaṇ*, m.: *wehṛā* m.
cousin, use brother: on father's side, *cācce bābbeõ bhrā*: mother's, *māmmeõ bhrā*, etc.
covenant, *kaul karār*, m.: *aihd*, m.: *shṭāmp*, m.: *rajistrī*, f.: *see* agreement, bond.
(1) cover, v. *kajjṇā*, *ḍhakkṇā*: *see* hide, screen.
(2) cover, n. (also lid) *ḍhakkaṇ*, m.: *ḍhakkṇā*, m.: for earthen pots, *capṇī*, f., *chūṇī*, f., *chūṇā*, m.: of dried earth, *cāppaṛ*, m.: for umbrella, hat, pillow, *uchāṛ*, m.
coverlet, *see* quilt.
covet-, -ousness, *lālac*, m. (*k.*): *tamā*, m. (*k.*): *see* desire, greed.
covetous, *lālcī*.
cow, *gā̃*: adj., *gōkā*: -dung, *gohā*, m.
coward, *ḍarākal*, *ḍarū*, *ḍarn-* [*wālā*.
cowherd, *chēṛū*, *wāggī*.
cowhouse, *kuṛh*, f.
coxcomb, *see* fop.
crack, n., *trēṛ*, f.: v., *trēṛ paiṇī* (*nū̃*): of glass, *tiṛakṇā*: china, *līk paiṇī*: wood, *kaṛkṇā*: (split, *pāṭṇā*, tr. *pāṛṇā*).
cradle, *panghūṛā*, m.
craft, *see* cleverness, deceit, profession
cram, *tunnṇā*.
(1) cramp, get, *bakhōṛ paiṇā*: *nāṛ caṛhnī*.
(2) cramped (no room), *sauṛā*, *taṅg*, *bhīṛā*.

crash, *ḍiggaṇ*, etc. *dā khṛāk*.
crawl: creeping things, use *dhiḍḍh parne turnā*: child, *riṛhnā*: go very slowly, *jū̃ dī tōr calṇā*: *see* creep.
crazy, *see* mad.
creak, *cī cī karnī*, *ciknā*: *see* squeak.
cream, *malāī*, f.
crease, *bhann*, f. (*paiṇī*): *see* fold.
create, *paidā k.*
creation, *khalkat* f.: *makhlūk*.
Creator, *Paidā karnwālā*, *Khālik*: *see* God.
credible, *mannanwālī gall*.
credit, *see* belief, trust: on c., *udhār*, *see* borrow, debt.
creditor, *laindār*, or use *laiṇā*.
credits, *laihnā*, m.
credulous, *shtābī mannanwālā*, *siddhā* (simple).
creed, *akīdā*, m.: *imān*, m.: brief M. sentences, *kalmā*, m.
creep, *see* crawl: -ing plant, *wēl*, f., *wall*, f.: -ing things: *see* insect, ant.
crest, on bird, *kalgī*, f.: *see* comb.
cricket, insect, *bīṇḍā*, m.: game, *kirkaṭ*, m.
crime, *jurm*, m.: *see* sin.
criminal, *see* guilty, prisoner: adj. (leg.), *faujdārī*, *see* civil.
crimson, *kirmzī*, *kirmcī*: *see* red.
cripple, *lunjā*, *ṭuhlā*: lame, *laṅgā*: *see* hand.
crisp, *kṛākēdār*.
crisis, *nāzak wakat*, m.
critical, *see* critical, crisis, delicate.
criticise, *nuks kaḍḍhnā*, *nuktācīnī karnī*, *ghuṭklā̃ chēṛnīā̃* or *kaḍḍhnīā̃*.
crocodile, *see* alligator.

crook, shepherd's, *ḍhāṅgā*, m.: *kalpā*, m.
crooked, *ḍiṅgā*, *ḍiṅg phaṛiṅgā*: bent at end, *muṛeā hoeā*: c. matter, *puṭṭhī* or *kuāsī* or *kasūtī gall*: *see* intricate.
crookedness, *ḍiṅg*, m.: *ḍiṅg phaṛiṅg*, m.
crop, n., *fasl*, m.: spring c. (*rabī'*), *hāṛhī*, f.: autumn c. (*kharīf*), *sauṇī*, f.: *see* produce.
crop-eared, *buccā*.
cross, *salīb*, f.: *sūḷī*, f. (lit stake): c. temper, *kauṛī tabīat*, f.
cross-examination, *jarhā*, f. (*k.*)
cross-legged, *caukṛī mārke baihṇā*: *see* squat.
crossroads (four), *curastā*, m., *curāhā*, m.; *caūk*, m. (in town).
crosswise, *cauṛē dā*: M. 128. 8: G. 122: *see* direction.
crow, v., *bāṅg dēṇī* (of cock).
crow-bar, *bārī*, f.
crowd, *kaṭṭh*, m.: *baṛā mulkh*, m.: *baṛā ādam*, *baṛī khalkat*: *jhurmaṭ* (*pāṇā*): *see* company.
crown, *tāj*, m.
crucify, *sūḷī* or *salīb utte cāṛhnā*.
crude, of word, *ḍagg*.
cruel, *bĕraihm*, *zālim*, *sakht*, *betars*.
cruel-ly, -ty, *bĕraihmī*, f.: *betarsī*, f.: *sakhtī*, f.: all w. *k.*, and *nāḷ*: *see* oppression.
crumble, (e.g. food, bricks, earthen pots), become powder, *bhurnā*: tr. *bhōrnā*.
crumb, *bhōrā*, m.: *krām*, collective term (K.).
crunch, *see* gnaw.
crush, *citthṇā*, *ghōṭṇā*, *dabāṇā*, *mandhāṛnā*: *see* squeeze, trample, pound, beetle.
crust, *krās* (K.).
cry, *see* call, weep, shout, scream.
crystal, *bilaur*, m.
cubit, *hatth*, m.
cucumber, *tar*, f., *khīrā*, m.
cud, chew, *ugāḷī karnī*.
cudgel, *see* stick.
cuff, *kaff*, f.: *see* blow (1).
culprit, *see* guilty.
cultivate, *wāhī karnī*, *khētī karnī*: *wāhṇā* (int. *waggṇā*): *see* plough.
cultivation, *wāhī*, f.: *khētī*, f.: leg, *kāshtkārī*, f.
cultivator, *wāhk*, leg, *kāshtkār*: *see* farmer.
cunning, *see* clever, deceitful.
cup, *pyālā*, m.: *see* drinking-vessel.
cupboard, *almārī*, f.
cupola, *gumbaz* m.
curb, *see* bit, bridle, restrain.
curdle, *jammṇā* (tr. *jamāṇā*): *see* rennet.
curds *dahī*, m.: *see* rennet.
cure, *wall k.*: *caṅgeā k.*: *see* treat.
curious, *see* strange.
curly, *challeāwāḷe wāḷ*: *see* hair.
(1) curry, food, *kārī*: c. and rice, *kārī cauḷ*, m. pl.
(2) curry, curry-comb (horse), *kharkṇā phērnā*.
curse, *bad duā dēnī* (*nū̃*): of God, *lānat karnī* (*nū̃*).
cursed, *lāntī*.
cursory reading, etc., *sarsarī nazr mārnī* (*te*).
curtain, *paṛdā*, m.: *see* screen, mosquito, cikk.
curved, *gōḷ* (round), *see* crooked.
custodian, *see* guardian, watchman.
(1) custom, gen., *dastūr*, m., *riwāj*, m.: esp. rel., *rīt*, f. *rasm*, f.: *see* habit, rule.

customer, *gāhk*, m. : *lainwāḷā*, m.
(2) customs, *maihsūl*, m. : *cungī*, f. (octroi) ; *see* tax.
cut, gen., *waḍḍhṇā* : clip w. scissors, *katrnā* : hair, *katrnā* (get cut, *katrāṇā*) : pay, *kaṭṭ-nā* : grass, *mārnā* (int. *mar-nā*), *khōtarnā* : teeth, *dandīā nikḷṇīā* (tr. *kaḍḍhṇīā*) : c. up fodder, *kutrnā* : c. up wood, *see* chop : *see* prune. A.
cutting (of flowers, trees for sowing), *kalam*, f. : of pay, *see* deduction.
cymbal, *channā*, m.

D

dagger, *khanjar*, m. : *churā*, m.
dacoit, *ḍākū*, m.
dacoity, *ḍākā*, m. (*mārnā*).
daily, *rōz*, *rōz dihāṛī*.
dam, n., *bann*, m.
damage, *nuksān*, m. : *see* loss, injure, hurt : leg., *see* A : v., *nuksān k.* (*dā*), be damaged, *nuksāneā jāṇā*, *nuksān h.* (*dā*).
damp, n., *sill*, f. · *sējjal*, f. : *see* moisture, wet : adj., *gillā* : become d., *sill* or *sējjal carhnī* (*nū̃*) : *sill ghattṇā*.
dance, gen., *naccṇā* : special d., *bhangrā* (*mārnā*) or *dhamāḷ* (*pāṇī*). [*ḍāṇḍī*, f.
dandy, *see* fop. : sedan chair,
danger, *khatrā*, m.
dangerous, *khatrewāḷā*.
dare, *dalērī karnī*, *jurat karnī*.
dark, n. and adj., *hanērā* : get d., *hanērā paiṇā* : at d., *hanēre paie* : very d., *ghup-ghēr*, m. : d. of colour, *see* A.
darling, *see* dear : rather spoilt, *lāḍlā*.
dash, *see* run, throw.
(1) date, fruit ; dried, *chuhārā*, m. : green, *khajūr*, f. : tree, *khajūr*, f.
(2) date, time : *tārīkh*, f. : *tarīk*, f. : *see* appoint : useful dates for computing middle-aged and old persons' age : *maine wāḷā sāl*, Apr. 1877 to Apr. 1878 : mutiny, *gadar*, m. (1857) : *Sikkhā dā rāj*, rule of the Sikkhs, later forties : *see* era, year.
daub, *see* plaster, smear.
daughter, *dhī* : leg. document, *bint* (always called *bannat*) : European's, *bāwī*, *miss bāwā* : d. in-law, *nūh*.
dawn, day, *diṇ* or *diũh caṛhnā*.
day, *dihāṛā*, m. (gen.) : *wār*, m. (day of week) : *diṇ*, *din*, m. (daylight, also 24 hours) : *rōz*. m. (rare except meaning daily) : *atth paihr*, eight watches, one day : d.'s work or wages, *dihāṛī*, f. : in course of day or less, *sādi-hāṛī* : by day, *diṇe* : day and night, *rātī dine*, *dēh rātī* : long days of hot weather : *mōkḷe dihāṛe*, *lamme dihāṛe*, *mōkḷī bahār*, f. : next d., *agle bhaḷak*, *dujje bhaḷak* : few days ago, *agle dihāṛe* or *diṇ* (the other day) : *see* time, year : that d., *ōddin* : what d., *kiddin* ? which d., *jiddin* : (or *ōddihāṛe*, etc.) : d. for fever, *wārī*, f. (turn). [die.
dead, *moeā hoeā*. *murdā* : *see*
deadly ; disease, *marnwāḷī*, *mautwāḷī* : snake, *zaihrī* : *see* fatal.
deaf, *ḍōrā*, *bōḷā* : *uccā suṇṇā*,

M. 129. 24: ears stopped, *jhappe aune* (*nū*), M. 117. 8.
deal, *see* associate.
dealings, *laihṇā dēṇā*, m., *lāho deī*, f., *laihṇ dēṇ*, m.: *kamm*, m.
dear; loved, *pyārā*, *azīz* (U.): money, *maihṅgā*, *pyārā*, *tēz*.
dearness, money, *maihṅgāī*, f. (pron. *maṅghāī*): *see* rise.
death, *maut*, f.: *see* die
bar, *see* forbid hinder.
debauchee, *sharābī*, *nashebāz*, *nashaī*, *luccā*.
debris, *malbā*, m. (also wood. bricks of house).
debt, *karz*. m.: get into d., *karz cukknā*, *de sir karz caṛhnā*: M. 118. 20: *see* owe.
debtor, *karzāī*.
decadence, *raunak ghaṭṇī*; *zōr*, etc., *ghaṭṇā*.
decamp, *cupp capītā nass jāṇā*.
decapitate, *see* behead.
decay, *trakknā*: *see* bad: get soft, *galṇā*: get spoiled, *wigaṛnā*: *see* decadence.
deceased, *see* dead, late.
deceit, deceive, *dhōkhā*, m. (*d.*, *nū*): *farēb*, m. (*k.*, *nāl*): *dhroh*, m. (*k.*, *nāl*): *ṭhaggī*, f. (*k.*, *nāl*): *ṭhaggṇā*, *luṭṭṇā* (both lit. rob): *see* trick: be d., *dhōkhā khāṇā*, *farēb khāṇā*: *see* put off.
deceitful, *dhōkhebāz*, *farēbī*, *dhrohī*, *ṭhagg*: *see* double (-tongued).
deceitfulness, *dhōkhebāzī*, f.
December, *dasambar*, m.: *poh*, m., about Dec. 13 to Jan. 12.
decide, *faislā karnā*: *see* settle, arrange, umpire.
decline, day, *diṇ ḍhalṇā*: *see* sink: in years, *umr ḍhalṇī*; *see* old: *see* refuse (1), decadence, lessen.
decorate, *see* adorn.
decrease, *see* lessen, decadence.
decree, *ḍigrī*, f.: *see* lose, command, regulation, law.
deduce, *natījā kaḍḍhṇā*.
deduct, *mujrā* m. (*mujre laiṇā*, *d.*): d. pay, *see* cut: *see* subtract.
deduction, of pay, *kāṭ*, f. (*k.*).
deed, *see* action: *amal*, m.: *kartūt*, f. (gen. bad).
deep, *ḍūṅghā* (water, thoughts, matters), *gaihrā* (thoughts, matters, U): *see* cunning.
deer, *harn*, fem. *harnī*.
defame, *see* accuse, slander.
defeat, v. int. *hārnā* (tr. *harānā*): n., *hār*, f.: *see* conquer, vanquish.
defect, *nuks*, m., *aib*, m., *kasr*, f.: *see* fault.
defective, *nākas*.
defence, *bacā*, m.
defenceless, *māṛā* (weak): *hathyār nehī*.
defend, *bacāṇā* (save): *hifāzat karnī* (protect).
deference, *lihāz*, m.: *ādar*, f.: *izzat*, f.: *see* consideration, favour, partiality.
deficient, *ghaṭṭ*, *kassā*, *kam*: *see* paucity.
defile (dirty) *mailā k.*: ceremonially, *palīt k.*: *bhēṭ chaḍḍṇā* (int. *bhiṭ jāṇā*): *choh chaḍḍṇā* (only by touch, int. *choh ghattṇā*): *see* unclean, abstain.
deformed, *see* cripple, hunchback.
defraud, *hakk dabāṇā* or *mārnā*, M. 123. 46.
defy, *laṛn nū teār k.*: *see* disobedient.

degrade, in rank, *trōrnā*, *tōṛnā* (int. *tuṭṭnā*).
degree, rank, *darjā*, m. : by degrees, *hōndeā hōndeā*, *hōndeā hawāndeā*, *hauḷī hauḷī*.
delay, *cir lāṇā* (int. *laggṇā*) : *dēr lāṇī* (int. *laggṇī*) : *ḍhill karnī*, *ḍhill mäṭṭh karnī*.
delete, *ḍhāṇā*, *miṭāṇā*, *lāhṇā* (int. *ḍhaiṇā*, *miṭṇā*, *laihṇā*) : strike off name, *kaṭṭṇā*, *khārij*.
delegate, *wakīl* ; *ēlcī*, (U.). [*k.*
deliberately, *jāṇke*, *sōc samjhke*, *jāṇ bujhke*, *aīwē nehī* : *see* purposely.
delicacy, esp. affected, *nazākatā*, f. pl. (*k*) : *nakhre*, m. pl. (*k.*) : *nakhrebāzī*, f. (*k.*) : real, use *bimār raihṇā*, *tagṛā nā raihṇā*, *nāzak*.
delicate, matter, person, *nāzak* *see* delicacy, weak : affectedly, *nazākatī*, *nakhrebāz*.
delicious, *suādlā*, *mazedār*.
delight, (int. sense,) *suād auṇā* (*nū̃*), *khush h.*, *rāzī h.* : tr., *khush-k.*, *rāzī-k.* : *see* charm, rejoice.
delightful, *see* good, beautiful, delicious, etc.
delinquent, *kusūrwār*, *see* guilty.
delirious (raving) *bĕhōshī wicc bakṇā*.
deliver, *chuḍāṇā* : d. address, d., *k.*, etc., or *suṇāṇā* : of midwife, *jamāṇā*.
deluge *see* flood.
delusion, *waihm*, m : *see* deceit.
demand, *see* ask, claim : commercial d., *māg*, f. ; *wikrī*, f. (sale).
demolish, *ḍhāṇā*, *ḍegṇā* : *see* destroy.
demoralised, become, *wigaṛnā*.
demur, *cū̃ carā karnī*, *kusakṇā* : *see* refuse (1).
den, animals, *khundhar*. f.
dense, trees, population, *sanhṇā* : *see* stupid.
dent, in metal, soft brick, *cibb*, m., (*paiṇā*, tr. *pāṇā* ; *see* straighten) : in wood, *ṭoā*, m. (*paiṇā*, tr. *kaḍḍhṇā*).
deny, *mukkarnā*, *inkārī karnī*, *namukkar jāṇā*, *nāh karnī*.
depart, *ṭur jāṇā*, *Allāh Belī h.* ; *alī panj h.* : *see* start, farewell.
department, *maihkmā*, m. : of education, *sarishtā e tālīm*, m.
depend, *see* confide, trust : my visit d. upon my getting leave, use " if " clause, or *shart*, f., condition : *see* condition. [*e.*
deplore, *menū̃ ohdā baṛā afsōs*
deport, *see* exile, banish.
deposit, n., *amānat*, f. : v., d. in bank, *jamā k.*, *rakkhṇā*.
depressed, *see* sad, sorry.
deprive, *khohṇā* : *see* defraud.
depute, *mukhtār banāṇā* : *wakīl karke ghallṇā*.
depth, *dunghiāī*, f.
deputy, *wakīl*, *naib*.
deride, *see* ridicule.
derogatory, *eh de wicc sāḍḍī bĕiztī e*.
descend, *laihṇā*, G. 64 : *utrnā*, *ḍhalṇā*.
descendant (s), *aulād*, f., *ulād*, f. : *āl aulād*, f., *ans*, f., *aūs*, f., *nasl*, f. : of Muhammad, *sayyad*, fem. *sayyadzādī* : *see* tree.
descent, *lahāī*, f. : *utrāī*, f.
describe, *bĕān karnā* (*dā*).
(1) desert, n., *rēgistān*, m. ; *ujāṛ*, m. : *barētā*, m., *barētī*, f., bit of dry sand in water : *see* waste : -ed, *ujjaṛeā hoeā*.

(2) desert, v., *nass jāṇā*, *chaḍḍṇā*.
deserve, *oh dā hakk e*.
design, *matlab*, m., *wiclā matlab* ; *see* intention : drawing, *nakshā*, m. (*banāṇā*).
desire, n., *cāh*, f. : *hirs*, f. : *shauk*, m. : *khāhsh*, f. : *rījh*, f. : *see* taste : v., above nouns w. *hōṇā* : *jī*, m., *rūh*, m., *dil*, m., all w. *karnā* (M. 119. 35, 37) : *cāhṇā* G. 67 : *auhlṇā* (w. hesitation) : *pucchaṇ pucchaṇ* (etc.) *k*., d. but hesitate to ask, G. 112 : cause to d., afflict, *tarsāṇā* : I wish for, want, *mĕnū cāhīdā e*, or *lōṛīdā e*, G. 67 : *see* long.
desist, *muṛnā*, *chaḍḍṇā*.
despair, *nāumēdī*, f. (*h*.) : *udāsī*, f., (*h*.).
desolate (place) *ujāṛ*, *wīrān* : *see* desert (1).
despatch, *see* send.
despise, *kujjh nā samjhṇā*, *kutte de barābar samjhṇā* : *see* contempt, scorn.
despot-, -ic, *see* cruel.
destiny, *see* fate.
destitute, *see* poor.
destroy, *barbād k*., *kharāb k*., *nās karnā* (*dā*), *cauṛ k*., *cauṛ capaṭṭ k*. ; *traṭṭī cauṛ karnī* (*dī*) : lay waste, *ujāṛnā* (int. *ujjaṛnā*) : money, *phūkṇā*, *uḍāṇā* : *see* demolish, devastate, waste, downfall, perish, ruin.
detail, n., *tafsīl*, f. : in d., *sārīā gallā*, *tafsīlwār* (U.), *mufassal* (U.) : v., *see* relate.
detain, someone, *bahāī rakkhṇā*, *khalhārī rakkhṇā*, *jāṇ nā d*.
detect, *tāṛ laiṇā*, *wēkh laiṇā*, *jāc laiṇā*, *samjhṇā* : *see* trace, discover.
detective, *khufyā pulswāḷā*.
detenu, *nazrband*, m. : *see* surveillance.
deteriorate, *wigaṛnā*, *kharāb hōjāṇā*.
determin-ation,-e, *pakkā irādā karnā* : *see* inten-d, -tion, purpose.
dethrone, *takhtō haṭāṇā*, *gaddīō lāhṇā*.
devastate, *wīrān k*., *ujāṛnā* (int *ujjaṛnā*) : *see* destroy, waste, desert (1).
devi-ce, -se, mechanism, *kalā*, f., *kalā*, f., : *see* arrange, plan, trick.
devil, *shatān*, m.
devote, time, *lāṇā*, *kharc k*. : *see* consecrate.
devoted, *see* love.
devour, *khā laiṇā*, *rugaṛ laiṇā*.
devout, *see* religious.
dew, *trēḷ*, f. (*paiṇī*).
dhak, tree, *chichrā*, m.
dialect, *bōlī* f.
dialogue, *see* conversation.
diamond, *hīrā*, m.
diarrhoea, *baṛe dast*, m. pl. (*laggṇe*, *nū* : *auṇe*, motions) : *see* dysentery. [f.
dice, *dāṇā*, m. : *pāshā*, m. : *nard*,
dictat-e. ion, (in school) *imlā likhāṇī* : gen., *kise nū koī gall likhāṇī*.
dictionary, *lugāt*, f. : *ḍikshnarī*, f. (educ.).
(1) die, v., *marnā*, *guzar jāṇā*, *pūrā h*. : trees, plants, *sukkṇā*, *marnā* : *see* death.
(2) die, n., *mohr*., f. (*lāṇī*) : *see* dice.
diet, *khurāk*, f. : *gazā*, f.
differ, *nā raḷnā*, *nā milṇā* : words for difference w. *hōṇā*.
difference, *fark*, m. : *wērwā*, m. :

great d., *zamīn asmān dā jark* : slight d., *rawāḷ jehā jark*.
different, *wakkhrā*, *hōr* : *see* differ, separate.
difficult, *aukkhā*, *mushkil*, *sakht*.
difficulty, *aukh*, m. : *aukhat*; f. : *mushkil*, f. : *aukkar*, f. : *see* inconvenience, trouble ; straits : w. d., adv., words for difficulty, trouble, etc., w. *nāḷ* : also *masā̃*, *masā̃ masā̃*, *kiwē̃*, *aukkheā̃ hōke*, *marke*, *see* scarcely.
dig, *puṭṭṇā* : *see* hoe, weed : d. hole, *ṭoā kaḍḍhṇā*.
digested, be, *pacṇā*, *hazm h.*, (tr. *k.*).
digestion, *hāzmā*, m.
dignity, (honour) *izzat*, f. : (rank) *darjā*, m. [*wāḷā*.
diligent, *mehntī*, *kamm karn-*
dim, *maṭṭhā*, *maddham* : sight, *maṭṭhī*, *māṛī*.
dine, *khāṇā khāṇā* : -ingroom, *khāṇā kamrā*, m.
dinner, *khāṇā*, m.
direct, adj., *see* straight : v., *rāh pāṇā* or *dassṇā* (*nū̃*).
direction, in what d.? *kehṛī guṭṭhe*, *kehṛe pāse*, *kehṛī sehde* : *see* north, south : lengthwise, *lamme dā*, M. 128. 8 : crosswise, *cauṛe dā* : in this way, *ēs dā*.
dirt, *gand*, m : *maiḷ*, f. : in well, *jīndar*, f. : *see* rubbish.
dirty, *gandā*, *maiḷā* ; *see* bad : of water, *see* muddy : of machine, *see* clogged : v., *gandā k.*, *maiḷā k.*
disabled, well, cart, animal, man, but not woman, *hanēkeā jāṇā* : for woman use ill, injured, etc.
disadvantage, *nuksān*, m. : *see* defect.
disaffected, *badniyyat*, *badkhāh* (U.) : *see* disloyal.
disagree, *khiāl nā raḷṇā* : *rā nā raḷṇī* : food, *menū̃ muāfik nehī̃*, *mēre lai caṅgā nehī̃*.
disagreeable, affair, *maṭṭhī* or *burī* or *mandī* or *kauṛī gall*.
disagreement, *see* discord, quarrel.
disappear, *disṇõ raih jāṇā*, *gaib hōjāṇā* : *see* run, visible.
disappoint, no exact word, *nāumēd k.*, *umēd jāndi rehī*, *umēd pūrī nehī̃ hoī*.
disapprove, *caṅgā nā laggṇā* (*nū̃*).
disaster, *hanēr*, m. : *see* calamity.
discharge, gun, arrow, etc., *see* fire : debt, *see* pay : servant, *juāb d.* (*nū̃*) : *see* dismiss.
disciple, *cēllā* (H.) : *murīd* (M.) : *shagird* : *see* pupil scholar.
discipline, *intizām*, m. (arrangement).
discomfort, *bēarāmī*, f. : *taklīf*, f. : *see* inconvenience.
discontented, *rāzī nehī̃* : *see* displeased.
discord (tune), *see* tune : unfriendliness, (*see* tune), *nāitfākī*, f. : *phuṭṭ*, f. : *wigāṛ*, m. : *see* enmity, quarrel
discordant, *see* tune.
discourage, *dil tōṛnā* (int. *tuṭṭṇā*), *bedil k.* (int. *h.*) : be d., *hauslā chaḍḍṇā*, *dil chaḍḍṇā*.
discover, *malūm k.* : *daryāft k.* (inquire) : by asking, *patā karnā* : by looking for oneself, *patā lāṇā* (int. *laggṇā*).
discuss, *gall karnī*, *salāh karnī*,

salāh mashwarā karnā : *see* argue.
disease, *rōg*, m. : *bamārī*, f. : *marz*, f : contagious or infectious, *lagganwāḷā*.
disembark, *see* land.
disgrace, *beiztī* f., *bepatī*, f., (both *k.*, *h.*, *dī*) : *namōshī*, f. (*h.*, *dī* or *aunī nū*, M. 117. 3) : *see* dishonour.
disgraceful, *sharm dī gall* : *see* bad, mean.
disguised, *bhēs badalke*.
disgust, *krīc*, f. : *kraiht*, f. : *nafrat*, f. : all w. *auṇā* and *wallō*, *tō*, M. 117.3 : or *k.* and *nāl*.
dish, *bhāṇḍā*, m., *bartaṇ*, m., *dīs*, m. (K.) : *kunāḷ*, m., *kunāḷī*, f. : *see* plate.
dishcloth, *jhāṛan*, m.
disheartened, *see* discourage.
dishonest, *beīmān*, *badniyyat* (in intention)
dishonour, *pat lāhṇī* (int. *laihṇī*, *dī*, M. 121. 19 : 122. 32) : *beiztī k.*, *dī* : *izzat lāhṇī* (int. *laihṇī*, *dī*) : *see* disgrace.
disinclined, *see* sick of.
disinfect, *pōcā pherṇā* (plaster) : *fanail chinkṇī* or *traūkṇī* (phenyle) : *see* fumigate.
dislike, *burā laggṇā* (*nū*, M. 121. 11) : *cangā* or *acchā nā laggṇā* (*nū*) : *see* disgust, annoy, displeased.
dislocated, be, of joint, *ṭalṇā laihṇā*, *utrnā* : adj., *ṭaḷeā hoeā*.
disloyal, *khairkhāh nehī* : *see* disaffected.
dismay, v., tr. *ghabrāṇā*, *ghabrā dēṇā* : int. *ghābbarnā*.
dismiss, *kaḍḍhṇā*, *tōr d.*, *juāb d.*, (*nū*) : permit to go, *rukhsat-karnā* (*nū*). A.
disobedient, *ākkhe nā laggṇā* : *gall na mannṇī* : *hukm nā mannṇā*.
disobliging, no word, say *putthā ādmī* ; *kise dā faidā nehī cāhndā* ; *badniyyat*.
disorder, *gaṛbaṛī*, f. : *bēintizāmī*, f. : *bētartībī*, f. : *see* confus-e, -ion, tidy, untidy.
dispensary, *haspatāḷ*, m. : *see* hospital.
disperse, *khalārnā*, *ēddhar ōddhar k.*, *urā parā k.*
display, *see* show.
displease, *narāz k.* : -d., *rinj*, *narāz*, *witreā hoeā*, *mūh waṭṭṇā* (*mēre wallō*) : *see* angry, annoy.
disposition, *tabīat*, f. : *mizāj*, f. : *see* pride. [*k.*
disprove, *jhūṭhā* or *galt sābit*
disqualify, *nā kaṭṭṇā* (*dā*). A.
dissension, *see* discord, quarrel, disturbance.
dissuade, *mōṛnā*, *manā k.*, *samjhāṇā*.
distance, *paiṇḍā* m. : *wāṭ*, f. : *witth*, f. (very small space) : *dūh pailīā dī wāṭ*, two fields' d. : *kukkaṛ uḍārī*, f., cock-fly, short d. : *see* near.
distant, *durāḍḍā* : *dūr* (fem., as *kinnī dūr* how far ?) : *see* far.
distinct, *see* different, separate.
distinguish, *nakhēṛā karnā*, *fark kaḍḍhṇā*, *pachāṇṇā* (pa. p. *pachā-ttā*, *-ṇeā*) : *tamīz karnī* (U.).
distinguished, *see* famous.
distressed, be, (heat, worry) *hussaṛnā* : *see* worry, trouble.
district, gen., *alākā*, m. : small, *tappā*, m., *halkā*, m. : Govt. d., *zilā*, m. : *taihsīl*, f. : *pargaṇa*, m. : *zail*, f.

disturbance, *raulā*, m. : *rattā*, m. : *rēṛkā*, m. : *rappha*ṛ, m. : *bakhēṛā*, m. (all w. *pāṇā*, int. *paiṇā*, *h.*) : *halcal*, f. (*paiṇī*, *h.*) : *rohlī*, f. (*macāṇī*, int. *macṇī*) : serious d., *fasād*, m. (*k.*, *h.*) : *daṅgā fasād*, m. (*k.*, *h.*) : *see* quarrel, noise, excitement, riot.

ditch, *ṭoā*, m. (*kaḍḍhṇā*) : *see* pit.

dive, *cubbhī mārnī* : go under accidentally, *gōtā khāṇā*.

diver, *ṭōbhā*, m.

divert, *dil parcāṇā* (int. *parcṇā*) : *dil bhulāṇā*, int. *bhullṇā* : *see* delight, please, game.

divide, *waṇḍṇā*, *taksīm-k.*

division, *taksīm*, f. : of school class, *farīk*, m. : *see* part.

divorce, paper of, *likhat*, f. (M.) : *tiāg pattrī*, f. (H.), *tiāg pattar*, m. (H.) : v. tr., *likhat dēṇī* (*nū̃*) : *tiāg dēṇā* (*nū̃*) : *tiāgṇā*, *talāk dēṇī* (*nū̃*).

divulge, *bhēt dassṇā*, *zāhr k.*

dizz-y, -iness, *nhērnī auṇī* (*nū̃*), *bhuāṭṇī auṇī* (*nū̃*), *sir cakrāṇā*, *sir cakkar khāṇā*, *akkhīā̃ agge nhērā auṇā*.

do, *karnā* (pa. p. *kītā*) : *see* accomplish, finish, work : d. without, *ohde bājhõ guzārā karnā* or *kamm calāṇā*.

docile, animal, *asīl*.

doctor, *ḍāgdār*, m. : *ḍākṭar*, m. : *hakīm*, m. : d.'s work, practice, *ḍākṭarī*, f.

doctrine, *tālīm*, f. (teaching) : *akīdā*, m. (creed) : *maslā*, m. (one point of d.).

dog, *kuttā*, m. : *see* puppy.

doll, *guḍḍī* f.

dome, *gumbaz*, m.

donation, *candā*, m.

donkey, *see* ass.

dooly, *ḍōlī*, f.

door, *būhā*, m., *darwāzā*, m. : rough wooden, *bhitt*, m. and *khiṛk*, m. : one side of double door, *bhitt*, m. : w. open doors, *latthī būhī*, G. 78 : w. shut d., *wajjī būhī* : indoors, *ghare*, *andar* : d.-frame, *cugāṭh*, m. : side of d., *muhāṭh*, f. : wood above, *sardal*, m. : below, *brū̃*, f. : lean against doorpost, *muhāṭhī laggṇā* (M. 120. 5) : through door, *būhe rāh* : *see* socket, pivot.

dot, *nukhtā*, *nuktā*, m.

double (size, price, distance, etc.) *dūṇā* : (two layers, etc.) *dohrā* : on both sides, *duallī*, thus *dūṇī sazā*, double punishment ; *duallī sazā*, punishment to both parties : *see* fold, time : v. tr., *dūṇā k.*, *dohrā k.* : d.-entendre, *domaihnī gall*, f. : double-tongued, *durangā*, *dubājrā* : *see* deceit-, -ful.

doubt, *shakk*, m. (*k.*, *h.*).

doubtful, *shakkī*.

doubtless, *beshakk*, *nishang*.

dough, *taun*, f., *guddhā hoeā āṭā* : for pudding, cake, scones, *māwā*, m.

dove-cot, *kābuk*, f. : in ground, *ghumail*, f. : roost, *chatṛī*, f.

down-, -wards, *see* below.

downfall, *nās*, m. : *barbādī*, f. : *see* destroy.

dowry, *dāj*, f. : *see* marr-y, -iage.

dozen, *darjan*, m.

drag, *dhrūhṇā*, *ghasīṭṇā* : d. in, *see* rake up.

drain, *waihṇī*, f. : *nāḷī*, f.

drama, *nāṭak* m.

draught, rough, of deed, etc., *masaudā*, m. (*baṇāṇā*).

draw, *khiccnā* : *see* drag : d. water, *bharnā*, rarely *kaḍḍhnā* : of tea, *rang aunā* (*nū*, M. 50. 4) : *see* drawing.

(1) **drawer**, *drāz*, f.

(2) **drawers**, *drāz*, f. sing. : very small, *jānghīā*, m. sing.

drawing, *taswīr*, f. (*khiccṇī*) : plan, map, *nakshā*, m. (*banāṇā*).

drawingroom, *gōḷ kamrā*, m.

dread, *see* fear.

dream, *khāb* f. m. : *sufnā*, m. (both *auṇā*, M. 117. 6, and *wēkhṇā*).

dress, n. v. : *see* clothes, clothe : lady's d., *drēs*, m. : d. wound, *paṭṭī bannhṇī*, *phāh lāṇā* (int. *laggṇā*) : *see* ointment. [m.

dressingroom, *sangār-kamrā*,

drill n., *kawaid*, f. (*k.*).

drill (hole) *chēk kaḍḍhṇā*.

(1) **drink**, *pīṇā* (pa. p. *pītā*) : caus. *piāṇā*, *piāḷṇā*.

(2) **drink**, intoxicating, *sharāb*, m. : *nashā*, m. (both w. *pīṇā*) : *see* drunk-, -ard.

(3) **drinking-vessel**, *channā*. m. : *kaul*, m. : *kaṭōrā*, m. : *gaṛwā* m. : *gaṛwī*, f. : *gilās*, m. : *see* cup.

drip, (of vessel, house. water), *cōṇā* : (of vessel, water), *wagṇā* : *see* ooze, trickle.

drive, horse, etc., *ṭōrnā*, *calāṇā* : d. fast, *bhajāṇā* : d. on or away, *hikkṇā* : *see* hammer.

drizzle, *phak*, f. : *phūhr*, f. (both *paiṇī*).

(1) **drop**, n., *būnd*, f. : *chiṭṭ*, f. (fr. splashed or falling water), both *paiṇī*.

(2) **drop**, v., *ḍiggṇā*, *paiṇā* : let fall, *ḍiggaṇ d.* : *see* drip.

drought, *rōṛā*, m. : *auṛ*, f. : *sōkā*, m. (all w. *laggṇā*).

drown, *ḍuobke marnā*, *ruṛhke marnā* (in flowing water) ; tr. *ḍōbṇā*.

drowsy, *see* sleepy.

drum, *ḍhōl*, m. : smaller, *ḍholkī*, f. : double, *tablā*, m. : all w. *wajāṇā* (int. *wajjṇā*).

(1) **drunk**, *matwālā*, *nashe wicc*.

(2) **drunkard**, *nashebāz*, *nashaī* (both also of drugs), *sharābī*.

drunkenness, *nashebāzī*, f.

dry, *sukkā* : d. bread, *rukkhī rōṭī*, f., bread alone : *sukkī rōṭī*, actually dry : *see* insipid.

due, n., *hakk*, m. : adj., d. to me, *menū aundā e* (money) : train due, *gaḍḍī āī cāhndī e*, (G. 112), *huṇ āī khlōṭī e*.

dumb, *gūngā*.

dumbbell, village, *bugdar*, m. : *mungḷī*, f., Indian club.

dung, horse, ass, *lidd*, f. : cattle, *gohā*, m., *gohā gaṭṭā*, m. : sheep, camel, rats, mice, *mengṇā*, f. pl. : dogs, human, *gūh*, m. : birds, *wiṭṭh*, f. (all w. *k.*).

dunghill, *rūṛī*, f.

dupe, *see* prey.

durable, *see* lasting.

dusk, *muhānjlā*, *mūh anhērā* m.

dust, n., *dhūṛ*, f. : *dhuddaḷ*, f. : *ghaṭṭā*, m. : of decayed body, *khāk*, f. : *miṭṭī*, f. : v., *jhāṛnā*, *jhāṛ pōc karnī* (*dī*) : *see* sweep.

duster, *jhāṛan*, m.

duty, *farz*, m. (*pūrā k.*) : of work, *naukrī* (*laggṇī*, M. 121. 7) : *dyūṭī*, f. (*h.*).

dwarf, *giṭh miṭhīā*, *ṭhingṇā*, *ṭhigṇā*, *gīnḍhā*, *wauṇā* (all for very small man).

dwell, *wassṇā*, *raihṇā* (pa. p. *rehā*) : *see* resident.

dye, n., *rang*, m. : for hair, beard, *wasmā*, m. and *kalf*, f., indigo : *mehndī*, f., red dye, (all with *lēṇā*) : v., *rangṇā*.

dyer, *lalār-ī*, fem. *-an*.

dysentery, *pēcish*, f. : griping pain, *marōṛā*, m. : *see* diarrhoea.

E

each, *see* every : two e., three e., etc., *dō dō* ; *trai trai*, etc., G. 24 : at certain rate for e., *sētī*, *picche*, *fī* (U.) : *e.g.* *jaṇe sētī*, per man : *see* per.

eager, *see* desire.

ear, *kann*, m. : w. cropped ears, *buccā* : poison ears, *see* incite.

early, *sawēḷe*, *sājhre*, *sawakhte* *see* morning.

earn, *khaṭṭṇā*, *kamāṇā* : *see* deserve, obtain.

earnings, *khaṭṭī*, f. : *kamāī*, f. : *see* advantage, profit.

(1) **earnest**, *sargarm*, *jōshwāḷā* : in e., truly, *saccī muccī*.

(2) **earnest money**, *saī*, f.

earth, *see* world, soil : filling up w. e., *bhartī*, (*pāṇī*) : e. coloured, *ghasmailṛā*, *khākī*.

earthquake, *bhucāḷ*, m.

ease (rest), *ārām*, m. : (easiness), *sukhall*, m., *asānī* f., at e., *maze wicc*, *maze nāḷ* : *see* rest, convenience.

easily, *saukh nāḷ*, *asānī nāḷ*, *cuṭkī wicc* ; *hāī māī*, used only in neg. sentences.

east, *caṛhdā*, m. : *caṛhdā pāsā*, m. : e.-wards, *caṛhde wall*.

easy, *sukhallā*, *saukhā*, *saihl*, *asān* : *see* chair.

eat, *khāṇā*, pa. p. *khādhā* : e. greedily, *ragaṛnā* : e. orange, lime, lemon, mango, sugar-cane, *cūpṇā* : parched grain, *cabbṇā*.

eavesdropping, *cōrī suṇṇā* : *see* overhear.

eccentric, *laihrī*.

echo, *dūhrī awāz*, f. (*auṇī*).

eclipse, *cugarn*, m. : solar, *sūraj* or *din dā* : lunar, *cann dā* : among educated people, *graihṇ*, e. (gen.) ; *cugarn*, lunar e.

economy, *sarfā*, m. (*k.*) : *ghaṭṭ kharc*, m. (*k.*)

edge, of instrument, *dhār*, f. : of river, lake, etc., *kanḍhā*, m., *dandā*, m. : of garment, *kannī*, f. : raised e. round roof, *banērā*, m.

educat-e, -ion, *see* teach : educated, *paṛheā likheā*.

efface, *see* delete : mental, *dūr k.*, *haṭāṇā*.

effect, *asar*, m. (gen.).

efficacious, *asarwāḷā* : *see* advantageous.

efficacy, *see* effect, advantage.

efficient, *see* able.

effort, *kōshish*, f. or *kōsht*, f. (*k.*) : *ṭill*, m. (*lāṇā*, int., *laggṇā*) : great e., *jataṇ*, m. (*k.*) ; *zōr*, m. (*lāṇā*) : w. an e., *ṭill nāḷ*, *zōr nāḷ* : *see* difficulty.

egg, *ānḍṛā*, m. : *āṇḍā*, m. : (lay, *d.*,) : white of, *safēdī*, f. : yellow, *zardī* f. : hatch e., *bacce kaḍḍhṇe* : e.-shell, *chill*, f.

egg-plant, *baṭāū*, m., *waiṅṅaṇ*, m. : *bhaṭṭhā*, m.

eight, *aṭṭh* : eighth, *aṭṭhwā̃* : G. 19-24 : eighth part, *see* time, wts. and meas.

eighteen, *aṭhārā̃* : -th, *aṭhāhrwā̃* : eighteen-finger shoe, *aṭhāhrī juttī*, f., G 19-24, 123.

eighty, *assī* : -one, *ikāsī* : -two,

beāsī: three, *tirāsī*: -four, *curāsī*: -five, *panj-* or *pacāsī*: -six, *cheāsī*: -seven, *satāsī*: -eight, *athāsī*: -nine, *unānwe*: G. 19-24, 123: ordinals: 80, *assīwā̃*: 81 to 88 end in *-āhsīwā̃* with high tone or occ. *āsīwā̃*: -nine, *unāhnwewā̃*: G. 22, 123.
either..or, *cāhe..cāhe*, *yā̃..yā̃ bhāwē....bhāwē*.
eject, *see* expel.
ekka, *yakkā*, m.
elapse, time, *laṅghṇā*.
elastic, *lifṇwāḷā*.
elbow, *ark*, f.
electric-, -ity *bijlī*, f.: e. light, *bijlī dī battī*.
elder, *waḍḍā*, *thõ waḍḍā*: *see* old: church-e., *ēlḍar*, m.
electroplate, *gilṭ*, m.
elephant, *hāthī*, fem. *hāthṇī*.
eleven, *yārā̃*: -th, *yāhrwā̃*: G. 19-24, 123.
eliminate, *kaḍḍhṇā*.
elope, of woman, *uddhaḷṇā*, *nikḷ jāṇā*: of man, *udhāḷṇā* w. woman as obj.
elopement, *udhāḷā*, m.
else (e.g., who e., what e.) *hōr*: *see* otherwise, course.
elude, *dhōkhe nāḷ nikḷṇā* or *bacṇā*.
emaciated, *baṛā māṛā* or *patlā*.
embankment, *bann*, m
embark, *jahāz utte suār-h.* or *caṛhnā*.
embers, *see* coal, ashes.
embezzle, *rupayyā khāṇā* (*beimānī nāḷ*).
embitter, *ohdā dil mere wallõ khaṭṭā k.*
embrace, *gaḷ nāḷ* or *hikk nāḷ lāṇa* (int. *laggṇā*, M. 1. 2. 31): *japphā*, *japphī mārn-ā*, *-ī*, *nāḷ*: *kaḷāwē wicc laiṇā*.

embroil, *phasāṇā* (int. *phasṇā*) w. word for quarrel.
emerge, *nikḷṇā*.
emergency, *see* crisis.
emigrate, *dujje mulkh wicc jāke wassṇā* or *raihṇā*.
emperor, empress, *see* king, queen.
(1) emphasis, particle of, *ī*, *hī*: also expressed by *chaḍḍṇā* (*chaṛnā*, *sarnā*), *dēṇā*, *laiṇā*, *suṭṭṇā*, *jāṇā* compounded w. verbs, G. 65, 110, 111: never by repetition of words, G. 71: *see* very.
(2) emphasise, *zōr dēṇā* (*utte*).
empower, *see* authorise.
empty, *sakkhṇā* (*k.*), *khālī* (*k.*): e. handed, *sakkhṇe hatth*: *see* unoccupied.
emulate, *rīs*, f. or *barābrī*, f. (*k.*).
enable, *es gall jogā k.* or *baṇāṇa*: *tākat dēṇī* (*nū̃*).
enamel, gen. *lohā*, m. (iron).
encamp, *ḍērā* or *tambū lāṇā* (int. *laggṇā*): *see* tent, camp.
enclose, a place, *duāḷe wāṛ dēṇī* or *jaṅgḷā baṇāṇā*: *see* shut up, hedge, railing.
enchant, *see* charm.
encourage, *dil wadhāṇā*: *see* comfort.
end, *akhīr*, m.: *ant*, m.: *natījā*, m. (result): to the e., *tōṛ tīkar*: in the e., *see* finally: *see* head, foot, object, edge, boundary.
endanger, *khatre wicc leauṇā*.
endeavour, *see* try.
endless, *beant*, *bēbahā*, *behadd*, *jehṛā* ' ə *nukke*.
endow, paraphrase, or *wazīfā dēṇā* (scholarship): *rupayye dēṇē*, etc.
endure, *jhallṇā*, *jhāgṇā*, *saihṇā*,

jarnā ; *bhugtṇā* (go through w.) : *see* remain, lasting, strong.
enemy, *wair-ī*, fem. *-an* : *dushmaṇ*, *dōkh-ī*, fem. *-aṇ* : deadly e., *jānī dushmaṇ* : *see* enmity, envy.
energetic, *cust*, *mehntī*, *himmatwāḷā*.
enervate, *see* weaken.
enforce, *zōre karāṇā* : *see* force.
engage, servant, *naukar rakkhṇā* : e. a seat, *thā rakhāṇā* : (but keep seat, *rakkhṇā*) : be e. to be married, *see* fiancé : be e. in work, *ḍaihṇā* (pa. p. *ḍehā*) : G. 67, 68.
engagement, (marriage), *kuṛmāī*, f. : *mangṇī*, f.
engine, *iñaṇ*, m. : small mechanical contrivance, *kalā*, f., *kalā*, f.
engrave, *ghaṛnā* : signet, *ukkarnā* (caus. *ukrāṇā*), *ukkhaṇṇā* (caus. *ukhṇāṇā*).
enjoy-, -ment, *suād*, m. : *mazā*, m. (both *auṇā*, *nū*) : *see* amuse, delight.
enlist, tr., *bhartī-k.* (int. *h.*) : *nāwā likhāṇā*, have one's name entered
enmity, *wair*, m. : *dushmaṇī*, f. : mutual ill-feeling, *aṇ baṇ*, f. : *see* envy.
enough, *bas*, *kāfī* (U.) : words for much : *jinnā lōṛīdā e* or *cāhīdā e* : *jinnī lōṛ e*.
enrage, *baṛā gussā duāṇā* (*nū*) : *see* excite, incite : be e., *baṛā gusse h.* : *see* angry, displeased, rage.
enquire, etc., *see* inquire, etc.
entangle, *phhāṇā*, *phasāṇā* (int. *phasṇā*).
enter, *waṛnā* (tr. *wāṛnā*) : *andar jāṇā* : e. name, *nā likhṇā* (caus. *likhāṇā*) : e. pupil in school, *dākhil h.* (of pupil) ; *dākhil k.* (of teacher) ; *dākhil karāṇā* (of guardian).
enteric, *mohrkā tapp*, m.
entertainment, *tamāshā*, m. : w. name, as *bhanḍā dā*, clowns' : *madārīā dā*, conjurers' : otherwise dancing-girls suggested : *see* amuse, delight.
enthusiasm, *jōsh*, m. : *sargarmī*, f.
enthusiastic, *baṛī cāh rakhdā e*, *baṛā shukīn*.
entice, *hirs*, f., or *tamā*, m., or *lālac*, m., *kujjh duāke manāṇā*.
entire, not broken or incomplete, *sābit* : *see* all, bag and baggage.
entitled, *see* right.
entrance fee, *see* fee.
entrails, *āndrā*, f. pl.
entreat, *see* beseech, ask.
entrust, *kōḷ chaḍḍnā*, *de pēṭe*, *de pāṇā*, *hawāle k.*
envelope, *lafāfā*, m.
envy, *khār*, f. (*h. nāḷ*) ; *kiṛ*, f. (*k. nāḷ*) ; *mērā sāṛā* (*ohnū paiṇā*) ; *dukh*, m. or *dukhwaidā*, m. (*h nāḷ*) ; *cōbh*, f. (*h. nāḷ*) ; or *mērā dukh k.* or *mēre nāḷ dukh rakkhṇā*, or *ohnū mērā dukh e* : this last also means sympathise : M. 130. 33-6 : *see* enmity.
epilepsy, *mirgī*, f.
equal, *barābar*, *barabbar*, *barōbbar* : in age, *hāṇī*, m., fem. *hānnaṇ* : *mēre jehā* (like), *jēḍḍā* (size), *jinnā* (amount, number), G. 91.
equality, *barābrī*, f.
equip, *sārā samān d.*, etc.
equipage, *see* retinue.
era, *sammat*, m., esp. that of

Wikrama Ditya, in which
·1975 = Apr. 13, 1918 to Apr.
12, 1919 : year A.D., *san
Īswī* : see date.
eradicate, *see* expel, annihilate,
destroy, exterminate.
erase, *see* delete.
erect, *khalhārnā* : *see* build.
err, error, *see* mistake.
escape, *bacnā, bac niklnā, chutt-
nā, mal jānā; phaṛā nā
dēnā, phaṛāi nā dēni* : *see*
run.
escort, *see* retinue.
especial, *khāss* : -ly, of set purpose, *ucēcā.*
espionage, *jāsūsī,* f. : *mukhbarī,*
f. : *see* spy.
essence, *asl* f.
essentially *asl wicc* : *see* real,
necessary.
establish, *kaim k.* : *see* build,
found.
estate, landed, *malkīyat,* f. :
jagīr, f. (given as reward):
jāēdāt, f. (property).
esteem, *izzat,* f. (*k.*) : *ādar,* f.
(k.) : *acchā* or *nēk samjhnā* :
see consideration, partiality.
estimate, n., *takhmīnā,* m. (of
cost, *banānā* or *lānā*) : *jāc,* f.
(*k.*, less formal, v., *jācnā*) : *see*
calculate, guess, approxi-
mately.
estrangement, *see* discord,
quarrel, enmity.
eternal, *hamēshā dā, azlī* (without beginning), *sadā dā,
abdī* (without end): *see* life.
eternally, *azlō abad tīkar* :
hamēshā toṛi, etc.
etiquette, *see* custom, rule.
Eurasian, *dōglā* : (jocular),
bērṛā, m.
evacuate, *see* empty, leave.
evade, *see* escape, put off.

evaporate, *sukk jānā.*
evasion, *see* evade.
even, not odd, *jist* : *see* level,
smooth.
even, adv. *sagō, wī, bī* : *see*
emphasis.
evening, *shām,* f. (sunset : in e.,
shāmī) : *tarkālā,* f. pl., about
half hour after sunset :
khaupīyyā, m., time of e.
meal, about 8 : *sōtā,* m.,
sleeping time, about 9 or 10 :
dūnghi shām, when full darkness comes : *see* afternoon.
event, *wākiā,* m : *gall,* f.
ever, *kade* : for e., *see* always,
eternal.
every, as in e. eighth day,
atthī dinī, atthwē (or *atthwē de
atthwē*) *dihāṛe.*
everyone, *har koī, sabbh koī,
hamā shamā, janā khanā* : *see*
all, people, common.
everything, *sabbh kujjh.*
everywhere, *sabbhnī pāsī, sabbh
dare, sabbhnī thāī* : *see* side.
evidence, *guāhī,* f. (*d., dī*) : *sabūt,* m. (proof, *d., dā*).
evident, *zāhr, sāf zāhr, ujāgar* :
self-e., *apū malūm hondā e.*
evil, adj., *see* bad : n. *bureāi,*
f. : *burāi,* f. : *kharābī,* f. :
badī, f. : *see* sin.
evil eye, be injured by; *nazreā*
or *nazrāṛeā jānā, nazr* or
nazrāṛ ghattnā : *tērī ohnū
nazr laggī.*
exact, *thīk, bilkul thīk.*
exact, v., *zōre lainā* or *ugrāhnā.*
exactly, *hū bahū, ain.*
exaggerate, *wadhānā.*
examin-e, -ation, in school, etc.,
imtihān lainā (*dā* of person,
subject) : be e., *imtihān d.
(dā* of subject) : e. books,
paṛtāl or *partāl karnī* (*dī*): e.

school, *muāinā karnā* (*dā*) : inspect (medical and in gen.) *mulāhzā karnā* (*dā*, U.) : cross-e., *jarhā karnī* : *see* pass, test.

examiner, *imtihān laiṇwāḷā*.

example, *namūnā*, m., moral, also pattern, sample : in grammar, etc., *misāl*, f. : for e., *maslan* : make e. of, say *dujjeā nū wī mat āwe*.

excavate, *see* dig.

exceedingly, *see* very.

excellent, *see* good : also *baṛā abbal*, *baṛā ḍabal* (strong, big), *fast klās*, *baṛ umdā sohṇā* (*baṛ* for *baṛā*).

except, *de bājhō*, *de suā*, *nū chaḍḍke*, *de bagair* (U.).

exception, *kaide de khalāf*.

excess, *bakāyā*, m. : *jinnā waddhe* : *lōṛ tō waddh* : amount in e. or defect, *wādhā ghāṭṭā*, m.

excessive, *haddō waddh* : -ly, *sakht* (for something undesirable) : *see* very.

exchange, *waṭānā* : *see* change : in e., *ohde thā̃* or *badle* : that may be e., *waṭāwā̃*.

excise, v., *waḍḍhṇā*.

excite, *jōsh duāṇā* (*nū*) : *ghabrāṇā* (confuse) : *see* incite, induce : be e.-ed, *jōsh wicc auṇā* : *ghābbarnā* (dismayed) : *halcal macṇī* (tr. *macāṇī*, lot of people).

excitement, *jōsh*, m., *hal cal paiṇī* or *macṇā* among lot of people : *see* disturbance.

exclud-e, -ing, *see* except, expel

excommunicate, *chēkṇā*, *zātō chēkṇā* : *hukkā pāṇī band karnā* (*dā*, int. *h.*) : remove ban, *hukkā pāṇī kholhṇā*, (int. *khulhṇā*).

excrement, *see* dung.

exculpate, *barī k.* : *see* acquit.

excursion, *sail*, m. or *sair*, m. or *sail sapaṭṭe wāste jāṇā*.

excuse, v., from doing, *muāf k.*, int. *h.* (*thō*) : *see* forgive : n., *uzar*, m. : you've no e., *terā koī caṅgā uzar nehī̃* : what e. have you ? *wajhā kī e* : a mere e., *huṭṭar*, m., *hīlā*, m., *jugat*, f. (quibble) : *see* pretence.

execrate, *nā̃ suṇke saṛnā* : *see* curse.

execute (hang), *phāhe d.* (*nū*) : *see* do, finish, behead.

executive, *intizāmī*.

exempt, v. tr., *muāf k.* (int. *muāf h.*, *thō*).

exercise, bodily, *warzish*, f. (*k.*) : *kasrat*, f. (*k.*) : practice, *mashk*, f. : e. book, *kāpī*, f.

exert, *see* effort.

exhausted, *see* faint.

exhibit-, -ion, *see* show, spectacle.

exhort, *nasīhat dēṇī* (*nū*) : *see* incite, encourage.

exile, v. n. : *see* banish and add : *mulkhō paṛ mulkh* (*karnā*, int. *hōṇā*).

exonerate, *see* exculpate, acquit.

exorbitant, *see* dear.

exorcist, *see* magician.

expect, *umēd*, f. (*h.*, *k.*) : person, *uḍīkṇā*.

expedient, *see* means, plan.

expedition, military, *lām*, m. (*laggṇā*, sometimes f.).

expel, *kaḍḍhṇā*, *bāhr dhikkṇā*, *banne saṭṭṇā* : see turn out.

expend, *see* spend, expense.

expense, *kharc*, m. : *lāgat*, f. :

see cost : at my e., *mēre pēṭe, mēre palleõ*, G. 34 : M. 129. 20 : marriage expenses paid to inferior castes, *lāg*, m.
expensive, *see* costly.
experience, *tajrabā*, m. (*k.*, *dā*).
experiment, science, *tajrabā*, m. (*k.*) : *see* test.
expert, *see* clever-, -ness.
explain, *samjhāṇā*, *bēān karnā*, *matlab dassṇā*, *sunāṇā*.
explicit-, **-ly**, *sāf*, *sāf saf*, *safāī nāḷ*.
expression, favourite, constantly used, *takīā kalām* m.
expressly, *see* especially, explicitly.
exquisite, *ḍāhḍā sohnā* : *see* excellent.
extensive, *mōkḷā*, *waḍḍā*.
exterminate, *aslõ* or *mūḷõ kaḍḍhṇā* : *see* destroy, annihilate, uproot.
extinguish, lamp, fire, *bujhāṇā*, (int. *bujjhṇā*) : for lamp also *waḍḍā k.*, G. 113.
extort, *see* force, confess.
extraordinary, *see* strange, wonderful.
extract, v., *kaḍḍhṇā* : n., from book, *ibārat*, f.
extraction, *kāḍh*, f.
extravagance, *fazūl kharcī*, f.
extravagant, *fazūl kharc*.
extremity, of trouble, heat, etc., *ākhar āī hoī e*.
exude, *see* ooze.
eye, *akkh*, f. (pl. *akkhīā*) : have bad eyes, *akkhīā auṇīā* (*dīā*), M. 116. 1 : evil e. *see* evil : pupil of, *dhīrī*, f. : healed ulcer in, *phōllā* (*paiṇā*), *ciṭṭā* (*paiṇā*).
eyebrows, *bharwaṭṭe*, m. pl.
eyelash, *pipṇī* f.
eyelid, *chappar*, m.
eye-witness, use *akkhī ḍiṭṭhī gall*, f. : *see* witness.

F

fable, *see* story.
face, *mūh* m. : *muhāndrā*, m. : *see* appearance : f. to f., *mūh drūhī* : *āhmo sāhmṇe*, *āhmṇe sāhmṇe* : to his f., *ohde mūh te* : f. downwards, *mūhdā*, *mūhdṛe mūh*, *mūhdṛe mūh* : (fall) on f., *mūh parne* : faces, *see* grimace.
facilitate, words for easy w., *karnā*.
fact, *saccī gall*, f. : *asl gall*, *wākiā*, m. (U.).
fail, gen. *ukkṇā* : (exam.) *fēhl h.* (*wicc*) : other things, *raih jāṇā*, *kujjh nā baṇṇā* : *see* bankrupt, deficient.
faint, *behōsh h.* ; feel f., *dil chappṇā* or *chōṭā h.*, *dil ghaṭṇā* : M. 128. 10 : exhausted through heat, thirst, etc., *hussaṛnā*, *ghābbarnā* : adj., of colour, *maddham*, *phikkā* : of light *maddham*.
fair, complexion, *gōrā* : f.-haired, *kakkā*.
faith, *imān*, m. : *see* believe, trust, confide, reliance, religion.
faithful, *namak-halāl*, *imān-wāḷā*.
fall, v., *ḍiggṇā*, *girnā* : something big, *ḍhaiṇā* : house, *ḍiggṇā*, *ḍhaiṇā*, (collapse, *baihṇā*) : hair, leaves, fruit, *jhaṛnā* : evening, darkness, night, dew, drops of rain, *paiṇā*.
fallow, *peā hoeā*.
false, *jhūṭhā* : *see* deceitful : coin, *khōṭā* : forged, *jāhlī* : *see* mistake : f. story, *gapp*, f. (*mārnī*).

falsely, *kuṛī mucci*, *jhūṭhī mūṭhī*.
fame, *nā̃*, m. (name): *see* famous.
familiar, too; cheeky, *bhūhe h.* or *caṛhnā*.
family, *ṭabbar*, m.: *bāl bacce*, m. pl.: *munḍe kuṛīā̃*, m. pl.: *kabīlā*, m. (U.): *horī* may be used, G. 82: wide sense, *khāndān*, m.: f.-man, *bāl baccedār*, *ṭabbarwālā*: *see* tree.
famine, *kāl*, m.: f.-allowance, *maihṅgāī*, f. (pron. *maṅghāī*), *kaihtsālī*, f., *kaiht*, m.
famous, *mashāhūr*, *manneā parwanneā*.
fan, *pakkhā* m.: *see* punkah.
fancy, silly, *waihm*, m.: person w., *waihmī*.
far, *see* distant: far side, *see* further.
fare, *bhāṛā*, m.: *karāyā*, m.
farewell, say f. to, *widyā-k.* (int. *widyā h.*): *see* leave, dismiss, salute.
farmer, (caste), *jaṭṭ*, *jaṭṭ būṭ*, *zamīndār*, *wāhī karnwālā* (actual farmer): leg. *kāshtkār*.
(1) fast, *see* swift: tight, *kasseā hoeā*: of colour, *pakkā*.
(2) fast, n., *rōzā*, m. (M.): *wart*, m. (H.): keep f., *rakkhṇā*: break f. at wrong time, *rōzā tōṛnā* or *bhannṇā*; at right time, *rōzā kholhṇā*.
fasten, *see* tie, shut: button, *bīṛā* or *baṭan mēlṇā* or *mārnā*.
fat, n., *carbī*, f.: adj., *mōṭā*: *see* grease, corpulent.
fatal, *marnwālā*, *jis thō mar jāīdā e*: *see* deadly.
fate, *takdīr*, f.: *kismat*, f.: *nasīb*, m (all M.): *lēkh*, m. (H.).
fated, *likheā hoeā*.
father, *pyō*, *cāccā*: f. in law, *sauhrā*: married woman's f.'s house or family, *pēke*, m. pl. (adj., *pēkā*): f. in law's f., *dadiauhrā*: f. in l.'s mother, *dadēhas*: f. in l.'s brother, *patiauhrā*, *patrauhrā*: *patiauhrā's* wife, *patēhas*: f. and mother of bridegroom are *kuṛm* and *kuṛmṇī* to f. and mother of bride, and vice versa.
fatigue, *thakewā*, m.: *see* tired.
fault, *kasūr*, m.: *see* mistake, defect, guiltless.
favour, *ahsān* (pron. *as-hān*) m.: *mehrbānī*, f.: out of deference to you, *tērā lihāz karke*: *see* grace.
favouritism, *see* partiality.
fear, n., *ḍar*, m.: *khauf*, m.: v., *ḍarnā*, *saihmṇā*: *ḍar laggṇā* or *auṇā* (*nū̃*): (tr., *ḍarāṇā*): be afraid and confused, *ghābbarnā*, (tr. *ghabrāṇā*).
fearless, *see* venturesome.
feast, *ziāfat*, f.: *khāṇā*, m.: *see* festival, invitation.
February, *farwarī*, f.: *phaggaṇ*, m. (about Feb. 13 to Mar. 12).
fee, fees, *fīs*, f.: entrance fee, *dākhlā*, m.
feeble, *māṛā*, *kamzōr*: *see* weak, ill, delicate.
feed (v. tr.), *khuāṇā* (gen.): poultry, int., *cuggṇā* (tr. *cugāṇā*): *see* graze. A.
feel, by touching, *ṭohṇā*, *chohṇā*, *hatth lāṇā* (*nū̃*): *see* cold, hot, hunger, thirst: f. angry, etc., simply use *be* angry, etc.: f. pulse, *nabz wēkhṇī*.

feeling, without f. in skin, etc., *sunn* : salvation not dependent on f., *najāt es gall wicc nehī pai sānū̃ ċarī khushī malūm howe yā nā howe.*
fellow-countryman, *watnī, mē watan* or *dēs* or *pinḍ dā.*
female, adj., *zanānā* : of sex (animals), *madīn* : *see* sex.
fence, *see* hedge, railing, enclose.
ferrel, at end of stick, *shām*, f.
ferry, *pattaṇ* m. : f. -train, *ṭhēl-lā*, m., *ṭhehlā*, m.
fertile, *see* soil (good).
festival, *īd*, f. (M.) : *tyohār*, m. (H.) : *see* holiday keep.
fetch, *see* bring.
fetter, *bēṛī*, f.
fever, *kass*, f. : *tāp*, m. : *bukhār*, m. : get f., these words w *caṛhnā* (*nū̃*) : f. go off, *laihṇā* : f.-heat, *bhakhā*, m. A.
few, *thōṛe*, *tā̃wā tā̃wā*, *wirlā wirlā*, *koī koī*, *ghaṭṭ waddh* (G. 28).
fez-cap, *turkī ṭōpī*.
(1) fiancé, *mangeā hoeā*.
(2) fiancée, *mang*.
fickle, *see* changeable, vacillate.
fie ! fie ! *tobā tobā*.
field, *paiḷī*, f. : *khēt*, m. (U.) : part of, *kiārā*, m. : division of arable land, *waṇḍ*, f.
fierce, *ḍāhḍā*, *sakht*, *waihshī*, *ḍarāṇwālā muhāndrā* (*see* face).
fife, *wanjhḷī*, f. : *bā̃srī*, f.
fifteen, *pandrā̃* : -th, *pandhra-wā̃* : fifteen finger long shoe, *pandhrī juttī* : G. 19-24, 123.
fifty, *panjāh* : -one, *ikwanjā* : -two, *bawanjā* : -three, *tar-wanjā* : -four, *curinjā* : -five, *pac- pach-wanjā* : -six, *cha-winjā*, *chiwanjā* : -seven, *sat-wanjā* : -eight, *aṭhwanjā* : -nine, *unāhṭh* : ordinals add -*wā̃*, 51 to 58 add also high-tone h, *ikwanjhawā̃*, etc., G. 19-24, 123.
fig, fruit and tree, *phagwāṛā*, m., *phagwāṛī*, f., *anjīr*, m.
fight, *laṛnā* : *see* quarrel : *bhiṛ-nā* (gen. of buffaloes) : n., *laṛāī*, f.
figure, *sūrat*, f. : *shakl*, f. : in arithmetic, *hinsā*, m. : *see* form, face.
file, n., *rētī*, f. : v., *rētṇā* : file papers, attach to file, *natthī-k.* [*bharke*.
fill, *bharnā* : one's f., *ḍhiḍḍh*
filth, *see* dirt, dirty, rubbish.
final, *chēkaṛlā*, *ākhrī*, *ōṛak dā*.
finally, *chēkṛe*, *chēkaṛ nū̃*, *ōṛak nū̃*, *nihait nū̃*, *ākhar*.
find, *labbh laiṇā* : int. *labbhṇā*, as *menū̃ labbhā*, I found it ; *milṇā* (*nū̃*) : f. out, *see* discover.
(1) fine, n., *ḍann*, m. : *caṭṭī*, f. : *jarīmānā*, m. : impose, f., *lāṇā*, int. *laggṇā*.
(2) fine, adj., *see* beautiful, good : not coarse, *mhīn*, *barīk* : f. fellow (ironical) *hazrat*, *bātshāh*.
finger, *ungaḷ*, f. : little f., *cīcī*, f. : *see* thumb, toe.
finish, *mukāṇā*, *pūrā k.*, *khatam k.*, *nabēṛnā* (settle) : *bhugtāṇā* (go through w.) : int. *mukkṇā*, *pūrā h.*, *khatam h.*, *nibbaṛnā*, *bhugtṇā*. Also by adding to root of verb *baihṇā*, *raihṇā*, *cukṇā*, *haṭṇā* ; G. 66 : or *chaḍḍṇā*, *dēṇā*, *laiṇā*, *suṭṭṇā*, *jāṇā*, G. 65, 110, 111 : it's all over, *syāpā mukk geā*, *khalāsī mukk geī* : the food is

finished, occ. *waddh geā*, G. 114.

(1) fire, n., *agg*, f. : light f., *agg bāḷnī* (int. *baḷnī*) : set on f., *agg lāṇī* (*nū*, int. *laggṇī*, catch f.) : *see* flame : slow fire, *see* slow.

(2) fire, v., gun, etc., *calāṇā* : missile, *mārnā*, *calāṇā* (bullet, arrow) : *see* stone, throw. A.

firefly, *ṭaṭāṇā*, m. *ṭanāṇā*, m.

fireplace, for fire or cooking, *angīṭhī*, f. : *culhā*, m.

firewood, *bāllaṇ* (note *l* in *bāllaṇ*, *ḷ* in *bāḷṇā*, light).

fireworks, *astbāzī*, f. : *ātashbāzī*, f. : fire off f., *calāṇā*, *chaḍḍṇā*, int. *calṇā*, *chuṭṭṇā*.

firm, stand, fixed, *ḍaṭṭṇā*.

first, *paihlā* : leader, *āggū*, *mohrlā* : at f., *paihlā*, *paihlū*, *paihle* : at f. go off, *paund*, *paund saṭṭe* : fr. the f., *muṇḍhõ*, *shurū tõ*.

firstborn, *pahlēṭhī dā* (pron. *palēṭhī*, *paḷēṭhī*).

fish, *macchī*, f. : catch f., *macchīā pharnīā*.

fisherman (water-carrying caste), *māch-ī*, fem. *-aṇ* (M.) : *jhiūr-*, fem. *-ī* (H.).

fist, *muṭṭh*, f., rarely *muṭṭhī*, f. : close f., *muṭṭh ghuṭṭṇī* : *see* handful

(1) fit, v., key, *see* key : clothes, shoes, etc., *pūrā auṇā* or *h.* (*nū*).

(2) fit, *see* able : f. for me, etc., *de laik*, *de jogā* (G. 38) : *de gōcrā* (G. 38) : *jogā* w. infl. inf., G. 95 : *see* proper, suitable.

fitting, *see* suitable.

five, *panj* : fifth *panjwā* : G. 19-24 : fifth part, *see* time : two-fifths and three-fifths in land tenure, *panj-duanjī*.

fix, in ground, *gaḍḍṇā* : f. day, date, *see* appoint.

flag, *jhaṇḍā*, m. : small, *jhaṇḍī*, f.

flame, *lāṭ*, f. : *lamb*, f. : *bhāhmbaṛ*, m. : in lamp-chimney, *lāṭ*, f. : flame up (lamp), *lāṭ nikḷnī* : fire, *bhaṛk uṭṭhṇā*, *bhāhmbaṛ uṭṭhṇā*.

flank, *pāsā*, m. : of animal, *wakkhī*, *pāsā*.

flannel, *falālain*, f.

flare up, *see* flame : get angry, *gussā bhaṛkṇā* (*dā*) : *see* angry.

flash, n., *lishk*, f. : *camak*, f. : *jhalak*, m. : v., *lishkṇā*, *camkṇā*.

flat, *cauṛā*, *caiṛā* : *see* level, plain.

flatter, *cāplūsī karnī* (*dī*).

flaw, *see* defect.

flax, *alsī*, f.

flea, *pissū*, m., *pissū*, m.

fledgling, *bōṭ*, m.

flee, *see* run.

flesh, *mās*, m. *gōsht* or *gōshat*, m. : for food, *see* meat, beef, mutton.

flexible, *lifaṇwālā*.

flinch, *sī karnī*.

float, *pāṇī utte tarnā*.

flock, sheep, goats, *ijjaṛ*, m. : birds, *ḍār*, m. : *taraṇḍā*, m. : *see* herd, swarm.

flog, *kōṛe mārne* (*nū*).

flood, *kāng*, f. : *haṛh*, m. : Noah's f., *Nūh nadī*, f. : *Nūh dī parlo*, f.

floor, *farsh*, m.

flour, *see* meal.

flourish, town, etc., *barī raunak*, etc.

flower, *phull*, m. : v., *phullṇā*, of crops, vegetables, *nissarnā*.

flower-bed, *khēḷ*, f., *kiārī*, f.

flower-pot, *gamlā*, m.
fluctuate, *waddhṇā ghaṭṇā*.
fluent, *far far karke boldā e*.
flute, *wanjhlī*, f. : *bā̃srī*, f. : double f., *jōṛī* f.
flutter, *phaṛkṇā* : of distress, *taṛafṇā*.
(1) fly, *uḍḍṇā*.
(2) fly, n., *makkhī*, f. : blue bottle, *makkh*, m.
foal, *wachērā*, m.
foam, *jhagg*, f.
fodder, *paṭṭhe*, m. pl. : *paṭṭhā daṭṭhā*, m. : very common kinds, *maiṇā*, m., *sinjī*, f.
fog, *dhundh*, f. (mist) : *gaihr* or *ghaihr*, m. (haze).
(1) fold, v., make f. in, *bhann pāṇī* (*wicc*), *bhannṇā* (*nū̃*) : f. in folds, *taih-k.* : roughly *kaṭṭhā k.*, *thappṇā* : f. double, *dohrā k.*, treble, *trehrā k.*, four fold, *cauhrā k.* : above four, *ehde panj*, *che taih kar*, (or fem., *ehdīā̃ taihā̃*), fold it five, six fold : f. up, *wuḷhēṭṇā* : *see* wrap, single.
(2) fold, n., in cloth, paper, *bhann*, f. : sheep, etc., *wāṛā*, m.
follow, *magar jāṇā*, *picche jāṇā* : worryingly, *magar paiṇā* : f. Christ or relig. leader, *pairwī karnī* (*dī*) : f. Christ, *Masīh de magar magar jāṇā*.
follower, *murīd* (M.) : *cēllā* (H.) : *mannaṇwāḷā*.
folly. *see* foolishness.
foment, limb, *sēk karnā* (*nū̃*), *see* toast (contrast word).
fond-, -ness, *see* like, desire.
fondle, *lāḍ k.* (*nū̃*) : *pyār d.* (*nū̃*) : *see* love, spoilt.
food, *khāṇā*, m. : *ṭukkar*, m. : *ṭukkar cappā*, m. : *rōṭī*, f. : *bhōjan*, m. (H.) : *ann pāṇī*, m. : *bhattā*, m. (midday meal taken to workers) : *see* diet : special for cattle, *gutāwā*, m. (mixture of straw, chaff, oilcake, water, meal) : for horses, *nihārī*, f.
fool, *aihmak*, *aihmakh*, *bewakūf* (last never to be used in address), *balēllaṛ*, *wāhyāt*, *bā-* or *mat-* or *hōsh-* or *akl-māreā*, *jhallā* : *see* mad, ignorant, stupid.
foolishness, *bewakūfī*, f. : *jhall-puṇā*, m. : *beaklī*, f. : *nadānī*, f.
foot, *pair*, m. . w. claws, *panjā*, m. : *see* paw, claw : crooked footed, *phiḍḍā* : on f., *ṭurdā*, *paidal* (U.) : fall at one's feet, *carnī ḍiggṇā*, *pairī paiṇā* : footfall, *pairā̃ dā khṛāk* : f. of bed, *puā̃dī*, f. : feet of bed, table, etc., *see* leg : f. of page, *hēṭhlā pāsā*, m. ; *see* bottom : f. of 12 inches, *fuṭ*, *fiṭ*, m. : *see* rule, tiptoe, wts. and meas.
fop, *bā̃kā*, *shukīn*, *jēṇṭal-main* : *ākkaṛ khā̃*.
for, *nū̃*, *wāste*, *laī*, *khātar*, *jogā*, *gōcrā* : *see* behalf, suitable, sake : gone for milk, *duddh nū̃ geā* : for of price, *tō̃*, *thō̃*, *thī*, G. 89, or loc. G. 9, 11, 78.
forbid *manā k.* : *see* hinder, stop : forbidden food, etc., *harām* or use *saūh*, oath : M. 107. 17-9.
(1) force, n., *see* power, oppression, effort : by f., *bado badī*, *malo maḷī*, *zōrī*, *zōro zōrī*, *zabardastī*, *majbūr karke*, *majbūrī gall*. *ic̄ārī gall*,

dhakke nāl : f.-ed labour, *wagār*, f. *wagyār*, f. : f.-ed labourer, *wagārī*, *wagyārī*.
(2) force, v. tr., *majbūr k.*, or causal v. w. word for "by force," G. 110 : f. him to do. *oh de kōḷō zōre karā*, etc. : *see* cause.
forenoon, about 8 or 9, *chāhwēḷā* : 10, *kūḷā bhattewēḷā* : 11, *bhattewēḷā* : 10 or 11, *rōṭī wēḷā* : *see* noon, morning.
forehead, *matthā*, m.
foreign, *horī mulkh dā*, *pardesī*, *ōprā*. *parāyā* : *see* strange.
foreknowledge, *see* prescience.
foremost, *āggū*, *mohrlā* : *see* first.
foresight, *dūrandesh-ā*, m., *-ī*, f.
forest, *ujāṛ*, m., *jaṅgal*, m.
forged, *jāhlī*.
forgery, *jāhlsāzī*, f.
forget, *wisārnā*, *wissarnā*, *bhullṇā* ; last two mean forget of person, or be forgotten of thing. A.
forgetfulness, *see* mistake.
forgive, *muāf k.*, *bakhshnā chaddṇā*, *jāṇ d.*, *muāfī dēṇī*.
fork, for table, *kāṇṭā*, m. : f.-ed stick, *dusāṅghī*, f. : f.-ed tree, *dusāṅghā*.
form, *shakl*, f. : *ḍauḷ*, f. : outline of body, *buṭ*, m. : *see* shape, face, appearance, system.
former, *see* previous.
formerly, *see* before.
fornicat-ion, -or, *see* adulter-y, -er.
fort, *kilhā*, m.
fortification, *kilābandī*, f.
fortress, *see* fort.
fortunate, *karmāwāḷā*, *çaṅgeā bhāgāwāḷā* (H.), *nasīb caṅge*, *kismat caṅgī* : *see* auspicious, unfortunate.
fortune, *see* fate : good f., *khush-kismatī*, f., *khush-nasībī*, f : *caṅge nasīb*, m. pl. : bad, *badkismatī* or *badnasībī*, f. : *bure nasīb*.
fortune-teller, *najūmī*, *ramlī*, *majūsī*.
forty, *cāḷī* : -one, *iktāḷī* : -two *batāḷī* : -three, *tartāḷī* : -four, *cutāḷī* : -five, *paītāḷī* : -six, *chatāḷī* : -seven, *saītāḷī* : -eight, *aṭhtāḷī* : -nine, *uṇwanjā* : ordinals add *-wā̃* w. high tone h, *cāhḷīwā̃*, *iktāhḷīwā̃*, *uṇwanjhawā̃*, G. 19-24, 123.
forward, *agā̃*, *agge* : *see* before : cheeky, *athrā*, *ḍhīṭh* : *see* impertinent, familiar.
forwardness, *see* boldness.
foundation, *nīh*, f. : *bunyād*, f. (latter word also metaphorical)
founder, *bānī*. [owner).
foundling, *lawāris* (without
fountain, *see* spring : artificial, *phuhārā*.
four, *cār* : -th, *cauthā* : fourth part, *see* time.
fourteen, *caudā̃* : -th, *cauhdāwā̃* : G. 19-24, 123 : fourteen finger long shoe, *caudhī juttī*.
fowl, for table, *kukkaṛ*, fem. *kukkṛī* : *see* cock, hen, chicken.
fox, *lūmb-aṛ*, fem. *-ṛī*.
frame, for door, picture, *cugāṭh*, f. : hanging f., for clothes, *taṅgṇā*, m.
fraud, *see* deceit, clever.
free, adj., *azād* : v. tr., *chuḍāṇā*, *chaḍḍṇā* : *see* leisure, gratis, liberty, release. A.
freeze, *jammṇā* : hands, feet, *see* cold

frequented, to be, of road, *wagṇā.* [ly.
frequently, *see* often, repeated-
fresh, *sajrā, tāzā* : green, *harā.*
fretful, *see* irritable.
friction, *see* discord : use *aṛnā, khaihke laṅghṇā, ragaṛke laṅghṇā.*
Friday, *jumā,* m. : *sukkar, shukkar, sukkarwār, shukkarwār,* (last four H.).
friend, *sajjaṇ, mittar, dōst, yār* (only one man of another), *bēlī* : *see* companion.
friendship, *dōstī,* f. : *yārī,* f. (between men) : strong f., *gūṛhī dōstī* : make friends w., *dōstī, yārī, pyār,* m., all w. *pāṇā* and *nāḷ* (int. *paiṇā, nāḷ*) : M. 120. 27 : 243. 5 : *dōstī rakkhṇī* (*nāḷ*), be friendly w.
frighten, *see* fear.
frill, *jhāllar,* f.
from, *tō̃, thō̃, thī̃, -ō̃,* G. 13, 36, 37, 88, 89 : fr. person, animal, *kolō̃.*
front, in, adv. *agge, mohre, agēre* : adj., *mohrlā* : prep. *sāhmṇe* : *see* face, forward, before.
frost, hoar, *kakkar,* m. : *see* freeze.
frontier, *sarhadd,* f. : adj., *sarhaddī.*
froth, *jhagg,* f.
frown, *treoṛhīā̃* or *ghurākīā̃* or *ghūrīā̃,* all with *waṭṭṇīā̃* : *ghurākī wekhṇā,* look angrily : *see* angry.
frozen, *see* freeze.
fruit, *phaḷ,* m. : raisins, etc., *mewā,* m.
fruitful *phaḷwāḷā.*
fruitless, tree, *apphaḷ* : *see* useless, vain.
fryingpan, *fraīpān,* m. (*K.*), Indian, *kaṛāhī,* f.
fuel, *see* firewood.
fugitive, *nasseā hoeā.*
fulfil, *see* finish.
full, *bhareā hoeā* : f. of Holy Spirit, *Pāk Rūh nāḷ bhareā hoeā* : f. brother, etc., *sakkā*
fumigate, *dhūkh* or *dhūf dēṇā* : *guggaḷ dhukhāṇā* : *gandhak* (sulphur) *dhukhāṇī* : *see* disinfect.
fun, *see* entertainment.
funeral, *janāzā,* m. (*paṛhṇā*).
funnel (engine, steamer, brick-kiln), *cimṇī,* f.
fur, *jatt,* f.
furious, *baṛe gusse wicc, bhakkheā hoeā* : *see* anger, rage.
furlong, *farlāṅg,* m.
furnace (with boiler) *bhaṭṭhī,* f. : for sugarcane juice, *cumbā,* m. [m. : *raihl,* f.
furrow, including ridge, *siāṛ,*
furniture, *mēz kursīā̃,* f. pl., *asbāb,* m. : old f.-seller, *kuāṛīā, kabāṛīā.*
further, *zyādā dūr, waddh dūr, paiṇḍā waddh e* : on far side, *parlā, pailā* : *parle* or *paile pāse* : *see* distant : moreover, *nāḷe.*
fuss, *raṭṭā* or *rēṛkā pāṇā* (int. *paiṇā*) : *see* disturbance, quarrel.
future, *agge nū̃, agge wāste.*

G

gain, *see* advantage, profit, obtain, earn, reach, succeed, win.
gait, *ṭōr,* f. : *cāl,* f.
gale, *see* storm.
galled, be (horse ass, mule) *läggā laggṇā* (*nū̃*) : M. 121. 14.

gallop, gentle, *poïā turnā*: vigorous, *sarpatt turnā*. A.
gallows, *sūlī*, f.: *see* hang, crucify.
gamble, *jūā khēḍṇā*: gambling, *jūā*, m.
gambler, *juāriā*, m.
game (gen.), *khēḍ*, f.: single g. or match, *bāzī*, f.: win g., *bāzī jittṇī*: lose g., *bāzī hārnī*, *bāzī ohde sir hōṇī*, *bāzī caṛhnī* (*nū*, M. 118. 24).
gaol, *see* prison.
gap, *khappā*, m., *witth*, f.
garden, *bāg*, m.: public g., *kaumpnī bāg*: g.-walk, *rāh*, m.: g.-bed, *khēḷ*, f.: *kiārī*. f.
gardener, *māl-ī*, fem. *-aṇ*: caste, *arāī*, fem. *araiṇ*; *maihr-*, fem. *-ī*.
garlic, *thōm*, f.
garrulous, *see* talkative
gasp, in death, *saihkṇā*: *see* pant; breath, out of.
gate, *phāṭak*, m.: *see* door.
gather, *see* collect, infer.
gender, *jiṇs*, f.
(1) general, n., *jarnail*.
(2) general, adj., *ām*, *mamūlī*.
generally, *aksar*, *ām*, *bauht karke*.
generation, *pīṛhī*. f.
generosity, *sakhāwat*, f. (U.).
generous, *sakhī*.
genius, *pujjke akl-wāḷā*: *see* sense.
gentle, no good word, *sharīf*, *ashrāf*, *bhalāmāṇas*: animal, *garīb*, *sāū*.
gently, *saihje saihje*, *saihe saihe*, *saihje nāḷ*, *saihe nāḷ*, *hauḷī hauḷī*: *see* quietly, slowly: speak g. *hauḷī*, *nimmhī*.
gentleman, *sāhb*, *sharīf*, *sharīf* or *ucce khāndān dā*: *see* gentle.
genuine, *see* real.
get, *see* obtain: g. something done, *see* cause. [*cōpaṛ*, m.
ghee, *ghyō*, m., occ. *thindhā*. m.,
ghost, *bhūt*, m., *jinn*. m. (M.): Holy Ghost: *see* spirit.
giant, no word, *baṛā lammā*, etc.
gibberish, *ĕwĕ bakṇā*.
gibe, *see* taunt.
giddy, *see* dizzy.
gift, to superior, *nazr*, f., *ḍhoā*, m., *ḍāhḷī*, f.: to inferior, *inām*, m., *bakhshīsh*, f.
gild, *mulammā-k.*: *giḷt-k.*
ginger, *adhrak*, f.: *sunḍh*, f. (dry).
girdle, *see* belt, griddle.
girl, *kuṛī*, *kākkī*, *jātkṛī*, *laṛkī*: occ. *bālṛī*: European, *miss bāwā*: *see* daughter.
girth, of saddle, *taṅg*, m.
gist, *khulāsā*, m.: *matlab*, m.
give, *dēṇā* (pa. p. *dittā*), *bakhshṇā*: g. in, admit defeat, *hār mannṇī*: lose heart, *see* discourage.
glad, *khush*, *rāzī*.
gladly, *khushī nāḷ*, *khush* or *rāzī hōke*.
glance, at book, letter, etc., *nazr mārnī* (*te*): just a g., *sarsarī nazr*, f.
glass, *kac*., f.: *shīshā*, m.: drinking g., *gilās*, m.: *see* mirror, drinking vessel.
glimmer, *thōṛī lishk* or *camak*, f.
glimpse, get g. of, *zarā nazrī paiṇā* (*ohdī*, &c.).
globe, of lamp, *hāṇḍī*, f.
glory, *jalāl*, m.: *see* splendour.
glove, *dastānā*, m.: G. 74.

glowworm, *taṭāṇā*, m., *ṭanāṇā*, m.
glue, *saṛēsh*, f. : v., *sarēsh lāṇī*, *sarēsh nāḷ jōṛnā* : *see* gum, paste. [frown.
gnash teeth, *dand pīhṇē* : *see*
glutton, *see* greedy.
gnaw, of rodents, *kutarnā*, *ṭukkṇā* : bone (dog), *khāṇā* : crunch, *kuṛkāṇā*.
go, *jāṇā* (pa. p. *geā*), *ṭurnā*, *calṇā* ; g. away, *ṭur jāṇā wag jāṇā*, *see* rise : g. out, *nikḷnā*, *banne jāṇā* : g. in, *waṛnā* : *see* start, walk, off.
goad, ox-, wooden, *parāṇī*, f. : v., *parāṇī nāḷ hujj mārnī* (*nū̃*) ; *see* prod : metaph., *see* incite, urge.
goal, football, hockey, polo, etc., *gōl*, m. : *see* aim, object.
goat, *bakr-ā*, fem. *-ī* : long-haired, *kāgānī bakrā* adj., *bākrā* : *see* kid.
gobble, *see* devour.
God, *Khudā*, *Rabb*, *Maulā* (all M.) : *Parmēshwar*, *Īshwar*, *Bhagwān* (H.) : god, *māhbūd*, m. (object of worship, M.), *dēotā*, m. (H.).
goddess, *dēwī*.
goitre, *gillhaṛ*, m. : man w. g., *gillhaṛwāḷā*.
gold, *syōnā*, m. : *sōnā*, m.
golden, *syōne dā*.
goldsmith, *sunyārā*.
gong, *see* bell.
(1) good, *caṅgā*, *acchā*, *umdā*, *wall*, *baṛā waddhīā* : *kharā* (genuine) : of character, *caṅgā*, *acchā*, *nēk*, *bhalāmāṇas*, *ashrāf* : of soil, *see* soil : coin, *see* coin : *see* excellent, very : interj., *caṅgī gall*, *kharī gall* n., God seeks our good, welfare, *bhalā*, m. : *see* welfare.
goodness, *nēkī*, f. : *bhaleāī*, f. : *bhalmaṇs-āī*, f., *-aū*, m.
goodbye, *see* farewell.
(2) goods, *asbāb*, m. : *laṭar paṭar*, m. : *nikk shukk*, m. : *see* property bag and baggage.
gooseberry, cape, *ṭipārī*, f.
Gospel, *Injīl*, f. : *Anjīl*, f. (the book) : G. message, *najāt dī khabar*, f.
gossip, *see* conversation, chatter.
govern, *hukūmat karnī*, *bādshāhī karnī*, *rāj karnā*.
governor, *hākim* : Lieutenant G., *lāṭ sāhb*.
grace, *fazl*, m. (M.) : *dayā*, f. (H.), *kirpā*, f. (H.).
gradually, *hundeā hundeā*, *hundeā hawāndeā*.
graft, n. (plant), *pyōnd-karnā*.
grain, *dāṇā* m. : *dāṇā phakkā* : wheat and barley, *gōjī*, f. : wheat, barley and gram, *bēṛṛā*, m. : receptacle for, *bharohlā*, m., *bhaṛohlī*, f., *kōṭhī*, f.
gram, *chōlle*, m. pl.
granary, *see* grain.
granddaughter, son's daughter, *pōtrī* : daughter's, *dohtrī*.
grandfather, paternal, *dāddā* : maternal, *nānnā* : *dadda's* father, *paṛdāddā* : *dadda's* mother, *paṛdāddī* : *nanna's* father, *paṛnānnā* : *nanna's* mother, *paṛnānnī* : *dadda's* house or family, *dādke*, m. pl. : *nanna's* house or family, *nānke*, m. pl. : adjj., *dādkā*, *nāṇkā*.

grandmother, paternal, *dāddī* : maternal, *nānnī*.

grandson, son's son, *pōtrā* : daughter's son, *dohtrā* : *potra's* son, *parpōtrā* : *potra's* daughter, *parpōtrī* : *dohtra's* son, *pardohtrā* : *dohtra's* daughter, *pardohtrī*.

(1) grant-in-aid, *grānṭ*, f. : *imdād*, f. : in receipt of g. (institution), *imdādī*.

(2) grant, *see* allow, give.

grape, tree and fruit, *dākh*, m. : *angūr*, m.

grasp, *hatth naḷ pharnā* or *phagarnā*.

grass, *ghāh*, m. : special kinds, *khabbal*, m. : *ḍeḷā*, m. : *dabb*, f.

grasshopper, *tridd*, m., *triddī*, [f.

grateful, *dā shukrguzār* : *see* thank.

grating, small iron, *janjrīā*, f. pl., *jhajjrīā*, f. pl. : larger bars, *jharne*, m. pl.

grat-is, -uitous, *muft*, *mukhat*, *muft dā*.

(1) grave, M. *kabr*, f. : saint's, *khāngāh*, f. : H. *marhī*, f. : *samādh*, f.

(2) grave, *see* serious, sober.

graveyard, *kabristān*, m.

gravel, single stone, *gīṭī*, f. : collective, *bajrī*, f., *kankrī*, f.: *see* pebble.

gravy, *grēbbī*, f. (K.).

graze, v. int. *cugṇā*, *chirnā* (go out to g.) : tr. *cārnā*, *cugāṇā*, *chēṛnā*.

grease, *thindheāī*, f. : *ciknāī*, f. (both words mean greasiness) : *see* fat.

greasy, *thindhā*, *ciknā*.

great, of size, age, dignity, *waḍḍā*, otherwise *baṛā* ; *see* very : G. 34.

greed- -y ; *see* covet-, -ous : *oh-dī nazr bhukkhī e.* : great eater, *baṛā khāū* or *khāṇ-wāḷā*.

green, *harā*.

greengrocer (woman) *arain* f. : *see* gardener. [-*ca*, *allhaṛ*

greenhorn, *anāṇā*, *siddhā*, *kac-*

greenness, *hareauḷ*, f.

greet, *see* welcome, salute.

gregarious, *kaṭṭhe raihṇwāḷe*.

grey, *see* brown : green grey, *sāwā* : of hair, *see* hair.

greyhound, *tāzī kuttā*. [m.

griddle, girdle, *tawā*, m. : *tajāl*,

grief, *dukh*, m. : *jhorā*, m. : *afsōs*, m. : *gam*, m. : *ranj*, m. (all w. *h.*, *afsōs* also w. *k*).

grieve, *jhurnā* : (*dā*) *dil dukhī hōṇā* : tr. *dil dukhāṇā* (*dā*) : *see* regret.

grimace, make to annoy, *cinghē lāṇe* : *ḍanḍīā cing-hāṇīā* : bad taste in mouth, etc., *bhaiṛā mūh baṇāṇā*.

grin, *dand kaḍḍhne*, *mūh aḍḍṇā*, *guṭak paiṇā*.

grind, fine, *pīhṇā* (int. *pīsṇā*) : coarse, *dalṇā* : g.-ing board, *sil*, f. : roller, *waṭṭā*, m. : *see* mill, grindstone, pin.

grindstone (for knives, etc.) *sāṇ*, f. : v., *sāṇ te lāṇā*.

grizzled, *see* hair.

groan, *aṛāṇā hūngṇā*.

grocer, *pasār-ī* fem. -*an*.

groom, *sīs* (often pron. w. low tone, *s-hīs*).

groove, *nāḷī*, f.

ground, *zamīn*, f. (*zimī*, *jīwī*, *jiwī*) : on the g., *bhuñē*, *bhūē* : *see* soil, foundation. [*nehī*.

groundless, *ehdī bunyād koī*

grow, *waddhṇā* : plants, *uggṇā*, begin to grow : *see* sprout.

growl, *hūngṇā*

grudge, *see* envy.
grudgingly, *see* reluctant.
grumble, *ū ū karnī*, *kuṛhnā*, *buṛ buṛ* or *bhus bhus karnī*.
(1) guard, *rakhwālī* or *rākhī karnī* : *caukīdārī karnī* : protect, *hifāzat karnī* (all *dī*) : be on g. against, *ohde wallō hushyār raihṇā* : *see* preserve, save.
(2) guard, in train, *gāḍ*, *see* sentry.
guardian, of things, *rākkhā*, *rakhwālā*, *caukīdār* : of persons, *sarprast*, *walī wāris* : leg. *wāris*, *see* saviour.
guess, *tukk lāṇī* : *ṭēwā lāṇā* : g. prove correct, *tukk ṭhīk wajjṇī* : *see* calculate, estimate, approximately.
guest, *parauhṇā*, m.
guide, *rāh dassṇā* or *wakhāṇā* set one on one's way, *rāhe pāṇā*.
guilt, *jurm*, m. : *see* fault.
guiltless, *bēgunāh*, *bēkasūr*, *see* innocent, acquit.
guilty, *mujram*, *kasūrwār*.
guitar, *sitār*, f. : *see* plectrum.
gulf, *khalīj*, m.
(1) gum, *gūnd*, f. : v., *gūnd lāṇī*, *gūnd nāḷ jōṛnā* : *see* paste, glue.
(2) gum (mouth), *masūṛā*, m. (gen. plur.). [*calṇī*) : *see* fire.
gun, *bandūk*, f., (*calāṇī*, int.
gunpowder, *barūd*, m.
gush (water) *zōr nāḷ wagṇā*.
gust, *see* storm.
gutter, *see* drain.
gyve, *see* handcuff.

H

habit, *bitar*, f., *gējh*, f., *wādī*, f., *ādat* f., (all with *paiṇī*) : *see* custom : make h. of, special verbal construction, G. 68, 69 : *gazā pakk jāṇī* (*dī*) : *see* accustomed.
haggle, *mull dī bābat jhagaṛnā*.
hail, n., *candrā*, m., *gaṛā*, m., *aihṇ*, f.
hair, *wāḷ*, m. (single h.) : very fine hair on body, each hair, *lū*, m. : fur, *jatt*, f. (also goat's h. etc.) : long hair, *chatte*, m. pl. : plaited lock, *mēḍhī*, f., *mēṇḍhī*, f. : curl, (special kind), *kalam*, f. : Sikkh's hair, *kēs*, m. : Hindu's lock, *bōddī*, f. : white hair, *dhauḷe* (*auṇe*, M. 117. 10), *citte* or *bagge wāḷ* : grey, *karṛ barṛe* or *karṛ barṛ wāḷ*, m. pl. : do one's h., *wāḷ suārne*.
hairless (on face) *khōddā* : beard, etc. not yet grown, *alū* : *see* bald.
half, *addhā*, *addh* : h. and h., *addh pacaddh*, approximately ; *addho addh*, exactly : in land tenure, *adhiāre te* : h. way, *adhwāṭe* : 1½, 2½, *see* one, two : above 2, *sāḍhe* w. number, G. 23 : *see* halve.
hall, in school, etc., *hāl*, m. : in house, *hāl kamrā*, m.
halo, round moon, *piṛ*, m., *cann piṛ malleā hoeā e*.
halt, *makām karnā*, *rāt raihṇā*.
halter, esp. cattle, *mohrak*, f. : horse, *talihārā*, m.
halve, *addho addh karnā*.
(1) hammer, *hathauṛā*, m. : wooden, *munghlī*, f. : sledge h., *wadān*, m.
(2) hammer, v., pegs, nails, *thōkṇā* : poles, *gaḍḍṇā*.
(1) hand, *hatth*, m. : without one or both h., *ṭuṇḍā* : h. of

watch, clock, *sūī*, f.: by h. *dastī*: *see* tie.
(2) **hand**, v., *phaṛāṇā*, *dēṇā*: *leā* (imperat. only).
handbreadth, *cappā*, m.
handcuff, *hatthkaṛī*, f., *kaṛī*, f.
handful, single, *lapp*, f.: double, *bukk*, m.: fistful, *muṭṭh*, f., rarely *muṭṭhī*, f.
handkerchief, *rumāl*, m.
handle, w. hole through it, of cup, dish, *kunḍā*, m.: button of lid, *ḍūḍḍan*, m.: latch -h., *lāṭū*, m.: others, *hatthā*, m., *hatthī*, f.: *muṭṭh*, f.: *dastā*, m.: cloth catch of chikk, *khūṭī*, f., *khuṭṭī*, f.
handsome, *see* beautiful.
hang, v. tr., *ṭaṅgṇā*, *lamkāṇā* (int. *lamkṇā*): h. person, *phāhe d.* (*nū̃*): h. oneself, *phāh laiṇā*: h. -ing frame for clothes, *ṭaṅgṇā* m.: hanging, *lamkdā*, *ṭaṅgeā hoeā*.
happen, *hōṇā*, *bītṇā*.
happy, *khush*, *rāzī*.
harass, *see* annoy.
harbour, *bandargāh*, f.
hard, *ḍāhḍā*, *sakht*.
hardly, *see* scarcely, difficulty.
hare, *saihā*, *sehā*, m.: also rabbit.
harm, *see* injure, loss, hurt.
harmless, *see* guiltless, innocent: also harm w. neg.
harmony, *see* tune, agreement.
harness, *sāz*, m. (*lāṇā*, int. *laggṇā*): v., also *jōṇā* (int. *juttṇā*, *juppṇā*).
harrow, *suhāggā*, m. (*phērnā*, int. *phirnā*).
harsh, *see* hard, rough.
harvest, *fasl*, m.: *see* reap.
(1) **haste**, n., *kāhl*, f.: *tāṛ*, f.: *utauḷī*, f.: *see* impatien-ce,-t.
(2) **hasten**, *kāhl* or *chētī* or *shtābī* or *jaldī* all w. *karnī*: *kāhḷā* or *utauḷā ṭurnā*: *see* headlong.
hasty, *kāhḷā*, *utauḷā*: *jaldbāz* (bad sense).
hat, *ṭōpī*, f.
hatch, *bacce kaḍḍhne*.
hatchet, *kuhāṛī*, f.: *see* axe
hate, *wair rakkhṇā*: *dushmaṇī rakkhṇī*: *see* dislike, disgust, envy.
haught-iness, -y.: *see* pride, proud.
haul, *see* pull.
have, *de kōḷ h.*: *see* keep: to h. to, inf. w. agent, G. 75, 97: or inf. w. *paiṇā* or aux. v. w. *hōṇā*, G. 96. 97: have something done, *see* cause: *see* possession.
hawker, *chābṛīwāḷā*.
haze, *see* fog.
he, *eh*, *oh*: his, her, *ehdā*, *ohdā*: also *s. sū*, G. 82-6: to him, her, *ehnū̃*, *ohnū̃*, also *s*, *sū*, G. 82-6.
head, *sir*, m.: of inanimate things, *sirā*, m.: sheep, goat, for eating, *sirī*, f.: bed, *sarhāndī*, f.: door, *sērū*, m.: of canal *hēḍḍ*, m.
heading, *see* title.
headlong, on one's head, *sir parne*: h. flight, paraphrase, as *khurī karke* or *annhe wāh* or *khitt dēke bhajj jāṇā*.
headman, *caudhrī*: of village, *lambaṛdār*: *see* lead-, -er.
headquarters, *hēḍkuāṭar*, m.: of canal, *see* head.
headstrong, *see* obstinate
heal, *see* cure, treat.
health, *tandrustī*, f.
healthy, *wall*, *caṅgā*, *acchā*, *tandrust*.
heap, *ḍhēr*, m., *ḍhērī*, f.: of

sugarcane, **straw**, **chaff**, **plastered** over, ***dhaṛ***, f. : *see* wood.

hear, *sunnā* : ***suṇāī dendā e***, he, she, they, etc., can hear : M. 238. 19.

hearing, of lawcase, ***pēshī***, f.

hearsay, ***suṇī suṇāī gall***, f.

heart, *dil* or *diḷ*, m. (lit. and gen.) : ***man***, m.

heartily, *dilõ wajhõ hōke*, *dil nāḷ*.

heat, *garmī*, f. : *tā*, m. (of fire) : fever h., *bhakhā*, f. : pungent heat, *see* hot : v. tr., ***garm k.***, *tāṇā* ; *tā pāṇā*, put burning coal into fire : ***tā d.***, make coal burn up : become very hot (of fire), *see* blaze and add tr. *bhakhāṇā* : *see* slow (fire), hot (fire)

heaven, *bihisht*, m. (gen.) : *surg*, m. (H).

heavy, *bhārā*.

hedge, *wāṛ*, f., *see* railing, enclose.

hedgehog, *jhāh cūhā*, m.

heel, *aḍḍī*, f.

height, *ucāī*, f. : of person, ***ucāī***, *lamāī*, f. : ***masātar***, f., height to tips of fingers above head (to estimate depth of water).

heir, *wāris*, m.

hell, *dozakh*, m. and *jahannam*, m. (M.) : *nark*, m (H.).

help, v., *madat*, f. (*k.*, *dī* : *d.*, *nū̃*) : *hatth phaṛnā* (*dā*) : also caus. of v. w. dat. of pers. and acc. of thing. G. 109 : without assistance, by himself, without being told to, *āpū̃*, *āpe*, *āpī*, *āpõ*, G. 88.

helper, *wasīlā*, m. : ***madadgār***, m.

helpless, ***lacār***, ***wacārā***.

hemorrhoids, *bawāsīr* f., bleeding, *khūnī*.

hemp, *san*, f. : *sankukṛā*, m. : *sūjjo-* or *sajjo-bhāṛā*, m. : intoxicating h., *bhang*, f., *cars*, f.

hen, *kukkṛī*, f.

hence, *ētthõ*, *ēttalõ*, *edharõ*.

henceforth, *edū̃ agge*, *agge nū̃*.

her, *see* he.

herb, medicinal, *būṭī*, f.

herd, cattle, *wagg*, m. : *see* flock.

herdsman, *wāggī*, *chēṛū*, *ḍāngrī* : *see* shepherd.

here, *ētthe*, *ēttal*, *eddhar* : *ure* or *urhā̃* (gen. of motion alone) : here it is, *āh wekhā̃* : h. and there, *kitale kitale*, ***kite kite***, ***kidhare*** *kidhare*.

hereditary, *maurūsī*.

hero, *bahādar* : *see* brave.

hesitate, *shakk wicc raihṇā*, *ḍōlṇā*, *ḍāwā ḍōl raihṇā* : *see* desire.

hiccup, *hiḍkī laggṇī* (M. 124. 50) or *auṇī*, (both w. *nū̃*).

(1) **hide**, *lukāṇā*, *chapāṇā* (int. *lukkṇā*, *chappṇā*) : hidden, *gujjhā*.

(2) **hide**, n., *see* skin.

hideous, *see* ugly.

high, *uccā* (gen.) : person, ***uccā***, *lammā*.

hill, *pahāṛ*, m. : small, *pahāṛī*, f. : v. small, *ṭibbā* m. : range of small hills, *pabbī*, f.

hilly, belonging to hills, *pahāṛī*.

him, *see* he.

hinder, *ḍakkṇā*, *rōkṇā*, *aṭkāṇā* : *see* stop, forbid, obstruct.

hindrance, material, *ḍakkā*, m. : abstract, *aṭkā*, m. *bāndhā*, m. : ***rukāwaṭ***, f. (gen.).

hinge, ***kabzā***, m. : *see* pivot socket.

hint, *ishārā*, m. (*k.*, *de wall*) : *see* hit, point.
hip, *lakk*, m.: h.-joint, *cūknā* m., *cūḷā*, m.. *cūkḷī*, m. : (carry) on hip, *ḍhākke*.
hippopotamus, *daryāi ghōṛā*, m.
hire, *bhāṛā*, m. : *karāyā*, m.: *see* wages.
hiss, snake, *shūkṇā*, *shūkarnā* : n., *shūkar* f., *shukāṭ*, f., (both *pāṇī*).
history, *tawārīkh*, f.
hit, int. *laggṇā* (stone, bullet, etc.) : *see* beat : h. at in speech, *nōk lāṇī* (*nū*, int. *laggṇī*, *wajjṇī*) : *see* hint, point.
hither, *ure*, *urhā* : *see* here.
hoarse, become, *saṅgh* or *wāz baihṇā* (*dā*) : M. 117. 15 : *wāz* or *awāz bhārā h.* (*dā*).
hobble, v. tr., *ḍhaṅgṇā* : v. int., *see* lame.
hoe, *gōḍṇā*, *gōḍḍī karnī* : n., small, *rambā*, m. : large, *kahī*. f.
hold, *phaṛī rakkhṇā*, *see* have, keep, seize.
hole, *mōrī*. f., (*kaḍḍhṇī*) : *chēk*, m. (*kaḍḍhṇā*) : in roof, *maggh*, m. : in wall, made by rain, etc., *gharl*, m. : in water-channel, *ghukkā*, m. (these last three w. *paiṇā*) : animal's burrow, *khuḍḍ*, f. (*kaḍḍhṇī*).
holiday, *chuṭṭī*, f. (leave) : *see* leave, festival.
hollow, *pōllā* (soft inside), *khoḷā khōkhlā* (U.).
holy, *pāk* (M.) : *pawittar* (H.) : *see* pure : h. man (H.), *sādhū*, *sanyāsī*. *gusāī*, *jōggī* : (M.) *aulīā*, *sāī*, *fakīr* : *see* priest.
home, *see* house : at h., *ghare* : gone h., *ghar geā*.
homesick, feel. *oddarnā* (*mā khuṇō* or *bājhō* or *thō*, for his mother).
homesickness, *udrēwā*, m.
honest, *dyānatdār*, *imānwāḷā*.
honey, *shaiht*, m., *mākhyō*, *mākhyō*, f. : *see* bee.
honeycomb, *mākhyō* (f.) *dā khaggā* or *pakkhā* or *kharkṇā* (or *dī challī*).
honour, *izzat*, f. (*k.*) : *ādar*, f. (*k.*) : *pat*, f., *see* esteem, respect.
honorary, *bētankhāh* : h. magistrate, *ānararī majasṭrēṭ*, m.
hoof, *khur*, m. (cloven) : *sum*, m. (uncloven).
hook, *kuṇḍā*, m. (gen.) : clothes, *hukk*, f. : fish-h., *kuṇḍī*, f.
hoop, boys', *reṛhā*, m., *cakkar*. m.
hoot, *oe oe karnī* : *see* clap.
hope, *umēd*, f. : *in shā Allā*, please God (M.) : *see* expect : *umēd*, expectation, seldom used for hope : I h. he will soon get well, *Khudā kare shtābī wall ho jāe* : I h. it did not hit him, *wajj nehī nā baiṭhā su* ? I h. you will not get wet on the way, *wāṭe bhijj nā nā jāē* : I h. your horse does not jib now, *huṇ te nehī ō nā ghōṛā aṛdā* ?
horn, *siṅg*, m. : -ed, *siṅgā wāḷā*.
hornet, *ḍehmū* m. : *see* wasp..
horse, *ghōṛā* : *waihtar*, m. (beast of burden, horse, mule ass).
horse-breaker, *cābuksuār*. m.
horse-race, *ghuṛdauṛ*, f.
hospital, *haspatāḷ*, m.
hostile, *see* enemy.
hot, *tattā*, *garm* : pungent in taste, *garm* (not *tattā* : n., *garmī*, f.) : feel h., *waṭṭ laggṇā*

(*nū̃*) : *garmī laggṇī* (*nū̃*) : *baṛā hussaṛ e* : cook at hot fire, *tēz tā̃ pakāṇā*.
(1) hour, *ghaiṇṭā*, m. : *ghaṛī*, f. (strictly 22½ min.).
houri, *parī*, f. : *hūr*, f.
(2) hourly, *see* repeatedly : *ghaiṇṭe ghaiṇṭe picche*.
house, *ghar*, m., *kōṭhā*, m., *makān*, m. : European, *kōṭhī* f., *banglā*, m. : *see* home, hut : cow-h., *kuṛh*, f. (for cattle) : pigeon -h., on pole, *kābuk*, f. : in ground, *ghumaiḷ*, f. : *see* roost.
how, *kīka-n*, *-nā̃*, *-r*, *-rā̃*, *kis tarhā̃*, *kiñ*, *kīkū̃* : *see* somehow.
howl, *rōṇā*. *cilāṇā*, *karlāṇā* : of jackal, *hawāṅkṇā*, *see* scream.
hubbub, *see* noise.
huff, take, *russṇā*.
hug, *see* embrace.
hum, *see* buzz.
humble, neg. of proud : h. oneself, *apṇe āp nū̃ nīweā̃ k.* : h. another, *ohdī lamb kaḍḍhṇī*, *ohdī ākkaṛ bhannṇī* : be humbled, *ohdī lamb* or *phūk nikḷnī* : *see* humiliation.
humiliation, *beiztī*, f. : *namōshī*, f. : v., *see* humble, disgrace, dishonour, pride.
hunchbacked, *kubṛā*, *kubbā*.
hundred, *sau*, *sai*, *saikṛā* : -th, *sauwā̃*, *sauhwā̃* : G. 20, 22, 93, 123 : *see* per cent.
hunger, *bhukkh*, f. (*laggṇī*, *nū̃*, G. 108).
hungry, *bhukkhā*.
hunt, *shikār k.* and *khēḍṇā* : *see* search, prey.
hunter, *shikārī*.
hurry, *see* hasten.
hurt (from blow, accident, etc.), *saṭṭ* f. (*laggṇī*, *nū̃*) : *see* wound, pain, damage, injury : of new shoes, medicine, etc., *laggṇā* (*nū̃*) : *see* strike.
hurtful, *nuksān* or *zyān* (*jān*) *karnwāḷā*.
husband, *khasm*, *gharwāḷā* : h. and wife, *miā̃ bīwī*, *dowē jī*, G. 122, M. 128. 16.
hush, *see* quiet ; h. up, *see* screen.
husk, *chill*, f. : v., *chaṛnā* : *see* peel.
hut, small house, *kullī*, f. : *jhuggī*, f. : thatched h. *chappar*.
hydrophobia, *see* rabies.
hypercritical, be, *ghutklā̃ cheṛnīā̃* or *kaḍḍhṇīā̃* : *see* criticize.
hypocrisy, *makārī*, f. : *pakhanḍ*, m. : *see* deceit.
hypocrite, *makār*, *pakhanḍī* : *see* deceitful.

I, *maĩ* : people like me or us, *hamātaṛ*, G. 28.
ice, *warf*, f. : *barf*, f.
idea, *khyāl*, m. : *see* thought, believe, opinion.
idiom, *muhāwrā*, m.
idiot, *see* mad.
idle, *sust*, *kamcōr* : out of work, *bekār*, *wehlā*.
idol, *but*, m. : *mūrat*, f. (picture).
idolator, *butparast*, *butā̃* or *mūratā̃ nū̃ pūjjaṇwāḷā*.
idolatry, *butparastī*.
if, *jē*, *agar*, *jēkar* : ask or see if, *pucch lai paī*, (never *jē*, *agar*).
ignite, *see* light.
ignorance, *añānpuṇā*, m. : *beilmī*, f. : *nawākfī*, f. : *see* foolishness, stupid.

ignorant, *beilm*. *añāṇā*, *jaihl*: *see* stupid.
iguana, *goh*, m.
ill, *bamār*, *wall nehī*; *māndā*, *rōgī* (habitually ill): out of sorts, *nimmā*, *nimmo jhūṇā*: of men, boys, animals, *maḷeā hoeā*, *ṭhangreā hoeā*, *hanēkeā hoeā*.
illegal, *kanūn de khalāf*: *see* unlawful.
illegitimate, child, *harām dā*: *see* illegal.
illfeeling, *see* envy (not distinguished). [*rōg*. m.
illness, *bamārī*, f.: *auhr*, f.:
illusion, *waihm*, m.: *see* deceit.
imagin-e, -ation, *khyāl karnā*, *farz karnā* (suppose): *waihm*, m. (foolish fancy, *h*.).
imaginary, *khyālī gall*, *farzī gall*.
imitat-e,-ion, *nakl*, f. (*k*.): copy at school, *nakl mārnī*, *k*.: of clown, *nakl utārnī*, *sāng utārnā*: in i. of, *ohde wallō wēkhke*, *ohdī wēkhā wēkhī* (U.): *see* counterfeit, copy.
immediately, *huṇe*, *ese weḷe*, *jhaṭ paṭṭ*: past time, *ōse weḷe*, *owē*.
immodest, *bēhayā*, *belajjā*.
immovable, *nehī halldā*: *see* lasting.
impartial, be, *raī nā karnī*, *sabbhnā nū ikkī akkh nāḷ wēkhnā*.
impassable, *langhaṇwālā nehī*.
impatience, *sauṛ*, f., *kāhḷ*, f. (both *paiṇī*): *see* hast-e,-en.
impatient, *kāhḷā*, or *sauṛā* (*paiṇā*), *bēsabr*: *sabr*, m., or *hauslā*, m., *nā k*.
impediment, *see* hindrance.
imperfect, *kaccā*, *nākas*, *mukkā nehī*.
imperfection, *see* defect, fault.
imperious, be, *hukm cāṛhnā*, *zōrāwarī karnī*: adj., *hākamānā*.
impertinent, *gustākh*, *shōkh*: *see* forward, rude.
implore, *see* beseech.
important, *bhārā*, *zarūrī*.
impossible, *namumkin*, *unhōṇī*: as interj., *mērī majāl e?* *majāl geī e?* *tōbbā!*
impress upon, *pakkī karnī* (*nū*).
impression, *nishān*, m.: on mind, *asr*, m.
imprison, *kaid-k*.: be -ed, *bajjhṇā*, *kaid-h*: *see* prisoner.
improper, *nāmunāsib*.
improve, int., *suddharnā*, *saurnā*: tr., *sudhārnā*, *suārnā*: *see* correct.
improvement, *see* progress: in disease, *riait*. f., *arām*, m., *armān*, m.
imprudent, *sōcdā nehī*.
impure, *see* dirty, unclean.
in, *wicc*, *andar*: on the inside, *andarwār*: from inside, *wiccō*, *andarō*: pass by way of inside, *wiccō* or *andarō dī langhnā*: of place, often loc., G. 9, 10, 77: in or after half an hour, three weeks, *addhe ghaiṇṭe* (*triūh hafteā*) *nū* or *picche*: within half hour, etc., *addhe ghaiṇṭe de andar*: often loc., *tinnī haftī*, in three weeks, so in the morning, evening, etc., G. 10, 34, 78.
inadvertently, *see* accidentally, carelessness.
inattentive, *dhiān nehī kardā*.
inauspicious, *see* auspicious.
inborn, *zātī*. A.
incantation, perform, *hāl khēḍ*-

nā, sir mārnā, mantar parhnā (K.).

incapable, incapacity, *see* able, worthless, useless.

incarnate, become, *deh dhārī h.* (H.): *autār dhārnā* (H.): *mujassam h.* (M.): *bandeā dī sūrat shakl wicc aunā.*

incense, n., *dhūf*, m., *dhūkh*, m.

incessant, *see* always, repeatedly, daily.

inch, *incī*, f.: *see* wts. and meas.

incite, *cukknā, bharkāṇā, macāṇā, paṭṭī paṛhāṇī* (*nū*): *kann wicc phūkṇā* (*de*): *see* induce, excite, urge, seduce.

incitement, *cukk*, f.

inclined to, *rūh* or *jī karnā*, (e.g. *cukkaṇ nū*, to lift, etc.): *see* desire, taste.

includ-ed, -ing, *de saṇe, wicc pāke, shāmil karke, ralāke.*

incoherent, *bemaihṇe.*

income, *āmdanī*, f.

incompetent, *see* able, worthless, useless.

incomplete, *see* imperfect.

incomprehensible, *samajh wicc nehī aundā, kujjh pir palle nehī peā.*

incongruous, *raldā* or *phabbdā nehī.*

(1) inconvenience, *wakht*, m.: *taklīf*, f.: *bēarāmī*, f.

(2) inconveniēnced, *khajjal, khajjal khuār, aukkhā*: *see* difficulty, trouble, straits.

(3) inconvenient, *sāḍḍe wāste mushkil e, eh wēlā ṭhīk nehī*: *see* convenience.

increase, int. *waddhnā, trakkī karnī*; tr., *wadhāṇā, trakkī dēṇī* (*nū*).

incredible, *mannaṇwālī gall nehī.*

incubate, *bacce kaḍḍhne.*

incurable, *koī ilāj nehī, lāilāj.*

indebted, *see* debtor: acknowledge obligation, *ahsān* or *ṭhākrā mannṇā.*

indecent, of words, *fohsh*; of persons, *luccā.*

indeed, is it so ? *halā, sacc e* ?

indefatigable, *anthakk, thakkaṇwālā nehī.*

indefinite, *ṭhīk patā nehī, ṭhīk faislā nehī, kaccī gall, kac pakk.*

independent, *khudmukhtār, āpū mālik e.*

index, *firist*, f.

indicate, *see* show.

indifferen-ce, -t, *see* carelessness.

indigent, *see* poor.

indigestible, *pacdā nehī.*

indigestion, *badhazmī*, f., *unpācā*, m.

indigo, *nīl*, f.

indistinct, *sāf nehī, maddham.*

induce, *manāṇā*: *see* incite, urge.

indulge (child), *lāḍ karnā* (*nāḷ*).

industrious, *mehntī.*

inevitable, *zarūrī, aṭall, kismat nāḷ nehī laṛdā*, etc.

inexperienced, *aṇāṇā*: *kaccā*: *nāī tajrabakār* (U.): *tajrabā nehī, allhaṛ.*

inexpert, *aṇāṇā, kaccā*: *see* clever.

infant, *kucchaṛ wicc, duddh pīṇwāḷā.*

infer, *natījā kaḍḍhṇā.*

infidel, *see* atheist: *kāfar* (M.).

infidelity, *kufr*, m. (M.): *bedīnī*, f.: *see* adultery.

inflammation, *sōj*, f. (swelling): v., *sujjṇā.*

influence, *rōhb*, m. (half fear): *rusūkh*, m.: *asr*, m.

inform-, -ation, *itlāh dēṇī* ; *kaiṛ karnī* : *khabar dēṇī*, (all *nū*).
ingenious, *see* clever.
ingenuity, *hikmat*, f.
ingratitude, *nāshukrī*, f. : *kirt·ghaṇī*, f. : *see* ungrateful.
inhabit, *wassṇā*, *raihṇā* : being i.-ed, *wassō*, f. : caus. v., *see* people (2).
inhabitant, *raihṇwāḷā* : *see* resident.
inherit, *wāris h.* : i.-ed, *maurūsī*.
inheritance, *wirsā*, f. : *mirās*, f.
inhuman, *insān nehī*, *bandā nehī* : *see* cruel, oppression.
injure, *tratṭī cauṛ karnī* (int. *hōṇī*, both *dī*) : *see* damage, hurt, loss.
injustice, *bēinsāfī*, f. : *bēniāī*, f. (H.). [m.
ink, *syāhī*, f : coloured i., *rang*,
inkstand, *duāt* f.
(1) inn, *sarā*, f. : European rest-house, *ḍāk banglā*, m.
innings, *wār*, f. (both individual and side : *laiṇī*, *dēṇī*).
(2) innkeeper, *bhaṭhyārā*.
innocent, *masūm* : *see* guiltless, acquit.
innuendo, *nōk lāṇī* (*nū*) : *ishārā k.* (*de wall*) : i. be apposite, *nōk wajjṇī* (*nū*) : *see* hint.
innumerable, *anginā*, *bē-bahā*, *-shumār*, *-hadd*.
inoculate, *ṭīkā lāṇā* (int. *laggṇā*, caus., *luāṇā*) or *ukhṇāṇā* (int. *ukkhaṇṇā*).
inquire, *see* ask, discover : i. after health, *surt laiṇī* (*dī*), *patā karnā* (*dā*), *pucchṇā* (*nū*).
inquirer, *mutlāshī* (or catechumen).
inquiry, investigation, *takīkāt*, f. (*k.*, *dī*).

insane, *see* mad.
insect, *kīṛā*, m. (often snake) : large ants, *kīṛe*, *ḍhak makauṛe*, m. pl.
insensible, *behōsh* : *see* numb.
inside, *see* in.
insipid, *bēsuādda*, *phikkā* : without sauce, etc., *rukkhā*
insist, *see* obstinate : *takrār karnā*, *maṇar paiṇā* (*de*) : *gal paiṇā* (*de*).
insistence, *takrār*, m. : *see* obstinate.
insistent, *khaihṛā nehī chaḍḍdā*.
inspection, school *muāinā karnā* (*dā*) : medical, etc., *mulāhzā karnā* (*dā*) : in gen. *phērā mārnā* (visit, etc.).
inspector, *inspiṭṭar*, *inspĕktar*.
instalment (money), *kishṭ*, f.
instance, *see* example. [*kisht*.
instant, n., *sakinṭ*, m. : *dam*, m. : *jhaṭ*, m. : *pall*, m.
instead, *de thā*, *de badle*.
instigate, *see* incite.
instinctively, *see* intuitively.
instruct-, -ion, *see* teach.
instrument, *racch*, m. *hathyār*, m. : *kalā*, f., *kalā*, f.. musical, *wājā*, m. : *see* play, tune,
insult, *see* disgrace. [tool.
insure, oneself, etc., *bīmā*, m. *karāṇā* (*dā*).
intelligent, *siāṇā*.
intelligence, *siāṇap*, f. : *see* sense, clever.
inten-d, -ntion, *manshā*, f. : *irādā*, m. : *nīyat*, f. : *matlab*, m. : *dalīl*, f. : *pucchaṇ pucchaṇ kardā sā*, intended to ask but hesitated, G. 112 : *see* object, desire.
intentionally, *see* deliberately, purposely.
intercede, *sifārish karnī* (*dī*) : *shafāt karnī* (*de-wāste*).

intercept, *rāh wicc phaṛnā.*
intercessor, *sifārish* or *shafāt karnwālā.*
intercourse, *sangat*, f. : *sohbat*, f. : *wāh*, m. : (*see* connection) : esp. eating, drinking *wartō*, f., *wartāwā*, m., ... *ṇā*, m. : coming and going, *auṇā jāṇā.*
(1) interest (gen. monthly), *byāj*, m., *sūd*, m. : *see* advantage, profit, benefit : self-i., *khudgarzī*, f. : *gaū*, m. : *see* object, intention.
(2) interested in, *dilcaspī*, f. (*menū ehde nāḷ e*), *ohdā shauk h.* (*nū*).
interesting, *suādlā*, *dilcasp.*
interfere, *dakhl dēṇā* (*wicc*).
intermingle, mix : *see* mix.
internal, *wiclā*, *wishkārlā*, *andarlā*, *andrūnī* (U).
interpose, *see* mediator, interfere, interrupt
interpret, *tarjmā karnā* (*dā*).
interpreter, *tarjmā karnwālā*, *mutrajjim.*
interrupt, *gall ṭukkṇī* (*dī*), *dī gall wicc gall karnī* : *see* interfere.
interval, time, *cir*, m. : *mohlat*, f. (days of "grace") : *wakfā*, m. (U.) : space, *paindā*, m. : *khappā*, m., *witth*, f., *wāṭ*, f.
intervene, *see* interpose.
interview, *mulākāt karnī* (*nāḷ*).
intimate, *pakkā dōst* or *yār* : *see* friend.
intimidate, *see* fear.
intolerable, *jehṛā nā jareā* (or *saiheā* or *jhalleā*) *jāe.*
intoxicant, *nashā*, m. : *nashe wālī cīz*, f. [(*kaḍḍhṇā*).
intrench, *khandak*, f. or *ṭoā*, m.
intricacy, *waḷ*, m., *pēc*, m. : *waḷ pēc*, m.
intricate, *pēcwāḷā*, *waḷ pēcwāḷā.*
intrigue, *see* plot.
introduce, person, *miḷāṇā* (*nāḷ*), *wākif karāṇā* (*nāḷ*) : *mēḷ karāṇā* (*dā*) : law, custom, money, *jārī karnā*, *ṭōrnā*, *kaḍḍhṇā.*
intrude, *see* interfere, interrupt.
intrust, *see* entrust.
intuitively, *uñ*, *āpū khyāl āeā*, *apṇī* (*apṇe*) *akl nāḷ*, *khāhmakhāh.*
invade, *mulkh wicc hamlā karke waṛnā.*
investigation, *see* inquiry.
invincible, *see* unconquerable.
invisible, *jehṛā nā disse.*
invit-e, -ation, *saddṇā*, *rōṭī ākhṇī* or *ṭhākṇī* or *warjṇī* (*dī*), *dāwat karnī* (*dī*) : *sāḍḍī ohde wall roṭī e.*
invoke, *kise dī duhāī dēṇī.*
involuntarily, *khāhmakhāh* : *see* force.
iron, *lohā*, m. : adj., *lohe dā* : (ironing) *istrī*, f. : iron, v. tr., *istrī-k.*
irony, *tāhnā mārnā* (*nū*), *nōk lāṇī* (*nū*), *makhaul nāḷ ākhṇā.*
irrecoverable, *geā guātā.*
irregular-, -ity, *bēkaid-ā* (n *-agī*, f.), *bēkanūn-* (n. *-ī*, f.), *bētartīb-* (n., *-ī*, f.).
irrelevant, *ehdā tallak nehī* (*nāḷ*).
irreligious, *bedīn* (M.) : *bedharm* (H.) : nouns add *-ī.*
irremediable, *dā ilāj nehī.*
irrigate, *see* water.
irritable, *ciṛhnwāḷā*, *kiṛnwāḷā.*
irritate, *see* tease.
island, *ṭāpū*, m. : *jazīrā*, m.
issue, order, *jārī-k.*, *kaḍḍhṇā.*

it, *see* he, she.
itch, n., v., *khurk*, f. (*h. paiṇī*).
item, *gall*, f.
itinerary, *safar*, m. : *safarnāmā*, m.
ivory, *dand khaṇḍ*, f.

J

jackal, *giddaṛ*, m.
jacket, *kōṭ*, m : *jākaṭ*. m.
jail, *see* prison.
jam, *jām*, m. (K., *banāṇā*) : *murabbā*, m. (*pāṇā*).
janitor, *caprās-ī*, m. fem. *-an*.
January, *janwarī*, f. : *māhṅg*, *māh*, m. (about Jan. 13 to Feb. 12).
jar, *see* pot.
jasmine, *cambā*, m.
jaw, *khakhwāṛā*, m. : *haṛbāccī*, f.
jealous-, -y, *see* envy, suspicious.
jeer, *see* mock.
jerk, *see* jolt.
jester (excess implied), *makhaulīā*, *ṭokī*, *maskharībāz* : professional, *bhaṇḍ* : *see* joke.
Jesus, *Yēsū*, *Īsā*, *Hazrat Īsā* (M.).
jet-black, v. black, *kāḷā syāh*, *kāḷā shāh*.
Jew, *Yahūd-ī*, fem. *-aṇ*.
jewellery, *gaihṇā*, m., *gaihṇe*, m. pl. : each piece, *ṭūmb*, f., also *gaihṇā*.
jib, *aṛnā*.
jingle, *chaṇ*, *chaṇ* *k.* : *see* tinkle.
join, *jōṛnā* (int. *juṛnā*) : person, *ralṇā* (*nāḷ*), *milṇā* (*nāḷ*, *nū̃*) : army, *bhartī h.*
joint, body, *jōṛ*, m.
jointly, *ralke*, *milke*, *katthe*.
joke, *hāsse dī gall* : *jugat*, f. (quibble w. slight sting) : rather objectionable, *makhaul*. m. : *maskharī*, f., *mashkarī*, f.
jokingly, *hāsse nāḷ*, *makhaul nāḷ*.
jolt, *hujjkā laggṇā* (*nū̃*) : *dhakkā khāṇā*.
journal, diary, *rōznāmcā*, m. (U) : *ḍairī*, f. ; *see* newspaper.
journey, *safar*, m. (*k.*) : *sair*, m. or *sail*, m. or *sail sapaṭṭā*, m., j. for pleasure, walk, etc. : *phērā*, m. (*pāṇā*, *mārnā*, int. *paiṇā*), esp. visit, useless j.
joy, *khushī*, f.
joyful, *khush*.
judge, n., *jaj*, *munsaf* (civil), *tasīldār*, (criminal and executive) : *see* magistrate : v., *faislā karnā*.
judgment-day, *kiāmat dā din*, m. (*kiāmat*, f., really resurrection).
jug, water or milk, *jagg*, m. : *see* pot.
juggler, *madār-ī*, fem. *-an*.
juice, *ras*, m.
juicy, *raswāḷā*.
July, *jaulāī*, f. : *julāī*, f. : *jaulā*, m. : *saoṇ*, m. (about July 13 to Aug. 12).
jumble up, *hēṭh utā k.*, *rauḷā mārnā*, *gaṛbaṛī karnī*.
jump, *ṭappṇā* (over, *nū̃* : on to, *utte*) : waves, water, *uchaḷṇā* : n., *chāḷ*, f. : *chalāṅg*, f. : *phalāṅg*, f. (all w. *mārnī*).
June, *jūn*, m. : *hāhṛ*, m. (about June 13 to July 12).
jurisdiction, *ikhtiār*, m.
just, *insāfwāḷā*, *niāī* : adv., *zarā* : j. now, *hune*.
justice, *insāf*, m. : *niā*, f.

K

kedgery, food, *khicṛī*, f.
keen, on sthg., *shukīn* : *see* desire, sharp.
keep, *rakkhṇā* ; in one's possession, *apṇe kabze wicc rakkhṇā* : animals *rakkhṇā* : k. seat, *see* engage : k. safe, *sāmbhṇā* : temporarily k. back money, wages, *hēṭh rakkhṇā* (G. 91) : *see* detain, hinder : kept tame animal, *rākhwā* : k. feast, *īd karnī* ; *see* celebrated
keeper, *see* guardian, watchman.
keepsake, *yādgār*, f.
kernel, *girī*, f. : (cocoanut, *garī*).
kettle, *kētlī*, f.
key, *kunjī*, f. : *cābī*, f. : fit, *laggṇī* (tr. *lāṇī*, try).
kick, by person, *thuḍḍā lāṇā* or *mārnā* (int. *khāṇā*, *laggṇā*) : also *thuḍḍī mārnā* : football, *kik mārnī* : by horse, etc., *dulattā mārnā*.
kid, *bagrōtā*.
kidney, *gurdā*, m.
kill, *mār chaḍḍṇā* or *saṭṭṇā*, *thā mārnā*, *jānō mārnā* : for food, *kohṇā* : *halāl-k.* (M.) : *takbīr paṛhnī* (*utte*, M.) : *jhaṭkā karnā* (*dā*, *nū*, H.).
kiln, *bhaṭṭhā*, m. : *āwā*, m. : *āwī*, f.
kilt, *ghaghrī*, f. : *see* skirt : k. -ed regiment, *ghāghrā palṭan*, f.
(1) **kind**, *mehrbān*.
(2) **kind**, n., *jins*, f. : *kism*, f.
kindness, *mehrbānī*, f.
kindred, *see* relati-ve,-onship.
king, *bādshāh* : *rājā*, *māhrājā*, *sultān*
kingdom, *bādshāhī*, f. : *saltanat*, f. (rule, etc.) : *rāj*, m.
kiss, *cummṇā* : n. *cummā*, m. : *cummī*, f. (all gen. w. bad meaning) : *see* caress.
kitchen, *baurcīkhānā*, m. : village, *culhānnī*, f. (M.) : *rasōī*, f. (H) : He's square, *caukkā*, m., *caũkā*, m.
kite, boy's, *guḍḍī*, f.
kitten, *bilūngā*, m.
knack, *jāc*, f. : *thauh*, m.
knead, flour, *gunnhṇā* (pa. p. *guddhā*, *gunnheā* : int. *gujjhṇā*) : clay w. hands or feet, *gōṇā*.
knee, *gōḍḍā*, m. : -cap, *cappṇī*, f., *chūṇī*, f.
kneel, *gōḍḍe niwāṇe* or *ṭēkne*, *goḍḍeā bhār* or *parne baihṇā*.
knife, *churī*, f. : *kard*, f. : pen-k., *cakkū*, m. : large k., *churā*, m. : -board, *takhtī*, f.
knob, *see* handle.
knock, at door, *khaṛkāṇā* (lit. rattle) : k. down, *ḍhāṇā*, *ḍēgṇā* : k. against, gently, *khaihṇā* (*nāḷ*) : *see* collide : be k.-ed about, *dhakke* or *bhambalbhūse khāṇe*.
knot, n., (tied or in wood) *gaṇḍh*, f. : v., *gaṇḍhṇā*, *gaṇḍh dēṇī* (*nū*) : open, *kholhṇī*.
know, *jāṇṇā*, *patā hōṇā* (*nū*), *malūm hōṇā* (*nū*) : make known, *patā dēṇā* ; spread abroad, *dhumāṇā* (int. *dhummṇā*) : k. languages, *jāṇṇā* ; adj., *-dān*, *fārsī-dān*, knowing Persian, etc.
knowingly, *see* purposely.
knowledge, *ilm*, m.
knuckle (hand or foot), *gaṇḍh*, f.

L

label, *ciṭṭ*, f.

labour, *mehnat*, f. : *see* force, effort, labourer.

labourer, *mazdūr*, m. : fields, *kāmmā* : employer or employee, wages in kind, *sēpī*, fem. *sēpaṇ* : all-time employee, *āthṛī* : one of menial classes, *kammī*, fem. *kamneāṇī* : condition of *sepī*, *sēp*, f. : *see* servant.

lace, boot, shoe, *waddhrī*, f. : *tasmā*, m. (U.).

lack, n., *thuṛh*, f. : *ghāṭā*, m. : v., *thuṛhnā*, *ghaṭṭṇā* (be insufficient).

ladder, *pauṛī*, f., *paṛsāṅg*, f. : *see* rung.

ladle, *see* spoon.

lady (European) *mēmsāb* : unmarried *miss sāb*, *miss*.

ladybird, *kummhā kīṛā*, m.

lake, *jhīl*, f., *sar*, m., *ḍal*, m.: *see* pond.

lamb, *lēllā*, m.

lame, *laṅgā*, *laṅgṛā* : walk l., *laṅgāṇā* : *see* cripple.

lament, *see* mourn, weep.

lamp, *lamp*, m. : *battī*, f. : wall-l., *duālgīr*, m. : earthen, *dīwā*, m.

lamppost, *munnā*, m. : *waḷā*, m.

lampstand, movable, *dīurī*, f. : in wall, *duākhā*, m.

lance, *see* spear.

(1) **land,** *zamīn* or *zimī* or *jīwī* or *jiwī*, f. : *see* soil, country.

(2) **land,** v., of ship, *kaṇḍhe* or *dande laggṇā* : of person, *jahāz uttō utarnā*

landlord, *mālik*, m.

lane, *galī*, f.

language, *bōlī*, f. : *zabān*, f. : *see* speech.

lantern, *lālṭaiṇ*, f., *hatth battī*, f.

lap, *gaḍḍ*, f. : *see* arm : *jholī*, f (front of garment, for carrying things in).

large, *see* big, roomy, loose.

(1) **last,** adj., *chekaṛlā*, *pishlā* : year, week, month, *see* year, week, month : last night, *ajj rāt nū̃*, *ajj dī rāt*, *rātī* : l. Monday, *pishle suār nū̃* : l. time, *aglī wārī*.

(2) **last,** v., boots, clothes, etc., *haṇḍhṇā* : last 2, 3 days, of food, *kaḍḍhṇā* (*dō trai din*) G. 118 : M. 119. 45 : of join in furniture, machinery, *khlōṇā*.

lasting, *pakkā*, *baṛā haṇḍhaṇwāḷā* : *see* permanent.

lastly, *see* finally.

late, adj., *cirkā*, *carākī* (but *carōkṇā*, of a long time ago), *pachētrā* : be l., *cir*, m., *ḍēr*, f. (both w. *lāṇā*, int. *laggṇā*), *paccharṇā* : *cirkā auṇā*, etc. (of train often *lēṭ auṇī*) : late, deceased, *marhūm* (M., U.), *bahishtī* (M), *surgī* (H).

lathe, *kharād*, f. : v., *kharādṇā*, *kharād k.* or *cāṛhnā*.

laugh, *hassṇā* : *hāssā auṇā* (*nū̃*), inclined to laugh, (M. 117, 6) : *guṭakṇā* (giggle) : derisive words, *mū̃h aḍḍṇā*, *dand kaḍḍhṇe* : *see* joke, ridicule.

law, *kanūn*, m. : relig., *sharā*, m. : *shariat*, f. (both M.).

lawful, *jāiz* : *halāl* (M., esp. food, money) : *see* legal.

lawsuit, *mukadmā*, m. : *see* case, lose, hearing : date of l., *tārīkh*, f. : *tarīk*, f.

lawyer, *wakīl*, m. : *bālishṭar*, m. : the practice or work, *wakālat*, f., *bālishṭrī*, f. : his pay, *mehntānā*, m.

lay, *see* place : eggs, *dēṇā*.

layer, fold, *taih*, m. f.: of bricks in building, *raddā*, m.

laziness, *ḍhill*, f., *ḍhill maṭṭh*, f.: *susti*, f.

lazy, *ḍhillā maṭṭhā*, *sust*, *kamcōr*.

(1) lead, *sikkā*, m

(2) lead, *mohre calṇā*, *agge calṇā*, *lai calṇā*, *āggū* or *mohrlā h.*: *see* guide.

leader, *sardār*: *see* lead, headman.

leaf, *pattar*, m.: of book, *warkā*, m.: of door, *bhitt*, m.

leak, *see* drip, ooze

(1) lean, adj., *māṛā*, *patlā*, *lissā*.

(2) lean on, *de sahāre calṇā* or *khlōṇā*: l. back, *nāḷ ḍhāsṇā lāṇā*, *ḍhoh lāṇī*: *see* stoop.

leap, *see* jump.

learn, gen. *sikkhṇā*: study in gen., *paṛhṇā*: lesson, *pakāṇā*, *yād-k.* (int. *pakkṇā*, *yād h.* or *auṇā*, M. 117. 4).

learned, *ālam*, *ilmwāḷā*: *maulwī* (M.): *paṇḍat* (H.): *see* expert.

lease, *paṭā*, m.: *ṭhēkā*, m. (contract): v., *paṭe* or *ṭhēke te dēṇā*.

least, *sabbhṇā* or *sāreā tō nikkā* or *ghaṭṭ*: at l., *ghaṭṭo ghaṭṭ*, *ghaṭṭ tō ghaṭṭ*.

leather, *camm*, m.: *camṛā*, m.: untanned, *khall*, f.: l.-worker, *mōc-ī*, fem. *-aṇ*: *cameār-*, fem. *-ī* (fr. the U.P.)

(1) leave, *chuṭṭī*. f. (*laiṇī*, *dēṇī*): take l. of, *widyā -h.*, *rukhsat -h.* (send off, *widyā -k.*, *rukhsat-k.*): l. off, *see* abstain: l. off work, *chuṭṭī karnī*: *see* liberty.

(2) leavings of food, *jūṭhā*, any food once begun is *jūṭhā*. adj.: n., *jūṭh*, m.

leaven, *khamīr*, m.

lecture, *dars*, m. (d.): *likcar*, m. (d.).

leech, *jōk*, f.

left, *khabbā*: l.-handed, *khabbā*.

leg, *latt*, f.: *liṅg*, m.: of furniture, *pāwā*, m.: of mutton, *lēk*, f. (K.): *see* calf, shin, thigh, muscle.

legal, *kanūn wallō jāiz*: *see* lawful.

legend, *kahāṇī*, f.

legitimate (child) *halāl dā*: *see* legal, lawful.

leisure, *wehl*, f.: *wāndak*, f.: *wānd*, f.: *fursat*, f. (U.): *see* leave: at l., *wehlā*, *wāndā*.

lemon, *see* lime.

lemonade, *lamnēṭ*, m., *miṭṭhā pāṇī*, m.

lend, money, *udhār -d.*: *see* debt. borrow

lender, *see* money-lender.

length, *lamāī*, f.: *lām*, m.: *lamittaṇ*, f.: l.-wise, *see* direction.

leopard, *cittrā*, m.

leper, *koṛhā*, fem. *koṛhī*.

leprosy, *koṛh*, m.: *waḍḍā rōg* or *dukh*.

less, *kamm*, *ghaṭṭ*, *kassā*.

lessen, *ghaṭāṇā*, *ghaṭṭ k.*, *kamm k.*: (int. *ghaṭṭ h.*, *kamm h.*, *maṭṭhā h.*): price, *riait karnī*.

lesson, *sabak*, m.: *see* learn, teach.

lest, *mate*, *cētā*, *ajehā nā howe pai*.

letter, *citthī*, f.: *khatt*, m. (often postcard): note, *rukkā*, m.: *parcī*, f.: official l., *rōbkār*, m.: of alphabet, *harf*, m.: *akkhar*, m. (H.).

lettuce, *salāt*, m. : *salād*, m.
leucoma, *see* eye-ulcer.
level, *padhrā*, *suāhrā*, *sāf*, *barābar* : *see* flat, plain.
lever, *tul* (*dēṇī*, l. up, raise).
liable, *see* prone.
liar, *jhūṭhā*.
libel, action, *izzat dā dāhwā* : *see* slander, accuse.
liberal, *see* generous : thought, *azād khyāl wālā*.
liberty, gen. *azādī*, f. : l. to do something, *khullh*, f., *ijāzat*, f. : *izn*, m. : take l., be familiar, *see* familiar : act without leave, *ijāzat tō binā karnā* : (or *bē* or *bilā ijāzat*).
library, *laibrerī*, f. : room in house, *daftar*, m.
licence, *laisans*, f. (a written l.) : *see* liberty.
lick, *cattṇā*.
lid, *ḍhakṇā*, m. : *ḍhakkan*, m. : for vessel, *cappṇī*, f., *chūṇī*, f., *chūṇā*, m.
(1) lie, tell, *jhūṭh bōlṇā* or *mārnā*.
(2) lie, down, *lammā paiṇā*, G. 64 (tr. *pāṇā*) : *saūṇā* (sleep) : remain lying, *peā raihṇā* A.
lieutenant, *laftain* : L.-Governor, *lāt sāb*.
life, (animal) *jān* : course of, *hyātī*, f., *zindagī*, f., *jindṛī*, f. : eternal l., *hamēshā dī zindagī* : past l., *guzrī hoī* or *pichlī zindagī* : biography, *hāl*, m., *hawāl*, m. : conduct *cāl caln*, m.
lifeless, *bejān*.
lift, *cukkṇā*, *uṭhāṇā*, *cāṇā* : *see* [carry.
(1) light, n. *lō*, f. : *cānnaṇ*. m. : *cānṇā*, m. : *rōshnī*, f.
(2) light, adj , not heavy, *haulā* : colour, *hawāī*, *nīm*.
(3) light, lamp, fire, *bālṇā* (int. *balṇā* : begin to burn, *bal paiṇā*) : *see* fire, burn.
lightning, *baddal lishkṇā* : *bijlī*, f.
(1) like, adj., *see* similar.
(2) like, v., *caṅgā laggṇā* (*nū̃*) : *see* desire, taste.
limbs, gen., *naiṇ prāṇ*, m. pl. : *haith pair*, m. pl. : *aṅg*, m. : *see* cripple.
(1) lime, lemon, large kind, *khaṭṭā*, m. : small, *nimbū*, m. : (thin rind) *kāgzī nimbū* : sweet, *miṭṭhā*, m. : small do , *nārgī*, f. : inferior l., *galgal*, f., *trunī*, f., *kimb*, m. : eat l., *cūpṇā*.
(2) lime, building, *cūnā*, m.
limestone, *rōṛ*, m.
line, *līk*, f. : *lakīr*, f. : in book, *satar*, f. : of poetry, *misrā*, m. : railway, *lain*, f. : of boys, etc., *katār*, f. (U.) : draw l., *khiccṇā* : a few lines (letter) *dō* or *cār harf*, m. pl.
lineage, *nasabnāmā*, m. (genealogy) : *see* descendants. tree.
lining, *lailan*, f.
link, of chain, *kunḍī*, m. : *caṅglī*, f. (rare).
linseed, *alsī*, f.
lion, *shēr babar*, *babar shēr*, m.
lip, *bull*, m. : *hōṭh*, m.
lisp, nearest word " stammer."
list, *firist*, f.
listen, *suṇṇā* : attentively, *kann lāke* or *dhyān karke* or *lāke suṇṇā* : l. for, *kaiṛ laiṇī* (*dī*).
literal, meaning, *lafzī*.
literary, *kitābī*.
literature, *kitābā̃*. f. pl.
litigious, *mukadmebāz*.
little, size, *see* small : quantity, *thōṛā jehā*, *zarā ku*, *kujjh*

kujjh, *ghaṭṭ waddh* (G. 28): v. l., *ruāḷ*, as *ruāḷ ku ātā*, v. l. flour: too l., *kassā*, *thōṛā*.
live, *jyūṇā* (pa. p. *jīweā*): dwell, *raihṇā*: l. good life, *cāl caln acchā e*: l. in ease, *arām wicc* or *nāḷ raihṇā*.
livelihood, *rozī*, f.: *rōzgār*, m.: *guzārā*, m.
liver, *kalejā*, m.: of animal, *kalejī*, f., *kalejā*, m.
livery, *wardī*, f.
living, *see* alive, livelihood.
load, *bhār*, m. (*laddṇā*): *bōjh*, m. (U.): *see* wts. and meas.
loaf, Indian, *rōṭī*, f.: *capāṭī*, f.: *parauṇṭhā*, m.: small, *gullī*, f.: European, *ḍabal rōṭī*, f.: *see* bread.
loafer, *awārā*, fem. the same.
loan, *see* lend.
loathsome, *ghinaoṇā*: words for disgust.
(1) lock, *jandrā*, m.: *tāḷā*, m. (both w. *mārnā*, *lāṇā*, int. *laggṇā*, *wajjṇā*): unlock, *jandrā lāhṇā* (int. *laihṇā*).
(2) lock, hair, *see* hair: Hindu's, *bōdī*, f.
locust, *makṛī*, f.
log, *gēllī*, f.: v. short, for fuel, *mōçhā*, m. (*pāṇā*, int. *paiṇā*): *see* sleeper.
logic, *manṭak*, f.
(1) loincloth, *laṅgōṭī*, f.
(2) loins, *see* waist.
lonel-y, -iness, use *kallā*, alone, and *see* homesick.
(1) long, adj., *lammā*: l. time, *cir*, m.: fr. l. time ago, *kadōkṇā*, *carōkṇā*, *jū*: *see* delay: longways, *see* direction: as long as, *jinnā cir*, *jicar*, *jicar tīkar*: long days (summer), *see* day.
(2) long for, *taṛafṇā* (great unrest): *saihkṇā*, (*nā*), *tarsṇā*: cause to l. f., afflict, *tarsāṇā*.
(3) long-lived, *waḍḍī umr dā*: *see* old.
look, *wēkhṇā* (pa. p. *ḍiṭṭhā*, *wekheā*), *takkṇā*: glance, *nazr mārnī* (*utte*): l. stealthily, *jhāttī mārnī*: *see* frown, search: l. after, *sāmbhṇā*, *sambhāḷṇā*: *see* watch, protect.
loom, *khaḍḍī*, f.: warp, *tāṇī*, f., woof, *pēṭā*, m.
loose, *ḍhillā*: get loose, machinery, masonry, *ukkhaṛnā* (tr. *ukhēṛnā*, *see* piece): clothes, *mōkḷā*.
lopsided, *see* weight.
loquacious, *see* talkative.
lord it over, lordly, *see* imperious.
lose, *guāṇā*, *khaṛāṇā*, *gum-k.* (U.): int. *guācṇā*, pa. p., *guātā* or *guāceā*: *kharācṇā*, pa. p. *kharātā*, *kharāceā*: *gum-h.*, (U.): also *jāndeā raihṇā*: l. game, *see* game: l. law-case, *ohdī* or *ohde-sir digrī hōṇī*, *mukadmā khārij hōṇā* (*dā*), *mukadmā hārnā* (*dā*).
loss, damage, *nuksān*, m., *jān*, m., *zyān*, m., all w. *h.*: financial, *mōs*, f., *ṭoṭṭā*, m., both w. *laggṇā*, *khāṇā*, *paiṇā*: *harj*, m. (*h.*), *caṭṭī*, f. (*painī*): *ghāṭā*, m. (*khāṇā*, *paiṇā*): make up l., *ṭōṭṭā* or *ghāṭā pūrā k.*: *kasr kaḍḍhṇī*: pay for l., *nuksān bharnā*: *see* damage.
lot, *see* fate: lots, draw, *guṇe pāṇe*.
lottery, *lāṭarī*, f.
loud, *zōr dā*.

loudly, *uccī uccī*, *uccī dittī*, *dabbke*, *zōr nāḷ*, *kaṛakke* (angrily) : *see* aloud.
louse, *jū*, f.
love, *mhabbat*, f. : (*rakkhṇī* or *k.*, *nāḷ*) : *pyār*, m. (*k.*, *nū*, *nāḷ*) : *see* fondle, indulge : *ishk*, m., *āshik h.* (*utte*) : *see* lover.
lover and loved one, *āshik mashūk* : words *ishk*, *āshik*, *mashūk* gen. bad meaning.
(1) low, adj., *nīwā* : -er, *heṭhlā*, *nīwā* : speak low, *see* gently : *see* mean.
(2) low, cattle, *aṛiṅgṇā*, *aṛāṇā*.
loyal, *khairkhāh*, *namakhalāl*.
luck, *see* fate, fortune.
lucky, *see* fortunate, rich.
lucrative, *baṛī khaṭṭī wālā*.
luggage, *see* baggage : -receipt, *bilṭī*, f.
luggage-van, *see* brake.
lukewarm, *see* tepid.
lump, of earth, *ḍhehm*, f. : in flesh, *giḷhṭ*, m. : *sunḍhā*, m. : *see* boil (1) : of meat, *see* piece.
lunch, *tipan*, m.
lung, *phēphṛā*, m.
lust, *lucpuṇā*, m. : *shahwat*, f. (U.).

M

macaroni, *makrūnī*, f.
machine, *mashīn*, f. : *kalā*, f. (mechanical device).
mad, *jhallā*, *pāgal*, *kamlā*, *shudāī*, : *bā* or *mat* or *hōsh mārī jāṇī*, hence adj., *bā mārēā*, etc. : *see* fool, foolishness : m. dog, *halkā kuttā* : *see* rabies.
magic, *jādū*, m. : *mantar*, m.
magician, *jādūgar*-, fem. *-nī* : *see* witch. [honorary.
magistrate, *majasṭrēṭ* : *see*
magnet, *miknāṭīs*, f.
magnificence, *see* splendour.
maiden, *see* girl, virgin, young.
mail, *ḍāk*, f. : m. train, *ḍāk gaḍḍī*, f. : Bombay, Calcutta m., *bambā* or *kalkattā mēl*, f.
maimed, *see* limb, cripple.
maintain, *pālṇā*, *parwarish karnī* (*dā*) : *kharc dēṇā* (*dā* or *nū*) : *see* assert.
maintenance, *rōṭī kapṛā*, m. *kharc*, m., *parwarish*, f.
maize, *makaī*, f. : *see* cob.
make, *banāṇā* (int. *bannā*) : *see* force, cause : ready-made, *baneā battreā*.
make-weight (for scales), *pāskū*, m. : *see* patch.
male, of animals, *nar* : adj., (men), *mardānā*.
malice, *see* envy.
mallet, *muṅglī*, f.
man, gen. *bandā*, *ādmī*, *insān*, m. : m.-kind, *insān* : m., not woman, *janā* : my good m., *bhāī*, M. 130. 32 : G. 125.
manage, *see* arrange : get along, *guzārā karnā*.
manager, *mainajar* : of land, *gumāshtā*.
mane, of horse, *jāddā*, f. pl.
manger, *khurlī*, f.
mango, *amb*, m. (tree and fruit) : eat m., *cūpṇā*.
manifest, *see* evident.
manner, *tarhā*, f. : *tarīkā*, m. : *ḍhaṅg*, m.
mansion, *mahall*, m. : *haweli*, f. : *waḍḍā makān*.
manufacture, *see* make.
manure, *mallhaṛ*, m. (*pāṇā*, int. *paiṇā*).
manuscript, *nuskhā*, m.
many, plur. of much : *see* much.

map, *nakshā* (*baṇāṇā*, *khiccṇā*).
marble, *sang marmar*, m.
(1) March, *mārc*, *mārac*, m.: *cēttar*, m. (about Mar. 13 to Apr. 12).
(2) march, v., *kūc karnā* (U.): *paindā mārnā*.
mare, *see* horse, pony.
margin, book, *hāshīā*, m.: *see* edge.
marine, *baihrī*, *samundar dā*.
mark, *nishān*, m.: exam., *nambar*: beating leaving no m., *gujjhī mār*, f.: Hindu m., *tikkā*, m., *tilak*, m.
market, *bazār*, m.: for special goods, *manḍī*, f: *see* purchases.
(1) marriage, whole celebration, *shādī*, f., *wiāh*, n.: actual m., *nikāh*, m. (M.): *see* marry
(2) marriage procession, *jañ*, f.: gathering, *mēḷ*, m.: member of *jañ*, *jāñī*: of *mēḷ*, *mēḷī*: m.-gift, *neōndrā*, m.: *bhāñī*, *bhānjī*, f.: m. settlement, *maihr*, m. (M.).
marrow, *mikkh*, f.
marry, M. *shādī k.*, *wiāh k.*, *nikāh paṛhānā* (all w. *nāḷ*): of priest, *nikāh paṛhnā*.

H., *lāwā̃ laiṇīā̃*, *phere laiṇe*: *wiāh k.*, *manḍū paṛhnā* (both w. *nāḷ*): of priest, *wiāh karānā* (*dā*), *wiāh paṛhnā* (*dā*): widow remarriage, *cādar pāṇī*, *cādrā pāṇā* (*nāḷ*), *karēwā*, m. (H.)

Gen. words, *khasm karnā* (marry husband), *zanānī karnī* (wife), or *karnā* w. person's name: *ghar wassṇā* (*dā*): man married second time, *duhājū* (no word for woman).

marsh, *jhīl*, f. (also lake).
martyr, *shahīd*, m.
martyrdom, *shahīd h.*
masculine, *muzakkar*.
mason, *rāj*, m.
massage, *see* shampoo.
mast, *mastaul*, m.
master, *see* owner, teacher, clever.
masterless, *see* ownerless.
mat, straw, *phūhṛ*, m.: *caṭāī*, f.: small *phūhṛī*, f.: for prayer, *masallā*, m. (M.): *see* rug, sack.
(1) match (lucifer), *tīlī*, f.: collective, *mācas*, m.: m.-box, *ḍabbī*, f.
(2) match, game, *maic*, m.
(3) match, v., *raḷāṇā*; int. *raḷṇā*.
matchless, *sabbhnā tō̃ cangā*, *waḍḍā*, etc.: *see* unique.
mate, *jōṛīdār*, *sāthī*: *see* companion.
materials of house, *malbā*, m.: minor m. for building, *masālā*, m.
mathematics, *hisāb*, m.: *riāzī*, f.
matter, *see* affair, pus: no m., *oh jāṇe*, *koī ḍar nehī̃*, *koī parwāh nehī̃*, *jāṇ dē*: *see* right (2).
matting, *see* mat.
mattress, *tulāī*, f.: *gadēlā*, m.: *see* quilt.
mature, *pūrī umr dā*, *pakkā*.
maund, *man*, m.: *see* wts. and meas.
May, *maī*, f.: *mēī*, f.: *jēṭh*, (about May 13 to June 12).
maxim, opinion, *maslā*, m.
maximum, *waddh tō̃ waddh* marks, *pūre nambar*.
me, *menū̃*.

meal, a, *khāṇā*, m. : one of two daily meals, *ḍaṅg*, m. : flour, coarse, *āṭā*, m. ; fine, *maidā*, m.

(1) **mean,** *kamīnā* : stingy, *shūm*, *kanjūs* (U).

(2) **mean,** v. *see* signify.

meaning, of word, *maihṇe*, m. pl. : sense, intention, *matlab*, m.

meanness, *kamīnā kamm*, m. : stinginess, *shūmpuṇā*, m.

means, *wasīlā*, m. : *see* income, livelihood : by m. of, through, *oh de wasīle*, *ohdī rāhī* : by all m., *see* certainly : you're welcome, *jam jam*, *jī sadke*, *sir matthe te*.

meanwhile, *inne* or *ōnne wicc*, *hālī*, *hālā*, *ucarā nū̃*, *icarā nū̃*.

measles, *khasrā*, m. : (*nikḷṇā*, *nū̃*).

(1) **measure,** v., *minṇā*, *kacchṇā*, *mēcṇā* : be m.-ed. by tailor, shoemaker, *nū̃ mēcā dēṇā* : n., *nāp*, m. : *mēcā*, m. : *pamaish*, f (*k.*).

(1) **measuring-tape,** *fītā*, m.

meat, for food, *mās*, m. : *gōshat*, *gōsht*, m. : *tarkārī*, f. : *laun*, m. : *see* mutton, beef, flesh.

meat-safe, *ḍōllī*, f.

mechanical, *kalā̃ nāḷ*.

mechanism, *kalā̃*, *kalā*, f. : *see* machine.

medal, *tagmā*, m. : *takmā*, m.

meddle, *see* interfere.

mediator, *wicōlā* : referee, *tarfain* : *see* umpire.

medicine, *duāī*, f. : *dārū*, m.

mediocre, *see* average, and add *mamūlī*, *aust darje dā*.

meditation, *dhiān*, m., *giān dhiān*, m

meek, use " not proud."

meet, *miḷṇā* (*nū̃*) : *ṭakkarnā* (*nū̃*, by accident) : *mulākāt karnī* (*nāḷ*, interview) : go to meet, *ohnū̃ aggōwāḷī* or *aggaḷwāhṇḍī miḷṇā*, *ohdī aggaḷwāhṇḍī nū̃ nikḷṇā*, *aggō lain jāṇā*.

meeting (someone), n., *ṭākrā*, m. : *mulākāt*, f. : relig. m., *mīṭiṅ*, f. : *see* assembly.

melody, *see* tune.

melon, musk, *khakkhṛī*, f. : water, *haduāṇā*, m. : Kabuli, *sardā*, m.

melt, v., int., *gaḷṇā* (also meat, rice, etc., getting too soft : tr. *gāḷṇā*) : *pagharnā* (esp. fat before fire : tr. *paghrāṇā*) : dissolve, as salt, sugar in water, tr. *ghōḷṇā*, *khōrnā* (int. *ghuḷṇā*, *khurnā*).

member, *sharīk*, m. : *mimbar*, m.

memorial, *yādgār*, f. : *see* memory.

memory, faculty, *cētā*, m. : (or *hāfzā*, m., U. : never *yād*) : bad m., *cētā kharāb* : within my m., *mērī hōsh sambhāḷ wicc* : *see* remember : in m. of, *dī yādgārī wāste*, or *wicc*.

mend, *see* repair, shoe.

menial, member of lower caste, shoemaker, barber, carpenter, sweeper, etc., *kam-mī*, fem. *-ṇeāṇī* : *see* servant.

mention, *dā zikr k.*, *dā nā̃ laiṇā*, *dī* (or *dā*) *carcā k.*

mercantile, *sudāgarī dā*, *tajārat dā*.

merchandise, *saudā*, m. : *saudā sūd*, m. : *māl*, m.

merchant, *sudāgar*, *byōpārī*, *tajārat karnwāḷā*.

merciful, *see* compassionate, mercy.

mercury, *pārā*, m.
mercy, *raihm*, m. (*auṇā* or *k.*, *utte*): *see* pity.
merely, *nirā*, *sirf* (not *khālī*).
merrymaking, *khushī karnī*.
message, verbal, *sanēhā*, m.: *sanāh*, m.: work, *kamm* m.: *buttī*, m.: *wiḍḍī*, f.
messenger, use "man."
metal, *dhāt*, f. [*see* manner.
method, *tarīkā*, m.. *kaidā*, m.,
metempsychosis, *awāgaū*, m.: *āwāgauṇ*, m.: *curāsī*, m. (all H.).
mew, cat, *miaūknā*.
midday, *see* noon.
middle, *wishkār*, m.: *addh wishkār*, m.: adj., *wiclā*, *wishkārlā*.
middle-aged, *adhkaṛ*.
middleman, *dalāl*.
middling, *see* average, mediocre.
midnight, *addhī rāt*, f.
midwife, *dāī*.
might, *see* power, strength, strong.
milch, *lawērī* (cow or buffalo).
mild, person, *halīm*, *narmdil*, *see* kind, compassionate, merciful.
mildness, *halīmī*, f.: *narmdilī*, f.
mile, *mīl*, m.: 1½ m., *kōh*: m., roughly, *kuhāṭrā*, m.: *see* wts. and meas.
milestone, *mīl*, m.
milk, n., *duddh*, m.: for first few days after calf born, *bauhlī*, f., *bauhlā*, m.: buttermilk, *lassī*, f.: v., *dhār kaḍḍhṇī* (*dī*); *cōṇā* (obj. both milk and cow): cow, etc. let herself be milked, *gā̃ milṇī*, M. 124. 1.
milkman, *dodh-ī*, fem. *-aṇ*; *duddhwāḷā*.
(1) mill, hand-, *cakkī*, f.: oxen, *khrās*, m.: water, *ghrāṭ*, m.: *see* millstone.
millet, *juār*, f.: *bājrā*, m.
million, *das lakh*: ten m., *karōṛ*, m.: ordinals, *das lakhwā̃*, *karōṛwā̃*.
millionaire, *lakhpatī*, *karōṛpatī*.
(2) millstone, *puṛ*, m.: to roughen m., *rāhṇā*.
mimic, *see* imitate, jester, grimace.
mince, *mins*, m. (*k.*, K.); *kīmā*, m. (*k.*).
mind, *dil*, m.: *jī*, m.: *man*, m.: *see* sense, intelligence: never m., *see* matter: not m. him, *ohdī parwāh nā karnī*.
mine, n., *khāṇḍ*, *khāṇ*, f.: *see* tunnel.
mingle, *see* mix.
(1) mint, herb, *pūdnā*, m.
(2) mint, for coin, *ṭaksāl*, f., *ṭaṅgsāl*, f.
(1) minute, n., *minṭ*, m.
(2) minute, fine, *see* fine. [m.
miracle, *karāmāt*, f.: *mohjzā*,
mirror, *shīshā*, m.
mischief, *sharārat*, f.
mischievous, *sharārtī*, *sharīr* (last three words applied to grown-up people mean wicked-, -ness).
miser, *shūm*, *kanjūs*, etc.
miser-able, -y, *see* poor, straits.
miserliness, *shūmpuṇā*, m.: *kanjūsī*, f.
misfortune, *badkismatī*, f.: *badnasībī*, f.: *see* calamity.
misjudge, *galt khyāl karnā* (*dā*, *dī bābat*).
mispronounce, *galt talaffaz bōlṇā* (*dā*)

mislay, *rakkhke bhull jāṇā*.

miss (aim), *ukkṇā*, *wār ēwē jāṇī*, *nishānā ēwē jāṇā*, *gōḷī* etc., *nā laggṇī* or *khunjh jāṇī*; m. train, *gaḍḍīō khunjhṇā* or *ghussṇā* or *raih jāṇā*: m. way, *rāhō khunjhṇā* or *ghussṇā*: feel person's absence, *ohde khuṇō* or *bājhō dil ōddarnā*: m. day, *diṇ chaḍḍṇā diṇ khālī jāṇā*.

mission, *mishn*, f.

missionary, *mishnarī*, *pādrī sāb*: lady m., *mishn dī miss sāb*.

misstate, *galt beān karnā* (*dā*).

mist, *see* fog.

mistake, *galtī*, f. (*k.*, *h.*): *bhull*, f. (*h.*), *bhull cukk*, f.: *bhulēkhā*, m. (*laggṇā*, *nū̃*): *ṭapḷā*, m. (*laggṇā*, *nū̃*): *khunjhṇā*, *ghussṇā*.

mistress, *see* teacher.

misunderstanding, *galtfaihmī*, f. (U.)

mix, v. tr., *raḷāṇā*, *miḷāṇā* (int. *raḷṇā*, *miḷṇā*): int. *āpe icc miḷde juḷde* (or *giḷde*) *ne*.

mix-ed, -ture, *raḷā miḷā*: *khicṛī*, f., *see* adulterate, -d.

moan, *see* groan.

mock, *see* imitate, jester.

mocker, *see* jester.

model, *see* pattern.

moderate, *see* average, mediocre.

modern, *inhā̃ dinā̃ dā*, *ajj kall dā*, *hāl de zamāne dā*: *see* new.

modest, *nēkbakht*, or *see* good.

moist, **moisten**, *see* damp, wet.

moisture, *see* damp: in soil for ploughing, *wattar*, m., G. 122: M. 129. 26·8: *wattar hō geā*, rain has wet soil enough for ploughing: *jiwī wattar ā geī*, (after v. heavy rain) soil dried enough to be ready for ploughing: *hēṭhlā utlā wattar raḷ geā e*, the m. from rain has reached down to the soil m.: *rēj*, m. (m. in earth of house after rain).

Monday, *suār*, m.: *somwār*, m.

money, *rupayyā paisā*, m.: *see* wealth.

money-lender, *sāhūkār*, *shāhūkār*, *shāh*.

mongoose, *neōḷ*, *nyōḷ*, m.

monkey, *bānd-ar*, fem. *-rī*.

monotheis-m, -t, *ikko Khudā nū̃ mann-nā*, *-aṇwāḷā*.

month, *mahīnā*, m.: last m., *pishle mahīne*. *see* next.

monthly, *mahīne dā*, *mahīne de mahīne*.

moon, *cann*, m.: full m., *pandhrawī̃ rāt dā cann*: light night, *cānnī rāt*. f: *see* rise, set.

morals, *cāl caln*, m.

more, *waddh*, *wadhīk*. *hōr*, *zyādā*, *wadhērā*.

moreover, *nāḷe*, *te nāḷe*

morning, *subā*, f.: *waḍḍewelā*, m.: *sarghī weḷā*, *parbhāt weḷā*, 1½ hrs. before dawn: *namāz weḷā*, ½ hour before dawn: *jhusmusṛā*, m., *muhānjḷā*, m., *mū̃h anhērā*, m., morning twilight: *dhammī weḷā*, m., time of dawn: *jhalānghe*, at sunrise: *fajr*, f., early m.: *see* forenoon.

morsel, *see* mouthful.

mortal, *fānī*: *see* deadly, fatal.

mortar for pointing, *pink*,

cūnā, m. : black, *simiḷṭ*, m. : *siminṭ*, m. : *see* point (4), pestle.
mortgage, v., *gaihṇe vāṇā* : *see* pawn.
mosque, *masīt*, f.
mosquito, *macchar*, m. : *guttī*, f. : -net, *machairī*. f., *jāḷī*, f., do. w. rods, *macchardānī*, f.
most, *sabbhnā̃* or *sāreā̃ tō̃ waddh*, *waddh tō̃ waddh*.
moth, *bāhmaṇ baccā*, m.
mother, *bēbbe*, *mā̃*, *māī*, *wāldā* (U.) : m. in law, *sass* : m. in law's father, *naniauhrā* (his wife, *nanēhs*) ; m. in law's brother, *maliauhrā* (his wife, *malēhs*) : mothers of bride and bridegroom are *kuṛmnī* to each other.
motion, *harkat*, f. : in meeting, *mōshn*, f. : *rā* f. : *see* move.
motive, *matlab*, m. : *wicclā matlab* ; *garz*, f
(1) mould, bricks, *saccā*, m. : pudding, *sā̃ncā*, m. (K.) : v. tr., *sacce wicc ḍhāḷṇā* (int. *ḍhaḷṇā*).
(2) mould (green), *ullī*, f. (*laggṇī*, *nū̃*).
mound, *ṭibbā*, m. : *ḍhērī*, f.
mount, *utte caṛhnā* (tr. *cāṛhnā*) : m. animal or vehicle, *suār h.* (tr. *k.*).
mountain, *pahāṛ*, m. : *parbat*, m. : *see* hill.
mountainous, belonging to mountains, *pahāṛī*.
(1) mourn, *mātam-k.*, *karlāṇā*.
(2) mourners, collective, *mukāṇ*, f.
(3) mourning, united, *mukāṇ*, f.
mouse, *cūhī*, f. (no word for male) : *see* rat
mouse-trap, *see* trap.
moustache, *mucchā̃*, f. pl. : beard and m., *daṛhī mucch*, f.
mouth, *mū̃h*, m. : at his m., through him, *ohdī zabānī*, G. 36, 37 : corner of m., *warāch*, f. : get sore m., *mū̃h pakk jāṇā* (*dā*) : do. horse, cattle, etc. *mū̃h auṇā* (*dā*), M. 117. 9 : *mū̃h pakk jāṇā*.
mouthful, liquid, *ghuṭṭ*, m. : solid, *barkī*, f., *burkī*, f., *garāh*, m., *garāhī*, f.
move, *hallṇā* (tr. *halāṇā*) : m. away, *haṭṇā* (tr. *haṭāṇā*) : m. a motion, *pēsh-k.* : without moving, gently, *aḍōl*, *malkṛī*.
moving, *see* pathetic, motion.
mow, grass, *ghāh mārnā* or *waḍḍhṇā*, *see* reap.
much, *cōkhā*, *bāhḷā*, *baukt*, *bathērā*, *ām*, *wāfar* : *see* more : many, use plur. of much : as m. as I, *mēre jinnā*, G. 91 92. : *see* number.
mucus, *balgam*, m
mud, *cikkaṛ*, m., *cikkaṛ cambhaṛ*, m. : half-dry, *khobhā*, m. : cake of m., *carēpṛī*, f. : m. for building, w. straw, *ghāṇī*, f. : without straw, *gārā*, m. : get covered w. m., *bharnā*, *miṭṭī nāḷ bharnā* : M. 118. 22.
muddy (water), *gandhḷeā hoeā*, *gandhḷā*.
muffler, *see* tie (2).
mug, *magg*, m.
mulberry, tree and fruit, *tūt*, m. : large-fruited, *shatūt* m.
mule, *khaccrā*, fem. -*car* (masc. rare) : *waihtar*, m. (also horse, ass) : man in mule corps, *khaccarpātrī*.
multiply (educ.), *zarb dēṇī* (*nā̃*,

nāḷ) : *see* increase : multiplication table, *pahāṛā*, m.
multitude, *see* crowd.
murder, *khūn*, m. (*k.*, *dā*).
murderer, *khūnī*.
murmur, *hauḷī bōlṇā*, *see* grumble.
muscle, no word, use *mās*, m. : *gōsht*, *goshat*, m. : m. of forearm, *bāh dī machḷī*, f. : of lower leg, *pinnī dī machḷī*, f. : m. to right and left of aesophagus, *rag*, f. : *see* biceps.
museum, *ajaib ghar*, m.
mushroom, *khumb*, f. : toadstool, *padd bhaiṛā*, m.
music, *see* tune, play, instrument.
musician, professional and gen. disreputable, *mirās-ī*, fem. *-aṇ* : *ḍūm-*, fem. *-ṇī* : singer (good meaning), *gawayyā*, (no fem.) ; *gauṇwāḷā*.
musk-rat, *cakcūhndar*, m.
muslin, *malmal*, f.
mustard, *rāī*, f., *auhr*, f. : growing, *sarhō*, *sarheō*, f. : *tārāmīrā*, m.
mutineer, *bāgī*.
mutiny, *bagāwat*, f. (*k.*) : *gadr*, m. (*k.*).
mutter, *see* murmur, grumble.
mutton, word for meat w. *nikkā*, small, or *bākrā*, of sheep or goat, prefixed *matan*, m. (K.).
muzzle, *see* snout, halter.
my, *mērā*.
mystery, *see* secret.

N

nail, finger, toe *nauh*, m. : small iron, *brinjī*, f. : *prēk*, f. : large, iron or wood, *killī*, f. : *kill*, m. : *mēkh*, f. : *see* hammer.
naked, *nangā*.
nakedness, *nang*, m.
name, *nā* m. : *nāwā*, m. (esp. in list) : v. tr., *nā rakkhṇā* or *dharnā* : *see* call : get a n. for, *all paiṇī* (*dī*) : getting bad n., *bhaṇḍī*, *badnāmī*, f. (both w. *h.*, *dī*) : *see* named.
named, *musamm-ī*, fem. *-āt* : be called Kammo, *Kammo akhwāndī* or *sadāndī e* ; G. 109 : *Kammo, Kammo karke saddde ne*.
nape, *see* neck.
napkin, *mēz dā tauliā*, m. : for infant, *nāpkin*, m.
narrate, *see* relate.
narrow, *sauṛā*, *bhīṛā*, *tang* : *ghaṭṭ cauṛā e* : of cloth, *bar chōṭā e*.
native, *dēsī* (Indian) : n. language, *mādrī bōlī* : *see* country.
natural, *kudratī*
naturally, *uñ ī*.
nature (around) *kudrat*, f. : *see* disposition.
naughty, *see* mischievous.
navel, *dhunnī*, f.
navigable, *jitthe kishtīā yā jahāz jā sakaṇ*. [(in plur.).
navy, *jahāz*, m. : *jangī jahāz*
near, *nēṛe*, *kōḷ*, *koḷe*, *nāḷ*, *karīb* : *see* distance : adj., *nāḷ dā*, *nēṛe dā*, *urlā*, fr. n., *nēṛeō*, *koḷō*, *nāḷō* : pass by n., *neṛe dū*, *nāḷdū* or *nāḷē dī*, *kōḷdū* or *koḷō dī* (*langhṇā*, *jāṇā*).
nearly, *karīban*, *karīb*, *kujjh ghaṭṭ* : *see* approximately.
necessary, *zarūrī*, *lāzarūrī* : *lōṛīdā* or *cāhīdā*, G. 67, 96 : *see* have to. [*ṛīā cīzā*.
necessaries, *zarūrī cīzā*, *lōṛīdī*-

necessity, *lōṛ* f. : *zarūrat*, f.
neck, nape, *gicī*, f. : *dhauṇ*, f. : *gāṭā*, m. : *munḍī*, f. : *gardan*, f. : front, *gal*, m. : *see* throat, Adam's apple, aesophagus.
necklace, *haikal*, f. : *hassī*, f. : *hass*, m. : *hasīrā*, m. : etc.
necktie, *naktāī*, f.
need, *see* necessity.
needle, *sūī*, f. : large, *sūā*, m.
neglect, *lāparwāhī*, f. : *gaflat*, f., *gāflī*, f. (all *k*.).
negotiation, *gall katth*, f. (*k*).
negro, *habsh-ī*, fem.*-aṇ*.
neigh, *hiṇaknā*.
neighbour, *guāhṇḍ-ī*, fem. *-aṇ*.
neighbourhood, *guāhṇḍ*, f. : *āhṇḍ guāhṇḍ*, f.
neither, *dohā̃ wiccõ koī nā* : n. ..nor, *nā*.. *nā* : *nā te*.. *te nā* : *nā*.. *te nā*.
nephew, brother's son, *bhatrīā* : sister's son, *bhaṇẽwā̃*, *bhaṇeā* : n.'s wife, *bhatrīõ nũh*, *bhaṇeweõ nũh*.
nest, *ālhṇā*, m.
net, fishing, *jāl*, m. : tennis n., *jālī*, f. : for straw, chaff, *traṅgaṛ*, m. : wire netting, *jālī* : *see* mosquito.
never, *kadī nā* : never ! interj., *majāl e*, *tōbbā tōbbā* : of incredulity, *hĕkkhā̃* ; (the reply is *hĕkkhā̃ kī* ?)
new, *nawā̃* : fresh, *sajrā* : n. or unwashed cloth, unused paper, waterpot, *kōrā*.
news, *khabar*, f. : incorrect, *gapp*, f.
newspaper, *akhbār*, f.
next, *nāl dā*, *dujjā*, *aglā*, *aglā* : n. week, month, year, *agle*, *auṇwāle hafte*, *mahīne sāl* : *aunde sāl* : this day n. week, *ajj de* or *ajōke dihāṛe*.
nib, *cunjh*, f. : *par*, m.

nibble, *kutarnā* : *see* gnaw.
nice, *see* good, tasty.
niche, *āḷā*, m.
nickel, *ciṭṭā trāmmā*, m.
nickname (to annoy) *cēṛh*, f. (*paiṇī*) : otherwise, say *nā̃ pai geā*.
niece, brother's daughter, *bhatrī* ; sister's, *bhaṇẽwī*, *bhaṇeī*. niece's husband, *bhatrīõ* or *bhaṇewīõ jawāī*.
night, *rāt*, f. (*paiṇī*) : by n., *rātī* . n. and day, *rātī diṇe*, *dēh rātī* : to-n., last n., *ajj rāt nū̃*, *ajj rātī* : n -clothes, *rāt de kapṛe*, m. pl. : *see* bedding.
nightmare, *daraoṇī khāb*, f.
nine, *nau* : -th, *nauā̃*, *nāwā̃*.
nineteen, *unnī* : -th, *unnhīwā̃*, G 22.
ninety, *nawwe*, *nabbe* : -one, *ikānwe* : -two, *bānwe* : -three, *tarānwe* : four, *curānwe* : -five, *pac-* or *panj-ānwe* : -six, *cheānwe* : seven, *satānwe* -eight, *athānwe* : -nine, *naṛinwe* : ordinals add *-wā̃* and high tone *h*, *nabbhewā̃*, *ikāhnwewā̃*, etc. : G. 20, 22, 123.
nipple, baby's indiarubber, *cūsṇī*, f., *cūpṇī*, f.
nitre, *shōrā*, m.
no, *nā*, *nehī*, *āhā̃* (w. glottal stop at end) : *see* nothing, nowhere.
no one, *koī nehī*.
nobility, *sharāfat*, f. : *see* noble.
noble, rank, *sharīf khāndān dā*, *āhlā raīs*.
nod, *see* sleepy.
noise, *rauḷā*, m. : *khapp*, f. : *dand*, f. : *rattā*, m. : *rēṛkā*, m. (all *pāṇā*, int. *paiṇā*) : *shōr*, m. (*k*.), *awāz*, f. (*auṇī* : *mārnī*,

call): *khṛāk*, m. (*auṇā*, of footsteps, cart, etc.): *see* splash, disturbance.
nomad, *pakkhīwās-*, fem. *-aṇ*: *ṭaprīwālā*; *see* tent.
nominal, *nirā nā ī e.*
nominate, *nā pēsh karnā* (*dā*).
nonsense: *see* never: *wāhyāt gall*, f.: *bakwās*, f.: *wāfrī*, f.: *wāfar gall*, f. (all *k.*): *yabbhā*, f. pl. (*mārnīā*): *fazūl* or *wāfar gallā*, f. pl. (*k.*): *gappā*, f. pl. (*mārnīā*): talker of n., *bakwās-ī*, fem. *-aṇ*.
noon, *dopaihr*, f.: at n., *dopaihrī*: *see* afternoon, forenoon.
nor, *see* neither.
north, *pahāṛ*, m.: *parbat*, m.: n.-wards, *pahāṛ* or *parbat pāse* or *wall*: n.-east, *pahāṛ te caṛhde dī gutth*: n.-west, *pahāṛ te laihnde dī gutth*.
nose, *nakk*; flat-nosed, *phīhnā*: blow n., *nakk suṇknā*.
nostril, *nās*, f.
not, *nā*, *nehī*.
note, *see* letter: bank-n., *nōṭ*, m.: make n. of, *likkhṇā*, *nōṭ k.*
notebook, *kāpī*, f.: *nōṭbuk*, f.
noteworthy, *sōccaṇ* or *suṇaṇ* or *yād rakkhaṇ jogā*.
nothing, *kujjh nehī*: n. at all, *kakkh wī nehī*: come to n., *guggaḷ jāṇā*.
notice, n., *ishtihār*, m.: v., *khyāl karnā* (*dā*): *dhiān karnā*: *see* advertisement.
notwithstanding, *bhāwē*.
nourish, *see* maintain.
novel, *see* new: book, *nāwal*, m.
November, *nawambar*, m.: *magghar*, m. (about Nov. 13 to Dec. 12).
now, *huṇ*, *huṇe*: at present, *hālī*, *hālā*: only n., *aje huṇe*: now now!, interj. (rebuke), *hāē*, *āhē*.
nowhere, *kitale nā* or *nehī*.
noxious, *see* injure, loss, hurt.
numb, *ṭhareā hoeā* (through cold, v. cold): *sunn* (also limb asleep).
number, *see* figure: *nambar*, m., of page, house, regiment, etc.: *tedād*, f., of people, etc.: what page? *kinnawā safā*? (so *jinnawā*, *innawā*, *ōnnawā*), also *kinnā*, *kehṛā*.
nurse, ayah, *āyā*, f.: European n., *nais miss sāb*: midwife, *dāī*.
nursery, of plants, *zakhīrā*.
nut, pistachio, *pistā*, m.: *see* walnut.

O

O, calling: woman to woman, *nī*, *aṛīe*: woman to man, *wē*: man to man, *ō*, *ōe*: man to woman, *ē*: all imply "*tū*": *see* oh.
oar, *cappū*, m.
oath, *saūh*, f.: *kasm*, f. (both *khāṇī*, *cukkṇī*): *Kurān cukkṇā*, take o. on Quran: administer o., *duāṇī*, *cukāṇī* (*nū*): be v. unwilling to, lit. take o. against, *eh kamm karn dī saūh hōṇī* or *cukkṇī*: M. 107. 17-9.
oats, *gandhaiḷ*, f.
obey, obedience, *tābedārī karnī* (*dī*); *ākkhe laggṇā* (*de*); *hukm mannṇā* (*dā*).
object, *garz*, f.: *see* intention, aim: secure o., *kamm* or *matlab kaḍḍhṇā*.
objection, *ehtrāz*, m. (*k.*): *uzr*, m. (*k.*), excuse.

obligation, favour, *ahsān*, m. (pron. *as-hān*) : *ṭhāhrā*, m. : admit o., *ahsān* or *ṭhāhrā mannṇā* (*dā*) : trade on another's o. to one, *ahsān* or *ṭhāhrā cāṛhnā* (*utte*) or *manāṇā* : *see* benefit.
oblige, *see* force, cause : *see* obligation.
obliterate, *see* delete, efface.
obscene, *gandā*, *fohsh*.
obscure, *see* dark, ambiguous : *matlab sāf nehī*.
observe, *see* notice, attend.
obstacle, *see* hindrance.
obstinacy, *zidd* (*bannhṇī*) : *khaih* (*rakkhṇī*) : *haṭṭh*, m., *aṛī*, f., *kabbpuṇā*, m. (all w. *k.*).
obstinate, *aṛyal*, *ziddī*.
obstruct-, -ion, *see* hinder, hindrance, and add *aṛekā*, m. : *mushkil*, f. : *aṛikk* or *aṛicc*, f. (all w. *pāṇā* : also *aṛicc ḍāhnī*).
obtain, *labbh laiṇā*, *laiṇā* : *menū labbhā* or *miḷeā*, *mere hatth āeā* : *see* secure, supply, produce.
obvious, *see* evident.
occasion, *maukā*, m. : *see* opportunity.
occur, take place, *see* place.
occurrence, *gall*, f.
ocean, *see* sea.
o'clock, what o ? *kī wajeā e*, *kinne waje ne* ? one o., *ikk wajeā e* : at 1 o., *ikk waje*, *ikk waje nāḷ* (about one) : M. 61.
October, *aktūbar*, m. : *kattē*, m. (about Oct. 13 to Nov. 12).
octroi, *see* tax.
odd, not even, *ṭāk* : *see* strange.
of, *dā* : material, *dā* : of himself, of his own accord, *see* help.
off, see o., *see* farewell : send o., *see* send : go o., *Allā Bēlī h.*, *alī panj h.*
offence, stumblingblock, *ṭhokkar* (*laggṇī*, *nū* ; *lāṇī*) : take o., *burā mannṇā* (at, *nū*) : *see* stumble, resent.
offer, *pēsh-k.*, *agge rakkhṇā* : sacrifice, *cāṛhnā*, *caṛhāṇā*.
offering, *caṛhāwā*, m., *nazr*, f. (both at shrine) : *see* gift, sacrifice.
office, room, *daftar*, m.
officer, *afsar* (military or any superior in office). [*ohdedār*.
official, adj., *sarkārī* : n., *afsar*,
officiat-e, -ing. : *iwzī*, *kaim makām*, *ohde thā kamm karnā*.
often, *aksar* : *see* repeatedly.
oh, pain, *hāl oe*, *hāe hāe* : displeasure, *hāē*, *āhē* : surprise, *halā*, *see* astonishment : protest, *tōbbā*, *lai*, *see* never.
oil, *tēl*, m : paraffin, *miṭṭī dā tēl* : for food, for rubbing, *mitthā* or *kauṛā tēl* (sweet or bitter, according to origin).
oilman, caste, *tēl-ī*, fem. *-aṇ*.
ointment, anoint, *malham*, f. (*lāṇī*, int. *laggṇī*) : *lēp karnā*, without bandage : *phāh lāṇā*, w. bandage (int. *laggṇā*) : *see* anoint.
old, *buḍḍhā*, *buḍhṛī*, *waḍḍā banḍā* ; *see* great : ancient, *purāṇā* : three years old, *triūh sālā* or *warheā dā* become o., *umar ḍhaḷṇī* (*dī*) : o. age, *pishlī umr*, *baṛī umr*, *buḍhēpā*, m.
old-fashioned, *purāṇe faishn* or *ḍhang* or *namūne dā*.

oleander, *kanēr*, m.
olive, *kaū*, m.
omen, *sagaṇ*, m. : random sentence in sacred book, *fāl*, f. (*kholhṇī*, *kaḍḍhṇī*, *pāṇī*) : *see* auspicious.
omit, *chaḍḍṇā* : miss a day, *see* miss.
omniscient, God, *sabbho kujjh jāṇdā e*, *ālam ul gaib* : man, *auliā* (M.).
on, *see* upon.
once, *ikk wārī*, *ikk ḍaṅg* (*see* meal) : at o., *see* immediately : all at o., *see* suddenly.
one, *ikk* ; G. 21 : all at o. time, adv., *ikko ṛikkī* : adj., *ikko ṛikkā* : 1½ *ḍēḍh*, *ḍūḍh* : adj. from these, *ḍeoḍhā*, *ḍeoṛhā*.
onion, *ganḍhā*, m.
only, *nirā*, *sirf* : *see* emphasis : o. son, no word in nom., obl. *ikkse* : for "*ikko*" *see* son.
ooze, *simmṇā*, *nikḷṇā* : *see* drip, trickle.
open, v. tr., *kholhṇā* (gen. : int. *khulhṇā*) : door, window, lock, *lāhṇā* (int. *laihṇā*) : eyes, *ughēṛnā* (int. *ugghaṛnā*) : mouth, *aḍḍṇā* : w. open doors, *see* door : o. school, shop, *kholhṇā*.
openly, *khulham khulhā*, *sāf sāf*, *khulhī gall* : *see* publicly.
operation, surgical, *aprēshan*, m. (*k.*).
ophthalmia, *see* eye.
opinion, *rā*, *rai*, f. : *khyāl*, m. : *kiās*, f. m. : in his o., *ohde agge*, G. 91, *ohde bhāne*, *ohde waṇḍe dā*, *ohde bhā dā* M. 127. 4-6.
(1) opium, *afhīm*, f. : *pōst*, m. (poppy).
(2) opium-eater, *afīmī*, *pōstī*.
opponent, *mukhālaf*, *see* enemy.
opportunity, *maukā*, m. : *tāṅg*, m. (both w. *laggṇā*, get) : seek o., *maukā wēkhṇā* or *jācṇā* or *tāṛnā*.
oppose, *mukāblā karnā* (*dā*) : *mukhālfat karnī* (*dī*) : *see* enemy.
opposite, prep., *de sāhmṇe* : *see* face : the o. of, *ohdā ulṭ*, M. 279. 18.
oppression, *zulm*, m. : *sakhtī*, f. : *dāhḍpuṇā*, m. : *taddī torī*, f. : *jabr*, m. f. : *sikkhā shāhī*, f. : (all w. *k.*, *utte* or *nāḷ*) : *see* violence, confess.
option, *ikhtiār*, m. : *marzī*, f.
optional, *ikhtiārī*.
or, *ke*, *yā* : *see* either.
oral, *zabānī*.
orally, *mūh zabānī* : heard o. fr. him, *ohdī zabānī suṇeā*.
(1) orange, Indian, *santarā*, m. : Maltese, *māltā*, m. : eat o., *cūpṇā*.
(2) orange, adj., *gutaī*.
ordain-, -ed, *see* preacher.
(1) order, written, *parwānnā* (for supplies, etc.) : *see* command, method, class, rank, arrange : in o. to, *ēs wāste paī*, *paī*, *tā jo* : also inf. w. *wāste*, *laī*, *nū*, etc. (G. 95), or simple inflec. inf : in line 17 of G. p. 95, for "in the past tenses of verbs" read "in the case of trans. verbs". Out of o. (machine, cart, well, etc.) *hanēkeā* or *wigṛeā hoeā* · *see* disorder.
orderly, n., *ardalī*, *capṛāsī*.
(2) orders, holy, *see* preacher.
ordinary, *see* common : every day, affair, *rōz dī gall*.
organ, *wājjā*, m. : play, *wajāṇā*.
origin, *asl*, f. : *see* beginning.

ornament, *see* adorn.
orphan, without father, *yatīm*, *pyō mhaitar* : without mother, *mā̃ mhaitar*.
orthodox, gen. *pakkā* : Hindu, *sanātanī*.
ostensible, *zāhrī* : only outwardly, *uttōwāḷī*.
ostentation, *see* show.
ought, *see* necessary, advisable, duty, require, have to.
other, *hōr*, *dujjā*.
otherwise, *nehī̃ te* : or use "lest."
out, *see* outside.
outbid, *wadhke bōlī dēṇī*.
outhouses, *naukarā̃ de ghar* : *see* stable, cowhouse.
outpost, *caukī*, f., *caũkī*, f.
outside, *banne*, *bāhr* : fr. o., *banneō̃*, *bāhrō̃* : by way of o., *banneō̃ dī*, *bāhrō̃ dī* : on the o., *bāhrwār*.
outwardly, *see* ostensible.
oven, *tanūrī*, *tandūrī*, f. : *bhaṭṭhī*, f., *tandūr*, m.
over, *see* above, upon, finish.
overawe, *see* threaten : be o.-ed, *dabbṇā*.
overcoat, *waḍḍā kōṭ*, m. : *brā̃ḍī*, f. (waterproof).
overcome, *see* conquer.
overflow, in vessel, *ucchaḷṇā* : boil over, *ubbaḷ jāṇā*, *ubbaḷke paiṇā* : river, *ucchaḷṇā*.
overhear, deliberately, *cōrī* or *malkṛī suṇṇā* : accidentally, *sbabb nāḷ* or *ẽwẽ suṇṇā*.
overlook, *nā khyāl karnā* (*dā*).
overseer, of labourers : *see* superintendent.
overshadow, *see* shade, shadow.
overtake, *jā raḷṇā* or *pharṇā* (*nū̃*) : *kōḷ appaṛnā*, *agge laṅghṇā*.
overturn, *see* upside down.
owe, he owes, *ōs dēṇā e* : he is owed, *ōs laiṇā e*, *ohnū̃ aundā e* : *see* debt.
(1) own, adj., *apṇā*.
(2) own, owner, *kih dā e*, *ehdā mālik kauṇ e*.
(3) ownerless, *lawāris*, *nikhasmā* : of animal temporarily separated fr. its owners, *luggā*.
(4) ownership, *mālkī*.
ox, *see* bull : pair for ploughing, *haḷ*, m., *jōg*, f.

P

pace, *kadam*, m. : *see* walk.
pacify, *rāzī-k.* : *sulhā karāṇī* (*dī*) : *see* calm (2), appease.
(1) pack, *asbāb teār-karnā* or *bannhṇā* : shove in, *tunnṇā*.
packet, postal, *pākaṭ*, *paikaṭ*, m. : *see* bundle, parcel.
(2) pack-horse, *lāddū ghōṛā*.
(3) pack-saddle, *sūṇḍkā*.
pad, on head, *innū̃*, m.
padlock, *see* lock.
page, *safhā*, m. : one double p., *warkā* (a leaf) : *see* sheet, paper.
pain, *pīṛ*, f. : *dard*, m. : griping, *waṭṭ* (*paiṇā*) : shooting, *trāṭ*, f. (*paiṇī*) : *see* grief, hurt.
painful, *dukhdā e*, *pīṛ kardā e*.
paint, *raṅg*, m. : (*lāṇā*, *nū̃* ; *k.*, *dā* or *nū̃* ; int. *laggṇā*).
painter, *taswīrā̃ banāṇwāḷā*.
pair, *jōṛā*, m. : of oxen, etc., *jōg*, f. : *hal*, m. (for ploughing) : the p. or fellow, *ehde nāḷ dā*.
palace, *mahall*, m.
palate, *tāḷū*, m.
pale, *pīḷā* (*paiṇā*, *h.*) : *raṅg laihṇā* (*dā*) : *bhussā*, p. ill : of colour, *see* light.

palm, hand, *taḷī*, f. : date-p., *see* date (1).
palpitate, fear, *dhaṛaknā* : excitement, longing, *taṛafṇā*.
palpitation, *dhaṛkī*, f.
palsy, *adhrang*, m. : man w. p., *adhrangī*.
pamphlet, *rasālā*, m.
pankha, *see* punkah
pannier, donkey's saddle-bags, *chaṭṭ*, f.
pant, *cheti cheti sāh laiṇā* : *see* breath, out of ; gasp.
pantry, *bōtalkhānā*, m.
paper, *kāgaz*, m. : sheet, *tā*, m. *see* news-p., page.
paragraph (educ.) *pairā*, m.
paralysis, *see* palsy.
paramour, *yār*.
parapet *banērā*, m.
parcel, *pārsal*, m. : *see* packet.
parch, tr., *bhunnṇā* : int. *bhujjṇī* : grain-parcher, *bhaṛbhūjā*.
pardon, *see* forgive.
pare, peel, fruit, vegetables, *chillṇā*, *chill lāhṇī* (int. *laihṇī*, *di* : nails, *lāhṇā*, gen. *luhāṇā*, get them done (A.).
parents *māpe mā pyō*, *wāldain*.
(1) part, n. *hissā*, m. : take p. in, *ralṇā*, *sharīk* or *shāmil h.* (*wicc*) : fifth p., sixth p., etc., *see* time.
(2) part, v., *see* divide.
partake, *see* part, share.
partially, as p. blind, *kujjh annhā* : *see* partly, partiality.
partiality, *raī*, f. : *tarfdārī*, f. : *lihāz*, m. (all w. *k.* and *dā*, *dī*).
particular, *see* special : -s, *see* detail.
partition, *see* part, divi-de, -sion.
partly, *kujjh te eh*..*te kujjh eh*, *abbaḷ te*.. or *ikk te*..*te phēr*.
partner, *sīrī*, *sānjhī*, *panjhāḷ*, *sāthī*, *jōṛīdār*, *hissedār* : half and half p., *ādhī*.
party, *farīk*, m. : *dhir*, f. : *pāssā*, m. : quarrelling clique, *dhaṛā*, m., *see* sect.
pass, *langhṇā* (tr. *langhāṇā*) : p. money, *lāṇā*, *calāṇā* (int. *laggṇā*, *calṇā*) : p. exam., *pās h.* or *k.* : p. time, *weḷā ṭapāṇā* (int. *ṭappṇā*), *jhaṭ* or *wakat langhāṇā* (int. *langhṇā*).
passage, in book, *ibārat*, f. : *see* tunnel.
passenger, *suārī*, f. : p.-train, *suārī gaḍḍī*, f. : *see* traveller, train (2).
passport, *pās*, m. : *rāhdārī*, f.
past, *jehṛā zamānā langh geā e.* : *purāṇā zamānā*.
paste, *lēwī*, f. (for gumming : *lāṇī*, int. *laggṇī*) : for pudding, *krās*, m. (K.) : *see* gum, glue.
pasture, *see* graze.
pat, v. tr., *thāpṛī mārnī* or *dēṇī* or *lāṇī*, (also *thāpṛā*, m.).
patch, cloth, leather, *ṭākī* (*lāṇī*, int. *laggṇī*) : metal, *ṭānkā* (*lāṇā*, int. *laggṇā*) : not a p. on him, *ohdā pāskū wī nehī*.
path, *paihā*, m. : *rāh*, m. : v. narrow (between fields, *see* boundary), *bannā*, m. : track, *ghāssī*, f. : *see* road, way.
pathetic, *rōṇ-* or *ruāṇ-wāḷī gall*, f. : *see* sad, touching.
patience, *hauslā* m. : *sabr*, m.
patient, adj., *hausle* or *sabr wāḷā* : n., *bamār*, *marīz* (U.).

patriotism, *watan dī mhabbat*, f.
pattern, *namūnā*, m.
paucity, *thuṛh*, f. : *ghāṭā*, m. : *kamī*, f. : *see* deficient.
paw, *panjā*, m. : p. ground (horse), *khaurū kaḍḍhṇā*.
pawn, v. tr., *gaihṇe* or *bandhe pāṇā* or *rakkhṇā*.
pay, *tankhāh*, f. (*tārnī*, *dēṇī* : int. *tarnī*, *milṇī*) : p debt, *dēṇā*, *lāhṇā* (int. *laihṇā*) : p. fine, *bharnā* : *see* strike off.
peace, between parties, *sulhā*, f. : in country, *aman*, m. : rest, *arām*, m. : of mind, *tsallī*, f., *tsallā*, f. : M. salutation, (*as-*) *salām alaikum* : reply, *wā alaikum* (*as-*) *salām*.
peacemaker, *sulhā karāṇwālā*.
peach, *āṛū*, m (tree and fruit).
peak, of mountain, *cōṭī*, f. : *sirā*, m. : *ṭishī*, f.
pear, *nākh*, f (tree and fruit).
pea, *maṭar*, m.
pearl, *mōtī*, m.
peasant, *see* farmer, villager.
pebble, *giṭī*, f. : *giṭā*, m.
peck, *cunjh* or *cinjh mārnī*, *ṭhūṅgā mārnā* : eat grain, etc., *cuggṇā*.
peculation, *gaban karnā*.
peculiar, *see* strange.
pedlar, *see* hawker.
pedigree, *nasabnāmā*, m. : tree, *shajrā*, m.
peel, *chill*, f. : v., *see* pare.
peep, *jhātī mārnī*.
peepul tree, *pippal*, m.
peerless, *sāreā tō wadhīā* or *awwal*, *ohde jehā* or *barābar koī nehī* : *bēnazīr* (U.) ; *lāsānī* (U.), *see* matchless.
peevish, *shtābī ciṛhnwālā*.
peg. *see* nail.
pellet, (small for *gulēl*), *gulēlā*, m. : (large, for *kubhāṇī*), *ḍhīṇḍhā*, m. : *see* sling, pebble.
pen, *par*, m. : *kalam*, f. : *see* nib : p. and ink, *kalam duāt*, f. : p.-tray, *kalamdān*, m.
pencil, *pinsal*, f. : *pilsaṇ*, f. : *rūl*, f. m.
penetrate, *see* enter, pierce, sink.
penknife, *cakkū*, m.
penman, *see* caligraphist.
pension, *pinshan*, f.
Pentateuch, *taurēt*, f.
(1) people, *lōk*, m. pl. : *lōkī*, m. pl. : Tom, Dick and Harry *jaṇā khaṇā*, *hamā shamā* : *see* common, everyone, all.
(2) people, v. tr., *abād-k.* (place) : *wasāṇā*, settle p. in a place
pepper, black, *kāḷī marc*, f. : *gōḷ marc*, f. : red, *lāl marc*, f.
per, *picche*, *sētī* (both after infl. noun) ; *fī* (before noun, U.) : in prices often loc., G. 78 : per man, *jaṇe sētī* : per house, *ghar picche* : at 6/- a maund, *chī rupaī maṇ* : *see* rate.
per cent, *saikṛā* (5%, *panj rupayye saikṛā*) : *fī sadī* : -age given to lambardar, zaildar, *panjōtrā*, m
peremptory, *see* imperious, urgent.
perennial, *jehṛā sārā sāl rawhe*.
perfect, *kāmal*, *pūrā* : *see* complete, guiltless.
perfection, *kamāl*, m.
perfid-ious, -y, *see* treacherous, treason.
perform, *see* do, finish.

perfume, *acohī bō*, f. : *khushbō*, f. (in villages this may mean also bad smell) : *cangī khushbō*, f. : *see* smell.

perfunctory, *kamm tarangarnā*.

perhaps, *shaid, shait, ho sakdā e*.

period, *zamānā*, m. : fixed p., *miād*, f., *mohlat*, f. : long time, *cir*, m. : *muddat*, f. : *bāmuddat*, f.

perish, *nās-h., barbād-h.* : *see* destroy, downfall : perish !, *bērā ruṛhī* (abuse).

perjury, *jhūṭhī saūh* or *kasm*, f. : *see* oath.

permanent, *see*, lasting : service, *mustakil, pakkī* (*naukrī*).

(1) permissible, *jāiz, hukm*, m., or *ijāzat*, f., *haiwe*.

(2) permi-t, -ssion, *see* allow, liberty.

perpendicular, *siddhā*, (straight) : *khaṛā*, steep.

perpetual, *hamēshā dā* or *wāste*.

perplex, *gallā nāl phasāṇā* (int. *phasnā*) : *see* confuse.

perquisite, *dastūrī*, f., on purchases : *kamīshan*, m.

persecut-e, -ion, *see* oppression.

persevere, *khaihṛā nā chuḍḍṇā, chaḍḍū nehī, pakkā*.

persist, *see* persevere. obstinacy, -te.

person, *see* man, etc. : in p., *āpū, āpe* : *see* self : the Spirit is a p., *nirā asr nehī, Rūh we*.

personal, *zātī* ; not used for "my p. Saviour," which is *mērā apṇā, mērā ī* : p. work, *jaṇe jaṇe nāl gall karke*, etc.

perspiration, *muṛhkā*, m. (*wagṇā* w. *dā*, *auṇā* w. *nū*) : *trēlī*, f. (through weakness or fear, *auṇī, nū*). [*ṇā*.

persuade, *manāṇā, samjhā-*

perturb-, -ation, *see* perplex, confuse.

perverse, *puṭṭhā, ulṭā*.

(1) pervert, v. tr., *wagāṛnā, gumrāh-k* (int. *wigaṛnā, gumrāh-h.*) : *see* excite, incite.

(2) pervert, n., *murtadd*.

pestilence, *bamārī*, f. : *see* plague.

pestle and mortar, *daurī ḍaṇḍā*, m. : *caṭṭū waṭṭā*, m. : *hamām dastā*, m. : in ground, *ukhlī mūhlī*, f.

pet, child, *lāḍlā* (spoilt). *pyārā* : animal, kept, *rākhwā, pāltū*.

petal, *pattī*, f. : *phull dī pattī*.

petition, *arz*, f., *suāl*, m. : leg., *arzī*, f. (written).

petticoat, *ghagghrī*, f. : *pĕṭikōṭ*, m. : *see* skirt, kilt.

pewter, *jist*, m.

philosopher, *failsūf* (U.).

philosophy, *failsūfī*, f.

photograph, *taswīr*, f. : *fōṭō*, m. f. (both *khiccṇā*).

phthisis, *tap dikk*, m.

physician, *see* doctor.

piano, *wājjā*, m. : play, *wajāṇā*.

pice, *paisā*, m. : half p., *dhēllā*, m. : quarter, *damṛī*, f. : third, *pāī*, f. : two p., *see* anna.

(1) pick, flowers, fruit, *khohṇā* (int. *khussṇā*), *cuṇṇā* : p. off sticky things, *lāhṇā* (int. *laihṇā*) : p. up, *cukkṇā* : *see* peck.

(2) pick, tool, *gaintī*, f.

pickle, *acār*, m. (*pāṇā* ; of, *dā*).

picture, *taswīr*, f. (*baṇāṇī, khiccṇī*), *mūrat*, f. (*baṇāṇī*).

piebald, *ḍabbā*, *ḍab khṛabbā*.
piece, *ṭōṭā*, m. : *ṭukṛā*, m. : of meat, *bōṭī*, f. : *ḍakkrā*, m. : take to pieces, undo, machinery, bed, masonry, *ukhēṛnā* (int. *ukkhaṛnā*) : see loose.
pierce, make hole, see hole : needle, thorn, see prick : pierce ears, nose, *winnhṇā* (pa. p. *widdhā* : int. *wijjhṇā*).
piety, *see* pious.
pig, *sūr*, fem. *sūrnī* : *bāhrlā*, *bāhr dī shai* : G. 114.
pigeon-house, *see* dovecot.
pigmy, *see* dwarf.
pigtail, *see* hair.
pile, *see* heap.
piles, *bawāsīr*, f., (also *mohkā*, m.) : bleeding, *khūnī*.
pilgrim, to Makkah, *hājī* ; Hindu, *tīrthī*, *jātrī*.
pilgrimage, to Makkah, *hajj*, m. (*k.*) : to Muslim shrine, *ziārat*, f. : to Hindu shrine *tīrath*, m. : *jātrā*, m. (all *k.*).
pill, *gōḷī*, f. ; *ṭikkī*, f. (flattened).
pillar, masonry or wood, *thammh*, m. : small, *thammhī*, f. (wood) : of brick, in house, *kauḷā*, m. : *see* support, boundary.
pillow, *sarhāṇā*, m. : *takīā*, m. : p.-slip or case *takīe dā uchāṛ* m.
pimple, *phimhṇī*, f.
pin, *pinn*, m. : rolling-p., *wēllaṇ* or *wēlṇā* m. : *see* rolling-board.
pincers, *sannhī*, f. : *see* tongs.
pinch, *cūndhī waḍḍhṇī* or *bharṇī* (*nū̃*).
pine, *diār*, m. : *biāṛ*, m. (both cedar) : pinus longifolia or excelsa, *cīhṛ*, f. : *cīhl*, f.
pinion, arms (tie), *mushkā̃ bannhṇīā̃* (*dīā̃*).
pink, *gulābī*, adj : *see* red.
pinnacle, of building *kiṅgrā*, m. : *see* peak.
pious, *Khudā-parast*, *dīndār*, *parhēzgār*, *bhagat* (H.).
pipe, *hukkā*, m. : *paip*, m. (European).
pirate, *daryāī cōr*, *baihrī cōr*.
pistol, *pistaul*, m. : *tamāñcā*, m. (both *calāṇā*, *mārnā*) : *see* shoot.
pit, *toā*, m. (also ditch, *kaḍḍhṇā*) : *khāḍḍā*, m. (*lāṇā*, int. *laggṇā*) : *khāttā*, m. (gen. an old *khāḍḍā*).
(1) **pitch**, tar, n., *lukk*, f. : *see* tune.
(2) **pitch**, tents, *lāṇā* : *see* strike.
piteous, *see* pathetic.
pith, *girī*, f.
pitiful, *see* compassionate, pathetic.
pity, *tars*, m. (*auṇā*, *k.*, *utte*) : *see* mercy, compassionate : it's a pity that, *afsōs e paī*.
pivot, *cūthī*, f. : of bed, *cūḷ*, m. : *see* socket.
(1) **place**, n., *thā̃*, m. f. : *jaghā*, f. : out of p., *kuthā̃-*, *-e*, *kojhā* : in right p., *thā̃ sir* : *see* instead, awkward.
(2) **place**, v., *rakkhṇā*, *dharnā* : p. bed, chair, water (before animal), *ḍāhṇā* (int. *daihṇā*, pa. p. *ḍatthā*) : *see* put A.
plague, *tāūn*, f. : *see* pestilence.
(1) **plain**, adj., *sāf* : *see* evident : simple, (both simple-minded and unornamented), *sādā*, *siddhā sādā* : *see* flat, level.
(2) **plain**, n., *madān*, m. : open space, no crops, *raṛā thā̃*, m., *raṛā*, m.
plainly, *sāf sāf*, *safāī nāḷ*.
plaintiff, *mudaī*.

plaintive, *see* pathetic, sad.
plait, v., *gundṇā* : rope, *waṭṭṇā* : n., *see* hair.
plan, *tajwīz*, f. : *hikmat*, f. (both *k.*) : *see* arrange : of building, etc., *nakshā*. m. (*baṇāṇā*). [*randṇā*.
plane, *randā*, m. (*phērnā*) : v.,
plank, *see* board.
plant, n., *būṭā*, m. : *būṭī*, f. : young for replanting, *panīrī*, f. (all w. *lāṇā*, int. *laggṇā*) : w. long tendrils, creeping, climbing, *wēl*, f. : *wall*, f.
plantain, *see* banana.
plaster, n., *see* mortar, mud : v., *limbṇā* : *lēmbī* or *lavāī karnī* (*dī*), *plastar karnā* (*dā*) : *see* mud, smear.
plate, gen. *bhāṇḍā*, m. : large, *plēṭ*, f. : smaller, *hāfplēṭ*, f. : still smaller, *kuāṭar*, m. : soup-p., *suplēṭ*, f. : Indian, *prāt*, f., *thāl*, m. : *thāḷī*, f. : *see* dish, drinking-vessel.
platform : *thaṛhā*, m. : *cabūtrā*, m.
(1) play, n., *khēḍ*, f. : drama, *nāṭak*, m.
(2) play, v., *khēḍṇā* : music, *wajāṇā* (int. *wajjṇā*).
player, *khaḍārī*.
playfellow, *see* companion.
pleader, *wakīl*.
pleasant, *dil nū̃ caṅgā laggṇā* : *see* good, tasty.
please, v. tr., *khush-k.*, *rāzī-k.* : int. *khush h.*, *rāzī h.* : p. do it, *mehrbānī karke* (very emphatic), *zarā* ; gen. omit : p. God, *in shā Allā*.
pleasure, *khushī*, f. : *marzī*, f. : w. p., *see* means.
plectrum, *mizrāb*, m.
pledge, *see* mortgage, pawn, promise.

plentiful, *see* much.
plenty, not famine, *sukāl*, m. : *see* much.
pliable, pliant, of thing, *lifaṇwālā*, *kūlā* : person, *jaldī mannaṇwālā*, *jehṛe pāse bhuāīe bhaundā e* : *see* changeable, vacillate.
plinth, *kursī*, f.
plot, *garmathā*, m. or *gall*, f. or *matā*, m. (w. *pakāṇā* : int. *pakkṇā*), M. 125. 16.
plough, *wāhṇā*, *hal wāhṇā* (int. *waggṇā*) : each ploughing, *sī lāṇī* (int. *laggṇī*) : *see* cultivate, train (1) : p.-ed land, *warihāl*, f. : *wāhṇ*, f. : *see* fallow.
ploughman, *hāḷī*, *wāhk* (plougher) : *see* farmer, cultivator.
pluck, *see* pick. [*laggṇā*).
plug, *ḍaṭṭ*, m. (*lāṇā*, int.
plum, *alūcā*, m. : (tree and fruit) : small, tree, *bērī*, f. ; fruit, *bēr*, m. : large grafted *bēr* (fruit or tree), *syō bēr* : small, *kāṭhā bēr* ; *bēr* bush, *malhā*, m.
plunder, *see* rob, steal
plural, *jamhā*, f.
P.M. *see* A.M.
pocket. *bojhā*, m. : *jēb*, m.
pocket-book, *pākaṭ buk*, f.
pocket-money, *jēb kharc*, m.
pod, *phaḷī*, f.
poem, *nazm*, f. : *shēhr*, m.
poet, *shairī*, *nazmā likkhaṇwālā*, *shāir* (U.).
poetry, *see* poem.
(1) point, *nōk* f. : p. of letter like *sīn* or *shīn*, *dandā*, *kiṅgrā*, m. : p. of story, etc., *matlab*, m. : be on the p. of, verbal form in *-wālā*, G. 98, 99 ; root of verb w. *caleā* G. 67 : *see* desire.

(2) point, v., *ishārā karnā* (*de wall*) : *see* hit at.
(3) point a building, *ṭīp karnī* (*dī*).
poison, *mauhrā*, m. : *zaihr*, m. : *wiss*, m.
poisonous, *zaihrī*.
poke, w. stick, goad, *hujj mārnī* (*nū̃*) : *see* goad.
poker, wooden, *kuḍḍhan*, m.
pole, north. *kutab*, m. : pole-star, *kutab tārā*, m.
pole, *ḍanḍā*, m., *bā̃s*, m. : *see* stick, post.
police, gen., *puls*, f. : *polīs*, f. : -man, *pulswālā*, *kanstebal* : p.-station, *thānā*, m. : -post, *caukī*, f., *caūkī*, f.
polish, *pālash*, m. (esp. boot-p.), blacking, *syāhī*, f. both *lānā*, int. *laggṇā*) : *see* varnish.
polite, *shaistā* : *see* courteous.
pollute, *see* dirty, defile, unclean.
polytheist, *mushrik*.
pomegranate, tree and fruit, *anār*, m.
pomelo, tree and fruit, *cakōdhrā*, m.
pomp, *see* show.
pond, *chappaṛ*, m. : *chappṛī*, f. (small, often dry) : *ḍhāb*, m. (big depression) : *see* lake.
ponder, *sōcnā* (*nū̃*) : *gaur karnā* (*utte*).
pony, small, *ṭaṭṭū*, fem. *ṭair*.
polo, *pōlō*, m.
pool, *see* pond.
poor, *garīb*, *muthāj* (seeking help), *maskīn*, *wacārā* (p. fellow) : *māṛā* (feeble, poor) : *daliddarī* (wretched) : *see* straits : of land, *niras*, *māṛī*, *raddī*, *maṭṭhī*, *narm* : *see* soil, waste : p. Panjabi, *ṭuṭṭī* *bhajjī* or *māṛī mōṭī Panjābī*, f., *see* smattering.
popcorn, *dhāhṇā*, f. pl. (barley).
poppy, *pōst*, m.
popular, *lōk baṛe khush ne ohde nāḷ* or *cāhnde ne* (*nū̃*) or *cangā jāṇde ne* (*nū̃*).
population, *abādī*, f.
populated, *abād*.
populous, *baṛī abādī*, *baṛe lōk*, *baṛā abād*, etc.
porcelain, *cīnī*, f.
porridge, *daḷīā*, m.
porter, *kulī*.
portion, *see* part.
portmanteau, *thailā*, m.
possess-, -ion, get p. of, *kābū-k.*, *mallṇā* : keep in p., *apṇe kabze wicc rakkhṇā* : *see* have.
possible, *mumkin*, *hō sakdā e* : see able.
(1) post (mail), *ḍāk*, f. : by post, *ḍāk wicc* : p. letter, *ḍāke* or *ḍāk icc pāṇā* (int. *paiṇā*) : travel post, *ḍāk bannhke safar karnā*.
(2) post, telegraph-, *waḷā*, m. : short p., *munnā*, m. : lamp-p., *waḷā*, *munnā* : *see* pillar.
(3) post, situation, *asāmī*, f. : vacancy, *asāmī khālī e* : service, *naukrī*, f.
(4) postage, *masūl*, m. : *ḍāk dā masūl*.
(5) postman, *ḍākwāḷā*, *ciṭṭhī rasān* (U.) : *halkārā*, runner.
(6) post-office, *ḍāk khānā*, m.
posterity, *see* descendants.
postpone, *multawī-k.*, (U.) : p. a week, *aṭṭhā dinā te gall pā dittī*, *aṭṭh din pāe* : *see* respite.
pot, earthenware, *ghaṛā*, m. : *jhajjar*, f. : large, *maṭṭ*, m., *cāṭī*, f. : long-necked, *surāhī*, f. : for cooking (earthen)

hāṇḍī, f., *tauṛī*, f., *kunnī*, f. : at well, *ṭiṇḍ*, f. : pot-stand (wooden), *ghaṛwanjī*, f., *ghaṛēthnī*, f. : metal pots, v. large, *kaṛāh*, m. ; smaller, *kaṛāhī*, f., *dēg*, f. ; small, *dējkī*, f. ; *gāgar*, f. (for water): put on pot, *cāṛhnā* (int. *caṛhnā*).

potato, *ālū*, m.

potsherd, *ṭhīkrā*, m. : small, *ṭhīkrī*, f.

potter, *kumhyār-*, fem. *-ī*.

pounce, *see* snatch, seize.

(1) pound, *kuṭṭṇā*, *ghōṭṇā* (w. liquid) : (p. and husk) rice, grain, etc., *chaṛnā* : *see* grind, beetle, pestle, rolling-board.

(2) pound, n., for cattle, *phāṭak*, m. : coin, *pauṇḍ*, m. : weight, *see* w s. and meas.

pour, *lhṇā* (int. *ḍulhṇā*) : *luddṇa* : p. out, *roṛhnā* (int. *ruṛhnā*) : *see* spill.

poverty, *garībī*, f. : *muthājī*, f. (seeking help, *k.*, *dī*) : *maskīnī*, f. : *taṅgī*, f. : *see* poor, difficulty, straits.

powder, gun-p , *barūd*, m. : *ḍārū*, m. : medicine, *puṛī*, f., *phakkī*, f. : no word for p. in gen.

power, *was*, m. : *mērī majāl e*? what p. have I (to do that)? *see* authority, strength : p. of attorney, *mukhtār-nāmā*, m.

powerful, *see* strong, strength.

practi-ce, -se, *mashk*, f (*k.*), *jāc*, f (knack, *auṇī*, *nū̃*) : *see* use.

praise, *waḍeāṇā*, *salāhnā*, *waḍeāī k.* (*dī*), *tarīf k.* (*dī*), *hamad karnī* (*dī*, only of God).

praiseworthy, *baṛā laik* : *see* good, excellent.

pray, prayer, gen., *duā maṅgṇī* or *karnī* : *namāz paṛhnī* (M.) : *prārthnā karnī* (H.) : prayers, *bandgī karnī*, *namāz paṛhnī* : p. for person, *duā dēṇī* (*nū̃*) ; gen , *de wāste duā karnī* or *maṅgṇī* : call to p., *bāṅg dēṇī* (M.) : *see* ask, beseech.

preach, in church, *wāhz* or *wāhd kar-nī* or *-nā* : to non-Christians, *manādī karnī*.

preacher, *wāhz* or *wāhd karn-wālā*, *pādrī*, *girjā karāṇ-wālā* : ordained person, *pādrī* ; ordain, *pādrī banāṇā* (int. *banṇā*) : *see* priest.

precaution, *khabardārī*, f. : *hōsh*, f., *ehtiāt*, (U.), all w. *k.*

precedent, *dastūr*, m., *rawāj*, m. : no p., *eṅ kadī nehī hoeā* : *see* custom, unexampled.

precept, *maslā*, m. : *see* advice.

precious, *pyārā* : *see* costly, good, excellent.

precipice, *khaṛā pahāṛ*, m. : *baṛī khaḍḍ*, f.

precipita-ncy, -te, -tion, *see* haste.

predestined, *Khudā dī marzī nāḷ* or *de hukm nāḷ* : *see* fate, fated.

preemption, right of, *hakk shufā*, m. (*k.*).

prefer, *eh menū̃ ohdū̃ caṅgā laggdā e* : *see* desire, like.

pregnant, woman, use *ohnū̃ umēdwārī e* : animals, *sūṇ-wāḷī*, *wakkōdī* (cattle).

prejudice, *tassab*, m. : *see* partiality.

prejudiced, *tassabī* : *see* partiality.

premature, *wakat tō paihlā*.

prepar-e, -ation, *teār-k.* (*nū̃*) : *teārī karnī* (*dī*) : *see* ready.

prescience, supernatural, *gaib-dānī*, f., *gaib dā ilm*, *ilhām*, m.
prescription, medical, *nuskhā*, m.
presence, *hāzrī*, f. (not absence): of superior, *huzūrī*, f.: *see* face, before: in p. of God, *Khudā dī huzūrī wicc*, *Khudā dī dargāh wicc*.
(1) present, adj., *hāzar* (esp. of inferior): *majūd*, (not absent): p. time, at p., *hāl dā zamānā*, m.: *hālī*, *hālā*.
(2) present, v., *dēṇā*, *pēsh-k*.
(3) present, n., *see* gift.
presentiment, *mēre dil wicc agdū eh gall āī sī* or *eh khyāl sī*.
preserve, *hafāzat nāl* or *sāmbhke rakkhṇā*: *see* jam: -d fruit, *murabbā*, m. (v., *pāṇā*).
(1) press, n., for books, clothes, plates, in wall or otherwise, *almārī*, f.: v. small in wall, *āḷā*, m.: for sugarcane, *wēlṇā*, m.: binder's p., *shakanjā*, m.: oil-p., *kolhū*, m.
(2) press, v., *dabāṇā* (int *dabbṇā*): *see* incite, urge, pressure, emphasise.
pressure, moral, etc., *dabā*, m.; *rōhb*, m. (both w. *pāṇā*, *utte*).
pretence, *bahānā*, m., *khēkhan*, m., *hīlā*, m., (all w. *k.*): *see* ostensible, put off, trifle.
pretty, *see* beautiful.
prevail, *phailṇā* (spread): *see* conquer, persuade.
prevaricate, *see* put off, trifle.
prevent, *see* stop, hinder, forbid.
previous, *aglā*, *paihlā*.
previously, *see* before.
prey, *shikār*, m.: dupe, v. tr. *jāḷ* or *shikār wicc phasāṇā*, (int. *phasṇā*), *shikār-karnā* (int. *hōṇā*): *see* hunt, shoot.
price, *mull*, m., *kīmat*, f.: *see* rate, cost, expense, spend.
priceless, use v. costly.
prick (needle, thorn), *cubbhṇā* (tr. *cōbhṇā*): tr., *sūī mārnī*, p. w. needle: p. up ears, *kann khaḷe karne* or *khalhār-ne*.
prickly-heat, *pitt*, f.; come out, *nikḷnī*; subside, *marnī*.
pride, (good) *fakhr*, m.: (bad) *magrūrī*, f., *shēkhī*, f., *ākkaṛ*, f., *mizāj*, f., *damāg*, m.: *see* proud, airs, conceit, take down p., *see* humble.
priest, Christian, *pādrī*; *fādar* (Rom. Cath.): M., *malwāṇā*, *miyyā̃*: H., *prōhat*: Cuhra, *gyānnī*, *fakīr*: Jewish, *kaihṇ*.
prince, *shāhzād-ā*, fem. -*ī*.
print, of printer, *chāpṇā*: caus. *chapwāṇā*: be p.-ed, *chapṇā*.
prison, *kaidkhānā*, m., *jēhlkhā-nā*, m.: *see* imprison.
prisoner, war or prison, *kaid-ī*, fem. -*an*: *see* imprison.
private, *sāḍḍī apṇī gall*, *prāiwēṭ*, *parde dī gall*: in p., *pasitte hōke*, *nawēkle hōke*.
privet, *sanatthā*, m.
privilege, *hakk*, m. (right): *ijāzat*, f. (permission): *riait*, f. (easement).
prize, *inām*, m.: v., *see* value.
probably, *wīh wiswe*, *umed e pai*.
probe, a matter, *phōlṇā*.
procla-im, -mation (causal) *ḍaunḍī piṭwānī*, *ḍhanḍōrā duāṇā*, *manādī karāṇī*: of actual crier, *ḍhanḍōrā d.*: make known, *ḍhumāṇā*, *suṇāṇā*.

procrastinate, *see* delay, put off.
procurable, *milda e.*
procure, *labbh laiṇā*, *see* obtain, produce (2).
prod, w. stick or knuckles, *hujj mārnī* (*nū̃*), *see* goad.
(1) produce, n., *paidāwārī*, f. (of land), *see* crop: *jo kujjh banḍā e.*
(2) produce, v., *paidā-k, banāṇā*: *see* secure, supply, obtain.
profan-e,-ity, *kufr bakṇā*.
profession, *kamm*, m. (men or women): *pēshā*, m., *kasab*, m. (these two not of women).
professor, *ustād*, *profēsar*.
proficient, *see* clever, able, intelligent.
profit, *khaṭṭī*, f., *labhat*, f., *nafā*, m: for his own advantage, *apṇe gaū̃ nū̃*: p. and loss, *nafā nuksān*, m: *see* advantage, excess.
profligate, *luccā*, *badkār*.
progress, *trakkī*, f. (*k.*): *see* advance.
prominent, *see* famous, conspicuous.
promise, *wāhdā*, m., *sukhan*, m., *karār*, m., *gall*, f., *zabān*, f. (all w. k.): break p., *apṇe wāhde*, *sukhan*, etc., *dā* or *thõ jhūṭhā h.*, *wāhdā troṛnā*: fulfil p., above words w. *pūrā k.*: *see* word.
promote, *trakkī dēṇī* (*nū̃*): a scheme, *calāṇā*, *madat dēṇī* (*wicc*).
prone, on face, *mū̃hdā*, *mū̃hdṛe mū̃h*, *mū̃h parne*: p. to, liable to, use *-wālā*; p. to forget, *bhullanwālā*: p. to fall, *ḍigganwālā*: to sickness, *bamār hōṇwālā*.
pronounce, letter, word, etc., *bōlṇā*, *bulāṇā*: be p.-ed, *bōlṇā*, *bōleā jāṇā*, *bulāeā jāṇā*.
pronunciation, *talaffaz*, m., (*bōlṇā*).
proof, *sabūt* (*dēṇā*, *dā*): *dalīl*, argument, *dēṇī*, *dī*): *see* prove.
prop, *sahārā*, m. (*d.*, *see* lean): for trees, *thūhṇī*, f.: *see* support, pillar.
proper, *munāsib*, *ṭhīk*, *see* suitable, right (2), advisable.
property, *māl*, m., *māl asbāb*, m.: estate, *jāēdāt*, f., *jāedād*, f.: *hasīat*, f., wealth: *see* wealth, rich.
prophecy, *nabuwwat*, f. (*k.*): *pēshīgoī*, f. (*k.*).
prophet, *nabī*, *pakambar*, *pagambar*.
propitiat-e, -ion, *see* conciliate, atone.
propos-e, -al, *rā* or *rai dēṇī*, *dassṇī*: in meeting, *rā* or *mōshn pēsh karnī*: *see* opinion, advise.
prose, *nasr*, f.
prosecute, *see* case.
prosper-, -ous, *see* advance, progress, rich: or say *ohdā kamm wāh wā caldā e.*
protect, *see* guard, preserve, save.
protector, *see* guardian, saviour.
protrude, *nikḷṇā*, *wadhṇā*: -ing, *nikḷeā* or *wadheā hoeā*.
proud, *magrūr*, *mizāj-* or *damāg-* or *ākaṛ-* *-wālā*: *see* pride.
proudly, words for pride w. *nāḷ*.
prove, *sābit-k.*: *see* proof.
proverb, *masāl*, f.: *akhāṇ*, m.
(1) provide, *see* obtain, supply, produce (2), secure.

(2) provided that, *jē* or *agar* (if): *jē te, hā par jē te*: *see* condition.
province, *sūbā*, m.
provision, rations, *rasad*, f., *rāsn*, f.
provo-ke, -cation, *see* annoy.
proxy, *wakīl*, m.
prune, v. tr., *chāṅgṇā*, *chaṅgāī karnī* (*dī*).
pry, *see* peep.
psalm, *zabūr*, m.; book of P., *zabūrā̃ dī kitāb*, f., *zabūr*, m. pl.: a volume containing the Ps., *zabūr*, f.
publicly, *khulham khulhā*, *khulhā*, *khulhā ḍulhā*, *lōkā̃ de sāhmṇe*: *see* openly.
publish, *chapwāṇā*: be p.-ed, *nikḷṇā*, *chapṇā*: *see* print, proclaim.
pudding, *putīn*, f.: *phutīn*, f.
pull, *khiccṇā*: punkah, *khiccṇā*: p. out hair, weeds, and other small things, *puṭṭṇā*: *see* drag.
pulley, *garāṛī*, f.: for well, *carakhṛī*, f.
pulpit, *mimbar*, m., *mēz*, *mēc*, m.
pulse, *nabz*, f. (*wēkhṇī*, caus. *wakhāṇī*, also *bā̃h*, f.).
pump, *naḷkā*, m.: railway, etc., *pamp*, m., *papp*, m.
pumpkin, *kaddū*, m.
punctual, *weḷe sir auṇā*: *wakat dā paband* (U).
puncture, (bicycle) *pancar*, m. (*h.*, *nū̃*).
pungent in taste, *see* hot.
punish-, -ment, *sazā*, f. (*d.*): capital p., *phāhe* or *phā̃sī* or *maut dī sazā*.
punkah, *pakkhā*, m.: to fan, *pakkhā jhallṇā*: pull p., *khiccṇā*; p.-coolie, *pakkhe-wāḷā*.

pupil, of eye, *see* eye: of wrestler, *paṭṭhā*, m.: *see* disciple, scholar.
puppy, *katūrā*, m.
purchases, *saudā*, m.: *saudā sūd*, m.: *see* buy, obtain.
pure, *see* clean: ceremonially, *see* holy: unadulterated, *nakhākhrā*, *khālas*: pure Panjabi, etc., *ṭhēṭh*. [A.
Purgative, *julāb*, *m.* (*laiṇā*, *d.*).
purify, words for clean, pure, holy, w. *k.*: *see* wash.
purity, *pakīzgī*, f. (U.): *see* cleanliness.
purple, *kāshnī* (violet), *kirmzī kirmcī* (red purple or crimson): purplish, *see* somewhat.
purpose, *see* aim, object, intention: for the p. of, *see* order: to no p., *dhigāṇe*, *ēwē*: *see* useless.
purposely, *ucēcā*, *jāṇke*, *samjhke*: *see* deliberately.
purse, *guthlī*, f., *gutthī*, f., *thailī*, f., *baṭūā*, m.
pursue, *magar bhajjṇā*.
pus, *pāk*, f. [(*nū̃*).
push, *dhikkṇā*, *dhakkā dēṇā*
put, *rakkhṇā*, *dharnā*: *see* place: p. in, *pāṇā* (int. *paiṇā*): p. away w. care, *sāmbhṇā*: p. off, *see* delay: p. off w. excuses, promises, *lāre* or *lāre lappe dēṇe*, *ṭālṇā* (int. *ṭaḷṇā*), *ṭāḷ maṭoḷā karnā*, *ṭāḷ ṭapoḷe karne*: p. off w. semi-jocular remarks, *jugtā̃ karnīā̃*: p. on clothes, on to oneself or child, *pāṇā*; to oneself, *utte laiṇā*; a shawl round one's head, *bukkaḷ mārnī*: make someone p. on clothes or let him put them on to oneself, *puāṇā*: *see* wear: p. out, *see* extinguish, annoy, eject.

putrid, *see* rotten, bad.
putty, *puṭīn*, f., *phuṭīn*, f.

Q

quadruple, *cauṇā*, *cār guṇā* : in four folds, *cauhrā* : *see* fold, time.
qualification, *liākat*, f. : *kī pās e*, what has he passed ?
quality of mind, *sift*, f. (also Divine attributes, attributes of mind) : q. of thing, *darjā*, or simply good, bad, etc.
quantity, *kinnā*, how much ? *ēnnā*, *ōnnā*, *jinnā*.
quarrel, *takrār*, m., *jhagṛā*, m., *laṛāī*, f. (all *k.*, *h.*) : mild q., *āpe icc rinj rāzī h.* : *see* disturbance, discord.
quarrelsome, *jhagṛnwālā*, *laṛākā*, *takrārī*.
quart, about *ikk sēr panj chaṭā-kāā*.
quartan fever, *cauthā*, m.
quarter, G. 23, *cauthāī*, f. : *cuhāī*, f., (esp. land) : *cauthā hissā*, m. : *pā*, m. (of *ser*, *see* wts. and meas.) : q. more than, *sawā*, as 3¼, *sawā trai* : adj., *suāyā*, used for one and q. : q. less than, *pauṇe*, as 1¾, *pauṇe dō* : q. of orange, etc., *see* section : ¾ of, *muṇnā*.
queen, *rāṇī*, *malkā*, f.
quench, fire, *bujhāṇā* ; int., *bujjhṇā* : thirst, *see* slake.
question, *suāl*, m. (*k.*), *see* ask.
quibble, *jugat*, f. (*k.*), *huṭṭar*, m. (*k.*), *hujjat*, f. (*k.*) : *see* argument, excuse.
quick, *see* swift, quickly.
quickly, *shtābī*, *chēṭī*, *jabde*, *jhabde*, *jhaw*, *shapāshapp* : of action *hallke*. *hīlā karke*, *wag tag* : go q., *khurī karnī*, *khiṭṭ dēṇī* or *mārnī*.
quicksilver, *pārā*, m.
quiet, *cup*, *cupkītā*, *cup cupītā*, *sun munn* : keep q., *aman karnā*, *sāh laiṇā*, *ḍanḍ nā pāṇī*, etc. (noise w. neg.), *cup k.* ; *see* screen.
quietly, *malkṛī*, *aḍōl*, *aṇchōp* : *see* gently, slowly.
quilt, *lēf*, m., *jullā*, m., *razāī*, f., *gudṛī*, f. : *see* mattress.
quince, fruit and tree, *bahī*, f.
quintuple, *panj guṇā*, *panjauṇā* : *see* fold, time.
quire, *dastā*, m. (24 sheets).
quite, *see* absolutely, altogether.
quiver, *see* tremble, shake.
quorum, *kōram*, m.
Quran, *kurān*, m. : one who knows by heart, *hāfaz* : for *hāfaj* *see* blind : Q-stand. *rehl*, f.

R

rabid (dog, etc.), *halkā*.
rabies, *halak*, m. (get, *kuddṇā*, *nū̃*).
race, *dauṛ*, f. : horse-r *ghuṛdauṛ*, f.
racquet, tennis, racquets, *ballā*, m.
radish, *mūḷī*, f.
raft, *bēṛā*, m.
rag, *līr*, f. : *cithṛā*, m.
rage, get into r., *agg laggṇī* (*nū̃*) : be angry inwardly, *lūsṇā* : *see* anger, enrage.
ragged, garment, *pāṭā hoeā* : man, *pāṭeā kapṛeā wālā*, *līrā patīrā wālā*.
railing, *jaṅglā*, m. : *see* hedge, enclose.
railway line, *laiṇ*, f. : *rēl dī saṛak* ; sometimes *pakkī saṛak* (also Grand Trunk Road) : *see* station, train.

rain, *mīh*, m. (*wassṇā*) : *jhaṛī*, f., (continued r., *laggṇī*): *pāṇī*, m. (*paiṇā*) : *kaṇīā*, f. pl. (*paiṇīā*) : *kaṇī muṇī*, f. (*h.*): *kaṇmaṇ*, f. (*laggṇī*); last three words mean slight rain: *bārish*, f. (U., continued r., *h.*) : *see* drizzle, storm.
rainbow, *piṅgh*, f., *guḍḍī guḍḍe dī piṅgh*, f. (*paiṇī*).
raise, *cukkṇā*, *uṭhāṇā* (int. *uṭṭhṇā*) : r. stick, *uggarnā* : r. wall, *usārnā* (int. *ussarnā*): r. dead, *jawāḷṇā*.
raisin, *sauṅgī*, f., *mewā*, m., (collective).
rake, *jandrā*, m. (*lāṇā*) : r. up a matter, *phōlṇā*.
ram, *chatrā*, m.
rampart, *duār*, f., *duāl*, f., *fasīl*, f.
ramrod, *gaz*, m.
rancid, *see* bad, rotten, smell.
random, at, *uñ*, *ēwē*, *bin sōceā*; *see* guess, reason.
rank, *darjā*, m., *ohdā*, m. : *see* line.
rankle, *dil icc khaṭakṇā*.
ransom, *fidyā*, m. : *see* save.
rap, *see* knock.
rapid, *see* swift.
rare, *ghaṭṭ wēkhīdā e* or *miḷdā e*.
rash, *jaldbāz* (U.) : *see* hasty.
rashness, *jaldbāzī*, f. (U.) : *see* haste.
rasp, *see* file.
(1) rat, *cūhā*, m. (no word for female) : *see* mouse.
(2) rat-trap, *see* trap.
rate, *bhā*, m., *nirkh*, m. : at r. of, *cuūh ānnī waṭṭī*, 4 lbs. for 4 annas, G. 78 : *rupayye dā cār ser*, 4 ser a rupee: *see* tariff, per.
rather, *see* prefer, than : r. white, etc., *ciṭṭā jehā*, G. 27, 92; or add *-ērā*, *waḍērā*, biggish : G. 18 : *see* somewhat : rather than, *nāḷō*.
ratify, *tasdīk karnī* (*dī*) : *see* confirm.
rations, *rāsn*, f., *rasad*, f.
(1) rattle, v. int., *khaṛkṇā*, *khaṛ khaṛ-k.*, tr. *khaṛkāṇā*.
(2) rattle, toy, *chaṇkṇā*, m.
raw, *kaccā* : *see* uncertain.
ray, of sun, *kirn*, f. (U.), *rashm*, f. (U.), also of cloth.
raze, *ḍhā chaḍḍṇā*.
razor, *ustrā*, m.
reach, *appaṛnā*, *paūhcṇā* : *hatth nehī appaṛdā*, cannot reach it : *see* obtain.
read, *paṛhnā* : r. it out, *paṛhke suṇāṇā*.
readmit, to rel. privileges, *see* excommunicate.
ready, *teār* : r. to do, *karn nū teār* : r. made, *baṇeā battreā* : *see* prepare.
real, *aslī* : r. gold, silver, *succā* : r. reason, *wiclā matlab*, *asl gall*, f.
reality, *hakīkat*, f., *aslīat*, f. : in r., *asl wicc*, *hakīkat wicc* : *see* root.
really, *see* reality.
reap, *waḍḍhṇā*, *wāḍhīā karnīā*, *lāīā karnīā* or *lāṇīā*.
reaper, *wāḍhā*.
reaping-hook, sickle, *dātrī*, f.
(1) rear, v tr., *pāḷṇā*, *parwarish karnī* (*dī*).
(2) rear, of horse, *sīkhpā-h*.
(3) rear, n., *pishlā pāsā*.
reason, *dalīl* (argument) : *see* cause, purpose, therefore, without any reason, *bēsbabb*, *uñ*, *ēwē*, *dhigāṇe* : *see* random.
reasonable, *mākūl*. [(U.).
rebel, *bāgī* ; *sarkash*, rebellious

rebellion, *bagāwat*, f., *gadr*, m.: *see* riot.
rebuke, *see* reprimand, forbid.
receipt, *rasīd*, f. (*likhṇī*, *dēṇī*): railway r.. *bilṭī*, f.
(1) receive, *milṇā* (*nū̃*), also for r. visitors.
(2) receiver of stolen goods, *cuṅg cōr*.
recent,-ly, *jabde*, *jhabde*, *jhaw jhaw*. *nawā̃*, *ajj kall dā*, *huṇ dī gall*, *thōṛeā̃ dihāṛeā̃ dī gall*, *thoṛā cir hoeā*.
reciprocal, *āpe icc*.
recite, *ākhṇā*, *suṇāṇā*.
reckless, *lāparwāh*.
reckon, *see* count, estimate.
recluse, *gōshā-nishī*, (M. relig. term).
recognise, *sihāṇṇā*, *sañhāṇṇā*, *pachāṇṇā* (pa. p. *sihātā*, *sāñhātā*, *pachā-ttā* or *-ṇeā*).
recognition, *sihāṇ*, f., *sañhāṇ*, f., *pachāṇ*, f.
recoil, *pishā̃ haṭṇā* (go back).
recollect, *see* remember.
recommend, no exact word, *safārish karnī*, beg for (*dī*); *cāl caln dī ciṭṭhī dēṇī*, give letter of character: *see* advise.
recompense, *badlā*, m., *iwzānā*, m. (both *d.*): *see* damage.
reconcile, *sulhā karāṇī* (*karnī*, *hōṇī*), *rāzī-k.*: be r., *āpe icc rāzī h.*; *huṇ rāzī e koī shikait nehī̃ kardā*, now r.-ed, no complaint.
record, *likhṇā*: n., *sanad* (f.) *rawhe*, that there may be a r
recover, get back, *phēr milṇā*, *phēr laiṇā*: get well, *wall* or *caṅgā h.*: r. oneself, *sambhaḷṇā*.
recruit, *raṅgrūṭ*: *see* enlist.

red, *lāl*, *sūhā*, *rattā*: v. red, *lāl sūhā*: of cattle, *gōrā*. A.
redeem, *chuḍāṇā* (from pawn, seizure, etc.): rel., *see* save.
Redeemer, *see* Saviour.
reduce, *see* degrade.
reduction in price, *riait*, f.
reed, *kānnā*, m.: various kinds, *kāhī*, f., *naṛ*, m., *sarūṭ*, m., *sirkī*, f., *ḍibb*, f.: *dabb*, f. (v. long grass).
reel, *ḍōlṇā*, *ḍōldeā̃ jāṇā*.
reference, *hawālā dēṇā* (*dā*).
refined, *shāistā* (manners).
reflection, in mirror, *parchāwā̃*, m. (*paiṇā*): *see* thought, shadow.
reform, v. tr., *sudhārnā*, int., *suddharnā*.
refrain, *parhēz karn-ī* or *-ā* (*tõ*): leave off, give up idea of, *muṛnā* (*tõ*), *chaḍḍṇā*: *see* abstain.
refuge, *panāh*, f.: *see* shelter.
(1) refuse-e, -al, *mukkarnā*, *namukkarnā*, *inkār karnā* (*dā*), *inkārī karnī* (*dī*), *nāh karnī*: *madē*, *machaḍḍ*, one who refuses to give, leave: *see* reject: receive refusal, *juāb milṇā* (*nū̃*): flat refusal *sukkā juāb*: answer back, *gall partāṇī*, *aggõ bōlṇā*.
(2) refuse, n., *see* rubbish.
refute, *jhūṭhā sābit-k*: *radd-k.* or *raddṇā* (*ohdī gall nū̃*): *see* reject.
regard, *see* esteem, consideration, honour, respect.
regeneration, *see* conversion.
regiment, *palṭaṇ*, f.: cavalry, *rasālā*, m.: artillery, *tōpkhānā*.
register, v. tr., *rajisṭrī karāṇī* (*dī*, said of sender: *karnī*,

of clerk): ·ed letter, *rajistri*, f.
regret, *pachtāwā*; *afsōs*, m. (*k.*), sorrow in gen.: *see* grief, repent, remorse.
regrettable, *afsōs dī gall*, or words like, *burī gall*, etc.
regular, *kaide nāl*, *kaide dī gall*, etc.: a r. thief, *pakkā cōr*.
regulation, *kaidā*, m., *hukam*, m.
reign, *saltanat*, f., *rāj*, m.
rein, *wāg*, f.
reinstate, *bahāl-k.*, *phēr rakkhṇā*.
reject, *radd-k.*, *raddṇā*, *raddī-k.*, *nāmanzūr-k.*: *see* refuse (1), refute.
rejoice, *khushī karnī* (*dī* of cause): *see* delight.
relate, *bēān karnā* (*dā*), *sunānā*.
relationship, *sākādārī*, f., *rishtedārī*, f.
relative, n. *sāk*, *rishtedār*: *see* full: be related to, word for relative w. verb subst. or *hōṇā*. G. 119, M. 121. 11
release, *chaḍḍnā*; *azād-k.* (U.): *see* acquit, free.
relent, *see* pity, mercy, compassionate.
reliable, *mohtbar*, *pakkā*, *imānwālā*: A: *see* untrustworthy.
reliance, *wasāh*, m., *māṇ*, m. (both w. *k.*, *dā*): *see* confide, trust, faith, untrustworthy.
relief, *see* ease, rest.: military, *badlī*, f.
relieve, *see* ease, rest.: of one's duty, *ralīw-k.* (int. *ralīw-h.*), *kamm chuḍānā* (*koḷō*).
religion, *mazhab*, m. (gen.): *dīn*, m. (M.): *dharm*, m. (H.).
religious, *dīndār* (M.), *namāzī* (praying much, M.): *dharmī* and *bhagat* (H.).
relinquish, *see* abandon.
relish, *see* enjoy, like, taste.
reluctant, use not wish, not desire, *rūh nehī̃ kardā*: *see* wish, oath, desire, sick of.
rely, *see* reliance, trust, confide.
remain, be left over, *bacṇā*, *waḍhṇā*, *bākī raihṇā*: r, behind, *picche raihṇā*: r. in one place, *ṭikṇā*: *see* stay.
remainder, financial, mathematics, *bakāyā*, m.: gen., *jehṛā bākī e.*
remedy, *see* treat, cure, recompense.
remember, not forget, gen., *cētā*, m. (*auṇā*, *raihṇā*, *nū̃*, M. 117. 11): *thauh*, m. (*raihṇā*, *nū̃*), *yād-raihṇā* (*nū̃*): suddenly r., *yād auṇā* (*nū̃*), M. 117. 4: r. is also *yād rakkhṇā* or *karnā*: note *yād rakkhṇā* is keep in mind: *yād karnā* is (1) r. a person, think of him: (2) used speaking respectfully of calling someone: (3) learn lesson: (4) r. after an interval: *see* memory.
remembrance, *see* memorial, memory.
remonstrance, *see* objection, reprimand, reproach.
remiss, *see* lazy, delay.
remorse, *pachtāwā*, m. (*laggṇā*, *h.*, *nū̃*), *afsōs*, m. (*auṇā nū̃*, *k.*): *see* regret.
remote, *see* distant.
remove, v. tr., *dūr-k.*, *laijāṇā*, *kharṇā*, *haṭāṇā*: int., to another house, city, *uṭṭh jāṇā*.
renegade, *murtadd* (M., rel.): *see* treacherous.
rennet, *jāg*, f. (*lānī*, int. *laggṇī*): tablet of r., *ṭikkī*, f.

(*dā*), *zimmewārī cukṇī* (*dī*), *bīṛā cukkṇā* (*dā*) : hold someone r. for, *ohde peṭe pāṇā*, G. 34 : *ohde zimme lāṇā* : *ohde māthe lāṇā* (blame for).
rest, *arām*, m. (*k.*), *cain*, m. (of mind, U.) : *tsallī*, f. (mind) : take a r., *sāh laiṇā* : give person r. by doing his work for short time, *sāh kaḍhāṇā* (*nū̃*) : let animal r., *sāh duāṇā* (*nū̃*) : for these three *see* G. 122, 109 ; M. 129. 22 ; 118. 32 : give person r., also *chaḍḍṇā* : *see* ease, convenience.
resthouse, *baṅglā*, m. or *ḍāk-baṅglā* : village, *dārā*, m. : a serai, *sarā*, f.
restless, *bēkarār*, troubled in mind ; *becain*, uneasy (both U.).
restlessness, *cintā*, *bēkarārī*, f. (U.), *becainī*, f. (U.) : *bēarāmī*, f. [hinder.
restrain, *see* stop, forbid,
resurrection, *jī uṭṭhṇā*, *kiāmat*, f. (often used for judgment-day) : *see* rise.
retail, *see* wholesale.
retinue, *nāḷ de bande*, *nāḷ de suār*.
retire, go back, *pishā haṭṇā* : *naukrī chaḍḍṇī*, *raṭair hō jāṇā* (*tō*).
return, v. int., *partṇā*, *part jāṇā*, *part auṇā*, *muṛnā*, *pishā̃ muṛnā* : v. tr., *partāṇā*, *pishā̃ mōṛnā*, *mōṛnā* : article that may be returned, *mōṛwā̃* : r. fare, *wāpsī karāyā*, m. : r. post, *wāpsī ḍāk*, f. : *see* turn back.
revenge, *badlā laiṇā* (*de koḷō*, *gall dā*) : *sijjhṇā* (*nū̃*).
revenue, *āmdan*, f.
revere, *see* acknowledge, respect, honour.
reverse, v. tr., *puṭṭhā-k.* ; turn back, *pishā̃ bhuāṇā* : *see* upside down, defeat.
revile, *burā ākhṇā* (*nū̃*), *gāhḷā̃ kaḍḍhṇīā̃* (*nū̃*).
revise, lesson, etc., *durhāṇā*, *rawaiz-k.* (*nū̃*) : look over again, *nazr sānī karnī* (*dī*, U.).
revive, *jān wicc jān auṇī*, *hōsh auṇī* (*nū̃*).
reward, *inām*, m. : *ajar*, m. (of God, U.).
rhyme, *kāfyā*, m. (*bannhṇā*, int. *bajjhṇā*).
rib, *pasḷī*, f : I'll break your ribs, *babbar bhannū̃gā*.
ribbon, *fītā*, m. : *rēshmī fītā*, silk r.
rice, growing, *munjī*, f., *dhān*, m. : grain, cooked or not, *cauḷ*, m. pl. : r. cooked w. milk, *khīr*, f. : cook r., *rinnhṇā* (pa. p. *riddhā* : int. *rijjhṇā*) : get soft in cooking, *baihṇā*.
ricochet, ducks and drakes, *tatto tārī*, f. (*khēḍṇī*).
rich, *amīr*, *ba<u>kh</u>tāwar*, *saukhā*, *paise-wāḷā*, *hasīat-wāḷā*, *dhanī* (H.), *daulatwand*.
riches, *see* wealth.
riddle, *kahāṇī* (*pāṇī*) : *bujhārat* (*pāṇī*) : *see* secret.
ride, *suār h.*, *suār hōke jāṇā*, *ghōṛe te jāṇā* : get ride, carriage, boys' back, anywhere, *hūṇṭe laiṇe* (*de*).
ridicule, mock, *makhaul karnā* (*nū̃*) : *hujtā̃ karnīā̃* (*nū̃*) : milder, *jugtā̃ karnīā̃* (*nū̃*) : *kise dīā̃ maskhrīā̃ karnīā̃* : *ok de wallō̃ wēkhke hassṇā* (also means laugh w. pleasure) :

sloping, *ḍhālwā*, and words for slope w. *-wāḷā*.
slow, *ḍhillā*, *matthā* : *see* lazy : s. fire, *matthe tā* (*pakāṇā*, *see* simmer).
slowly, *hauḷī hauḷī*, *saihje* : go s. *jū dī ṭōr ṭurnā* : *see* steadily.
slowness, *ḍhill*, f., *ḍhill matth*, f.
slur, *dhabbā*, m., *dāg*, m. (both *lāṇā*, int. *laggṇā*).
small, *nikkā*, *chōṭā* : of person, *see* short, dwarf.
smallpox, *mātā*, f. (*nikḷnī*).
(1) **smart**, adj., *sajā sajāeā*, in appearance; and words for show : *cust* in action.
(2) **smart**, ache, *see* pain, hurt.
smartly, *custī nāḷ*.
smash, v. tr., *ṭōṭe ṭōṭe k.*, *phīṭe phīṭe k.*, *cūr cūr k.* (all *nū̃*) : int., same words w. *h.* : *see* collide, knock.
smattering, speak language badly, *ṭis mis karnā* : *see* poor.
smear, w. oil, butter, etc., *cōpaṛnā* : *see* plaster.
(1) **smell**, v. tr., *sunghṇā* : int. (bad s.) *bō chaḍḍṇī* or *karnī*, *bō auṇī* (*tō̃*).
(2) **smell**, n., sweet, *see* perfume : bad, *mushk*, f. : *bō*, f. (by itself means bad s.).
smile, *muskṛāṇā* : jocular words, *guṭaknā*, *guṛhkṇā*.
(1) **smoke**, n., *dhū̃*, m. : *see* soot.
(2) **smoke**, v. int., *dhū̃ nikḷṇā* : s. pipe, hukka, tobacco, etc., *pīṇā* : of hukka also *chikkṇā* : have turn at hukka, *sūṭ*, m., *sūṭā*, m., *wārī*, f. (all w. *lāṇā*), *wārī laiṇī*.
smooth, to touch, *kūḷā* : road, ground, *padhrā* : gen. *sāf*, *suāhrā*.
smother, *sāh band karke mārnā*, *saṅgh ghuṭṭke mārnā* : *see* choke, strangle, stifle.
snaffle, *kazāī*, f.
snake, *sapp*, fem. *sappṇī* : -skin, cast off, *sappkunj*, f.
snake-charmer, *sapyādhā*.
snap, fingers, *cuṭkī mārnī*. [A.
snare, *phandhā*, m. : net, *jāḷ*, m.
snatch, kite, cat, hand, *jhuṭāh mārnā*, *jharāṭ* or *jharuṭṭ mārnī* : *see* seize.
sneer, *tāhne mārne* (*nū̃*) : *mehṇā dēṇā* or *mārnā* (*nū̃*).
sneeze, *nicch mārnī* : severe w. cough, *dhrañṇā*, *drā̃sṇā*.
snore, *ghurāṛe mārne*. [f.
snout, *būthī*, f. : pig's, *thunnī*,
snow, *warf*, f., *barf*, f. : fall, *paiṇī*.
snuff, *naswār*, f.
so, *see* thus : so and so, *falāṇā*, *see* such and such : so so, *ajehā kajehā* ; in indifferent health, circumstances, *heṭhā uṭā*.
soak, v. tr., *bheõṇā*, int. *bhijjṇā* : *see* wet.
(1) **soap**, *sabūṇ*, m. : *sāban*, m. (U.).
(2) **soap-nut**, *rēṭhā*, m., *rēṭhṛā*, m.
sob, *hatghōre laiṇe* or *bharne*, *bilkṇā*.
sober, *hōsh wicc* : *sanjīdā* (solemn).
sociable, *milṇwāḷā*, *maḷāprā*.
society (also *a* society), *susaiṭī*, f. : M. *anjuman*, f. : H. *sabhā*, m., *samāj*, m.
sock, *julāb*, f., *jurāb*, f., *jarēb* f., *mauzā*, m. : *massī*, f.
socket, *ghūā*, m. : *see* pivot.
soda, *sōḍā*, m. : s.-water, *sōḍā*, m., *khārā pāṇī*, m. : bottle of, *khārī bōtal*, f., *sōḍe dī bōtal*.

ohnū tauṛī mārnī : *see* taunt, imitate, laugh, jester, clap.
rifle, *rafal*, f., *bandūk*, f.
(1) right, not left, *sajjā* : r.-handed, *sajjā*.
(2) right, not wrong, *ṭhīk*, *durust*; and words for good, etc. : all right, *khair sallā*, *khair mehr e*, *cangā*, *halā* : *see* matter.
(3) right, n., *hakk*, m. : person w. a. r., *hakdār*.
righteous, *nēk* : *see* religious, good.
rigid, *sakht*, *ḍāhḍā*, *jehṛā nā life*.
rind, *see* peel, pare.
(1) ring, n., large or small, without stone, *challā*, m. : small w. stone, *mundrī*, f., *chāp*, f. (see stone) : ear-r., *wāḷī*, f., *murkī*, f. : thumb-r., *ārsī*, f.
(2) ring, v. tr., small bell, etc., *chaṇkāṇā* (int. *chaṇakṇā*) : large bell, gong, coin or pot to see if sound, *wajāṇā* (int. *wajjṇā*) : also *bulāṇā*, *khaṛkāṇā* : coin, etc., rings, *wajjdā e*, *bōldā e* : does not r., *bōḷā e*. *nehī bōldā*, or *wajjdā*, *ḍorā e*.
ringworm, *dhaddar*, *daddar*, m.
rinse, mouth, *kurlī karnī* : vessel, etc., *haṅgālṇā*.
riot, *balwā*, m. (*k.*, int. *h.*) : *see* disturbance.
rip, *see* undo.
ripe, *pakkā* : half r., *āhbū* ; *ḍaddrā* (also half cooked).
rise, *uṭṭhṇā* : note following pairs : *uṭṭhke bauh*, get up into sitting posture : *uṭṭh bauh*, get up (gen. implying " and go away ") : *uṭṭhke khlō*, (also *khlō jā*), stand up : *uṭṭh khlō* rise (and move away) : *uṭṭhke geā*, he rose and went away ; *uṭṭh geā*, he removed (to another house) : r. fr. dead, *jyū paiṇā*, *jī uṭṭhṇā* (*murdeā wiccō*).
rise, sun, moon, stars, *caṛhnā*, *nikḷnā* : r. late. of moon on 15th day, *gōḍḍā mārnā* or *lāṇā* (int. *gōḍḍā laggṇā cann nū*), G. 119 : M. 121. 17.
rise, of price, *wadhṇā* : dearness, *maṅghāī*, f., *maihṅg*, f., *tēzī*, f., *pyār*, m. : *see* dear.
rise, of wind, *wagaṇ lagī e*.
rise, originate, *shurū-h*.
risk, *khatrā*, m.
rites, *rīt rasm*, f. (*pūrī karnī*).
rival, *jehṛā mukāblā kare*.
river, *daryā*, m. : *see* stream.
rivet, *kāblā*, m. : r.-screw, *dhibrī*, f. : *see* patch.
(1) road, metalled, *pakkī saṛak* : unmetalled, *kaccī saṛak*, f. : village, *paihā*, m. : *see* path, way : centre of metalled r., *goḷā*, m. : sides, *paṭrī*, f. : dip in metalled r. for water-flow, *gaib*, f. : *see* roughness.
(2) road-metal, *rōṛ*, m.
(3) road-mender, *māhwāriā*, m.
roar, of animal, man in anger, *gajjṇā*.
roast, *bhunnṇā*, int. *bhujjṇā* : r.-meat in bazar, *kabāb*, m. : r. vegetables or rice, *bhuṇā*, m.
rob, *luṭṭṇā*, *dhāṛā mārnā*, *luṭṭ mārnī* or *macāṇī* : metaph. *ṭhaggṇā* : *see* steal.
robber, *ḍākū*, *dhāṛwī*, *luṭērā* (esp. metaph.).
robbery, *ḍākā*, m. (*mārnā*, int. *paiṇā*).
robust, *taṛ*"*ā* : *see* strong.

rock, no word, *caṭān*, f. (U.), *see* stone.
rocket, *hawā̃*, f. (*calāṇī*, *calnī*).
rod, *see* stick: iron r., *kandḷā*, m., *sīkh*, f.
rogue, *see* blackguard.
(1) roll, call, *see* attendance and call.
(2) roll, v. int. *riṛhnā* (tr. *reṛhnā*).
(3) roller, iron, *rūl*, m., *rōlar*, m.
(4) rolling-board, *phaṭṭā*, m.: -pin, *wēlṇā*, m.; of stone, for grinding, *siḷ* f., *waṭṭā*, m.
roof, *chatt*, m., *kōṭhā*, m.: v. tr., *chattṇā*.
(1) room, *kamrā*, m.: in village house, *kōṭhṛī*, f.: front r. in do., *pasār*, m.: spare-r., *musāfar kamrā* or *khānā*, m.: r. on roof, *cubārā*, m.: *see* bath-, bed-, dining-, drawing-r.
(2) room, space, *thā̃* m. f., *jaghā*, f., *gunjaish*, f.
roomy, *mōkḷā*: non-r., *sauṛā*, *tang*.
root, *jaṛ*, f.: *see* uproot: get to root of thing, *kuṇh kaḍḍhṇī* (*dī*), *aslīat* or *hakīkat dā patā lāṇā*.
rope, *rassā*, m.: for drawing water, *lajj*, f.: round the *bair*, *baraṛ*, m.. round *bair* for *tindā̃*, *māhl*, f.: for well, gen., *khabbaṛ*, m., *chillaṛ*, m. (also *dullaṛ*, *tillaṛ*, m.): for horse's heels, *pachāṛī*, f.; for his forelegs, *agāṛī*, f.: *see* string, thong.
rosary, *tasbī*, f. (M., *phērnī*, *raḷṇī*): *māḷā*, f., (H., *phērnī*, *simarnī*, *raḷṇī*).
rose, *gulāb*, m.: colour, *gulābī*.
rot, decompose, *trakkṇā*: begin to r., *bō chaḍḍṇī*: get soft, *gaḷṇā*: allow to rot, decompose, *tarkāṇā*.
rotten, *see* rot, bad.
rough, *kharhwā*: r. work, *mōṭā kamm*: r. and ready, *jaṭkā*, *jaṭkā hisāb*, m.: *ḍagg jehā*: r. road, *see* roughness.
roughness, unevenness, in ground, *aḍḍokhōṛā*, m., *khṛappā*, m., *khṛōc*, m.
(1) round, adj., *gōḷ*: adv., *duāḷe*, *āḷe duāḷe*, *cufere*, *cār cufēre*, *cāre pāse*, *sabbhnī pāsī*.
prep., *de duāḷe*, *de āḷe duāḷe*, *de cufēr*, *de cār cufēre*, *dī caũh pāsī*.
pass by way of round, *duāḷeō̃ dī langhṇā*, pass beyond and round, *waḷṇā*: go r. and r., esp. involuntarily, *cakkar khāṇā*.
(2) round, n., a long round, *waḷā* (*paiṇā*, *nū̃*): *waḷe wāḷā rāh*: *cakkar laggṇā* (*nū̃*): of ladder, *see* rung.
roundness, *guḷeāī*, f.
rouse, *see* wake, incite, excite, urge.
rover, *awārā* (bad sense), fem. the same: *see* nomad.
row, *see* line.
royal, *bādshāhī*, *shāhī*.
rub, *malṇā*, *mālish karnī* (*nū̃*); *ragaṛnā* (roughly): gently in passing, *khaihṇā* (*nāḷ*): skin get rubbed and sore, *ucchṇā ambṇā*: *see* chafe; rubbed off, *chill ghattṇā*: anything get rubbed, *ghasar laggṇī* (*nū̃*): get rubbed away, *ghass jāṇā*: r. out, *see* delete.
rubber, *rabaṛ*, m., *rabaṭ*, m.
rubbish, refuse, *kūṛā*, m.: r.-heap, *rūṛī*, f.: *see* nonsense.
ruby, *lāl*, m.

rude, *see* impertinent, forward: answer back, *gall partāṇī*, *aggõ bōlṇā*: rough and r., *waihshī*; *see* rough and ready.
rudeness, *gustākhī*, f., *shōkhī*, f.: *see* rude.
rug, *galīcā* m., *namdā*, m.
(1) ruin, *see* destroy, downfall; perish: add *tabāhī*, f., *kharābī*, f.
(2) ruins, of house, only walls, *khole*, m. pl.
(1) rule, *kaidā*, m., *kanūn*, m. (both *baṇāṇā*): *tarīkā*, m. (method): *see* custom, govern. [*futtā*, m.
(2) rule, foot-rule, *dufuṭṭā*, m.,
(1) ruler, *hākim*, m.
(2) ruler, wooden, *rūl*, f. m.
rumble, of wheels, etc., *khṛāk auṇā*: noise of *hukkā*, camel, *buṛhkṇā*.
ruminate, *chew cud*, *ugāḷī karnī*.
rumour, *afwāh*, f. (*uḍḍṇī*, tr. *uḍāṇī*): *see* spread.
run, *bhajjṇā*, *dauṛnā* (caus. *bhajāṇā*, *duṛāṇā*): r. away, *bhajj jāṇā*, *maḷ jāṇā*, *nass jāṇā* (caus. *nasāṇā*), *khiskṇā* (caus. *khaskāṇā*): go off quickly, *wag jāṇā* (caus. *wagāṇā*); *see* swift: run, of water, *wagṇā*: run, of sore, nose, *wagṇā*: of eyes, *akkhīā wiccõ pāṇī wagdā e*.
rung of ladder, *ḍaṇḍā*, m.
rupee, *rupayyā*, m., *rupeā*, m., jocular, *chill*, f., *chillaṛ*, f.: r.'s worth of change, *rupayye dā bhanghaṛ*, or *bhān*: but bring back the change, *bākī lai ā*.
ruse, *dā*, m., (*lāṇā*, int. *laggṇā*, *khāṇā*): *see* deceit, trick.
rush at, *ṭuṭṭke paiṇā* (*nū̃*): *hatthī paiṇā* (*oh dī*): *mārn paiṇā* (*nū̃*).
rust, n., *jaṅgāḷ*, m.: v., *jaṅgāḷ laggṇā* or *khāṇā* (*nū̃*).
rut, of wheels, *gail*, f.: metaph., paraphrase w. habit, custom.

S

sabre, *see* sword.
sack, *bōrā*, m.: *bōrī*, f.: *gūṇī*, f.: -cloth, *ṭrappaṛ*, m.: *see* pannier.
sacred, *pawittar* (H.): *pāk*, *mukaddas* (M.).
sacrifice, n., *kurbānī*, f. (M.): *balidān*, m. (H.): v., *kurbān-k.*, *balidān-k.*
sad, *udās*, *nimmo jhūṇā*: *see* sorry, grief.
saddle, *zīn*, f., *kāṭhī*, f. (wooden): put on s., *pāṇī*: to s. something on anyone, *see* responsible.
saddle-bags, *see* pannier.
sadness. *udāsī*, f.: *gacc*, m. (*auṇā*), almost weeping.
safe, *salāmat*, *sahī salāmat*. A.
safety, *salāmtī*, f., *bacā*, m.: *see* guard, preserve, save.
sago, *sāgū*, m.
sail, n., *bādbān*, m.; v., *jahāz wicc sail* or *safar karnā*.
sailor, *beṛīwālā malāh*.
saint, *see* holy and add *pīr*, (M.): *rishī*. *munī*, *warāgī* (H.).
sake, *de wāste*, *de wāte*, *de laī*, *dī khātar*: in prayer *Masīh dī khātar*.
sale, *wikrī*, f., *farōkht*, f. (U.).
saliva, *thukk*, m.: *lab*, m.
salt, *lūṇ*, m., *namak*, m. (U.): s.-cellar, *lūṇ-* or *namak-dān*, m.: s. water, *khārā pāṇī*, m.: s. opposed to sweet in food,

salūṇā : without s., of something which should have s., *phikkā* (*see* insipid) : s. meat, *namkīn* : to s., *namkīn-k.*
saltpetre, *shōrā*.
salute, salutation, *salām*, f. m. (*k.*) : *bandgī*, f. (*k.*) : acknowledge s., *salām dā juāb d.* : s. with guns, *salāmī*, f.
salvation, *najāt*, f. (M.) : *mukti*, f. (H.).
same, *īho*, *īhoī*, *ūho*, *ūhoī*, *oh ī* : *ose* or *ese tarhā̃ dā*, *eho-* or *ūho-jehā* : of same age, *see* equal : *see* resemblance.
sample, *namūnā*, m.
sanction, *manzūrī*, f. : obtain, *laiṇī* : grant, *dēṇī*, also *manzūr-k.*
sand, *rēt*, f : stretch of s. in water, *barēt-ā*, m., *-ī*, f.
sandy, *rētlā*.
sarcasm, *see* taunt.
Satan, *shatān*.
satiat-e, -ed, -y, *see* satisfy, etc., appease (hunger) in A.
satin, *see* silk.
satisfaction, *tsallī*, or *tsallā*, f. (comfort) : *rāzī* or *khush h.* : having had enough food, drink, water (said of land, trees, people, cattle), of someone's society, etc., *rajj*, f. : *see* satisfy, satiate.
satisfactor-y, -ily, *khātarkhāh* : *see* good.
satisfy, *rāzī* or *khush k.*, (int. *h.*), *tsallī* or *tsallā hōṇī* (*dī*) : w. food, etc. (*see* satiate, satisfaction) *rajāṇā*, *sēr-k.* (U.), be s.-ed, *rajjṇā*, *sēr-h.* (U.):
Saturday, *haftā*, m. : *abbal haftā*, m. : Hindu words, *saniccar*, *saniccarwār*, *chanicchar*, *chaniccharwār*, *chinchin*, *chinchinwār*, all m.
sauce, *sās*, f. : *grēbbī*, f. (gravy), chutney, *catnī*, f.
saucer, *pirc*, f.
savage, *waihshī*, *jānglī*.
save, *bacāṇā* : of Christ, *bacāṇā*, *najāt dēṇī* (*nū̃*) : be s.-ed, *bacṇā*, *najāt milṇī* (*nū̃*).
Saviour, *bacāṇwālā* (also human), *Najāt Dēṇwālā*.
saw, n., small, *ārī*, f. : large, for two men, *kalwattar*, m., *ārā*, m. : large, in frame, two men, *parnāhī*, f. : v., *cīrnā* (*ārī nāl*, etc.).
sawdust, *būrā*, m.
say, *ākhṇā*, *ākhṇā wēkhṇā*, *kaihṇā* : caus., *akhwāṇā*, *bulāṇā*, G. 109.
saying, n., *akhāṇ*, m.
scab, *khrīṇḍ* (*bajjhṇā*) : *see* scar.
scabbard, *miān*, m.
scald, *sāṛnā*, int. *saṛnā*.
scales, small, *trakkṛī*, f. : large, *kaṇḍā*, m. : weighing machine at station, etc., *kaṇḍā*, m. : goldsmith's, *kaṇḍī*, f., one side of basket s., *chābbā*, m.
scandal, use slander and spread, *see* spread, slander.
scar, *zakhm dā nashān* or *dāg*, m. (both also of fresh mark) : *see* scab.
scarce, *see* rare.
scarcely, *masā̃*, *masā̃ kiwē̃*, *masē̃ kiwē̃* : *see* difficulty.
scarcity, *see* famine, rare.
scarecrow, *daraoṇā*, m.
scarlet, *shōkh lāl*, *lāl sūhā*, *gul anārī*.
scatter, v. tr., *khalārnā*, *khanḍāṇā* ; int. *khillarnā*, *khinḍṇā*.
scattered, few, *see* few.
scene, *see* sight, view : s. of crime, *maukyā*, m.

scenery, *see* scene.
scent, *see* perfume, smell.
scholar, learner, *paṛhnwāḷā*, *tālib ilm* (U.) : *skūl dā muṇḍā* : learned, *see* learned.
scholarship (money), *wazīfā*, m. : learning, *ilm*, m. : *see* learned, know.
school, *skūl*, m., *madarsā*, m. : special Hindu, *pāṭhshālā*, m. (for girls, *puttrī pāṭhshālā*).
schoolboy, *see* scholar.
schoolfellow, *jamāt-ī*, fem. *-aṇ*.
school-master, -mistress, *see* teacher.
science, gen., *ilm*, m : physical s., *sains*, f.
scissors, *kaincī*, f.
scold, *see* reprimand.
scorch, v. int., *saṛnā*, *jhalūhnā* : tr., *sāṛnā*. [93.
score, twenty, *wīh*, G. 21, 22,
scorn, *hikārat dī nazr nāḷ wekhṇā* : *see* despise.
scorpion, *ṭhūhā*, m.
scoundrel, *see* blackguard.
scrape, *khurcṇā*, *khōtarnā* (esp. clean by scraping).
scraper, for horse, *kharkṇā*, m.
scratch, for itch, *khurkṇā* : get a s., *jharīṭ paiṇī* (*nū*) : *see* scrape.
scream, *cīkṇā*, *cīk mārnī*, *caṅghāṛnā*, *caṅghāṛ mārnī* : *see* howl.
screen, *see* chikk, curtain : anything to s. fr. sight, wind, etc., *ohlā*, m. : v. tr., *see* save, preserve, guard : hush up, *paṛdā pāṇā*, *pōcā phērnā* (both *gall utte*) : *see* quiet.
screw, *pēc*, m. (*lāṇā*, *kassṇā*).
screw-driver, *pēckass*, m.
scrub, *kūcṇā* : metal vessel, *mānjṇā* : table, chair, etc., *dhōṇā*, *ragaṛke dhōṇā*.
scuffle, *āpe icc hatthī paiṇā* or *khaihṇā* : *see* rush.
scullion, *masālcī*.
scum, *jhagg*, f.
scythe, *see* sickle.
sea, *samundar*, m. : *see* shore.
seal, *mohr*, f. (*lāṇī*, int. *laggṇī*).
sealing-wax, *lākh*, f. (*lāṇī*, int. *laggṇī*).
search, *labbhṇā*, *ḍhūṇḍhṇā*, *talāsh karnī* (*dī*) : turn over things, *phōlṇā* : police s. of house, person, for stolen goods, *talāshī*, f. (*laiṇī*, *dī*).
season, *bahār*, f., *mausam*, m.
(1) **seat**, n., in railway carriage, *banc*, f., *thā*, m. f. : *see* chair, stool, bench.
(2) **seat**, v. tr., *bahāṇā*, *bahāḷṇā* : *see* teach, sit.
(1) **second**, *dujjā*, *dūsrā*.
(2) **second**, motion, *tāīd karnī* (*dī*).
second-hand, *purāṇā*.
second-sight, n., *gaibdānī*, f. : possessing s., *gaibdān*.
secret, *bhēt*, m., *bhēt wāḷī gall*, f. : *see* hide : adj., *gujjhā* : s. agent or one in the s., *bhēt-ī*, fem. *-aṇ*.
secretly, *cōrī*, *cōrī chappī*, *bhēt nāḷ*.
sect, *firkā*, m. : *see* party.
section, *see* part : of orange, lime, lemon, pomelo, etc., *phāṛī*, f.
secure, firm, *pakkā*, *ṭhīk*, *tagṛā*, *huṇ khlōwegā* : *see* safe, servant.
security, *see* bail, safety, trust.
sedition, *see* mutiny.
seduce, *baihkāṇā* (pron. *bak-hāṇā*), *wagāṛnā*, *warglāṇā* : *see* incite.
(1) **see**, *wēkhṇā* (pa. p. *ḍiṭṭhā*,

wēkhṇā), *wēkhṇā cākhṇā* : we shall see, *wēkhi jāpegī* : be seen, *see* visible : able to see, not blind, *sujākhā*.

(2) seeing that, *see* since.

seed, *bī*, m.: (v. tr. s. cotton, [*wēlṇā*.

seek, *see* search.

seem, *jāpṇā*, *malūm h.*, *zāhr h.* : *see* visible, evident.

seize, *phaṛnā*, *phagaṛnā*, *khōhṇā* (int. *khussṇā*), *nappṇā*, *napaṛnā*, *mallṇā*. *zore laiṇā* : *see* snatch, confiscate.

seldom, *ghaṭṭ*, *ghaṭṭ waddh* : *see* sometimes.

select, *cuṇṇā*, *pasand-k*.

(1) self, myself, himself, etc., *āpī*, *āpū̃*, *āpe*, *āpõ* : genit. *apṇā* (when distributive, *apṇā apṇā*, *āpo dhāpṇā*, *āpo apṇā*) : acc. *apṇe āp nū̃* : G. 27, 28, 87, 88.

(2) self, n., (relig. sense, evil self), no word, use, *apṇī marzī*, *apṇe khyāl*, *gunāh*, m.

selfish, *khudgarz*. *matlabī*, *garzī*.

selfishness, *khudgarzī*.

sell, v. tr., *wēcṇā* : int. *wikṇā*.

semolina, *samlīnā*, m. (K.).

send, *ghallṇā*, *ṭōrnā*, *apṛāṇā*, *pucāṇā* : s. for person, *sadd ghallṇā* : thing, *maṅgā ghallṇā*, *maṅg ghallṇā* : s. and ask, *pucch ghallṇā* : send message, *ākh ghallṇā*, *sanēhā ghallṇā*.

senior, *waḍḍā*.

sensation, *see* feeling, astonish, surprise.

sense, *hōsh*, f., *akl.*, m. f., *sudh*, f., *budh*, f., *magz*, m., *ṭhēṭh*, f. : *see* understanding : come to senses, *hōsh auṇī* (*nū̃*), M. 117. 7 : out of senses, *see* mad, fool : meaning, *see* meaning.

senseless, *behōsh* (unconscious) : *see* mad, fool.

sensual, *luccā*, *shaihwatī*.

sentence, in book, *jumlā*, m., *fikrā*, m. : of judge, *hukm*, m.

sentry, *santrī*, *paihrewālā*.

separate, adj., *wakhrā*, *aḍrā*, *aḍḍ*, *wakkho wakkh*, *aḍḍo aḍḍ*, *walo walī*, *nawēkḷā*, *alaihdā*, *alagg* : *see* apart.

v., *naikheṛnā* (int. *nikkhaṛnā*), also any adj. for s. w. *karnā* : int. *wiccharnā* (w. sadness), or any adj. for s. w. *hōṇā*.

separation, *alaihdgī*, f., *judāī*, f. : *wachōṛā*, m. (w. sadness).

September, *satambar*, m., *assū*, m. (about Sept. 13 to Oct. 12).

series, *silsilā*, m.

serious, solemn, *sanjīdā* : important, *bhārā*.

sermon, *wāhz*, f. m.: *wāhd*, f. m. : *khutbā*, m. (M) : *see* preach.

servant, *naukar* (fem. do), *ṭaihlīā* : Govt. s., *mulāzam* : s. of God, *Khudā dā bandā*, *sēwak*, (H.) : person rendering services for fixed amount of grain, *sēp-ī*, fem. *-aṇ* (master also called *sēpī*) : night and day s. of farmer, *āthṛī* : farm s., *kāmmā* (fem. *kāmmī*) : secure s., *banāṇā*. A.

serv-e, -ice, *naukrī*, f., *ṭaihl*, f., *mulāzmat*, f., *khidmat*, f., *sēwā* : s. of *sēpī*, *sēp*, f. : all ... : day labour, *mazdū-rī* ... ī, *dihāṛīā̃ karnīā̃* : rel... vice, *bandgī*, f., *duā* *ba*... *girjā*, m. (church) : all ... *īṇā* of clergyman, *ka*... worshippers : *see* at

set, *lāṇā*, int. *laggṇā* : *see* place, put : s. limb, *jōṛnā*, int. *juṛnā* : s. jewel, *jaṛnā* : of sun, moon, stars, *ast h.*, *ḍubbṇā* : s. table, *see* table : of cement, etc., *ḍāhḍā h.*, *pakkā h.*

settle, *see* arrange, decide : dispute, *faislā karnā*, *see* umpire : s. matter, *nabēṛnā*, int. *nibbaṛnā* ; *bhugtāṇā*, int. *bhugtṇā* : of earth in water, *baihṇā*, *see* clear : of building, earth (sink), *baihṇā* : dwell, *wassṇā* : debts, *see* pay : not quite settled, *see* uncertain.

settlement, *faislā*, m. : land-s, *bandobast*, m. (*k.*) : *see* assess-, -ment, tax. [m.

settler, *raihṇwāḷā*, *wassaṇwāḷā*,

seven, *satt* : -th, *satuā̃* : G. 19.

seventeen, *satārā* : -th, *satāhrwā̃* : shoe s. fingers long, *satāhrī juttī* : G. 19–24, 123.

seventy, *sattar*, *s-hattar* : -one, *ak-hattar* : -two, *bahattar* : -three, *tihattar*, *tarhattar* : -four, *cuhattar*, *curhattar* : -five, *panjhattar* : -six, *chĕhattar* : -seven, *satattar*, *sathattar* : -eight, *aṭhattar*, *athhattar* : -nine, *unāsī*, ordinals add *-wā̃* : 79 adds high tone h, *unāhsīwā̃* : G. 19–24, 123.

several, *kaī*, *kujjh* : *see* few.

severe, *ḍāhḍā*, *sakht*, *zōr dā*.

severity, *ḍāhḍpuṇā*, m., *zōrāwarī*, f., *sakhtī*, f. : *see* oppress.

sew, *syūṇā*, pa. p. *sītā*.

sewing, *salāī*, f. : -machine, *mashīn*, f., *syūṇwāḷī mashīn*.

sex, *jins*, f. : use man, woman ; for animals, *see* male, female.

shade, *chā̃*, f. : in the s., *chā̃we* : *see* shadow.

shadow, *parchāwā̃*, m. : overshadow, of tree, *sāyā pāṇā* (int. *paiṇā*, *utte*).

shady, *chā̃wāḷā*.

shaft, of carriage, *bamb*, m.

shake, v. tr., *halāṇā*, int. *hallṇā* : *see* wobble, tremble : s. hands, *hatth malāṇā* or *suttṇā* (*nāḷ*), *panjā suttṇā* (*nāḷ*).

shallow, water, *pāṇī thōṛā e* or *laṅghaṇwāḷā e* : of person, *kaccā*, *sōcdā nehī̃*.

sham, *see* pretence, imitation : adj., *naklī*.

shame, *sharm*, f. : *namoshī*, f. (humiliation) : both w. *auṇī*, *nū̃*, M. 117. 3 : feel ashamed, *bhaiṛā paiṇā*, M. 125. 7 : *see* shy : for s. ! *tōbbā tōbbā*, *hoe hoe*, and words for bravo used ironically.

shameless, *besharm*, *behayā* (strong words, of woman mean immoral).

shameful, *sharm dī gall*, f.

shampoo, *mutthiā̃ bharnīā̃* (*nū̃*) : w. feet, *laṭāṛnā*.

shape, *see* form.

share, *hissā*, m. : *see* part, divide, partner, common.

sharp, not blunt, also of sight, intelligence, *tēz*.

sharpen, knife, axe, etc., *candṇā*, *tēz-k* : *see* grindstone.

sharpness, *tēzī*, f.

(1) **shave**, *munnṇā* : get shaved, *munāṇā* (w. word for beard, head, etc.) : -ed patch on head, *tāḷū* (*kaḍḍhṇā*, caus. *kaḍhāṇā*).

(2) **shavings** of wood, *sak*, m., *sakṛā*, m.

shawl, *see* sheet : *loī*, f., *cutahī*, f., *khēs*, m., *dushāllā*, m. : wrap s. round head, *bukkal mārnī*.

she, *eh*, *oh*.
sheath, *see* scabbard.
shed, *dhārā*, m.: railway s., *chidd*, m.
sheep, *bhēd*, f., *bhēdī*, f.: fat-tailed, *dumbā*, m.: *see* ram: adj., *bākrā* (or goat's).
sheepfold, *wārā*, m.
sheeshum tree, *tāhlī*, f.
sheet of paper, *tā*, m.: of cloth, *cādar*, f. (*palangh dī*, *manjī dī*, of bed): pull s. over one, *cādar utte laiṇī*: *see* cloth.
shelf, niche, *ālā*, m.: on wall, *ṛarchattī*, f.: in wall-press, *drāz*, f.
shell (sea, river) *sippī*, f.: cowrie *kauḍḍī*, f.: explosive, *gōlā*, m.: *see* husk, peel.
shelter, *ōhlā*, m. (esp. against something coming from side): *ḍakkā*, m. (gen.): *bacā*, m. (gen.): *sāyā*, m. (someone's protection): *see* guard, save, preserve.
shepherd, *ājṛī*, *chēṛū*, *ayālī*.
shield, *ḍhāl*, f.
shin, *sukṛanj*, f.
shine, *lishkṇā*, *camakṇā*.
ship, *jahāz*, m.
shipwreck, *jahāz ṭakkar khāke ṭuṭṭ geā*.
shirker, *kamm cōr*, *see* lazy.
shirt, *kamīz*, f., *jhiggā*, m., *kuṛtā*, m.
shiver, *see* tremble, chatter.
shock, sorrow, etc., *saṭṭ* (*laggṇī*, *nū̃*), *sadmā*, m. (U. *h.*, *nū̃*), *see* grief, collide.
shoe, *juttī*, f.; English, *būṭ*, m.: pair of s., *juttī*, *jōṛā*, m., *būṭ*: G. 73, 74: Hindu wooden s., *paūā*, m., *khṛā*, f.: repair s., *gaṇḍhṇā*: put on, *pāṇā*: take off, *lāhṇā*: horse-s., *khurī*, f., *nāl*, m.: cattle-s., *khurī*, f.: old worn-out s., *chittar*, m.: size, of s., thirteen, fourteen to eighteen finger-breadths, *tehrī*, *cauhdī*, *pandhrī*, *sohlī*, *satāhrī*, *aṭhāhrī*, G. 123; small 14, *narm cauhdī*: large 16, *pakkī sohlī*.
shoeless, *see* bare.
(1) **shoot**, *see* fire (2), and add following: *calāṇā* (int. *calṇā*) and *mārnā* used of both gun, cannon, etc., and missile (bullet, arrow, etc.), also *chaḍḍṇā* of gun, cannon, etc.: but *calāṇā* and *chaḍḍṇā* mean merely "fire," "fire off," whereas *mārnā* implies hitting (w. *nū̃* of thing, person hit): go shooting, *shikār khēḍṇā* or *karnā*: *see* stone.
(2) **shoot**, of tree, *gullā*, m.
shop, *haṭṭī*, f., *dukān*, f.: keep s., *haṭṭī* or *dukān karnī*: start s., *haṭṭī pāṇī* or *kholhṇī*.
shopkeeper, *haṭṭīwālā*, *baṇīā*, *dukāndār*.
shore, *kaṇḍhā*, m., *dandā*, m. (lit. edge).
(1) **short**, things in gen., *see* small: person, *madhrā*, *mandhrā*, *nikkā*: *see* dwarf: letter, speech, *see* brief: in short, *muddā*, *gall kāhdī*: in s. time, soon, *thōṛe cir nū̃*, *zarā ku nū̃*.
(2) **short-lived**, *thōṛe cir dā*, *chōṭī umar icc moeā*, *thōṛā cir rehā*: *see* transient.
shot, grains of, *charrā*, m.: *see* shoot (1).
shoulder, n., *moṇḍhā*, m.: v., *moṇḍheā te* or *kaṇḍhāṛe* or *dhangāṛe cukkṇā*: *see* back, also back in A.: s. one's

way, ***dhakke nāḷ laṅghṇā*** (also means by force): ***see*** **shove.**

shout, *awāz mārnī*, *kūk mārnī*: *see* call, scream: speak loudly, *uccī* or ***zōr-nāḷ*** or ***dabbke kūṇā***, *uccī ditlī bōlṇā*: loudly or angrily, *karakke kūṇā*.

shove, *dhakkā dēṇā* (*nū̃*), *dhikkṇā*: s. off (esp. in water), *ṭhelhṇā*, int. *ṭhillhṇā*.

shovel, *bēlcā*, m.: *karch*, m. (v. large iron spoon).

(1) show, v., *dassṇā*, *wakhāṇā*.

(2) show, n., *wakhāḷī*, f., *dakhāwā*, m.: for s., *wakhāṇ wāste*, *apṇī izzat wadhāṇ wāste*: display, grandeur, *chūkā shākī*, f. (*k.*): *tash* or *tash ṭush kaḍḍhṇī*: *ḍaddh kaḍḍhṇī* (affect style) M. 120. 48: *see* splendour, sit.

shriek, *see* scream, shout.

shrill, *tēz*.

shrine, (M.) ***khāngāh***, f. (tomb): (H.) ***sthān***, m., *mandar*, m. (temple).

shrink, v. int., cloth, etc., *saṅgarṇā*: through pain, *sī karnī*: s. back, *pishā̃ haṭṇā*.

shrivel, *see* wither, wrinkle.

shroud, n., for burial, ***khapphaṇ***, m.

shrub, *jhāṛī*, f.: small, ***bucc***, m.

shun, *parhēz karn-ī*, *-ā* (*tō̃*, esp. of food, actions): ***bacṇā*** (*koḷō̃*): *dūr raihṇā* (*tō̃*): *see* avoid, abstain.

shunt, train, ***shanṭ karnā***.

shut, *band-k.*: s. door, window, *mārnā* (int. *wajjṇā*): fasten hook of door, etc., ***kunḍī mārnī*** (*dī*): ***hukk mārnī***, (*dī*): ***kunḍā mārnā*** (*dā*): close door, etc., ***see*** close: s. up, ***band-k.***

shy, be, *saṅgṇā*, ***jhakṇā***, ***jhijhakṇā***: adj. *saṅgā wāḷā*: ***see*** **ashamed, shame, shyness.**

shyness, *saṅgā*, f.: ***jhākkā***, **m.** (both w. *auṇā*, *nū̃*): *see* shy.

sick, *see* ill, sorry, vomit: be s. of, *jī* or *rūh* or *dil caṛhnā* (*tō̃*): *see* tire, (tired of).

sickle, *dātrī*, f.

side, direction, *pāsā*, m., *lāhmb*, f., *bāī*, f., *bāhī*, f., *guṭṭh*, f. (corner): get to one s., *lāhmbe* or *ikkī pāse hōjā*: in what direction, *see* direction: on all sides, *sabbhnī pāsī*, *çawhī pāsī*; everywhere, *sabbh dare*, *har kite*: round, near, *āḷe duāḷe*: *see* round: on this s., *urār*: on that s., *pār*: s. of body, *wakkhī*, f.: *see* party, bed, door.

sideboard, *sālbōṭ*, *m.* (K.).

side-dish, *dōṅghā*, m.

siege, *muhāsrā*, m. (*k.*), *ghērā*, m. (*pāṇā*).

sieve, *chāṇnī*, f.

sift, *chāṇṇā*: separate husk fr. grain, *chaṭṭṇā*.

sigh, *hāhukā mārnā*.

sight, eyesight, *nazr*, f.: view, *nazārā*, m.: spectacle, *tamāshā* (*see* entertainment): of holy place or person, *see* visit.

sign, *nishān*, m. (*k.*, mark): *ishārā*, m. (*k.*, sign): *see* effect, proof, result.

signal, railway, *saṅgal*, m.: go down, *hōṇā ḍaun h. hatth*, m. (*ḍiggṇā*:) *see* sign.

signature, *daskhaṭṭ*, m.

signet, *mohr*, f. (*lāṇī*, *laggṇī*): engrave, *see* engrave.

signify, *ohde maihṇe kī ne*, *ohdā matlab kī e*: *see* meaning: it does not s., *see* matter.

silence, *cup-cāp*, f., *khamōshī*, f. (U.).
silent, *cupcapītā*, *cup*, *cupkītā*.
silently, *cup capītā*, *cup cāp*, *maikṛī*, *hauḷī hauḷī* : *see* secretly.
silk, *paṭṭ*, f., *rēsham*, m., *ṭassar*, m. : adj., these words w. *dā*, also *rēshmī*, *ṭassarī*.
silly, *see* fool.
silver, *cāndī*, f., *ruppā*, m.
silversmith, *sunyārā*.
similar, *wāṅgar*, *wāṅgū*, *wargā*, *hār*, G. 35 : *jehā*, G. 91, 92 : *ajehā*, *ehojehā* : like what ? *kehā*, *kehojehā* : relative, *jehā*.
simmer, *maṭṭhe tā pakkṇā*.
simple, *sādā* (not ornamented) : of person, *bholā*, *siddhā*, *sādā*, sometimes *bātshāh*.
simultaneously, *ikse weḷe*, *nāḷo nāḷ*, *kaṭṭhā*.
sin, *gunāh*, m. (*k.*) : *pāp*, m. (*k.* H.) : *see* evil, wickedness.
since (1), time, *jadō dā*, *jis weḷe tō* : *jadō dī oh āī e*, *maī ohnū nehī̃ ḍiṭṭhā*, I have not seen her since she came : time since, pa. p. with *nū̃* : *ohnū̃ khote tō ḍiggeā dō dihāṛe hoe ne*, it is two days since he fell from the donkey ; G. 79, last line : *see* ago.
(2) reasoning, *see* because, also *jis hāl wicc*, *jadō*.
sincere, *saccā*, *dilī*.
sincerely, *dil nāḷ*, *dilō wajhō hōke*.
sinew, *nāṛ*, f. (also vein, artery).
sinful, *see* sinner.
sing, *gauṇā*.
singer, *see* musician.
singe, v. tr., *sāṛnā*, int. *saṛnā*.
single, one fold, *akāhrā*, *ighrā*, *see* fold, bachelor.
singly, *ikk ikk karke*.
singular (grammar), *waihd*, f. : *see* strange, wonderful.
sink, in water, *ḍubbṇā* (also of sun, etc. : tr. *ḍōbṇā*) : in something soft, mud, etc., *khubbhṇā*, tr. *khōbhṇā* : *see* drown.
sinless, *bēgunah* ; faultless, *beaib*, *bēkasūr* : innocent, *masūm*, *mashūm*.
sinner, *gunāhī*, *pāpī* (H.).
siris tree, *see* acacia.
sister, *bhaiṇ*, *hamshīrā* (U.) : s.-in-law : wife's s., *sāḷī* : wife's brother's wife, *sāḷehā-r*, *-j* : brother's wife, *bhāhbī*, *bharjāī* : husband's sister, *naṇān*, *nanāṇ* : husband's elder brother's wife, *jaṭhāṇī* : younger do., *darāṇī*.
sit, *baihṇā*, pa. p. *baiṭhā*, G. 64 : sitting, *baiṭhā hoeā*, G. 108 : *see* squat : s. on eggs, *baihṇā* : sit up, *see* rise : at someone's feet as scholar, *baihṇā*, M. 117. 13, 19 : *see* teach : sit upon, reprimand severely, (jocular), *khabar laiṇī* (*dī*), *makkū ṭhappṇā* (*dā*), *lamb kaḍḍhṇī* (*dī*), *sukṛanjā̃ bhannṇīā̃* (break shins, *dīā̃*), *babbar bhannṇe* (break ribs, *de*), *ākkaṛ bhannṇī* (take down pride, *dī*). N.B.—In some places *lamb kaḍḍhṇī* means "affect style" : *see* reprimand, reproach.
site, *jaghā*, f.
sittingroom, *baiṭhak*, f. : *see* drawingroom.
situated, simply say *kitthe we*, [etc.
situation, service, *naukrī*, f. ; *asāmī*, f. (vacancy) : place, *jaghā*, f. (also for service).

six, *chē* : -th, *chēwā* : G. 19–24.
sixteen, *sōḷā* : -th, *sohḷwā* : sixteen finger shoe, *sohḷī juttī* : G. 19–24, 123.
sixty, *saṭṭh* ; -one, *akāhṭh* : -two, *bāhṭh* : -three, *trehṭh* : -four, *cauhṭh* : -five, *paĩhṭh* : -six, *cheāhṭh* : -seven, *satāhṭh* : -eight, *aṭhāhṭh* : -nine, *unhattar* : ordinals add *-wā*, *saṭṭhwā*, etc., G. 19–24, 123.
size, of person, *kadd*, m. (U.) : of boot, shoe, *see* shoe : in gen. no word, use *ēḍḍā*, *ōḍḍā*, so large ; *kēḍḍā*, how large ; *jēḍḍā*, as large : *see* big.
skein, *gunjī*, f.
skeleton, *pinjrā*, m., *pinjar*, m.
skewer, *sīkh*, f (also iron bar).
skill, skilful, skilled, *see* clever-, -ness.
skim, milk, *malāī lāhṇī*.
(1) skin, n., *camm*, m. : *camṛā*, m. : hide, *khall*, f. : water-s., *mashk*, f. ; do. for crossing river, *sarnāhī*, f. : of fruit, vegetable, *see* peel.
(2) skin, v. tr., *camm lāhṇā*, *khall lāhṇī*, *khullṇā* (used by scavengers) : *see* pare.
skirmish, *laṛāī bhiṛāī*, f.
skirt, *gagghrī*, f., *laihngā* m., *kōrā*, m. (2nd and 3rd ornamented) : worn by men and women, *taihmat*, m., *luṅgī*, f., *lācā*, m., *dhōttī*, f. (H.).
skull, *khōprī*, f.
sky, *asmān*, m.
slack, *ḍhillā*. loose : *see* lazy, [careless.
slake, thirst, *treh maṭṭhī karnī* or *bujhāṇī*.
slander, use *jhūṭhā*, false, w. " accusation " : *bakhīlī k.* (*dī*), *tohmat* (*lāṇī*, *utte*, U.), *nakhiddhṇā*, *mukāḷā k.* (*dā*), *kulāhṇā*.
slant, m., *urēb*, m., *see* slope, sloping.
slanting, *kuāsā* ; *ḍiṅgā*, crooked, *see* slope.
slap, *capēṛ*, f., *caṇḍ*, f., *dhapphā*, m. (*mārnā*, *khāṇā*).
slate, *slēṭ*, f. : wooden, *takhtī*, f.
slaughter, *see* kill.
slave, *gulām* : slavery, *gulāmī*, f.
sledge-hammer, *see* hammer.
(1) sleep, n., *nīndar*, f. (sleepiness), *see* sleepy.
(2) sleep, v., *saūṇā*, pa. p. *suttā*, G. 64 : fast asleep, *ghūk suttā hoeā* : sleeping, *suttā hoeā*, G. 108 : to have just fallen asleep, *akkh laggṇī* (*dī*) : to be getting up fr. s., *suttā peā utthṇā*, M. 125. 8 : go to s., of limb, *saūṇā*.
sleeper, wooden, *gellī*, f., *see* log.
sleeplessness, *unīndrā h.* (*nū*) : *jagrāttā kaṭṭṇā* : *see* vigil.
sleepy, feel, *nīndar auṇī* (*nū*), M. 117. 5 : *uṅghlāṇā*, *uglhāṇā*, nod drowsily : *jāgo mīṭī*, half asleep on one's bed.
sleeve, *bāh*, f.
slice, of bread, *tōs*, m. (whether toasted or not) : of fruit, *phāṛī*, f. (whether cut as in melon, or section of orange, etc.).
sling, n., *gulēl*, f. (like bow) : *kubhāṇī*, f. (real sling) : *see* pellet.
slip, *tilhkṇā* : down, *riṛhnā*.
slipper, *gurgābī*, f : *slīpar*, m.
slippery, *tilhkaṇwāḷā*, *cīhkṇā*.
slit, n., *trēṛ*, f., (*paiṇī*, *nū*) : v. tr., *cīrnā*, *pāṛnā* (also tear) : *see* cut.
slope, *nuāṇ*, m., *salāmī*, f., *ḍhaḷwāṇ*, m., *urēb*, m. : *see* slanting.

renounce, *see* abandon: r. claim, *dāhwā chaḍḍṇā* (*dā*). A.

repair, *marammat karnī* (*dī*): *see* shoe, require.

repeal, laws (of God), *mansūkh-k.* (M.): *see* abolish, cancel.

repeat, *phēr ākhṇā*: r. after me, *mēre picche picche ākh, mērī gall durhāndā jā, jo maĩ ākhā tū̃ wī ākhdā jā*: r. or recite poetry, etc., *ākhṇā, paṛhnā*.

repeatedly, *bhaũ caũ, jhaṭe binde, ghaṛī ghaṛī, ghaṛī muṛī, jhaṭe jhaṭe, bauht wārī, baṛī wārī, kinnī wārī* (for *wārī* also *wērī*): do thing repeatedly, special verbal construction. *see* G. 68, 69.

repent, *tobā karnī* (*dī, tõ*): *pachtāṇā* (*tõ*): *kannā nū̃ hatth lāṇā, nakk nāḷ līkā* (or *kaḍḍā*) *kaḍḍhṇīā* (caus. *kaḍhāṇīā*). [f. (*k.*).

repentance, *tobā*, f.: *pacchōtāp,*

repetition, *see* repeat, repeatedly.

report, *khabar*, (*d., dī*): *rapōṭ,* f. (*d., dī*). [delegate.

representative, *see* ambassador,

reprieve, *see* forgive, respite.

reprimand, *jhiṛak*, f., *jhāṛ*, f., *taṛī*, f., *ghurkī*, f. (all w. *d.*, *nū̃*): also *ohnū̃ jhāṛ kītī* or *pāī*, or *ohdī jhāṛ kītī*: *jhāṛnā, jhiṛkṇā, ghurkṇā, dābbā cāṛhnā* or *d.* (*nū̃*), *ṭhākṇā*: *see* reproach, sit upon.

reproach, *ulāhmā dēṇā* (*dā* of cause, *nū̃* of person): *phiṭkā dēṇīā* (v. mild abuse).

reprove, *see* reprimand.

republic, *jihde wicc kamēṭī kamm calāndī e, bādshāh koī nahī*: (U., *jamhūrī riāsat*, f.).

repudiate, *see* renounce, refuse (1), abandon.

request, *see* ask, beseech.

require, *see* ask, desire, advisable, necessary: r. to be done, often verbal part. in *-wāḷā, juttī gandhanwāḷī e,* shoes r. to be repaired, G. 45.

resemblance, *upe icc raḷde ne, ikko jehe ne, miḷde juḷde ne*: of face, *muhāndrā raḷdā e*: *see* same.

resent, *burā mannṇā* (*gall nū̃*): *see* offence.

reserve, *rakkh chaḍḍṇā.*

resident, *raihnwāḷā*; *wasanwāḷā*: leg. *sākan*, fem. *saknā*: *see* dwell, inhabit.

resign, *istīfā dēṇā* (*kamm tõ*): *kamm chaḍḍṇā*, sometimes *chuṭṭī mangṇī*.

resin, *gūnd*, f., *rāḷ*, f.: *see* gum.

resist: oppose, objection, fight.

resolute, *ḍāhḍā, rāṭh, pakkā.*

resolution, *faislā*, m. (decision): firmness, *ḍāhḍpunā*, m., *ḍaḍhippaṇ*, m.: *see* intend.

resolve, *see* decide: in meeting, *faislā karnā* (int. *hōnā*): *tajwīz karnī* (int. *hōnī*).

respect, *adab*, m., *izzat*, f., *ādar*, f., (all w. *k.* and *dā, dī*): word of respect, *horī*, m. pl., G. 27, 73. 82.

respectable, *izzatdār, sharīf. ashrāf* and words for good.

respectful, *adab wāḷā, adab nāḷ kūnā.*

respite, give r. of two months, *do mahīne pāe*; M. 126. 23: *mohlat*, f., (U): *see* postpone, forgive.

responsible, *zimmewār*: make oneself r. for, *zimmā cukkṇā,*

sofa, *waddī kursī*, f. : *kauc*, m.
soft, *kūlā*, tender of flesh, meat, skin, trees, shoots, leaves, bones (of children, young animals), smooth of skin, cloth : *narm*, soft of heart, cloth, skin, leather, also of meat if result of cooking : *pōllā*, of earth, soil.
softly, not loudly, *see* gently.
(1) **soil**, *zamīn*, f., *jīwī*, f., *bhoē*, f., *mittī*, f. : good, damp s., *chambh*, f., *rohī*, f. : also good, *mairā*, m., *pakkī jīwī* : not good, *rētā*, m. : barren, *rakkar*, m., *banjar*, m., *kallar*, m.
good, adj., of soil, *saras*, *caṅgī*, *missī*, *bhōrī* : bad, *mārī*, *niras*, *karlāthī*.
(2) **soil**, soiled, *see* dirty.
solder, *kalī karnī* (*nū̃*) : *see* patch.
soldier, *sipāhī*, *faujī ādmī* : English, *gōrā* : *see* officer.
sole, of foot, *talī*, f. : of boot, shoe, *talā*, m.
solemn, *see* serious, sober. [U.).
solid, *piddā*, *thōs* (not hollow,
soliloquise, *sōcnā*, *see* think, meditation.
solitude, *see* alone, lonely.
solve, sum, problem, *hall-k.*, *kaddhnā* : riddle, *bujjhnā* (guess).
some, *kujjh*, *bāze*, *koī*, *koī koī* (G. 87), *ikknā* (only oblique), G. 28 : some . . . others, *koī* . . . *koī*, G. 87 : *see* few.
somehow, *kiwē*, *kise tarhā̃*, *masā̃* : *see* difficulty, scarcely.
someone, *koī* : s. or other, *koī nā koī*.
something, *kujjh* : s. or other, *kujjh nā kujjh*.
sometimes, *kade*, *kadē kade*, *kadī kadāī* (implies seldom).
somewhat, rather, -ish, *jehā*, G. 27, 92 : or add *-ērā*, as *wadērā*, biggish, G. 18 : colour, yellowish, blackish, etc., *pīlī* or *kālī bhai mārdā e*.
somewhere, *kite*, *kitale*, *kidhare* : s. else, *hōr kidhare*, *hōr dare*.
son, *puttar*, *bētā*, leg. *wald* : Europeans', *bāwā* : s.-in-law, *juāī*, *juātrā*, *majnān* : *ikko puttar mar geā*, only one son died : *ikkse puttar dī saūh*, oath by only son.
song, *gaun*, m., *gīt*, m.
soon, *jabde*, *jhabdē*, *jhaw jhaw*, *thōre cir nū̃*, *zarā ku nū̃*, *hune*, *jaldī*.
soot, *kālakh*, f. : *dhū̃*, m. (smoke).
soothe, *see* comfort, condole, add *dalāsā dēnā* (*nū̃*), *piṭ matthī karnī* (*dī*).
soothsayer, *najūmī*, *see* astrologer, magician.
soporific, *suāṇwālī duāī*, f.
sorcerer, *see* magician, astrologer, soothsayer.
(1) **sore**, n. (wound), *phaṭṭ*, m., *zakhm*, m : (blow), *saṭṭ*, f., on back of horse, mule, etc. *lāggā* (*laggṇā*, M. 121. 14) : *see* boil (1).
(2) **sore**, adj., *see* chafe, painful.
sorrow, *see* grief.
sorrowful, *see* sad.
sorry, *see* sad, grieve, regret : s. for oneself, *nimmā* (*jāpṇā*).
(1) **sort**, n., *jins*, f., *kism*, f.
(2) **sort**, v. tr., *chāṇṭṇā*.
so so, *see* so.
soul, *rūh*, m : often *dil*, m., heart ; *jān*, f., life.

(1) sound, n., *ăwāz*, f., *wāz*, f.: *see* noise.
(2) sound, adj., horse, etc., *bilkul tagṛā*.
(3) sound, v. int. *ăwāz dēṇī*, *shōr karnā*: v. tr., a person, *patā lāṇā* (*koḷō* of person, *dā* of thing): coin, pot (to test it), *see* ring: a letter, *see* pronounce.
soup, *shuruā*, m.: -plate, *suplet*, f. (K.).
sour, *khaṭṭā*: milk become s., *phiṭnā*, *saurnā* (G. 113), *kharāb hō jāṇā*, *wigaṛnā*.
source, spring, *cishmā*, m., *cashmā*, m.: origin, *jaṛh*, f., *asl*, f., *muṇḍh*, m.
sourness, *khaṭeāī*, f.
south, *dakkhaṇ*, *dakkhaṇ pāsā*, m.: -wards, *dakkhaṇ wall* or *pāse*: south-west, *dakkhaṇ te laihnde dī guṭṭh*: south-east, *dakkhaṇ te caṛhde dī guṭṭh*.
sovereign, *see* king: coin, *pauṇḍ*, m., *asharfī*, f.
sovereignty, *rāj*, m., *bādshāhī*, f., *saltanat*, f., *hukūmat*, f.
(1) sow, n., *see* pig.
(2) sow, v. tr., *bījṇā*: sowing, n., *biāī*, f., *bijāī*, f.
space, *khappā*, m., *witth*, f., *thā̃*, m. f. (place): *wāṭ*, f., *paiṇḍā*, m. (distance).
spacious, *mōkḷā*: *waḍḍā* (big).
spade, *bēlcā*, m: inverted, *kahī*, f.
span, *giṭṭh*, f.
(1) spare, adj., *fāltū*, *waddh*.
(2) spare, v. tr., do without, *ohde bājhō̃ guzārā karnā*: *see* forgive.
sparingly, *sarfe nāḷ*, *thōṛā*.
spark, *ciṅgāṛā*, m. (from fire): *ciṇag*, f., from flint, iron, etc., also small fr. newly kindled fire.
sparkle, *lishkṇā*, *camakṇā*.
sparse, *wirlā*, *ṭāwā ṭāwā*, *thōṛā*.
spatter, *chiṭṭā pāṇīā*, int. *pai-ṇīā*: *chaṭṭe mārne*: *see* splash, sprinkle.
spavin, *haḍḍ mūtrā*, m.
speak, *kūṇā* (pa. p. *koyā*), *kūṇā saihṇā*, *bōlṇā*, *bōlṇā cālṇā*, *gall karnī*, *kuskṇā*: also note *maĩ ohde nāḷ ā̃*, I am speaking to him: *see* speech: s. against, *see* accuse, slander.
spear, *barchā*, m., *barchī*, f., *nēzā*, m.
special, *ucēcā*, *khāss*.
specially, *ucēcā* (of set purpose), *khāskar* (U.).
species, *jins*, f., *kism*, f.
spectacle, *see* sight, entertainment.
spectacles, *aiṇak*, f.; wear, put on, *lāṇī*: take off *lāhṇī*.
spectator, *wekhaṇwāḷā*: *see* audience.
speech, *see* language, and add speak lang., *bōlṇī*; know, *jāṇṇī*, *auṇī* (*nū̃*), M. 117. 2: speak badly, *see* smattering: make a s., *spīc dēṇī*: *see* conversation.
speed, *kinnā tēz*, *kinnī jaldī*: *see* swift.
spell, *see* charm: s. a word, *jōṛ karnā* (*dā*), *hijā karnā* (*dā*).
spelling, *jōṛ*, m., *hijē*, m., *spĕl*, m.
spend, money, *kharc-k.*, *lāṇā*, *puṭṭṇā*: be spent, *laggṇā*, *kharc-h.*: s. time, *weḷā laṅghāṇā* (pass time), *wakat lāṇā*, *dihāṛe lāṇe* (int. *laṅgh-ṇā*, *laggṇā*): *see* squander.
spices, *masālā*, m.

spider, *bambo... .a*, m.
spike, *see* nai
spill, v. int., *ruhṇā*, *ruṛhnā* (in tr. mea... pour, *see* pour): tr. *dulhan* ... *uṛhan dēṇā*.
(1) spin, *kattṇā* (object thread or spinning wheel): *see* spinning-bee, spinning-wheel, turn, top.
spinach, *sāg* m., *pālak*. f.
spindle, *see* spinning-wheel.
spine, *kaṅgrōṛ*, f. [*bhohrā*, m.
(2) spinning-bee, *triñan*. m.,
(3) spinning-wheel, *carkhā*, m: needle, *trakḷā*, m.
spirit, *rūh*, m: Holy Spirit, *Pāk Rūh*, m.: in phrases like "s. of pride" or "faithfulness." omit "spirit": intoxicating, *sharāb*, m., *nashā*. m.
spirited, poor-s., *dil chōṭā*, G. 122: M. 128. 9.
spiritual, *ruhāni*.
spit, *thukkṇā*: *see* saliva, vomit.
spite, *see* envy, hate.
splash, n., *chaḷak*, m.: noise of, *ghṛam*, m.: v. int., *chaḷakṇā*, *chiṭṭā paiṇiā* (drops): tr. *chaḷkāṇā*, *chaṭṭe mārne*, *chiṭṭā pāṇiā*: *see* spatter, sprinkle.
spleen, *tiḷī*. f., *lif*, f.
splendour, *bhaṛak*, f., *rauṇak*, f. (many people): *see* show, glory.
splice, *bannhṇā*: village style, *gāṇḍhā lāṇā* (*nū̃*, int. *laggṇā*).
splinter, wood, *chiltar*, f.: brick, stone, *ciṭṭh*, f.
split, *pāṛnā* (int. *pāṭṇā*), *cīrnā*: *see* tear, cut, chop.
spoil, *wagāṛnā*, int. *wigaṛnā*; *kharāb-k.*, int. *h.*: be spoiled, of matter, affair, *guggaḷ jāṇā*: *see* destroy, rob, steal.
spoilt, child, *lāḍḷā*.

spoke, in wheel, *ār*, m.
sponge, spane, m. [*āpō*.
spontaneously, *āpū̃*, *āpe*, *āpī*,
spoon, *cimcā*, m., *cammac*, m., *ḍoī*, f. (wooden), *kaṛchī*, f., *kaṛch*, m. (v. large).
sport, *khēḍ*, f. (game): shooting, fishing, etc., *shikār kheḍṇā*.
sportsman, *shikārī*: player, *khaḍārī*.
spot, *see* stain: drop, *chiṭṭ*, f. (*paiṇī*): *see* spatter, splash.
spotted, *dāgwāḷā*, *ḍabbā*, *ḍab khṛabbā*.
spout, of teapot, etc., *ṭūṭī*. f.: on roof for rainwater, *pāṛchā*, m., *parnāḷā*, m.
sprained, be, foot, *moh ghattṇā*, *mohcā jāṇā*, *moh nikḷnī* (*dī*): other parts, *waḷ paiṇā* (*nū̃*): *see* strain.
spread, carpet, cloth, *wachāṇā*, int. *wichṇā*: separate out, *khalārnā*, int. *khillarnā*: s. abroad, *phalāṇā*, int. *phailṇā*: s. rumour, *dhumāṇā*, int. *dhummṇā*.
(1) spring, season, *cētar wasākh*, m., *basant*, f.
(2) spring, steel, etc., *kamānī*, f.
(3) spring, water, *sōtā*, m., *sumb*, m., *cishmā*, m., *cashmā*, m.
(4) spring, *see* jump.
sprinkle, *chiṇakṇā*, *traũkṇā*; *see* splash, spatter.
sprout, *phuṭṭṇā*, *puṅgarnā*: grow, *uggṇā*.
spur, *kāṇṭā*, m. (*mārnā*).
spurious, *jhūṭhā*, false; *jāhlī*, forged.
spurn, *see* scorn, despise.
spy, *jāsūs*; *mukhbar* (informer): *see* espionage.

squander, *uḍāṇā*, *phūk chaḍḍṇā*, *ujāṛnā*, *luṭāṇā* (often of extravagant alms): *see* waste, destroy.
square, *curas*, *murabbā*: of land, *murabbā*, m.
squash, *ciṭhṇā*, *napiṭṭṇā*; *cūrk.*, into small pieces: *see* squeeze, burst, crush.
squat, on heels, *pairā̃ bhār baihṇā*: cross-legged, *caukṛī mārke*: w. legs stretched out, *nisḷīā̃ karke*: on knees and feet, *gōṭh mārke*, *kuṭṭe baihṇī baihṇā*, *ūṭh baihṇī baihṇā*, *goḍe mū̃dhe mārke baihṇā*.
squeak, *cī̃ cī̃ karnī*, rats, mice, etc.: *see* creak.
squeeze, *ghuṭṭṇā*: wring, *nacōṛnā*, *napīṛnā*; press, *dabāṇā*: so as to burst, *phehṇā*, int. *phissṇā*, *see* burst: s. sugar-cane, oil, etc., *pīṛnā*; of fruit, *nacōṛnā*, *napīṛnā*: *see* squash, press, crush.
squib, *paṭākā* (*calāṇā*, int. *calṇā*).
squint (eyed), *bhaiṅgā*: v., *bhaṅgāṇā*.
squirrel, *gālhaṛ*, m., *gālhaṛ cūhā*, m.
stab, *talwār*, f., *khanjar*, m., *churī*, f.: all w. *mārnā* and *nū̃* [*astabal*, m.
stable, *tawēlā*, m., *stabal*, m.,
stack of hay, *kupp*, m.
staff, *see* stick.
stag, *harn*, fem., *harnī*: *bārā̃-siṅgā*, m.
stage, *paṛā*, m., *manzal*, f.
stagger, *ḍōlke ṭurnā*, *ḍigdeā ṭurnā*.
stagnant, *khlōtā hoeā*, *gandā* (dirty).
stain, both moral and lit., *dāg*, m., *dhabbā* (moral), m.: both w. *lāṇā*, int., *laggṇā*: *see* delete.
stair, *pauṛīā̃*, f. pl.: one step, *pauṛī*, f.
stake, for impaling, *sūḷī*, f., *sīkh*, f.: *see* nail.
stale, *behā* from yesterday; *tarbehā* from day before: *behā*, also gen.
stalk of wheat, barley, *nāḷī*, f., millet, maize, sugarcane, *ṭāṇṇā*, m.
stallion, *sāhn*, m.
stammer, *thathlāṇā*.
stammerer, *thatthā*.
stamp, seal, etc., *mohr*, f. (*lāṇī*, int. *laggṇī*): postage, *ṭikaṭ*, m. f. (*lāṇā*, int. *laggṇā*).
(1) stand, *khlōṇā*, pa. p. *khlōtā*, *khaḷā*: standing, *khlōtā*, *khaḷā*, G. 108: caus. *khalhārnā*: *see* rise.
(2) stand, I won't stand that; paraphrase: *eh mĕnū̃ manzūr nehī̃*; *maĩ tĕnū̃ ēs tarhā̃ nehī̃ karn dēṇ lagā*; *maĩ ēs tarhā̃ nehī̃ hōṇ dēṇ lagā*; *ēs tarhā̃ mērī tērī nehī̃ nibhaṇ lagī*.
(3) stand, n., for tumtums, carriages, etc., *aḍḍā*, m.
standard, *see* flag.
star, *tārā*, m.: *see* rise, set, comet: for names *see* A.
starch, *kalf*, f., *māyā*, m.
stare, *tāṛī lāṇī*; angrily, *ghurā-kī wēkhṇī*, *ghūrnā*.
(1) start, be startled, *ṭraihṇā* (pa. p. *ṭraṭṭhā*), *trāh nikḷṇā* (*dā*): *see* startle.
(2) start, set out, *ṭur paiṇā*, *ruāṇā h.*, *Illāh bēlī h.* (God be your, his friend, farewell): *alī panj h.*
startle, v. tr., *trāhṇā*, *see* start (1).
starvation, *baṛī bhukkh*, f.

starve, *baṛā bhukkhā h.*, *bhukkh nāḷ marnā*, *bhukkhā marnā*.

state, *hālat*, f., *hāl*, m., *hāl hakīkat*, f.: Native State, *riāsat*, f.: *rāje dā rāj*.

stately, building, *waḍḍā te sohṇā*.

statement, *beān*, m., *ākhṇā*, m

statesman, *bādshāh dā salāhkār*

station (railway), *ṭeshn*, m., *stēshn*, m.

stay, *ṭhaihrnā*, *raihṇā*, *ṭikṇā*: *see* wait: place where one can stay, friend's house, etc., *ṭhāhr*, f. A.

steadily, go slowly but s., *raḷakdā jāṇā*.

steal, *cōrī karnī*, gen.; *curāṇā* (must have object): *see* stealthily, receiver.

stealthily, *cōrī*, *cōrī chappī* (or *chappe*), *cup capītā*: *see* quiet- -ly, silent-, -ly.

steam, real or vapour from kettle or hot food, *hawāṛ*, f.: from ground, *bhaṛās*, f.

steamer, *jahāz*, m.

steel, *aspāt*, m., *fulād*, m.

steep, *siddhī caṛhāī*, f.; *siddhā uttā jāndā e*; *sakht caṛhāī*, f.

stench, *see* smell.

(1) **step**, *kadam*, m.: stepping-stone, *paintṛā*, m.: *see* stair, ladder.

(2) **step**, in s.-son, brother, etc., *matrēā*, fem. *matrēī*: step brother or sister on father's side, *pyōō mātar*; on mother's, *māō mātar*: wife's child by former husband, *pishlagg*.

stew, n., *ishṭū*, m. (K.): v., *rinnhṇā*, (pa. p. *riddhā*, int. *rijjhṇā*).

(1) **stick**, n., *sōṭī*, f.: cane, *baint*, m.: stout, s., *sōṭā*, m. (short), *ḍaṅgōrī*, f. (for old people); *ḍāṅg*, f. (long), *ḍanḍā*, m. (short): *see* switch.

(2) **stick**, v., gen. *laggṇā*, tr. *lāṇā*: s. in mud, etc., *khubbhṇā*, tr. *khōbhṇā*.

sticky, *see* viscous.

stiff, dough, *ākṛā*: proud, *ākaṛwālā*, *ākṛeā hoeā*.

stifle, v. int., *baṛā waṭṭ laggṇā* (*nū̃*): *see* sultriness: tr., *see* smother.

(1) **still**, yet, *aje*, *phēr wī*, *tā̃ wī*.

(2) **still**, *halldā nehī̃*, *see* quiet, calm (1).

sting, *ḍaṅg mārnā*, (*nū̃*), int., *laggṇā* (*nū̃*); *laṛnā* (*nū̃*).

stingy, *see* miser-, -liness.

stink, *see* smell.

stipulation, *shart*, f., *karār*, m. (promise).

stir, *see* excite, disturbance: fire, *bhakhāṇā*.

stirrup, *rakāb*, f.

stitch, *trōppā*, m. (*lāṇā*, int. *laggṇā*): *see* patch.

stocking, same as sock, or add *lammā*, long.

stomach, *ḍhiḍḍh*, m., *pēṭ*, m.

(1) **stone**, *waṭṭā*, m., *patthar*, m.: *see* pebble, limestone: in bladder, *patthrī*, f.: in fruit, *giṭak*, f., *hikkaṛ*, f.: pip of orange, apple, etc., *bī*, m.: in ring, *thēwā*, m.: throw s., *saṭṭṇā*, *mārnā* (hitting someone or -thing).

(2) **stone**, v. tr., fruit, *giṭkā̃ kaḍḍhṇīā̃*: person, etc.: *see* stone (1).

stony, *waṭṭeā̃wālā*.

stool, *ṭūl*, m., *caukī*, f.: village, *pīṛhī*, f., *pīṛhā*, m.: of reeds, *mūṛhā*, m.: *see* chair, seat.

stoop, *uṛnā*, *nyūṇā*, *jhukṇā*,

nīwā h., sir jhukāṇā: *see* bend, lean (2), crooked.
stop, v. tr., *see* hinder, forbid, leave off, and add *mōṛnā*, int. *muṛnā*; *ṭhākṇā*: int. *rukkṇā*.
stopper, in bottle, plug, *ḍaṭṭ*, m.: *see* lid, cork.
store, *zakhīrā*, m., *khazānā*, m. (treasure): stores, *saudā*, m.; European, *shtōr*, m. (K.).
store-room, -house, *gudām*, m.
storey, *see* story (2).
storm, wind, *hanērī*, f., *jhānjhā*, m.: gust, *jhakkhaṛ*, m.: heavy rain, *phāṇḍā*, m., heavy squall of rain, *sharlāṭā*, m.
(1) story, narrative, *kahāṇī*, f. (*pāṇī*, *suṇānī*): *bĕān* (*karnā*).
(2) story, of house, *chatt*, m. (ceiling), *manzal*, f.: two-, three- four-storied, *du-*, *tar-*, *cu-chatta* or *-manzilā*.
stove, *angīṭhī*, f.
straight, *siddhā*, *suāhrā*.
(1) strain, (sift), *chāṇṇā*: strain through cloth, *puṇṇā*: cloth for straining, *pōṇā*, m.
(2) strain, arm at socket, through throwing, etc., *bāh* w. *chanak jāṇī*, *cuṭak jāṇī*, *chan jāṇī*, *chankī jāṇī*, *chanak ghaṭṭṇī*.
straits, in, *awāzār*, *tang*, *aukkhā*, *khajjal* (going here and there), *khajjal khuār*: *see* knock, difficulty.
strange, *ōprā*; *bagānā* and *parāyā* (not one's own): *ajīb*, *ajaib*, *anōkhā*; *see* stranger wonderful.
stranger, *ōprā*, *obbhaṛ*, *parāyā*, *pardēsī*.
strangle, *sangh* or *gaḷ ghuṭṭṇā*: *see* hang, smother, choke.
strap, *waddhrī*, f., *tasmā*, m.
stratagem, *dā* (*lāṇā*, int. *laggṇā*, *khāṇā*): *see* trick, deceit.
straw, *see* chaff.
straw-coloured, *kakkā*.
stray, v. int., *khunjhṇā* (*rāhō*, etc.), *ghussṇā* (*rāhō*, etc.), *ṭhaṛukṇā*: *see* astray, wander.
stream, *nadī*, f., *nāḷī*, f.: *see* river.
street, *bazār*, m., *gaḷā*, m.: lane, *gaḷī*, f.
strength, *zōr*, m., *tākat*, f.: *see* power, strong.
stretch, *see* spread, pull: s. oneself, *ākaṛnā*, *ākaṛ auṇe* (*nū̃*).
strict, *kaide dā paband*, *sakht*, *ḍāhḍā*, *karṛā*.
(1) strike, *see* beat, blow, mark, prod: add *saṭṭ lāṇī*: of missile, *laggṇā* (*nū̃*): M. 244. 26: of stick, etc., *wajjṇā* (*nū̃*), *laggṇā* (*nū̃*): s. tent *puṭṭṇā*: s. off name, *see* delete; do. on payment of debt, *nāwā waḷṇā* or *lāhṇā* (int. *laihṇā*), *āgat pāṇā* or *karnā* (int. *paiṇā*).
(2) strike, refuse to work, *kamm chaḍḍṇā*.
(1) string, *rassī*, f., *ḍōrī*, f., *sūtrī*, f.: on bed, *wāṇ*, m.: on *ṭiṇḍ* at well, *warhī*, f.: bundle or ball of, *pinnā*, m., *gunjī*, f.: as sold. *chaṛā*, m.
(2) string, together papers, *natthī-k*.
strip, clothes, bark, etc., *lāhṇā*.
stripe, *dhārī*, f.: mere line, *līk*, f.
strive, *see* effort.
stroll, *sail*, m., *sair*, m., *sail sapaṭṭā*, m. (all *k.*).
strong, *tagṛā*, *tākatwāḷā*: of things, *mazbūt*, *ḍāhḍā*: of

tea, *sañhṇī*, *gūhṛī*: *see* strength, power.
struggle, *see* scuffle, effort.
stud, collar, shirt, *gudām*, m.: *see* button.
student, *see* scholar, disciple.
studious, *mehntī*.
study, v., *paṛhnā*, *sṭaḍī karnī*: n. (room), *daftar*, m.
stuff in, *tunnnā*.
stumble, *ṭhuḍḍā laggṇā* (*nū*) or *khāṇā*.
stumblingblock, *see* offence.
stump of tree, *muṇḍh*, m.: jagged bit of wood, *khuṅghī*, f., *muḍḍhī*, f., *muṇḍhī*, f.
stun, *behōsh-k.*, int. *h.*
stupid, *beakl*, *allhaṛ* (inexperienced), *ḍhaggā*: *see* fool.
stupidity, *see* foolishness.
subject, n., persons, *raīyat*, f., *parjā*, f. (both always sing.): of book, letter, *mazmūn*, m.
submerge, *ḍōbṇā*: *see* sink.
submission, *see* obedience.
subordinate, *mataiht*.
subscri-be, -ption, give, *candā dēṇā*: raise, *ugrāhṇā* (int. *uggharnā*).
subside, building, *baihṇā*: *see* collapse, lessen.
subsist-, -ence, *guzārā*, m. (*k.*, *h.*).
substitute, *iwzī*: *see* exchange, change, relief.
subterfuge, *see* trick, deceit, stratagem.
subtract, *tafrīk karnī*, *minhā-k.* (educ.), *ghaṭāṇā*.
(1) **succeed**, *kamm tōrnā*, *matlab kaḍḍhṇā*; *kāmyāb h.* (U.).
(2) **succeed**, *ohde thā auṇā*, *ohde magar auṇā*.
such *ajehā*, *ehojehā*: s. and s., *falāṇā*.
suck, *cuṅghṇā*, *cūpṇā* (fruit): *see* eat, suckle.
suckle, *duddh piāṇā* or *cuṅghāṇā*.
suddenly, *acāṇcak*, *cāṇcakke*, *accaṇcēt*, *awāghatt*.
suffer-, -ing, *see* endure, pain, grief.
sufficient, *see* enough.
suffocate, *see* choke, hang, smother.
sugar, *miṭṭhā*, gen.: ground fine, *būrā khaṇḍ*, f.: not so fine, *dāṇedār khaṇḍ* (or both simply, *khaṇḍ*, f.; European variety, *cīnī*, f.): tablets, *mishrī*, f.: unrefined, *guṛ*, m.: finer than *guṛ*, *shakkar*, f.: without s., of tea, etc., *phikkā*.
sugar-cane, *kamād*, m.: each cane, *gannā*, m.: different kinds, *pōnnā*, m. (very thick), *pēṭkū*, m., *trēṛū*, m., *dhauḷū*, m., *cinkhā*, m. (v. thin, also called *kāṭhā*, m.): s. juice, *rauh*, f.: eat s., *cūpṇā*.
suggestion, *see* hint, say.
suicide, *phāh laiṇā*, hang oneself; *gaḍḍī agge baihke marnā*, sit before train: gen. *khudkushī*, f. (U.).
(1) **suit**, in law, *mukadmā*, m.: *see* case, lose.
(2) **suit**, clothes, *jōṛā*, m., *sūṭ*, m.
(3) **suit-, -able**, v., *phabbṇā*, *munāsib h.*, *caṅgā laggṇā* also *de gōcrā*, *de jogā*, *de laik*, G. 38; *jogā* w. infl. infin. *see* proper, right, advisable.
sulk, *russṇā*, *mūh waṭṭṇā*: *see* displeased.
sulphur, *gandhak*, f.
sultriness, (outside) *gummā*,

gõmmā, gum, ghummā, ghõmmā, cumāsā (all m., *laggṇā, nū̃*): (in room or outside), *watt* (*laggṇā, nū̃*): physical feeling, *hussaṛ*, m. (*h., nū̃*), and v. *hussaṛnā*.

sum, in arithmetic, *suāl*, m.: of money, *rakam*, f.: total, *jõṛ*, m., *jamhā*, f., *mizān*, f. (U.). [m., *samṛī*, f.

summary, *nacõṛ*, m., *khulāsā*,

summer, *garmīā̃*, f. pl.: often *hāṛh*, m. (lit. the month June 13–July 12), *unhāḷ*. m.

summer-school, *paṛhāī*, f.

summit, *see* pinnacle, peak.

summon, *see* call.

summons, leg., *samman*, m.

sun, *sūraj*, m., *dyūh*, m., *din* or *din*, m.: s. come out fr. cloud, *dhupp laggṇī*: have five or six days of sunshine, *panj che dhuppā̃ laggṇīā̃*, G. 125: M. 129. 27: warm oneself in sun, *see* bask: put it in the sun, *dhupp icc rakkhṇā, sukṇe pāṇā*: *see* sunshine.

sunday, *aitwār*, m.

sunshine, *dhupp*, f.: *see* sun.

superfluous, *wā̃far, wā̃dhū, fāltū*; *fazūl* (useless).

superintend, *kamm wekhṇā* (*dā*), *nigrāṇī karnī* (*dī*, U.), *nigābā̃nī karnī* (*dī*, U.).

superintendent, *kamm wekkhaṇwāḷā, mainajar*: head workman, *mēṭ*.

superior, *see* good, better, one's s. officer, *afsar*.

superstition, *waihm*, m.

superstitious, *waihmī*.

supervise, *see* superintend.

supine, lying or fallen on one's back, *utāṇā, kaṇḍ parne* or *bhār*.

supper, *safar*, m. (K).

supplant, *dhokhe nāḷ thā̃ mallṇā*.

supple, *lifaṇwāḷā, kūḷā*.

supply, *apṛāṇā, pucāṇā*: *see* produce, obtain, secure.

support, *see* prop, pillar, lean: gen. *sambhāḷṇā, madad dēṇī* (*nū̃*): hold up, *cukkī rakkhṇā*: provide for, *pāḷṇā, parwarish karnī* (*dī*): *see* endure.

suppose, *farz karnā*: *see* think, guess, calculate, what if.

suppress, *see* hide, stop, hinder.

suppurate, *pakkṇā, pāk paiṇī*.

sure, *see* certain.

surety, *see* bail, certain.

surgeon, *see* doctor, operation.

surpass, *wadhṇā, de nāḷõ caṅgā h.*

surprise, *see* astonish-, -ment.

surrender, *hār mannṇī*: *hathyār saṭṭṇe*.

surreptitiously, *see* stealthily.

surround, *waḷṇā, ghērnā, gherā pāṇā* (*de duāḷe*).

surveillance, *nazr*, f.: keep under s., *nazr icc rakkhṇā*: *see* detenu.

survey, measure land, *kacchṇā pamaish karnī* (*dī*): *see* look, measure.

suspect, *see* suspicion.

suspend, *muattal-h.* (U.).

suspicion, *shakk karnā* (*dā*), *zan karnā* (*dī bābat*), *badgumāṇī karnī* (*dī bābat*).

swagger, *ākaṛke calṇā*.

swaddling-clothes, *põṛe*, m. pl.

swallow, *nigaḷṇā, laṅghāṇā*: *see* anger.

swamp, *see* marsh.

swarm, of bees, *ghaṇ*, m.: of flies, *ḍār*, m.: *see* flock.

swear, *see* oath.

sweat, *see* perspiration.
sweep, *jhāṛū phērnā* or *dēṇā* : s. up leav..., papers, etc., *hūnjṇā*.
sweeper, *mehtar*, *jhāṛū dēṇwāḷā*, addressed often as *jamādār* : caste, *Cūhṛā*, *Kāḷakh dās* : one who has become Muhammadan, *musall-ī*, fem. *-aṇ* ; Sikkh, *mazbhī Sikkh-*, fem. *-ṇī*, or simply *mazbh-ī*, fem. *-an*.
sweet, *miṭṭhā*, both of people and things : s. drink, *sharbat*, m.
sweets, gen., *miṭhāī*, f. : many kinds.
swell, flesh, etc., *sujjṇā* : something hollow, as stomach, *āpharnā*.
swelling, *sōj*, f. : *aphrā*, m. : *see* swell : fr. bite of insect, *dhrapphaṛ*, m. : *see* lump.
swift, *trikkhā*, *tēz* : in a hurry, *kāhlā* : go swiftly, *khurī karke jāṇā*, *khiṭṭ dēṇī* or *mārnī*.
swim, *tarnā* : water deep enough to s. in, *tārū pāṇī*, m.
swimmer, *tārū*.
swimming, the art, *tārī*, f. (*auṇī*, *nū*).
(1) swing, n., *pīngh*, f.
(2) swing, on a swing, *pīngh caṛhāṇī*, *pīngh de hūnte laiṇe* (tr. *dēṇe*) : gen., *ṭangke halāṇā* (int. *hallṇā*) : *see* hang.
switch, little stick, *chamak*, f. *chūjak*, f., *shūshak*, f. : *see* stick.
swoon, *see* faint.
swoop, *see* pounce.
sword, *talwār*, f. (*mārnī*, int. *laggṇī*, *nū*).
sympathiser, *dardī*.
sympathise w., *ohdā dard karnā*, *ohnū ohdā dukkh hōṇā* (this may mean envy) ; G. 125 : M. 130. 34–6 : *hamdardī karnī* (*nāḷ*) : or *ohnū ohdā dard hōṇā* or *auṇā*.
sympathy, *see* sympathise.
sympathetic, *dardī* ; *hamdard* (U.).
symptom, *nishānī*, f.
syringe, *pickārī*, f. [*ṭrīkal*, m.
syrup, *shīrā*, m. : golden,
system, *kaidā*, m. : *tarīkā*, m.

T

table, *mēz*, m., *mēc*, m. : lay, set t., *mēz lāṇā* (int. *laggṇā*) : take away things, *mēz cukkṇā*.
tablecloth, *mēz dī cādar*, f.
tablet, *takhtī*, f.
taciturn, *gall nehī kardā*, *cuppū*, *mūh wattdā raihndā e*.
(1) tack, n., *brinjī*, f. : *see* nail.
(2) tack, sew, *kaccī suāī karnī*, *kaccā karnā* (*nū*).
tail, *pūshal*, f. : of bird, fish, *būṇḍā*, m. : tailless, *lunḍā*.
tailor, *darz-ī*, fem. *-an*.
tainted, be, *bō chaḍḍnī*, *trakk caleā*, *wigaṛ caleā*, *muss caleā* ; of milk, *wigaṛ caleā*, *phiṭ caleā* : *see* bad, sour. A.
take, *laiṇā*, G. 64 : t. away, *khaṛnā*, *lai jāṇā* : *see* seize, conquer ; t. out stain, *see* delete : t. off clothes, hat, shoes, *lāhṇā*, sometimes, *wadhāṇā*, G. 113.
talc, *abrak*, m. (mica).
tale, *see* story : t.-bearer, *cugalkhōr* (U.), *bakhīlī* or *cuglī karnwāḷā* : *see* accuse, slander.
(1) talent, money, *tōṛā*, m. (1000 rupees).

(2) talent, *see* ability, able, clever.
talisman, *tilism*, m. (U.).
talk, *see* conversation.
talkative, *galāhdar*, *gappī* (esp. of what is untrue), *bakwāsī*, *bariā gallā karnwālā*: *see* chatter.
tall, *lammā*, *uccā*.
tallow, *see* fat.
talon, *see* claw.
tamarind, *imblī*, f.
tambourine, *ḍaph*, f., smaller, *ḍaphṛā*, m., *ḍaphlī*, f., *khanjarī*, f.: *see* drum.
tame (quiet), *asīl*, *garīb*: kept, not wild, *rākhwā*.
tank, *talā*, m.
tap, *nalkā*, m.: *see* spout.
tape, *fītā*, m.: for beds, *nuār*, f. (adj. *nuārī*): for fastening drawers, *nāḷā*, m.: *see* measuring -t.
tapioca, *tāpiū*, m. (K.).
tar, *lukk*, f.
target, *takhtā*, m.
tariff, *nirkh*, m.: *bhā*, m.: t.-list, *nirkhnāmā*, m
tassel, as in fez cap, *phummaṇ*, m.: as in the cloth called *khēs*, *bumbal*, m.
(1) taste, *suād*, m., *mazā*, m. (U.): t. for, inclination towards, often used in connection with stealing, *jhass*, m., *caskā*, m. (both *paiṇā*, and *dā*): *see* desire.
(2) taste, v. tr., *cakkhṇā*.
tasteless, *see* inspid, add *alūṇā*, *belūṇā*.
tasty, *suādlā*, *mazedār*, *karārā* (well-spiced).
tattoo, *ukkhaṇṇā guddṇā*, both w. thing tattooed as obj.
taunt, *tāhne mārne* (*nū*), *mehṇā dēṇā* or *mārnā* (*nū*, *kise gall dā*), *nōk lāṇī* (*nū*, int. *wajjṇī*, *laggṇī*): *see* ridicule.
taut, *see* tight.
tax, *masūl*, *maihsūl*, m.: octroi, *cuṅgī*, f., *cuṅgī dā masūl*: (octroi post, *cuṅgī*, f.: octroi official, *masūlīā*, *cuṅgīwāḷā*): land-t., *muāmlā*, m.: (collect t., *laiṇā*, *ugrāhṇā*): on sales, *āṛhtal*, f., *dhaṛth*, m.: *see* collect, assess, settlement.
tea, *cāh*, f.: *see* teapot.
teach, *paṛhāṇā*, *sikhāṇā*, *tālīm dēṇī* (*nū*), *sikkhyā dēṇī* (*nū* H.): sit at feet of teacher to learn, *baihṇā* (caus. *bahāḷṇā*).
teacher, *ustād*, *māsṭar*, *munshī*: of Persian, Arabic, *maulwī*: of Sanskrit, *paṇḍat*: relig. t., M. *murshad*, *maulwī*: H. *gurū*, *paṇḍat*: female t. in school, *ustādṇī*.
teaching, *see* teach and add *paṛhāī*, f.
teapot, *cāhpōcī*, f.: vessels of similar shape, *astāwā*, m., *satāwā*, m., *lōṭṭā*, m.
(1) tear, v. tr., *pāṛnā*, int. *pāṭṇā*. [pl.
(2) tear, n., *atthar*, f., *hanjū*, f.
tease, *chēṛnā*, *satāṇā*, *dikk-k.*: t. by disappointing, *jhakhāṇā*: *see* annoy.
teat, animal, *thaṇ*, m.: *see* nipple.
teaze, *tumbṇā*: *see* card (1).
telegram, *tār*, f.
telegraph, *tār ghallṇī* or *dēṇī*: -wire, *tār*, f.: -post, *waḷā*, m.
telescope, *dūrbīn*, f.
tell, *ākhṇā*, *dassṇā*.
temper, tempered good-, *caṅge subhā wāḷā*, *saihndaṛ* (patient): bad-, use easily angry, annoyed.

temperament, *tabīat*, f.
temperate (person), *parhēzgār*.
temperature, *garmī*, f. (heat): of body, do., and *bukhār*, m. (fever).
temple, *mandar*, m., *shiwālā*, m.
temporary, *thōṛeā̃ dinā̃ wāste*, *ārzī* (of employment, U.): t. piece of work *calā̃wā̃ kamm*, m.
tempt, v. difficult idea, *azmā-nā*, *warglānā*, *bakāṇ dī kō-shish karnī*, *khiccṇā* (draw): *see* incite, test, seduce.
temptation (idea difficult), *azmaish*, f., *partāwā*, m., *khice*, f. (drawing).
ten, *das*: -th, *daswā̃*: G. 19–24.
tenaciously, *cambaṛke*, *khaihṛā nā chaḍḍke*.
tenant, *sāmī*, f., *asāmī*, f.
tender, soft, *kūḷā*, *see* soft: loving, *mhabtī*.
tendon, *see* sinew.
tendril, *wall*. f., *wēl*, f.
tenet, *akīdā*, m., *asūl*, m.: point of doctrine, *maslā*, m.
tent, *tambū*, m., *dērā*, m., servants' t., *chōldārī*, f.: nomads' small, *pakkhī*, f., *tap-rī*, f.: *see* nomad: wall of t., *kanāt*, f.: put up t., *lāṇā*: strike, *puṭṭṇā*.
tentatively, *wēkkhan wāste*, *azmāṇ wāste*.
tepid, *kōssā*, *khūh-nuāyā*.
terrible, *ḍarnwāḷā*, *jis tō̃ ḍar āwe*, *ḍarauṇā*.
terrify-, **-ing**, *see* fear, terrible.
terror, *khauf*, m., *ḍar*, m.
tertian fever, *treīā*, m. (*caṛhnā*. come on: *laihṇā*, go off).
test, *azmāṇā*, *parkhṇā*, *wēkhṇā*, *azmaish karnī* (*dī*): examine, *imtihān lainā* (*dā*): test exam., *ṭēsṭ*. m., *ṭēsṭ* or *azmaishi imtihān*, m. (educ.).
testament, *see* will: New T., *Nawā̃ Aihdnāmā*, m., *Injīl*, f., *Anjīl*, f.: Old T., *Purāṇā Aihdnāmā*, m.: *see* Pentateuch, Psalms.
testi-fy, **-mony**, *see* witness, evidence.
testimonial, *sāṭifkaṭ*, m., *sanad*, f.
than, *nāḷō*. *thō̃*, *tō̃*, *thī*, G. 18: *see* rather, comparison, time.
thank, *shukr karnā* (*dā*): t. you: *tuhāḍḍī mehrbānī e*: t. God, *shukr e*, *Khudā dā shukr e*: the strange phrase *Rabb dā bhalā howe* is often heard.
thankful, *shukrguzār*: *see* obligation.
(1) **that**, conj., *pai*, *ke*: sometimes *akhe*, *makhe*, G. 121, 40: M. 127–42.
(2) **that**, pron., *oh*, *parlā*, *pailā*: that is, *yānī*.
thatch, *chappar*, m.
the, *eh*, *oh*. or omit.
theft, *cōrī*, f.: *see* robbery.
their, *ohnā̃ dā*, *ehnā̃ dā*, *ne*, *ṇe*, G. 82–6.
them, *ohnā̃ nū̃*, *ehnā̃ nū̃*, *ne*, *ṇe*, G. 82–6.
then, reasoning, *whalā*, *tā̃*, *te*, *phēr*, *khā̃* (only with imperat.), *tadde*: time, *odō̃*, *odū̃*, *ōsweḷe*, *ōtweḷe*, *tadō̃*, *tadū̃*.
thence, *ōtthō̃*. *see* there.
theolog-y, **-ical**, *see* A.
theory, *maslā*, m., *dalīl*, f.
there, *ōtthe*, *oddhar*, *parhā̃*; *ōttal* (gen. motion to): there it is, le voilà, *oh wekhā̃*.
therefore, *ēs wāste*, *ōs wāste*, *tā̃ ī*, *tadde*, *tā̃ karke*, *tā̃hīē*.
they, *eh*, *oh*.

thick, liquid, *gūṛhā*, *gāṛhā*, *saṅhnā*: dirty water, *gandhḷeā hoeā*, *see* dirty: dense, trees, crowd, *saṅhṇā*: close friendship, *gūṛhī* or *pakkī dōstī*: not thin, *mōṭā*.
thickness (not thinness), *muṭeāī*, f.
thief, *cōr*: *see* robber, receiver.
thigh, *paṭṭ*, m.
thimble, *aṅgūṭhī*, f.
thin, not fat or thick, *patlā*; *lissā* (persons, animals only): not coarse, *mhīn*: fine and small, *barīk*: ill-looking, *māṛā*, *lissā*.
thing, *cīz*, f., *cīz wast*, f., *shai*, f.
think, *sōcṇā*, *gaur karnā* (consider), *dhiān karnā* (meditate): I believed or thought, *maĩ ākheā*, *maĩ samjheā*.
third, *see* three: t. day fever, *see* tertian.
thirst, *treh*, f., G. 108: (intense) *bhaṛkī*, f.: *andar saṛdā e*.
thirsty, *trihāyā*.
thirteen, *terā̃*: -th, *tehrwā̃*, G. 19–24, 123: thirteen-finger shoe, *see* shoe.
thirty, *trīh*: -one, *akattī*, *akattrī*: -two *battī*, *battrī*: -three, *tettī*, *tetrī*: -four, *cauttī*, *cautrī*: -five, *paĩtī*, *paĩtrī*: -six, *chattī*, *chattrī*: -seven, *saĩtī*, *saĩtrī*: -eight, *aṭhattī*, *aṭhattrī*: -nine, *unṭālī*, *unṭāḷī*.
ordinals add *-wā̃* with tonic *h*, (*trīh* already has it): as *akattīhwā̃*, *untāhḷīwā̃*, G. 19-24, 123.
this, *eh*, *urlā*.
thither, *see* there.
thong, *wadhrī*, f.
thorn, *kaṇḍā*, m.: t.-branch, *ḍhīṅgar*, m., *ḍhīṅgrī*, f., *moṛhā*, m., *moṛhī*, f.: tiny thorny plant injurious to rubber tyres, *bhakkhṛā*.
thorny, *kaṇḍeā̃wāḷā*.
thoroughly, *bilkull*, *pūrī tarhā̃*, *pūre taur nāḷ*: *see* absolutely, altogether.
thou, *tū̃*: people like thee or you, *tumhātaṛ*, G. 28.
though, *bhā̃we*, *bhā̃we jīkar*.
thought, gen., *sōc*, f., *sōc wacār*, f.: *khyāl*, m., idea, opinion: *gaur*, m., consideration; *dhiān*, m., meditation: *dalīl*, f., reasoning: *see* anxiety.
thoughtful, *sōcā̃ icc*, *dalīlā̃ icc*.
thoughtless, *lāparwāh*, *sōcdā nehī̃*: *bēparwāh*, beyond need of caring, as God, rich man.
thousand, *hazār*: -th, *hazārwā̃*: hundred t., *lakkh*: -th, *lakkhwā̃*: G. 20–4, 93.
thread, *dhāgā*, m., *tand*, f.: sacred Hindu t., *janeo*, m.: three-fold t., *paṛkatteā*, *dhāgā*: *see* string.
threat-, -en, *dhaūs dēṇī* (*nū̃*), or *cāṛhnī* (*utte*) or *wakhāṇī* (*nū̃*), *dhamkī dēṇī* (*nū̃*), *dabbā dēṇā* (*nū̃*), *dabkāṇā*, *ghurkī dēṇī* (*nū̃*), *ḍarāṇā*: *see* reprimand, frown.
three, *trai*, *tinn*: third, *trījjā*, *tīsrā*: G. 19–24: t.-fold (actual layers), *treohrā*; three times as big or much, *trīṇā*, *trai hisse waddh*: *see* time, thread: thrice, *trai wārī* or *werī*.
thresh, v. tr., *gāhṇā*, int. *gaihṇā*.
threshingfloor, *piṛ*, m. A.
threshold, room at, *ḍeoḍhī*, f.: of door, *brū̃*, f., *dalhīz*, f.
throat, outside, *gaḷ*, m., *gaṭṭā*, m.: inside, *saṅgh*, m.: *see* neck and add *saṅghī*, f.

throne, *ta<u>kh</u>t*, m.: of ruling princes, *gaddī*, f.
throttle, *see* strangle.
through, *wiccdū*, *wiccõ dī*: t. Jesus Christ, *Yesū Masīh dī rāhī* or *de wasīleõ*: t. door, window, *see* way: *see* because of, means.
throw, *saṭṭṇā*, *suṭṭṇā*, *mārnā*: t. away, *suṭṭ* or *saṭṭ charnā* or *chaḍḍṇā*): t. away liquid, *roṛh charnā*, *ḍolh charnā*: t. at, strike w., *mārnā* (acc. of missile, *nū* of person.)
thrust, stuff in, *see* stuff in: t. out, *dhikkṇā*, *kaḍḍhṇā*.
thumb, *angūṭh*, m., *angūṭhā*, m.: affix t.-mark, *angūṭhā lāṇā* (int. *laggṇā*).
thunder, v. int., *baddaḷ gajjṇā* (sometimes *kaṛakṇā*).
Thursday, *jumerāt*, f., *wīr* or *wīrwār*, m. (H.).
thus, in this way, *eñ*, *iñ*, *aiñ*, *eõ*, *eñ karke*, *aikkaṇ*: in that way, *owẽ*, *aukkaṇ*, *uñ*: (*owẽ* also just then, immediately).
thy, *see* you.
(1) tick, n., in dogs, etc., *ciccaṛ*, m.
(2) tick of clock, etc., *ṭik ṭik*, f. (*k*.).
ticket, *ṭikaṭ*, m. f.: return t., *wāpsī ṭikaṭ*, *auṇ jaṇ dā ṭikaṭ*: (travel) without t., *barang*, *beṭikṭā*.
tickle, v. tr., *kutkutāṛī kaḍḍhṇī* (*dī*), int. *nikḷṇī* (*dī*), often in plur.
tidy, *sāf suthrā* (clean), *ṭhīk sāhmke rakkhṇā*. *koī shai kuthāẽ nā howe*, *thā̃ pathā̃ī rakkhṇā*: *see* untidy.
(1) tie, v. tr., *bannhṇā*, pa. p., *baddhā*, int. *bajjhṇā*: *see* knot: tie arms or hands behind back, *mushkā̃ bannhṇīā̃* (*dīā̃*).
(2) tie, n., muffler, *guḷūban*, m.: *see* neck-tie.
tiffin, *ṭipan*, m.
tiger, *shēr*, fem. *shērnī*.
tight, *kasseā hoeā*, *ghuṭṭeā hoeā*: *see* narrow.
tighten, *kassṇā*, *ghuṭṭṇā*.
tightly, *kasske*, *ghuṭṭke*.
tile, *khaprail*, f. (U).
(1) till, v. tr., *see* plough, cultivate.
(2) till, up till, *ṭikar*, *tāṇī*, *toṛī*, *tāṛī*, *tāī*, *tākar*, *sīdhā*.
(3) till, conj., *jicar ṭikar* (or *tāī*, etc.), *jicar nū*, *jicar* .... *nā*.
tilt back, of carriage, *ullarnā*: *see* weight.
time, gen., *wakat*, m., *weḷā*, m.: the present, past or future age, *zamānā*, m., *samā*, m.: fixed period, *miād*, f.: length of t., *cir*, m.: short t., *jhaṭ*, m., *ghaṛī*, f. (*see* short, long): in t., at the right t., *weḷe sir*, *wakat sir*; at the wrong t., late, *kuweḷe* (*see* late): this t., *aitkī*, *aitkā̃*, *es wārī*, *es werī*, *es phēre*: *see* meanwhile. o'clock: for A.M., P.M., *see* A.M.

time in four, five times, etc., *wārī*, *werī*: the first, second t., *paihlī*, *dujjī wārī* or *werī*, *paihlā phērā*, etc.

five, six times as big, *panj hisse waddh*, etc., or reversing it, *ohdā panjwā̃ hissā* (a fifth part of it): fr. two to five, special words, *dūṇā*, *trīṇā*, *cauṇā*, *panjauṇā*.
time-server, *matlabī*, *garzī*.
timid, *see* coward.

tin, material or a tin, ***tīn***, m.: for soldering, ***kalī***, f. (*k.*): canister, ***kanastar***, m., ***pīpā***, m.: bath-tin, ***bhabkā***, m.

tinkle, ***chanaknā, wajjṇā, chan chan karnī***.

tip, ***nōk***, f.

tiptoe, on, *pabbā̃ bhār* (*pabb*, m., is ball of foot).

tire, v. int., ***thaknā***, (***thakā-nā̃***): tired, ***thakeā hoeā***: *see* faint: get tired of, ***akknā*** (***tō̃*** tr. ***akānī̃***), *see* sick of.

title, of book, etc., ***nā̃***, m.: heading, ***surkhī***, f.: of person, *lakab*, m.: honorary t. given by Government, ***khatāb***, m.

to, dat., ***nū̃***: of place, ***nū̃***, often loc. case, G. 9, 10, 77: of purpose, infin w. ***wāste, laī, nū̃***, up to, *see* up.

toast, n., ***tōs***, m. (slice whether toasted or not); v., ***tōs sēk-nā rōṭī sēknī***: foment or heat limb at fire, ***sēk karnā*** (***hatth nū̃, latt nū̃***, hand, leg): *see* warm.

tobacco, ***tamākū*** (***pīṇā, chikk-nā̃***).

to-day, ***ajj***: a week fr. t., *see* week: emphatic, *ajjo, ajjo ī, ajje ī*.

toe, ***ungal***, f.: big t., *angūṭh*, m., ***angūṭhā***, m.: little t., ***cīccī***, f.: fleshy part of t., ***pōttā***, m.: ball of toe, *see* tiptoe.

together, *katthe, ralke, nā̃lo nā̃l*.

toilsome, *taklīfwāḷā*, *see* difficult.

toll, *masūl*, m.: *see* tax.

tomato, *ṭamāṭar*, m.

tomb, *see* grave, shrine.

to-morrow, ***bhaḷke, kall***: *see* yesterday (last clause): day after t., *parsō̃*: day after that, *cauth*: fifth day, ***panj-auth***: sixth day, ***cheauth***: (*satauth, aṭhauth*, seventh, eighth day, are perhaps jocular); also ***panjwā̃ din***, etc.: t. week, *see* week.

tonga, *ṭā̃ngā*, m.

tongs, *uccā*, m., *cimṭā*, m.: *see* pincers.

tongue, *jībh*, f., *zabān*, f.: *see* language: t. of bell, *see* bell.

to-night, *ajj rātī̃, ajj rāt nū̃*, also last night.

(1) **too**, as in too much, etc., gen. omit, show by context, *bauhtā tattā*, too hot, etc.

(2) **too**, also, *wī, bī*, *see* moreover.

tool, *hathyār*, m.: pl., *racch kā̃ṇ*, m.: barber's t., *racch*, m.

tooth, *dand*, m.: double t., back t., *hanhū̃*, f.: show teeth (dog in anger, or derisively of person laughing), ***dand kaḍḍhṇe***: tooth in saw, *dandā*, m.: *see* dentist in A.

toothbrush, *dā̃ttan*, f.

toothed, *dandeā̃wāḷā*.

(1) **top**, of box, lid, *ḍhakkaṇ*, m.: of chest of drawers, bookcase, etc., *chatt*, m.: of page, *sirā*, m., *see* bottom, foot.

(2) **top**, plaything, *lāṭū*, m.: spin t., *lāṭū saṭṭṇā, wagāṇā* or *bhuā̃ṇā*; int. *wagṇā, bhaū̃ṇā*.

topsy turvy, *hēṭh utte* (one on top of other); *ugrā dugrā, agaṛ dugrā, wigḷeā shigḷeā*: *see* untidy, upside down.

torch, *mashāl*, f.: t.-bearer in marriage, *mashālcī*.

torment, *see* tease, annoy, torture.

tortoise, *kaccukummā*, m., *kha-cōprā*, m.

torture, *puls ohde nāḷ burī kītī*, (not used of woman); *mārnā*; *sakhtī karnī (nāḷ)*: see tie.

total, *jamhā*, f., *mizān*, f. (U.), *jōṛ*, m.

totter, *see* stagger.

touch, *hatth lānā, chohṇā*: feel, *toṇnā*: t. heart, *dil utte asar karnā*.

touching, *see* pathetic, sad, and add *afsōswāḷā, dil te asar karnwāḷā*.

touchstone, *ghaswaṭṭī*, f.

tough, no word; say *camm wāṅgar* or *lif jāndā e par uṅ ḍāhḍā e, pāṭdā nehī*.

tour, on duty, *daurā*, m. (*k.*): pleasure, *sail* or *sair*, m. (*k.*): very brief, *phērā*, m. (*mārnā*)

tow, *see* hemp.

towards, *de wall, de wallō* (only w. look, see, otherwise *wall*); *dī sedh, de pāse*.

towel, *tauliā*, m.; *nhauṇwāḷā tauliā, gusl dā tauliā*: t.-horse (or rail) *tauliā dī ghōṛī*.

tower, *burj*, m.: small, *burjī* f.

town, *shaihr*, m., *naggar*, m. (large village).

toy, *khaḍauṇā*, m.

trace, *patā*, m. (for verbs, *see* discover), *nishān (labbhṇā, dā)*; *sūh (kaḍḍhṇī, dī)*: *see* track, path.

track, of wheels, *gail*, f.: of feet, hoofs, etc., *khurā*, m.: v. tr., *khurā kaḍḍhṇā*, *see* path, trace.

tracker, *khōjī* (chiefly for cattle, horses, etc.).

trade, *tajārat*, f., *byopār*, m., *wanj byopār*, m., *sudāgrī*, f. (all w. *k.*): *see* profession, merchandise.

trader, *see* merchant.

tradition, gen., *rawait*, f.: *hadīs*, f. (M.): *waḍḍeā dī gall*.

traffic, *auṇā jāṇā*, m.: *rauṇak raihndī e*.

(1) train, v. tr., *see* teach: t. animals for ploughing, also metaph. boy for work, *hāḷī kaḍḍhṇā*, int. *nikḷnā*: for burden bearing, *lādū kaḍḍhṇā*, int. *nikḷnā*.

(2) train, n., *gaḍḍī*, f.: mail, t., *ḍāk gaḍḍī*; Bombay mail, *bambā mēl*, f.; Calcutta mail, *kalkattā mēl*, f.: passenger t., *suārī gaḍḍī, psanjar*, f.: local t., *lōkal*, f., *nōkal*, f.: goods t., *māl gaḍḍī*: the Lahore, Wazirabad, t. has come, gone, *Lahaur (Wazīrābād) āeā e, ṭur geā e*.

trait, *sift*, f.

traitor, no good word, *see* treacherous, treason.

trample, upon, *mindhṇā, mindhāṛnā, latāṛnā, utte ṭurnā, utte pair rakkhṇā*, *see* crush.

transaction, *kamm*, m., *laihṇ dēṇ, laiṇ dēṇ*, m.

transfer, *badlī karnī, hōṇī*.

transfigured, be, *sūrat badal jāṇī (dī)*.

transform, *sūrat, shakl badalnī (dī)*.

transient, *fānī, caūh dihāṛeā dā*, *see* shortlived.

translate, *tarjmā karnā* (*dā*, int. *h.*).

translation, *tarjmā*, m.: literal t., *lafzī tarjmā*.

translator, *tarjmā karnwālā, mutrajjam* (for *mutarjim*

transmigration, *awāgaū*, m., *āwāgauṇ*, m., *curāsī*, m. (all H.).

transport, *bārbardārī*, f. : man engaged in mule t., *khaccar-pātrī* : ser tence to transportation, *k e pānī dā hukm dēṇā* (*nū̃*) *āle pānī ghallṇā*.
trap, *kuṛikkī* f., *pinjrā*, m.
trash, *raddī cīz*, f. : *see* useless, worthless, nonsense.
travel, *safar karnā* ; for pleasure, *sail* or *sair karnā* : t. distance, *paiṇḍā mārnā* or *k.* (esp. walking) ; go a stage, *paṛā jāṇā* (but *paṛā karnā*, halt).
traveller, *rāhī*, *musāfar*.
traverse, *see* travel.
tray, *trēḷ*, f. (K.) : t.-cloth, *trēḷ dī cādar*.
treacher-ous, -y, no good word, *namak-harām*-(n., *-ī*, f.), *dil icc bāgī*, *beīmān*-(n., *-ī*, f.) : *see* treason.
treacle, *ṭrīkal*, m. (also golden syrup).
tread, *see* trample.
treason, use *bagāwat*, f., *bādshāh* or *sarkār dā badkhāh* : *see* treacherous.
treasure, *khazānā*, m.
treasury, *khuzānā*, m.
treasurer, *kh zāncī*, m.
treat, well, badly, kindly, *kise de nāḷ caṅgā*, *burā*, *mehrbānī dā salūk k.* : t. disease, sick person, *alāj karnā* (*dā*) ; be treated (sick person), *duāī karnī* (by, *dī*), *alāj karāṇā* (by, *kolõ*).
treatment, *see* treat.
treaty, *aihd*, m., *āpe icc likhke karār karnā*.
treble, *see* three.
tree, *rukkh*, m., *būṭā*, m., *darakht*, m. : bark, *chill*, f., *chillaṛ*, f. *raṅg*, m. : piece of bark, *sakk*, m., *sakṛā*, m. : family tree, *shajrā*, m.
tremble, *kambṇā*, *kambṇī lagg ṇī* (*nū̃*) : *kambṇī chiṛnī* (*nū̃*), begin trembling.
trial, leg., *mukadmā*, m. : each appearance, *pēshī*, f. : send up for t., *calān k.* (*dā*) : *see* test, try, examine.
triangular, *targuṭṭhā*, *tarnukrā*.
tribe, *kaum*, f.
tributary of river, *shākh*, f., *sūā*, m. : *see* canal.
trick, n., v. *pakhaṇḍ*, m. (*khēḍṇā*, *nāḷ*), *chaḷ*, m. (*khēḍṇā*, *nāḷ*) ; *dā*, m. (*lāṇā*, *nū̃*, int., *khāṇā*, *laggṇā*) ; *dā farēb karnā*, *nū̃*) ; *khuṭṭar*, m. (*k.*, *nāḷ*) ; *waḷ pēc*, m. (*k.*, *nāḷ*) ; *luṭṭ*, m., or *luṭṭ*, *khruṭṭ* (*k.*, *nāḷ*) ; *dhōkhā* m (*d.*, *nū̃*), (int., *khāṇā*) ; *hīlā*, m. (*k.*, *nāḷ*), *ḍhaṅg*, m. (*k.*, *nāḷ*).
trickle, *cōṇā* : n., *coā*, m. (*paiṇā*) : *see* drip, ooze.
tricky, *pakhaṇḍī*, *khuṭṭarī*, *ḍhaṅgī*.
trident, *tarsūl*, m.
trifle, n., *nikkī cīz*, f., *nikkī gall*, f. : v. small amount, *ruāḷ jehā* : he's only trifling w. you, *hujtā* or *jugtā* or *huṭṭar kardā e* : *see* waste.
trigger (also cock), *ghōṛā*, m.
trim, hair, *katrnā* : trees, plants, *chāṅgṇā*, *katrnā*.
Trinity, *Taslīs*, f.
trip, make stumble : v. tr., *ṭhuḍḍā lāṇā* (*nū̃*, also kick), int. *laggṇā* (*nū̃*).
triple, *see* three.
trivial, *see* trifling.
trolly, on railway, *ṭhēllā*, *ṭhelhā*, m., *ṭrāllī*, f.
trooper, *suār*.
trot, *duṛkī calṇā* or *ṭurnā* : tr *lāṇā*, *ṭōrnā*, *calāṇā*.
trouble, *taklīf*, f., *janjāḷ*, m., *kaziā*, m., take t., *taklīf k.*,

sir khapāṇā (mental): experience t. in getting something done, *khajjal h.*, *khajjal khuār h.*, *bhambaḷ bhūse khāṇe*: give t., *taklīf d.*: *see* inconvenience, difficulty, straits, annoy.
trough, same as manger.
trousers, Indian for men, *tambī*, f., *salwār*, f. (baggy), *sutthaṇ*, f. (baggy), *ghuṭannā*, m., *pajāmā*, m.: for women, *sutthaṇ*: English, *patlūn*, f.
trowel, *rambā*, m., *khurpā*, m.
true, *saccā*: t. to his word, *gall dā pakkā*, *see* promise, word: t. friend, *pakkā* or *saccā* or *dilī* or *jānī dōst*: t. Sahib, *pakkā Sāhb*: *see* real, truthful.
truly, *saccī muccī*.
trumpet, *turam*, m., *turī*, f., *bigal*, f., all *wajāṇā*, int. *wajjṇā*.
(1) trunk, of tree, *pōrī*, f.: of men, animals, *dhaṛ*, m.
(2) trunk, of elephant. *suṇḍ*, f.
(3) trunk, *see* box.
trust, n., *wasāh*, m., *bharosā*, m., *āsrā*, m.: in t., *amānat wicc*: v., t. to sthg., *ohdā mīn k.*: *see* faith, believe, confide, reliance, untrustworthy. [*see* worthy.
trustworthy, *ehtbārwāḷā*, *pakkā*,
truth, veracity, *sacāī*, f., *saccāī*, f.: reality, *hakīkat*, f.: *see* real, reality.
truthful, *saccā*, *see* true.
try, *koshish karnī*, *kōsht karnī*: t. hard, *see* effort, difficulty: t. one's best, *apṇe wallō ghaṭṭ nā karnī*.
tube, *naṛī*, f. (of reed): *phūknī*, f. (blowpipe); *naḷkā*, m.: bicycle t., *ṭūp*, f., *ṭyūb*, f.
tuft, of Hindu's hair, *bōddī*, f.: *see* crest.
Tuesday, *mangaḷ*, m., *mangaḷwār*, m.
(1) tumbler, acrobat, *naṭṭ*-, fem. -*ṇī*: *bāzīgar*-, fem. -*nī*.
(2) tumbler, glass, *gilās*, m.: *see* drinking-vessel.
tumour, *giḷṭī*, f.: *rasauḷī*, f.: *see* boil (1)
tumult, *see* disturbance, riot.
tune, air, *rāg*, m.: pitch, *sur*, f.: in t., *ṭhīk sur nāḷ*, *sur raḷāke*: out of t., *besur*, *besurā*, *sur nehī raḷdī*, *sur ṭhīk nehī*: being out of t., *besurī*, f.: tune, v. tr., *sur raḷāṇī*, *sur ṭhīk karnī*; *see* play, instrument. Note also *mērī ohde nāḷ sur nehī*, we are not friendly.
tunnel, *ṭanḍaḷ*, m., *surangh*, f.: for water, *saifal*, m.
turban, *pagg*, f., *pagṛī*, f., *sāfā*, m.: red or black, *cīrā*, m.: blue and white, *lunṅī*, f.: put on t., *bannhṇā*: take off, *lāhṇā*, *wadhāṇā*, G. 113.
turbulent, *fasādī*: *see* rebel, rebellion, riot.
turmeric, *hardaḷ*, f., *wasār*, f.
(1) turn, n., *wārī* f.: my t., *mērī wārī*: take one's t., in game, *wār laiṇī*: by turns, *wārī wārī*, *wāro waṭṭī*: t. in canal, road, *mōṛ*, m., *goshā*, m.: t. or twist in road, *waḷā*, m., *warāṅglā*, m. (all four *paiṇā*, tr. *pāṇā*).
(2) turn, v., *bhaūṇā*, G 64 (tr. *bhuāṇā*); *phirnā* (tr. *phirāṇā*, *phērnā*): tr. also *ghumāṇā*: t. in lathe, *see* lathe: t. cattle, horses, by heading them off, *waḷṇā*, *waḷke leauṇā*: t. wheel, esp. well, *gēṛnā* (int.

giṛnā, caus. *gaṛānā*); *see* spin: t. out., *see* expel and add *hikkṇā*, *see* excommunicate: t. out, prove, *nikḷṇā* (t. out thief, *cōr nikḷnā*): t. back, *muṛnā* (tr. *mōṛnā*), *see* return: t. over papers, etc., *phōlnā*: t. round (head), *see* dizzy: t. upside down, *see* upside down.

turnip, *gōṅglū*, m.

turnscrew, *pēckass*, m.

turquoise, *firōzā*, m.

turtle, *kaccūkumhā*, m., *khacoprā*, m.

twelve, *bārā*: twelfth, *bārhwā̃*, G. 19–24, 123.

twenty, *wīh*: twentieth, *wīhwā̃*, G. 19–24, 93, 123.

twice, *see* two.

twig, *see* branch.

twilight (morning), *mū̃h anhērā*, m., *muhānjlā*, m.: (evening) *hanēre paiē*.

twins, *jauṛe*, m. pl.: he is one of t., *jauṛeā̃ dā e*, *jauṛeā̃ wiccō e*, *jauṛeā̃ dā bhrā* or *puttar* (t. brother or son). A.

twine, v., *see* twist, cling: n., *see* string.

twinkle, *camaknā*.

twist, *marōṛnā*, *waṭṭnā* (t. round and round, esp. of rope, etc.).

two, *dō*, *see* second: t. and a half, *ḍhāī*: adj. fr. *ḍhāī* is *ḍhāyā*: G. 19–24: t.-fold, actual layers, *dohrā*, *see* fold: double, *see* double: twice, *dō werī*, *dō wārī*; twice as big as, *dūṇā*, *dō hisse waddh*, *see* time.

typewriter, *likkhaṇwāḷī mashīn*, f.

tyranny, *see* oppress.

tyrant, *see* cruel.

tyre (bicycle, etc.), *ṭair*, m.

U

udder, *hawānnā*, m.: *see* teat.

ugly, *kojhā*, *bhaiṛī sūrat wāḷā*: *see* awkward.

ulcer, *see* boil (1), eye-ulcer.

ultimate, *see* last (1).

ultimately, *see* finally.

umbrage, *see* offence.

umbrella, *chatrī*, f.: u.-cover, *uchāṛ*, m.: put up u., *lāṇī*: take down, *band-k*.

umpire, *tarfain*, m.: in game, *ampair*, m.: *see* mediator.

unadulterated, *see* adulterat-e, -ed, pure.

unanimous, use *sāreā̃ dī salāh* or *rā*: *itfāk nāḷ*, *mutfik hōke* (U.).

unanimity, *itfāk*, m. (U.).

unaspiring, *chote dil wāḷā*.

unaware, *bekhabar*, *patā nehī*: *see* ignorant.

unbeliever, *kāfar* (M.).

unblemished, *beaib*, *bedāg*: *see* defect, fault.

uncertain, *shakk e* (*wicc*), *pakkī khabar nehī*.

uncertainty, *kacc pakk*, m.

uncharitable, *badzan*.

uncivilised, *waihshī*, *jāṅglī*, *ḍhaggā jehā*.

uncle, father's elder brother, *bābbā*, *tāeā* (H.): father's younger do., *cāccā*: mother's brother, *māmmā*: father's sister's husband, *phupphaṛ*: mother's sister's do., *māssaṛ*: husband's or wife's uncle, *see* father.

unclean, *see* dirty: ceremonially, *palīt*, *napāk*, *mlēcch* (H.): morally, *napāk*, *palīt*: *see* pure, holy, clean.

uncleanness, *palītī*, f., *napākī*, f.

uncommon, *see* strange.
unconquerable, *jehṛā nā hāre.*
uncooked, *kaccā* : half-cooked, *daddrā* : *see* ripe.
uncover, any word for lid or covering with *lāhṇā* or *uttõ lāhṇā* : *naṅgā-k.*
uncultivated, *peī hoī zamīn,* [*raṛā,* m.
under, underneath, *see* below.
undergo, *see* suffer. [*bhohrā,* m.
underground room, cellar,
understand, *samjhṇā, samajh auṇī* (*nū̃*), M. 117. 4: be understood, of thing, *sujjhṇā* (*menū̃*, etc.); *palle paiṇā, piṛ palle paiṇā,* M. 129. 10: G. 112 (last two only in negative and interrogative sentences).
understanding, n., *samajh,* f., *thauh,* m. : *see* sense, wis-e, -dom, intelligen-ce, -t, clever.
undertake, *zimmā cukkṇā* (*dā*), *bīṛā cukkṇā* (*dā*), *zimmewār h.* (*dā*).
undo, sewing, *udhēṛnā* (int. *udhaṛnā*) : gen. *kholhṇā* : bed, machinery, *ukhēṛnā* (int. *ukkharnā*) : *see* destroy.
undress, *kapṛe lāhṇe, wadhāṇe* G. 113 : caus. *luhāṇe.*
undutiful, of children, *kuputtar* : servants, *see* lazy, unfaithful.
uneas-iness, -y, *see* restlessness.
uneducated, *anpaṛh.*
uneven, *see* rough, level, smooth.
unexampled, *es tarhā̃ dā hõr koī nehī̃, eñ kadī nehī̃ hoeā* : *see* unique.
unfaithful, gen. *bēwafā* : of subordinate, *namak-harām.*
unfavourable, opinion, report, *de khalāf, de barkhlāf, caṅgā* or *acchā nehī̃.*

unfit, ***laik nehī̃, dī laik dā nehī̃, nafiṭṭ*** : *see* able.
unfortunate, gen., ***wacārā*** (v. mild word): **unlucky,** ***badkismat, mandeā̃ bhāgā̃ wāḷā.***
unfortunately, ***afsos e pai, badkismatī nāḷ*** : the opposite is ***abihāre,*** luckily.
unfounded, ***ohdī bunyād*** or ***as līat koī nehī̃.***
unfruitful, trees, etc., *apphal* : morally, *apphal* : *see* barren.
unfurnished, *samān koī nehī̃, bussā* : *see* empty.
ungrateful, *nashukrā, kirtghan.*
ungrudgingly, *khushī nāḷ, khulhe dil nāḷ.*
unhappy, *see* sad.
unholy, *see* holy, unclean.
uniform, *wardī,* f.
uninhabited, of house, *khālī* : *see* unoccupied : of place, desolate, *suñā, bēabād.*
uninteresting, *suād koī nehī̃, besuādā* : *dilcasp nehī̃* (U.).
uninvited, *bin saddeā̃, saddeā̃ binā.*
unique, *bēnazīr* (U.), *lasānī* (U.) : *see* unexampled, matchless, peerless.
unjust, *bēinsāf, bēniā̃.*
unjustly, *nahakk, bēinsāfī nāḷ.*
unkind, *beraihm* ; *betars.*
unknowable *bandeā̃ dī samajh wicc nehī̃ aundā.*
unlawful, gen., *najaiz* : *harām,* forbidden by religion, gen. food (M.): illegal, *kanūn de khalāf.*
unlimited, *behadd* : *see* endless, innumerable.
unload, *bhār lāhṇā.*
unlock, *see* lock.
unluck-y, -ily, *see* unfortunate-, -ly.
unmarried, *kuārā,* fem. *kuārī* :

carā, carā chānd, carā murā (last three also "alone"), *see* alone.
unmentionable, *dassan de laik* (or *dī laik dā*) *nehī*, *jihde ākkhaṇ tõ sharm aundī e*, (*gall*) *karnwālī nehī*.
unmerciful-, -ly, *beraihmī nāḷ*, *betarsī nāḷ*: *see* unkind.
unmindful, *see* careless.
unnecessary, *lorīdā nehī*, *ohdī lōṛ nehī*, *zarūrī nehī*: (spare) *fāltū*, *wadhīk*, *wādhkū*.
unoccupied, house, *wehlā*, *khālī*: out of work, *wehlā*, *wāndā benaukar* (out of service).
unpleasant, of matter, word, etc., *mandī gall* (or *kauṛī*, *maṭṭhī*, *burī*)
unpopular, *oste koī khush nehī*, *sāre ohdī shikait karde ne*.
unravel, *see* solve, undo.
unreliable, *see* untrustworthy.
unripe, *kaccā*: half-ripe, *see* ripe. [obedient.
unruly, *sarkash* (U.): *see* dis-
unsafe, *see* danger-, -ous.
unseasonable, *see* untimely.
unstable, *see* shake, vacillate, wobble.
unsteady, *see* unstable.
untidy, *see* topsy turvy, and add *samān ēwē peā hoeā e*, *cīzā ēwē peīā hoīā ne*, *betartībī nāḷ*.
until, *see* till.
untimely, adv., *kuweḷe*, *bewakt*: n., *kuweḷā*, m., *kuwēḷ*, f.
untrustworthy, *beatbārā*, *wasāh de laik nehī*.
unused, leather, blank paper, water-pot, cloth (or unwashed), *korā*: *see* new.
unventilated, *wā dā koī rāh nehī*, *bārī nehī*, *see* ventilate.
unwilling-, -ly, *see* force, reluctant, sick of, oath.
up, *utte*, *utā*: up to, *tīkar*, *tāṇī*, *toṛī*, *tākar*, *sīdhā*, *tāī*: *see* upon. [proach.
upbraid, *see* reprimand, re-
uphold, *see* maintain, support.
upon, *utte*, *de utte*, *te*: upon arriving, *see* while.
uppermost, *utlā*.
upright, *see* perpendicular, stand, good, honest.
uproot, *ukhēṛnā* (int. *ukkhaṛnā*), *jaṛhõ puṭṭṇā*.
upset, *ḍēgṇā*, *garāṇā* (U.).
upside down, *mū̃hdā*, *puṭṭhā*: on one's face, *see* face: turn u., *mū̃hdā mārnā* or *k.*, *puṭṭhā k.*; of bricks, bread, *thullṇā*: *see* topsy turvy.
upwards, *see* up.
urge (warn against forgetting), *pakkī karnī* (*nū̃*), *jhī karnī* (*nū̃*): (emphasise) *gall utte zōr dēṇā*: (annoy) *tang-k*: (keep on) *khaihṛā nā chaḍḍṇā*, *picche paiṇā*: *see* excite, incite, emphasise.
urgent, *zarūrī*: of command, *takīdī*.
us, *sānū̃*: *see* we.
usage, *see* custom, treat.
use, v. tr., *wartṇā*, *istemāl-k*. (U.): u. unnecessarily, of big words, etc., *wāhṇā*, G. 121, M. 127. 34: have no u. for, *maī jarebā̃ kī karnīā̃ ne*, what use have I for socks? G. 118: be used of road, *wagṇā*: become used to, state of being used to, *see* accustom.
useful, *baṛe kamm dā e*, *baṛā kamm dendā e*: *waddhrīā̃ baṛe* or *baṛīā̃ kamm aundīā̃ ne*, thongs are v. useful.

useless, *kisc kamm dā nehī*, *raddī* : *see* worthless.
uselessly, *dhigāṇē*, *ēwē*.
usual, *see* custom, common, ordinary.
usually, *aksar*, *ām*, *bauht karke*.
usurp, *hakk mārnā* or *dabāṇā* or *laiṇā* or *dabbṇā* : *see* seize.
utmost, *jitthō toṛī hō sake*, *apṇe wallō ghaṭṭ nā karnī*.
utterly, *see* absolutely, altogether, thoroughly.

V

vacancy, *see* post.
vacant, *see* empty, unoccupied, uninhabited.
vacation, *see* leave.
vaccinate, *ṭīkā lāṇā*, int. *laggṇā*; caus. *luāṇā*, *ukhṇāṇā*. A.
vacillate, *galle galle phirnā*, *dalīlā badaldeā raihṇā*, *ḍōldeā raihṇā*, *ḍāwāḍōl*, *lāī lagg* (easily persuaded) : *etthe kujh te otthe kujh*, *see* back out, wobble, changeable, pliable.
vagabond, *awārā* (fem. the same), *see* nomad.
vain, *nazāktī*, *nakhreā wālā*, *baṛī mizāj wālā*, *baṛe damāg wālā* : *see* conceit, delica-cy, -te, air, proud : in v., *muft dā* (or *mukhat dā*), *ēwē*, *dhigāṇe*, *befaidā*.
valet, *baihrā*.
valid, *thīk*, *jāiz*, *kamm dā*, *aje caldā e*, still current, etc.
valley, *wādī*, f. : pass, *darā*, m.
valuable, *see* costly, good, excellent.
value, n., *see* cost : v., *mull ṭharhāṇā* (fix price), *kadr pāṇā* (*dā*) ; esteem, hold dear.
valueless, *see* useless, worthless.
vanish, *see* disappear.
vanquish, *see* conquer, defeat, win : in argument, *lājuāb-k*, *bōlaṇ jogā nā chaḍḍṇā*.
vapour, *see* steam.
variable, *see* vacillate, changeable.
variation, *wādhā ghāṭā*, m. : *see* change.
varicose vein, *see* vein.
variety, *kism*, f., *jins*, f. ; *see* various, change, variegated.
variegated (colours), *rang barangī*.
various, *kism kism dā*, *bauht kism dā*, *wakkho wakkh* : *see* variety, change, variegated.
varnish, n. and v., *rogan karnā* (*nū*).
veer, *see* vacillate, changeable.
vegetable, *salūṇā*, m., *sabzī*, f., *bhājī*, f., *sāg pattar*, m. (*tarkārī* means meat) : v.-bed, *see* flower-bed : v.-curry, *chichkī*, f. (K.).
vehemently, *zōr nāḷ*, *zore* : *see* force.
vehicle, *see* carriage, cart, train.
veil, *cādar*, f. : H. woman's, covering body, *addharwanjhā*, m., *sāṛhī*, f. : M. woman's, all over, *bhurkā*, *burkā*, m. : v. oneself, *ghuṇḍ kaḍḍhṇā* : draw v. over, *see* screen.
vein, *nāṛ*, f. (also sinew, artery) : varicose v., *phullī hoī nāṛ*.
velvet, *makhmal*, f.
venerate, *mannṇā* : *see* honour.
vengeance, *see* revenge.
venomous, *zaihrī*.
ventilate, *būhe bārīā lāhṇīā*, *wā nū andar auṇ dēṇā* : *s.* sultry.
venture, *himmat karnī*, *dalērī karnī*, *haūslā karnā* (all *dā*, *dī*).

venturesome, *dalēr, bekhauf.*
veracity, *see* truth.
verandah, *barāṇḍā*, m.: on the v., *barāṇḍe icc.*
verb, *fehl*, m.
verbal-, -ly, *zabānī*: hear v. from him, *ohdī zabānī suṇṇā*: G. 37.
verbatim, *lafaz lafaz.*
verdant, *see* green, verdure.
verdigris, *ullī*, f. (*laggṇī, nū̃*).
verdure, *hariaul*, f., *harā*, m., *sabzī*, f.
verge, *see* edge: on the v. of doing, *see* about, almost, nearly.
verif-y, -ication, *tasdīk karnī* (caus. *karāṇī, dī*).
vermicelli, *warmselī*, f.: native, *sēwīā̃* (*waṭṭṇīā̃*, make).
verse, of Bible or other sacred book *ait*, f.: *see* poem: of poetry, *wars*, m. (educ.).
very, *baṛā* (G. 34, never *waḍḍā*), *dāhḍā, bauht, bāhlā, cokhā, bauhtā, tagṛā, pujjke, parle darje dā, sagō*: also *wāhwā* (used of good things alone); *see* emphasis.
vessel, domestic, *bhāṇḍā*, m., *bartaṇ*, m.: *see* ship, boat.
vest (under-), *banyāṇ*, f., *baṇaiṇ*, f.: *see* waistcoat.
vestige, *see* trace.
veterinary, surgeon (native), *salōtrī.*
vex, *see* annoy, tease, angry, displeased.
viâ, *de rāh, hoke.*
viaduct, *pul*, m.
(1) **vice**, *burī ādat*, f.: *see* sin, evil, bad.
(2) **vice**, blacksmith's, *jamūr*, [m.
Viceroy, *mulkhī lāt* (also Lt.-Gov.). *waḍḍā lāt.* Lt.-Gov. is often *choṭā lāt.*
vicinity, *see* neighbourhood, near.
vicious, *see* bad, blackguard: of horse, *cak mārnwālā* (biter), *dulatte mārnwālā* (kicker).
victory, *jitt*, f., *fatāh*, f.
view, scene, *nazārā*, m.: *see* opinion.
vigil, *jagrātā* (*kaṭṭṇā, raihṇā*): *see* wake, sleeplessness.
vigilance, *hushyārī*, f., *khabardārī*, f: *see* care.
vigorous, *see* vigour.
vigour, *tākat*, f., *zōr*. m.: *see* power. strong.
vile, *makrūh*, *see* bad, unclean, dirty.
village, *piṇḍ*, m., *grā̃*, m.: large, *naggar*, m.
villager, *piṇḍ dā, pēṇḍū* (slightly contemptuous).
vindicate, *saccā sābit-k.*
vine, *dākh*, f., *angūr dī wēl* or *dā būṭā.*
vinegar, *sirkā*, m.
vineyard, *dākh dā bāg.*
violence, *see* oppression and add *dhakkeshāhī*, f.: by v. (physical or mental), *dhakke nāḷ, zore*: *see* confess, force.
violent, *see* violence, severe.
violet, flower, *binafshā*, m., *binashkā*, m.: colour, *kāshnī.*
virgin, *kuārī.*
virtue, *see* goodness.
virtuous, *nēk, pāk, bhalā lōk*: *see* good.
viscosity, *lēs*, f.
viscous, *lēslā.*
visible, to be, *dissṇā, nazrī paiṇā, labbhṇā, wakhāḷī dēṇī*: come into sight, *hun dissaṇ* (or other verb) *lagā* or *lagg peā*: cease to be v., *see* disappear and add *akkhīā̃ thī*

ohle hō jāṇā, nazrõ ghuss jāṇā, chaī maī hō jāṇā.
visit, *miḷn jāṇā* (*nū̃*), *mulākāt nū̃ jāṇā* (*dī*) : go away from home, *wāhṇḍā jāṇā* : v. holy place or person, *ohde dīdār* or *ohdī ziārat* (M.) or *ohde darshaṇ* (H.) *nū̃ jāṇā* : v. of inspection, often simply *phērā mārnā* : *see* inspect.
visitor, *mulākātī* : on a visit, *wāhṇḍā* : *see* guest.
vital, *nāzak thā̃* (v. place) : *see* important
viva voce, *zabānī, mū̃h zabānī, takrīrī* (U.).
vivid, of colour, *see* bright, colour.
vocabulary, *firist*, f., *see* dictionary.
voice, *awāz* or *wāz*, f. m. : *see* call, hoarse.
void, make, become, *see* abolish, cancel, repeal : fizzle out, *guggaḷ jāṇā, fisk hō jāṇā.*
volcano, *ātshī pahāṛ*, m., *agg wāḷā pahāṛ*, m.
volley, *wāṛ*, f. (firing).
volume, *jild*, f.
voluntarily, *apṇī marzī* or *khushī nāḷ, āpū, āpõ, āpī, āpē, khushī razāī* : *see* gladly.
volunteer, v., use words for voluntarily w. *jāṇā*, go, etc. : n., *wālanṭīr*.
vomit, *ulṭī auṇī* (*nū̃*), *uttõ suṭṭṇā, kai karnī* ; *jī uṭā auṇā*, feel inclined to v. (*dā*), G. 117, M. 117.7: v. up, *ugalṇā, uglācṇā* : vomiting and diarrhoea, *haizā*, m. (*h.*, *nū̃*).
vote, n. and v., *rā dēṇī, woṭ dēṇā.*
vow, n., *mant*, f., *nazr*, f. : make v., these words w. *mannṇī* : fulfil v., same w. *pūrī karnī, cāṛhnī.*
voyage, *samundar dā safar*, m.
vulgar, of person, *waihshī jehā, jaṭkā, kamīnā* : of word or thing, *ḍagg, jaṭkā, moṭā.*

W

waft, *udāke laijāṇā.*
wager, *see* bet.
wages, *tankhāh*, f. : of day labourer, *mazdūrī*, f. : each day's, *dihāṛī*, f.
wagon, *see* carriage, cart.
wail, *see* weep, mourn.
waist, *lakk*, m.
waistcoat, *phatūhī*, f., *salūkā*, m., *kuṛtī*, f., *wāskaṭ*, f.
wait, *uḍīknā, ṭhaihrnā, baihṇā* (sit), *khlōṇā* (stand) : w. for, *uḍīknā, uḍīk rakkhṇī* (*dī*), *rāh wekhṇā* (*dā*, look out for) : caus., *uḍīk karwāṇī*, or use *uḍīknā peā* : lie in w., *dhrumbhḷā hōke baihṇā* : w. at table, *khidmatgārī karnī* : *see* attend, serve : w. a bit, *khlō jā* : *see* waiting.
waiter, *khidmatgār*, m.
waiting for, n., *uḍīk*, f. : *see* wait.
wake, waken, v. int., *jāgṇā* : w. up, *nīndar uggharṇī* (*dī*), *jāg auṇī* (*nū̃*), *jāg uṭṭhṇā* : v. tr., *jagāṇā, uṭhāṇā* : to stay awake, *unīndrā raihṇā* (*nū̃*) : observe vigil, *see* vigil : to have just got up fr. sleep, *suttā peā uṭṭhṇā* : half-awake, *jāgo mīṭī, jāgo mīṭā, jāgo nūṭā.*
(1) **walk,** v., *ṭurnā* : *see* go : go for w., *wā bhakhṇī, sair* or *sail karnā, sail sapaṭṭe jāṇā* : walking, on foot, *ṭur-*

dā, *paidal*: to w. a horse, *kadmī lāṇā* or *tōrnā* (*nū*).
(2) walk, n., style or rate of walking, *tōr*, f.: garden-w., *rāk*, m., *paṭrī*, f.
walking-stick, *sōṭā*, f.: *see* stick.
wall, *kandh*, f.: *dūāl*, f.: roof-less, crumbling w., *khoḷā*, m.: w. of tent, *see* tent.
walnut, *khrōṭ*, m., *akhrōṭ*, m.: w. very thin shell, *kāgzī khrōṭ*.
wander, *bhaundeā raihṇā*, *awārā phirnā* (idle and useless, fem. *awārā*); *see* astray, stray: be knocked about, *see* knock.
wanderer, wandering, *see* nomad and add *pharautū*.
wane, *ghaṭṇā*: *see* lessen.
want, *see* desire, long for, lack: be wanting, *nā hōnā*: for w. of, *khuṇō*, sometimes *bājhō*, *see* without.
war, *laṛāī*, f. (also battle): *lām*, m., expedition, (occ. f., *laggṇā*): *jang*, m (U.); H. holy war, *judh*, m.; M., *jihād*, m.: civil w., use *āpe icc*, among themselves: go to the w., *lām icc jāṇā*.
wardrobe, *kapṛeā wāḷī almārī*, f.
warehouse, *gudām*, m., *māl gudām*, m.: *see* storeroom.
warm, *see* hot, tepid: w. oneself at fire, *agg sēkṇī*; in sun, *suyyā sēkṇā*, *dhupp sēkṇī*.
warn, *khabrdar-k.*: *see* tell, inform, caution.
(1) warp, v. int., of frame, bed, etc., *kāṇō pai jāṇī* (*nū*), *ḍingā h.*: tr. *ḍingā k.*: *see* twist, crooked, bend.
(2) warp, n., *see* loom.
warrant, for arrest, *waranṭ*, m. pl. (*kaḍḍhṇe*, *nikḷṇe*): authority, *see* authority: guarantee, *see* bail, responsible.
wart, kind of, *mohkā*, m.
wary, *hushyār*, *samajhdār*: *see* caution.
(1) wash, clothes, separate parts of body, things in gen., *dhōṇā* (int. *dhuppṇā*, *dhuccṇā*): *see* bathe: ceremonial, *see* ablution: *see* scrub, clean.
(2) washerman, *chīmbā*, *dhōbbā*, *dhōbbī*: fem. *chīmbī*, *dhōbbaṇ*.
(3) washing, single w., set of clothes for one w., *jugān*, f.
wasp, *dhamūṛī*, f.: long, thin, *ghurain*, f.: *see* hornet.
(1) waste, adj., gen., as w. paper, *raddī*; *see* useless, worthless: w. land, *ujāṛ*, m., *raṛā* (not used), *kallar*, *banjar* (both barren), *see* soil, barren, desert.
(2) waste, v., *see* squander, destroy, devastate, lose.
(1) watch, timepiece, *ghaṛī*, f.
(2) watch, v., *see* look, guard, wait, wake.
(3) watchful, *see* wary.
(4) watchmaker, *ghaṛīsāz*.
(5) watchman, *see* sentry, guardian; village w; *barwāḷā* (caste), *rabṭī* (lit. reporter), *caukīdār*.
(1) water, n., *pāṇī*, m.: in eyes, blister, etc., *pāṇī* (*paiṇā*): in food, *pāṇī*, *tarī*, f., *shōrā*, m. (soup), *lās*, m. (soup): *see* shove off.
(2) water, v. tr., land, *piāṇā* (int. *picṇā*), *chiṇṇā*: w. basket by hand, *jhaṭṭā jhaṭṭṇā* or *chiṇṇā* (the basket is *jhaṭṭā*, m.): *see* sprinkle; cattle,

larger animals, *pāṇī ḍāhṇā* (*nū*); human beings, smaller animals, *pāṇī piāṇā* or *dēṇā* (*nū*): also *pāṇī dassṇā* (animals); place for giving people water free as charity, *chabīl*, f. (*lāṇī*, int. *laggṇī*): land watered by rain (not irrigated), *barānī*; by well, *cāhī*; by canal, *naihrī*.

(3) water-carrier, M. *māshk-ī*, fem. *-aṇ*; caste, *mācch-ī*, fem. *-aṇ*: H. *jhiūr-*, fem. *-ī*.

(4) water-channel, -course, in fields, from canal, *khāḷ*, m. (*khāḷṇā*): v. small w., *āḍ*, f. (*kaḍḍhṇī*): drain, *see* drain.

(5) water-fowl, *see* dabchik, duck, etc., under heading "bird."

(6) watering-can, *phuhārā*, m.

(7) water-man, *see* water-carrier, sailor.

(8) water-melon, *see* melon.

(9) water-mill, *ghrāṭ*, m.: *see* mill.

(10) waterpot, *see* pot.

(11) waterproof (material), *barsātī*, f.: coat, *barsātī*, *brāṇḍī*, f.

(12) water-tax, *ābyānā*, m.

watery, gen. and food, *jihde wicc pāṇī baṛā e*: food, *patlā*: *see* damp, moisture, wet.

(1) wave, n., *ṭhallh*, f., *ṭhāṭh*, f.: v. small, *laihr*, f.

(2) wave, v. tr., *halāṇā*.

waver, *see* hesitate.

(1) wax, n., *mōm*, m.: sealing-w., *lākh*, f.: in ears, *kannā dī maiḷ*, f.

(2) wax-candle, *see* candle.

(3) wax-cloth, *mōmjāmā*, m.

way, actual and metaph., *rāh*, m.; *see* path, road: manner, *see* manner, method: half way, *adhwāṭe*: show the w., *see* guide: off the w., lose w., *see* astray, stray: by w. of the door, window, *būhe rāh*, *bārī rāh*; by w. of the house, well, *ghar*, *khūh de uttō dī*.

wayfarer, *rāhī*.

waylay, *see* wait, lie in.

we, *asī*: people like us, *hamātaṛ*, G. 28.

weak, gen. *māṛā*; *kamzōr*: of people, animals, *māṛā*, *lissā*: w. in character, *kaccā*, *gallā dā kaccā*, *see* vacillate: w. tea, *patlī*: heart become w or faint, *dil ḍubṇā* or *chapṇā* or *ghaṭṇā*.

weaken, words for weak w. *karnā*.

weal, on body, *laūs* or *lās* (*paiṇī*).

wealth, *daulat*, f., *māl*, m., *hasīat*, f., *dhan*, m.

wealthy, *see* rich.

wean, child, *duddh chuḍāṇā* (*dā*): from habit, fault, *chuḍāṇā*.

weapon, *hathyār*, m.

(1) wear: put on, *pāṇā*, *lāṇā*: he wears a waistcoat (is in the habit of putting on), *phatūhī pāndā hondā e*: is wearing trousers, has put on, *tambī pāī hoī e*; or *pāke lagā jāndā e*, etc.: put on, bed-clothes, shawl, etc., *utte laiṇā*: v. int., wear (well or badly), *haṇḍhṇā*: tr. *haṇḍhāṇā*, wear out or for certain time (only of things that one wears): *see* wear out.

(2) wear away, *see* rub.

(3) wear out, int., *haṇḍh jāṇā*, tr., *haṇḍhāṇā*, *haṇḍhā chaḍḍṇā*: (n., *haṇḍhepā*, m.), of non-wearable things, *purāṇā*

hōjāṇā: wear out a person w. words, *sir khapāṇā* (*dā*), *kann khāṇe* (*de*); int. *sir khappṇā* (*dā*): *see* tire, weary.

wearisome, *thakāṇwāḷā*, *akāṇwāḷā*, *see* weary, tire, sick of.

weary, *thakkā hoeā*: *see* tire, sick of.

weather, no word, *see* climate, season, spring, summer, autumn, winter, rain: fine w., *kharā*, after rain, *wānd laggṇī*, *nimbal h.*, *kharā ho jāṇā*, *farakkā laggṇā*.

weave, *uṇṇā*, *khaḍḍī uṇṇī*: *see* loom.

weaver, *julāh-*, fem.-*ī*.

web, cobweb, *jāḷā*, m.

wed, wedding, *see* marriage, marry.

wedge, *phāṇṇā*, m., *cappar*, f.

Wednesday, *buddh*, m., *buddhwār*, m.

weed, v. tr., *gōḍḍī karnī*, *gōḍṇā*: n., *būṭī*, f., *jāṅgḷī būṭī*. Names of common weeds:—
(i) occasionally eaten: *bughāṭ*, m., *jaũsāg*, m., *maiṇā*, m., *maiṇī*, f., *mrikkaṇ*, f., *papoḷī*, f., *saũcaḷ* f.
(ii) not eaten: *āthū bāthū*, m., *billī būṭī*. f., *dodhak*, f., *katittaṇ*, f. (dock-leaf), *lēlhī* f., *madhrāṇī*, f, *naṛī dodhak*, f.

week, *haftā*, m., *aṭṭh din*, m. pl., *aṭhwārā*, m (rare): next w., *agle hafte*: last w, *pishle hafte*: this day next or last w, *ajj dā dihāṛā*, *ajōkā dihāṛā*: tomorrow w., *bhaḷak de dīhāṛe*. A.

weekly, adv. *aṭṭhwē de aṭṭhwē dihāṛe* or *din*, *aṭṭhī dinī*, *aṭṭhī dī aṭṭhī dinī*: adj., use adv., also *haftewār* (U.).

weep, *rōṇā*, *aṭṭhrū wagāṇīā*, *karlāṇā* (gen. aloud): slightly, *aṭṭhrū wagṇīā* (*dīā*): sadness, almost crying, *gacc* (*auṇā*, *nū*): w. for person or thing, *rōṇā* (*nū*).

(1) weigh, *tōlṇā* (int. *tulṇā*): estimate weight by lifting, *hāṛnā*, *jācṇā*: w. anchor, *cukkṇā*: metaph., *see* consider, think.

(2) weighing-machine, at railway station, *kaṇḍā*: *see* scales.

weight, *bhār*, m., *wazn*, m.: weight too much forward, *dābū*, m.: too much back, *ulār*, m.: weight for scales, *waṭṭā*, m.; two-ser w., *duserī*, f., *waṭṭī*, f.: weights and measures, *see* A.

welcome, v., *wēkhke khush h.*, *mhabbat* or *khushī nāḷ milṇā* (*nū*): welcome! *jī āeā nū*, *see* means, gladly, willingly.

welfare, *khair*, f., *khairīat*, f., *sukkh sāṇd*, m. (ask after, *pucchṇ-ā*, -*ī*): *see* health, healthy, well (2).

(1) well, n., for irrigation, *khūh*, m.: for drawing water, no Persian wheel, *khūhī*, f.: deserted w, *ḍall*, f.: w. steps down, *baolī*, f.: the chief parts of a w. are vertical cogged wheel, *ḍhōl*, m.: horizontal do., *carhakḷī*, f., *cuhakḷī*, f: wheel w. pots, *baiṛ*, m.: pole through last two, *laṭṭh*, f.: earthen wall, *cannā*, m.: pole across above, *kāṇan*, f.: rope for pots, *māhl*, f.: pot, *ṭinḍ*, f.: ox-walk, *padāṇā*, *purāṇā*, m.: hand-pulley, *carakhṛī*, f.: work w. *wāhṇā* (int.

wagnā): turn by hand, *gēṛnā* (int. *giṛnā*).

(2) well, adv., *caṅgī* or *acchī* or *wall tarhā̃ nāḷ*: adj., in good health, *wall*, *caṅgā bhalā*, *rāzī*, *caṅgā*: *see* welfare, health, healthy: all's well, *khair e*, *khair mehr e*: all being well, e.g. where are you going, all being (I hope) well? *kitthe khair nāḷ* or *khairī mehrī* (H. *sukkh nāḷ*) *caleā ẽ*? Well done! *see* bravo: v. well, all right, *halā*, *caṅgā*, *acchā*.

(3) well, particle of reasoning, *khair*, *whalā*.

well-bred, *see* courteous, polite.

well-dressed, use *acche kapṛe*, m. pl.: *see* fop.

well-known, *mashāhūr*: *see* common, famous.

well-meaning, *nēknīyyat*.

well-wisher, *khairkhāh*.

west, *laihndā*, *laihndā pāsā*: westwards, *laihnde*, *laihnde wall* or *pāse*.

wet, adj., *wattreā hoeā*, *see* damp, moisture: v. tr., *bheōṇā* (int. *bhijjṇā*).

wet nurse, no word, use *duddh piāṇwāḷī*, etc.: occ *dāī*.

wharf, *ghāt*, m.: *bandargāh*, f. (harbour).

what, *kī*: (obl. *kāh*, *kās*): what if (depreciatory), lest, *mate*, *cētā*, *par je*: but what, *kī par*: what else (often means why not), *te hōr*.

whatever, *jō kujjh*.

wheat, *kaṇak*, f.: different kinds, *dāgar* f., *nikkī kaṇak*, f., *waḍāṇāk*, f., *kaṇkū*, m.: *see* grain.

wheedle, *dhokhā dēke manāṇā*, *gallā̃ icc phasāke manāṇī* *see* coax.

wheel, *piñ*, m., *pahīā*, m., *cal* *kā*, m.: Persian w., *see* wel w.-barrow, *reṛhī*, f.

when, *jad*, *jadō̃*, *jis wele*, *j* *ghaṛī*: inter. *kadō̃*, *kad*.

whence, inter. *kitthō̃*: rel. *jitth*

whenever, *jad kadī*, *bhāwē̃ kad*

where, inter. *kitthe*: motion to *kitthe*, *kittal*, *kiddhar*: re *jitthe*, *ji'tal*, *jiddhar*.

wherever, *jitthe kite*, *bhāw* *jitthe*.

whet, whetstone, *see* sharpen, grindstone: metaph., *wadhāṇā*.

whether, conj., *pai*: w. . . . or, *bhāwē̃* . . . *bhāwē̃*, *cāhe* . . . *cāhe*.

which? *kehṛā*? which, *jehṛā*.

while; repetition of infl. pres. part.: w. walking, *ṭurdeā̃ ṭurdeā̃*. G. 80: w. going, returning, *jāndī wārī*, *partdī wārī*, M. 239. 22; 268. 17: while or upon; upon arrival, *appaṛdeā̃ sār*, G. 91, *appaṛdeā̃ ī*, M. 273. 40, 41 (and so w. other verbs): cf. *lō laggdeā̃*, while it was getting light; *lo hondeā̃*, while it was light: *see* when.

whimper, *ū̃ ū̃ karnī*, *see* groan.

whine, *see* whimper.

whip, lash, *trāṭṭ*, m., *chāṭ*, m.: wooden part, *parāṇī*, f.: English w., *cābak*, m.: v. tr., these words w. *mārnā*, *nū̃*: *see* bea flog, strike: w. cream, beat eggs, etc., *phēṇṭnā*.

whirlpool, *cakkī* f., *ghummaṇghēr*, m.

whirlwind, *wā warōḷā*, m.

whisper, no real word: *kann*

icc ākhṇā: **koī kuskeā wī nehī**, no one even whispered.
whistle, *sīṭī* (*mārnī*). both the sound and the instrument.
white, *ciṭṭā*, *baggā*, *safēd*: whitish, *see* somewhat: w. of egg, *safēdī*, f.: w. hair, *see* hair: w. and black, *see* A.
whitewash, *safēdī*, f. (*karnī*): brush for w.-ing, *kūcī*, f. (*phērnī*).
whither, *see* where.
whitlow, *phimmhṇī*, f.: *see* boil (1).
who, *kauṇ*, obl. *kih-*, *kis-*.
whoever, *jehṛā koī*, *jō koī*.
whole, unbroken, *sābat*, *sābat sabūt*: all, *see* all, complete.
wholesale (sell), *katthā* (*wēcṇā*); *thōk* (U., *wēcṇā*): retail, *parcūṇ* (*wēcnā*).
wholesome, *see* good, advantageous, profit.
wholly, *bilkul*, *see* altogether.
whooping-cough, *kāḷī khangh*, f. (*h*, *nū̃*).
why, *kāhnū̃*, *kāhde jogā*, *kāhde laī*, *kāhde wāste*, *kyū̃*, *kis karke*, *kehṛī galle*.
wick, *battī*, f. (also lamp)
wicked, *see* bad, blackguard, sinner, and add *ucakkā* (especially robber).
wickedness, *see* badness, evil, sin, and add *sharārat*, f.
wide, *cauṛā*, *caiṛā*, *mōklā*.
widow, *ranḍī*, *bewā* (villagers use former).
widower, *ranḍā*.
width. *cuṛāī*, f., *pēṭ*, m.: of cloth, *bar*, m.
wife, *wauhṭī*, *suāṇī*, *ṭabbar*, m., (*mēre*, etc. *gharō̃*); *zanānī*, *bīwī* (w. educated people first three uncommon); sometimes *wāif*, wife: wife, *saukaṇ*. Note that *ṭabbar* (lit. family) is masc.
wild, *waihshī*, *jāṅglī*: of plants, animals, *jāṅglī*.
wilderness, *see* desert (1), wood, forest.
wilful-, -ness, *see* obstina-te, [-cy.
will, n. (written), *wasīatnāmā*, m.: *see* bequeath, inheritance.
willing, *rāzī*, *mannaṇwāḷā*.
willingly, *khushī nāḷ*, *see* voluntarily: by all means, *see* means.
willingness, *razā*, f., *khushī*, f.: *see* pleasure.
win, *jittṇā*: game, *see* game.
wince, *see* flinch.
(1) **wind**, *wā*, f., *hawā*, f.: east w., *purā*, m., west, *pacchō̃*, f.: hot summer w., *lō*, f.: blow, of w., *wagṇā*: in the w., open air, *waule*: absence of w., *see* sultriness: strong w., *see* storm; contrary w., *wā sāhmṇī e*: favouring w., *wā picche we*.
(2) **wind**, watch, clock, v. tr., *cābī* or *kunjī dēṇī* (*nū̃*): twist, *see* twist.
winding-sheet, *khapphaṇ*, m.
window, *bārī*, f.: through the w., *bārī rāh*: *see* open, shut.
wine, *sharāb*, m., *dārū*, m. (both any wine or spirit, latter also medicine), *nashā*, m. (any intoxicant).
wing, *par*, m.
winged, *parā̃wāḷā*.
wink, *akkh mārnī*.
winnow, in open fields, *uḍāṇā*: with basket in hand, *chaṭṭṇā*: winnowing, *uḍāīā*, f. pl.: winnowing basket, *chajj*, m.: *see* sift.

wipe, *pūnjhṇā*.

wire, *tār*, f.: wire-gauze or netting, *jāḷī*, f.

wisdom, *danāī*, f., *akl*, f. m., *siāṇap*, f.: *see* sense, intelligen-ce, -t, understanding, philosophy.

wise, *danā*, *aklwāḷā*, *siāṇā*: *see* wisdom, clever.

wish, *see* desire.

wits, *see* wisdom, sense.

witch, *cuṛel*, *ḍaiṇ*, *jādūgarnī*.

with, along with, *nāḷ*, *sane sang*, *see* together: instrument, *nāḷ*; for parts of body existing in pairs, loc. plur., as *akkhī*, *kannī*.

wither, plants, etc., *kurmāṇā*, *kumlāṇā*.

within, *see* in.

without, *bin*, *binā*, *de binā*, *tō binā*, *bājhō de bājhō*, *bagair*, *de bagair*, *khuṇō*: do without, *see* do.

witness, person, *guāh*, *see* eye-witness: from hearsay, use *suṇī suṇāī gall*: evidence, *see* evidence.

wizard, *see* magician.

wobble, *ḍōlṇā* (tr. *ḍulāṇā*): *see* vacillate, changeable, back out, shake.

wolf, *bhageāṛ*-, fem. -*ī*.

woman, *zanānī*, *janānī*, *buḍḍhī* (married, of any age), *aurat*: "womankind," *khodāmhain*, m. (slightly jocular): my good woman, *whaī*, M. 130. 32: G. 125: adj. *zanānā*, as *zanānī gaḍḍī*, carriage for women only: *zanānā kamm*, women's work.

womanish, *zanānī tabīat dā*.

womb, *kukkh* f., *dharn*, f., *rehm*, m. (U., all uncommon). *ḍhiḍḍh*, m., *peṭ*, m., both meaning stomach, may be used.

wonder, feeling of, *see* astonish-, -ment: wonderful thing, *tajjab dī gall*, *harānī dī gall*: I w. if he'll come, *patā nehī khabre āwe ke nā*, *wēkhīye āwe ke nā*.

wonderful, *ajaib*, *acarj*, *anōkhā*: *see* strange.

wood, gen., *lakkaṛ*, f, *lakṛī*, f., *kāṭh*, m.: firewood, *bāllaṇ*, m.: heap of for sale, *ṭāl*, m.: piece of split firewood, *phāṅg*, f. (*k.*), cut across, *mochā*, m. (*pāṇā*); any piece, *ṭōṭṭā*, m.: *see* log, beam: saw w., *cīrnā*, *see* chop: lot of trees, *see* forest, copse: forest of dhak trees, *ḍhakkī*, f., *see* dhak: wood and grass land near river, *bēllā*, m.

wood-boring insect, *ghuṇ*, m.

wooded, use *baṛe rukkh ne*.

wooden, *lakkaṛ dā*, *kāṭh dā*.

woof, *see* loom.

wool, *unn*, f.: soft hair or fur, *jatt*, f.: silky w., *pashmīnā*, m.

(1) woolly, *unn dā*: *pashmīne dā*, of silky wool.

(2) woolly insect, destroys clothes, *lehā*, m.

word, single word *lafaz*, m., *lafs*, m.: phrase, matter, thing, speech, *gall*, f.: one's w., promise, *see* promise and add *kalām*, f. m., *kaul karār*, m.: Word of God, *Khudā dī Kalām*: w. by w., *see* verbatim, literal: a few words, written, *dō cār harf*: of conversation, *see* converse.

(1) work, n. *kamm*, m., *kamm dhandā*, m. *kamm kāj*, m.: literary w., use *kitāb*, f.,

book; *rasālā*, m., pamphlet, etc.: work involved in message, *see* message: w. turn up to be done, *kamm paiṇā* (*nū*), M. 125. 6: G. 120: w. go on, *calṇā, ṭurnā* (tr. *calāṇā, ṭōrnā*) M. 126. 29: out of w., *see* unoccupied: leave off w., *see* leave: permanent w., *see* permanent in A.

(2) work, v., *kamm karnā, kamm kāj, kamm dhandā karnā*: literary, *likhṇā*: finish work badly, w. carelessly, *traṅgaṛnā*: he has begun working, is at work, *oh kamm lagg peā e*: work out at per rupee, maund, etc., *baihṇā*, M. 117. 12, 14: G. 117: work, be working, of machine, etc., *calṇā, ṭurnā*; of well, *wagṇā*.

workman, skilled, mason, builder, etc., *rāj*: unskilled, *kulī, mazdūr*: paid by day, *dihāṛīdār*: *see* labourer, servant, clever.

workmanship, *kamm*, m., *kārīgarī*, f., *banāwat*, f.

workshop, *kārkhāṇā*, m.

world, earth and people, *dunyā*, f., *jahān*, m.: H. sometimes *jagat*, m., *jagg*, m.: the earth, *dunyā*, f., *zamīn*, f., H. *dhartī*, f.: the next w., *aglā jahān, parlōk*, m. (H.): *aglā jagg* (H.): *see* heaven.

worldly, *dunyāwī, dunyā dā*.

worm, *kīṛā*, m.: blindworm, slow-worm, *dumūhī*, f.: *see* ant, snake.

worry, worried *see* annoy, angry, bore, displease, tease, trouble, inconvenience, difficulty, straits.

worship, Christian, *bandgī karnī, duā bandgī karnī, girjā karnā, duā namāz karnī* (of officiating person, *karāṇī, karāṇā*), occ. *namāz paṛhnī*: H. and M., *see* pray: *pūjā karnī* (*dī*), w. idols.

worshipper, use words for worship w. ending *-wālā*, or paraphrase: *pujār-ī*, fem. *-an*, worshipper of idols.

worth, *see* value, cost.

worthless, *see* useless and add (things) *bakār, bakārā, nikammā, kujjh nehī*: matter, words, *see* nonsense: persons, *raddī, kucajjā* or *becajjā* (doing things badly), *nighreā hoeā, nāmurād, bēhadzitā* (rather strong word): *see* bad, etc.

worthy, man, *bhalāmāṇas*, fem. *bhalīmāṇas*, *see* deserve, right.

would that, use *Khudā kare pai*; *kadī kare* (*kare ā, kardā*) *kehī sohṇī gall howe* (*howe ā, hondī*), what a good thing, if he does it, did it or were to do it: M. 270. 36, 37.

wound, *phaṭṭ*, m., *zakhm*, m.: blow, *saṭṭ*, f: v. tr. use beat, strike, etc.. *ohde lāṇ* or *mārn nāḷ phaṭṭeā geā* or *zakhm hoea*: be w., *phaṭṭeā jāṇā, zakhm h.* (*nū*), w. the feelings, *dil dukhāṇā*: *see* grieve.

wrap, *walhēṭṇā*: *see* fold.

wrath, *see* anger.

wreak, *see* revenge.

wreck, of ship, *ṭuṭṭṇā, ṭakkar wajjī te ṭuṭṭ geā*: *see* ruin, destroy, downfall.

wrestle, *ghulṇā*: wrestling match, *ghōḷ*, m.

wrestler, *ghulāṭīā, palwhāṇ*.

wretch, *kambakht*: *see* bad, wicked.

wretched, *see* poor, straits.
wring, out water, etc., *nacoṛnā*: twist round, *maroṛnā*: *see* squeeze.
wrinkle, in face, *jhurṛī* (*paiṇī*); gen. plur.: *see* crease, fold, frown.
wrist, *guṭṭ*, m.: w. and forearm, *wiṇī*, f.
writ, *samman*, m.
(1) **write**, *likhṇā*: enter in book, *likhṇā*, *darj-k.*: *see* caligraph-y, -ist, copyist.
(2) **writer**, *see* author, clerk, copyist: petition-writer, *arzī nawīs*: appeal-w., *apīl nawīs*.
(3) **writing**, handwriting, *khatt*, m.: act or price of w., *lakhāī*, f.
wrong, adj., *galt*: *see* bad.
v., *hakk mārnā* (*dā*), *see* damage. [loss.
n., *see* damage, injure,
wrongfully, *nahakk*, *dhigāṇe*, *befaidā*, *ẽwẽ*.

Y

(1) **yard**, length, *gaz*, m.: *see* wts. and meas. A: a yard measure, *gaz*, m.
(2) **yard**, *see* courtyard.
yawn, *ubāsī laiṇī*, M. 122. 35 *ubāsī auṇī* (*nū̃*), M. 117. 5.
year, *warhā*, m., *sāl*, m.: of era, *san* m.: every y., *sāl de sāl*, *warhe de warhe*, *warhe dinī* (G. 78), *har sāl*: in a y., *warhe dinī*, *warhe nū̃*, *sāl nū̃*, *warhe din icc*: next y., *aunde sāl*: last year, *par*, *parū̃*, *par de sāl*, *parōke sāl*: y. before last, *parār*.
yearly, *sālānnā*, adj., *see* year.
yearn, *see* long (2).
yell, *see* scream, shout.
yellow, *pīlā*: pale y., *khaṭṭā*: dark, *see* orange: of egg, *see* yolk: yellowish, *see* somewhat.
yes, answering question, *āho*, *ākho*, *āh*, *hā̃*: answering call, *hā̃*: G. 93, 94.
yesterday, *kall* (never *bhalke*): day before y., *parsõ*: day before that, *cauth*: fifth day, *panjauth*: sixth, *chcauth*: seventh, eighth *see* week, tomorrow: *satwẽ*, *atthwẽ dihāṛe* or *din*, etc., are also used.
yet, *see* still (1), besides.
yield, *see* give in, surrender: owing to threat, *dabb jāṇā*: n., *see* produce.
yoke, n., *panjāḷī*, f.: v., *jōṇā*, *jōtṇā* (int. *juppṇā*, *juttṇā*), *haḷ jōṇā* (for ploughing).
yolk, of egg, *zardī*, f.
you, *tū̃*, *tusī*: acc. *tenū̃*, *tuhānū̃*: your, *terā*, *tuhāḍḍā*: for acc., and your, also pronom. suff. (sing.), *-ū̃*, *-ī*, *-ā*, *-ī*: (plur.), *je*: G. 82–6.
young, *thoṛī umr dā*, *nikkā*, *chōṭā*: the y. of anything, *baccā*, m.: *see* child: y. man, *gabhrū*, *juān*: y. woman, *muṭeār*, *juān aurat*.
youth, state of, *juānī*, f.

Z

zeal, *sargarmī*, f., *jōsh*, m.
zealous, *sargarm*, *joshwāḷā*.
zero, figure, *sifar*, m.
zest, *shauk*, m. (desire, keenness,): *suād*, m., *mazā*, m. (both taste): *see* taste.
zinc, *jist*, m.
zoological gardens, *ciṛīā ghar*, m.

APPENDIX I.

ADDITIONS TO PANJABI MANUAL: Second Part, Grammar.

GENDER.

p. 1. To words both masculine and feminine add the following:—

lām, expedition, war.
kadr, value.
kiās, opinion.
manshā, intention.
taih. fold.
Panjāb, the Panjab.

awāz, *wāz*, voice, sound is fem. except in the expression *wāz bhārā hōṇā (dā)*, become hoarse.

Note.—*sarkār*, meaning either the Government or "your honour." is always fem. sing.; *hazūr*. your honour, is generally masc. plur., but villagers sometimes make it fem. sing; *ādmī*, occasionally used for wife, woman, and *waihtar*, beast of burden, are masc.; *mukāṇ*, mourners or mourning, is fem.

p. 2, paragraph (3). Gender different from Urdu: omit *magz*, which is masc. and means intelligence: add

sharāb, m., wine, spirit.
fasl, m., harvest.
Urdū, m., Urdu.
gār, f., cave.
jang, m., war.
lām, gen. m., war, expedition.
gūnd, f., gum.
takrār, m., fuss, quarrel.

p. 10, paragraph (4). Add *fajrī* or *fajrī*, in the morning: *ḍīgarī* or *ḍīgarī*, in the afternoon.

After the word *Bāgrīē* read "and adjectives in agreement, which would have ended in -ī, also change to -īē." For *cāḷīē*, *cāḷī*, read *cāhḷīē*, *cāhḷī*.

p 11, paragraph (2). Vocative: instead of the first four lines read "A feminine in the sing. generally makes the vocative by adding -e."

p. 15. Doublets. Many other examples will be found in the vocabulary.

p. 16. The genitive prep. *dā* always has *dī* for the loc. plur. See p. 9 of Grammar.

sabbh: one sometimes hears *hamhnū acchā* for *sabbhnā tō acchā*, *habbhe weḷe* for *sabbhe weḷe*, and *samhnā*, *samhnī*, for *sabbhnā*, *sabbhnī*.

p. 22. Ordinals, see also note on p. 123. The tonic h is omitted in 60, 80 and by some people in 79, 81–8.

p. 27, line 19 read:—*hōr*, other, has *horī* or *hōr* in the sing. oblique.

p. 34. *baṛā* and *waḍḍā*. *waḍḍā* means big in size, great in age or dignity.

VERBS.

p. 43. Add (see also causal verbs near end of App. I.).

udhaṛnā, be ripped (sewing, etc.), *udhēṛnā*, rip.

ukkhaṛnā, get loose, come to pieces, of machinery, masonry,	*ukhēṛnā*, loosen, etc.
uggharnā, be collected, of money,	*ugrāhṇā*, collect.
wagṇā, *wagṇā*, flow,	*wagāṇā*, cause to flow, etc.
wagṇā, *wagṇā*, be ploughed, be worked, of well or cattle,	*wāhṇā*, plough, etc.

With *bajjhṇā*, be fastened, imprisoned, *bannhṇā*, tie, cf. *wajjṇā*, be struck, etc., *wajāṇā*, strike, etc.

Infinitive: after *l*, *lh*, the ending is *-ṇā* if the accent is on the last syllable of the root, otherwise it is *-nā*, as

kholhṇā, open: *ḍōlṇā*, wobble, shake: *ḍulhṇā*, be spilt, but *badalnā* change.

p. 48. Add *rōṇā*, weep, pa. p. *runnā*, *roeā*.

dhōṇā, wash, pa. p. *dhōttā*.

With *gunnhṇā*, knead, pa. p. *guddhā*, compare *gundṇā*, plait, pa. p. *gundeā*.

p. 50. Imperative, plur. also *takkeā je*. This form *must* have *je*.

p. 52, line 2. *kardīē* or *kardī*.

line 6, *kardīo* is correct; omit note on p. 126.

p. 59, line 8: passive part. *dasseā hoeā*, or in Siāḷkōṭ and Jammū *dasseādā*, see p. 49, lines 6–9.

p. 62, last line but two. *tū dassdī* or *dassdīē*.

„ last line but one. *dassdīo* is correct; omit note on p. 126.

p. 65, (1). Emphasis or thoroughness: add "or completeness.

Habit.

p. 69 first line. After (i), add ***karnā*** :

,, under (ii) read :—***hōṇā***, tenses formed from the present part. ; both verbs in the same tense, the verb substantive (auxiliary verb) when it occurs, inserted only once.

To the examples add—

maĩ wehnnā honnā wā, I am in the habit of looking.

Note.—The idea of habit may be expressed also by means of *gijjhṇā* or *hiḷṇā*, to get accustomed :

oh iṭṭā̃ ḍhōṇ gijjhī hoeā e or *hiḷeā hoeā e*, he is accustomed to carrying bricks, he has got used to it, is in the habit of doing it.

jāṇā, go.

p. 70. Paragraphs (2) and (3) may perhaps be better expressed thus :—(2) when *jāṇā* is used with the root of intransitive verbs to express completeness it does not add the idea of "going," but the idea may be inherent in the root itself.

Exception : *uṭṭh jāṇā*, go away, move to another house or city.

(3) With transitive verbs *jāṇā* adds the idea of "going."

Exceptions : *samajh jāṇā*, understand : *pī jāṇā*, drink up or drink and go.

The Repetition of Words, p. 71.

Another meaning expressed by repetition is that of the English word "nice" in phrases like "nice and fresh," "nice and warm", always something agreeable.

pāṇī leā, ṭhaṇḍā ṭhāṇḍā leā,	bring water, bring it nice and cool.
ṭhaṇḍī ṭhaṇḍī wā wagdī e,	a nice, cool breeze is blowing.
sajrī sajrī malāī,	nice, fresh cream.
tatte tatte cauḷ,	nice, hot rice.
jhaw jhaw ā,	come (nice and) soon.

It will be noticed that in this connection it never has a bad meaning.

p. 74, last line. Instead of *pharāī dittī* we may have *phaṛā dittā* with the accent on the first syllable of *phaṛā*. This must be distinguished from *phaṛā dittā* with the accent on the second syllable which is the causal of *phaṛnā*, seize.

saṇḍhe phaṛā nehī̃ dittā (accent on *phaṛ*),	the buffalo did not allow itself to be caught.
os saṇḍhā phaṛā dittā (accent on *ṛā*),	he caused the buffalo to be caught.

The first *phaṛā* is a noun, meaning catching, the second a verb.

Locative Case, p. 78.

The use of the loc. to indicate instrument or means appears to be confined to those parts of the body which are found in pairs.

goḍī̃ arkī̃ riṛhdā sī peā,	he was crawling on knees and elbows.
akkhī̃ ḍiṭṭhā te kannī̃ suṇeā,	he saw with his eyes and heard with his ears.
hatthī̃ cukkeā,	he lifted it with his hands.

p. 82. *Horī* may also suggest the family a person serves, as *Jhaṇḍe horā dīā̃ pleṭā̃*, the plates of Jhanda's master. For *horī*, *horā*, some people say *warī*, *warā*.

Pronominal Suffixes, pp. 82–6.

To avoid confusion it should be remembered that, while these suffixes never indicate the nominative case, they do indicate the agent case, which Europeans often think of as the nominative. As the use of the suffixes is always found difficult it will be well to give the conjugation of the whole verb with the suffixes attached. Some parts do not usually take a suffix. but usage on this point is not invariable.

With Auxiliary Verb or Verb Substantive.

Examples :—

maĩ sajjaṇ ū̃ ?	I ask thee, am I a friend ?
maĩ sajjaṇ sū,	I am his friend.
tū̃ naṇān sū ?	art thou her sister-in-law ?
asī̃ jhalle ū̃,	I tell thee we are mad.

Present Tense.

Person.	*Possible suffixes.* SINGULAR.	*Possible suffixes.* PLURAL.
First ..	(*maĩ*) *ū̃*, *je*, *sū*, *ne*,	(*asī̃*) *ū̃*, *je*, *sū*, *ne*.
Second..	(*tū̃*) *sū*, *ne*,	(*tusī̃*) *sū*, *ne*.
Third ..	(*oh*) *ī* (or *ā*), *je*, *sū*, *ne*;	(*oh*) *nī̃*, *je*, *sū*, *ne*.

Emphatic :—

First .. *hai ū̃, je,*   *hai ū̃, je.*
Second.. none,   none.
Third .. *hai ī, je, sū, ne,*   *haiṇ nī, je, sū, ne.*

Past Tense.

First .. *(maĩ) sāje, sāsū, sāṇe,*   *(asĩ) sāje, sāsū, sāṇe.*
Second.. *tū̃, none,*   *tusĩ, none.*
Third .. *(oh) sāī, sāje, sāsū,*   *(oh) sāṇī, sāje, sāsū, sāṇe.*
       sāṇe,

WITH TRANSITIVE VERBS.

Suffixes with *dassṇā*, show.

Imperative.

tū̃ dass or *dassī sū, ne,*   *tusĩ dasso* or *dasseo sū, ne.*

Present Conditional, I may show, etc.

maĩ dassū̃, dassā̃ je, sū, ne,   *asĩ dassiye je, sū, ne* (not *ū̃*).
tū̃ dassē sū, ne,   *tusĩ dasso sū, ne.*
oh dassī, dasse je, sū, ne,   *oh dassan ī, je, sū, ne.*

Future, I shall show.

maĩ dassā̃-gā (fem. *-gī*) *je, sū, ne* : also *dassū̃-gā* (fem. *-gī*), *dassje-gā* (f. *-gī*).

tū̃ dassē-gā (f. *-gī*) *sū, ne.*

oh dasse-gā (f. *-gī*) *je, sū, ne* : *dassīgā, dassjegā, dassūgā, dassṇē-gā* (f. *-gī*).

asĩ dassāge je, su, ne (f. *-gīā̃*) : *dassūge, dassjege* (f. *-gīā̃*).

tusĩ dassoge sū, ne (f. *-gīā̃*).

oh dassange je, sū, ne (f. *-gīā̃*) : *dassṇīge, dassjege, dassūge, dass-ṇēge* (f. *-gīā̃*).

The future may also end in *-dā, -dī, -de, -dīā̃.*

Past Conditional, I should show, if I showed, etc.

Suffixes are used only with the *-o* forms: see Grammar, pp. 104–7.

    maĩ dass-do (f. *-dīo*) *ī, je, sū, ne.*
    tū̃ dass-dō (f. *-dīō*) *sū, ne.*
    oh dass-do (f. *-dīo*) *ī, je, sū, ne.*
    asĩ, none.
    tusĩ dass-deo (f. *-dīo*) *sū, ne.*
    oh dass-dēo (f. *-dīō*) *nī, je, sū, ne.*

Present Indicative, I am showing, I show.

maĩ dass-nā ū̃, dass-dā je, sū, ne : f. *-nī ū̃, -dī je, sū, ne.*
tū̃ dass-dā sū, ne : f. *-dī sū, ne.*
oh dass dā ī, je, sū, ne : f. *-dī ā, je, sū, ne.*

Imperfect.

maĩ dass-dā (f. *-dī*) *sāje, sāsū, sāne.*
tū̃ dassdā sāsū : f. *dassdī sāsū.*
oh dass-dā (f. *-dī*) *sāī, sāje, sāsū, sāne.*
asī dass-de (f. *-dīā*) *sāje, sāsū, sāne.*
tusī dass-de (f. *-dīā*) *sāsū, sāne.*
oh dass-de (f. *-dīā*) *sānī, sāje, sāsū, sāne.*

In the past indefinite, present perfect, pluperfect and future perfect of transitive verbs, tenses in which the passive participle is used, agreement is with the logical object (except, of course, where agreement is blocked by *nū̃*), and the use of pronom. suff. is generally confined to the 3rd sing. and plur. suffixes to indicate the agent. Occasionally the 2nd sing. and plur. suffixes are used when the logical nominative is *maĩ* or *asī* to express the idea "I am (or we are) speaking to thee" or "you."

Note.—To express the simple past with a suffix we must use the *-o* form or the pluperfect. The ordinary past if followed by a suffix, has the force of a present perfect.

Present Perfect.

The following cases therefore arise :—

maĩ ṭukkar khādhā ī (je),	I tell thee (you) that I have eaten my food.
maĩ roṭī khādhī ā (je),	I tell thee (you) I have eaten bread.
maĩ dō paraunṭhe khādhe nī (je),	. . . . two chapatis (masc.).
maĩ dō roṭīā khādhīā nī (je),	. . . . two chapatis (fem.).

Instead of *maĩ* we may have *asī*, we.

ṭukkar khādhā sū (ne),	he has (they have) eaten food.
roṭī khādhī sū (ne),	. . . . bread.
dō paunṭhe khādhe sū (ne),	. . . . two chapatis (masc.).
dō roṭīā khādhīā sū (ne),	. . . . two chapatis (fem.)

For the simple past use *-o* forms or pluperfect, *ṭukkar khādho sū (ne)*, he (they) ate food : *roṭī khādhīo sū (ne)*, he (they) ate bread.

Pluperfect (also means simple past).

The above sentences will become—

maĩ or *asā̃ khādhā sā̃* (*sāje*).	I etc. ate or had eaten.
maĩ or *asā̃ khādhī sā̃* (*sāje*),	do. do.
maĩ or *asā̃ khādhe sā̃ṇī* (*sāje*),	do. do.
maĩ or *asā̃ khādhīā̃ sā̃ṇī* (*sāje*),	do. do.
khādhā (fem. *khādhī*) *sāsū* or *sāṇe*,	he (they) ate or had eaten.
khādhe (f. *khādhīā̃*) *sāsū* or *sāṇe*,	do. do.

Future Perfect.

maĩ khādhā howīgā (*hojegā*),	I tell thee (you) that I shall have eaten.
maĩ khādhī howīgī (*hojegī*),	do. with fem. sing. object.
maĩ khādhe hoṇīge (*hojege*),	do with masc. plur. object.
maĩ khādhīā̃ hoṇīgīā̃ (*hojegīā̃*),	do. with fem. plur. object.

So also with *asā̃*, we.

khādhā hosūgā (*hoṇegā*),	he (they) will have eaten.
khādhī hosūgī (*hoṇegī*),	do. fem. sing. object.
khādhe hosūge (*hoṇēge*),	do. masc. plur. object.
khādhīā̃ hosūgīā̃ (*hoṇēgīā̃*),	do. fem. plur. object.

If the future in *-dā* is used the forms will be *howīdā*, *howīdī*, *hosūdā*, *hoṇēdīā̃*, etc., with *d* substituted for *g*.

The suffixes may also follow the verb as mentioned above.

Infinitive.

maĩ ṭukkar khāṇā ī (*je*),	I tell thee (you) I have to eat food,
maĩ roṭī khāṇī ā (*je*),	do. fem. sing. object,
maĩ khāṇe nī (*je*),	do. masc. plur. object,
maĩ khāṇīā̃ nī (*je*),	do. fem. plur. object,

and so on. The infinitive may be used all through the present, past and future exactly in the same way as *khādhā* except that *khāṇā*, *khāṇī*, *khāṇe*, *khāṇīā̃* occur instead of *khādhā*, *khādhī*, *khādhe*, *khādhīā̃*: thus—

asā̃ roṭīā̃ khāṇīā̃ sāje,	we tell you that we had to eat chapatis.
paraunṭhe khāṇe sāṇe,	they had to eat chapatis (masc. plur.)
maĩ caul khāṇe hoṇīge,	I tell thee I shall have to eat rice.
roṭīā̃ khāṇīā̃ hosūdīā̃,	he will have to eat chapatis.

WITH INTRANSITIVE VERBS.

The only difference is in the past tenses where with intransitive verbs the agent case is not used. It must be observed that even in intr. verbs the agent case is regularly found with the agent-infinitive, thus—

kikaṇ turnā sāsū ?	how was he to walk ?
roṭīā laike jāṇīā ne,	they have to take the chapatis and go.

Here we should have expected *jāṇā ne*, but the infin. is attracted into the form of the noun which is the object of *laike* : see Grammar. p. 98.

Present Perfect.

Examples :—

maĩ geā ū̃,	I tell thee I have gone.
maĩ geā sū ghar,	I have gone to his house.

We get the following forms (using *geā*, went)—

maĩ geā ū̃, je, sū, ne,	*asī̃ gae ū̃, je, sū, ne.*
tū̃ geā sū, ne,	*tusī̃ gae sū, ne.*
oh geā ī, je, sū, ne,	*oh gae nī, je, sū, ne.*

Fem. change *geā* to *geī* and *geā* to *geīā* otherwise exactly the same except that 3rd sing. is *geī ā*, not *geī ī*.

Simple past : use *-o* forms :—

jaṇā geo sū ghar,	the man went to his house.
janānī geīo sū ghar,	the woman went to his house.

Pluperfect (also means simple past).

maĩ geā (f. *geī*) *sāje, sāsū, sāṇe,*	*asī̃ gae* (f. *geīā*) *sāje, sāsū, sāne.*
tū̃ geā (f. *geī*) *sāsū, sāne,*	*tusī̃ gae* (f. *geīā*) *sāsū, sāne.*
oh geā (*geī*) *sāī, sāje, sāsū, sāṇe,*	*oh gae* (f. *geīā*) *sāṇī, sāje, sāsū, sāṇe.*

Future.

In addition to the following forms we may have *maĩ geā howā̃gā ī, oh geā howegā je*, etc., with the pronom. suffixes after the verb.

maĩ geā hoū̃gā, hojegā : fem. *geī hoū̃gī, hojegī*.
tū̃, none.
oh geā howīgā, hojegā, hosūgā, honegā : fem. *geī howīgī*, etc.
asī̃ gae hoū̃ge, hojege : fem. *geīā hoū̃gīā, hojegīā*.
tusī̃, none.
oh gae honīge hojege, hosūge, honege : fem. *geīā honīgīā*. etc.

Pronominal Suffixes in Negative Sentences.

With the negative nā: (for the interrogative *nā*, and *nehī nā* see lower down). The rule is the same as for affirmative sentences. *nā* comes before the verb as a rule, occasionally after the suffix, in which case it is strongly accented.

je nā mārdo sū,	if he had not struck him.
ḍitthā sū nā,	he has *not* seen him.
ākhī sū nā,	do *not* say it to him.

The second and third sentences, if *nā* is unaccented, will mean "he has seen him, hasn't he?" and "just say it to him, won't you?"

With the negative nehī. Two cases arise—

(1) Tenses not containing the past auxiliary *sā*, *saī*, *sī*, etc

(i) *First rule*. The suffix follows *nehī* (almost always).

nehī je bhanneā?	did you not break it?
nehī sū hikkaṇ lage,	they will not drive it out.

(ii) *Second rule*. The 2nd sing. suffix is always *ō*, no matter what it was in the affirmative sentence

labbhā ī? hast thou found it?	*labbhī ā?* (fem. object).
nehī ō labbhā (*labbhī*)?	hast thou not found it?
labbhe nī (fem. *labbhīā*)?	hast thou found them?
nehī ō labbhe (*labbhīā*)?	hast thou not found them?
maĩ dassnā ū,	I am telling thee.
maĩ nehī ō dassdā,	I will not tell thee.

(2) Tenses with past auxiliary.

Rule. The suffix is attached to *sā*. *sī*, etc. which become. as in affirmative sentences, *sāī*. *sāṇī*. *sāje*. *sāsū*, *sāṇe*. These words are preceded by *nehī*.

nehi sāī muṛnā?	wert thou not going to stop?

Unaccented interrogative nā.

Rule. The *nā* follows the suffix.

huṇe chāṅgṇā ī, nā?	you're going to prune now, aren't you?

Interrogative nehī nā.

Rule. The suffix generally comes between *nehī* and *nā*; *nehī ō nā ḍiggā?* I am asking thee, it has not fallen, has it? Cf. *nehī ē nā ḍiggā*, thou hast not fallen, hast thou?

p. 84 end of paragraph third. *Add* Exception: the 1st sing. or plur. agent with 2nd sing. or plur. pronominal suffix, is fairly common in the pluperfect and infin., and is sometimes heard in the past indef. and pres. perf. Examples have been given above pp. 146–7.

INFINITIVE.

p. 94, line 12 from foot. For second "nominative" read "infinitive."

p. 95, middle of p. The two lines beginning "In the past tense" should read thus:—The infinitive in agreement often expresses purpose. It may occur with any tense.

-o FORMS.

p. 106, middle of p. After the two lines beginning "Sometimes we find," add "This is common in the 3rd pers. of trans. and 2nd pers. of intrans. verbs."

Additional examples:

kyũ geõ (geĩõ, geo, geĩo) ? Why didst thou go (thou, f., you, m. pl., you, f. pl.) ?

But we hear also

bhrā geo ī ?	did thy brother go ?
kī kīto ī ?	what didst thou do?
gall eñ hoịo je,	I tell you, the matter happened thus.

COMPOUND VERBS, p. 110.

chaḍḍnā, as the second verb of a compound, is often pronounced *charṇā*, *sarnā* or *sharṇā*, but when it has its separate sense of "leave" it is always *chaḍḍṇā*.

ōs khēḷ gōḍ sarī e,	he has hoed the flower-bed.

Europeans employ intensive compound verbs to excess. The general rule is that they are uncommon in interrogative sentences and very rare in negative ones.

āeā e ? ā geā, aje nehī āeā,	has he come ? He has. He has not.
ḍāhṇ waḍḍhe nī ?	hast thou cut off the branches ?
nehī waḍḍhe,	I have not (cut them off).
waḍḍh chaṛe ne,	I have.

If the compound is used in an interrogative sentence it rather definitely implies completion or thoroughness. Thus we might have *ḍāhṇ waḍḍh sare nī* ? have you finished cutting off the branches ?

P. 126, omit the notes referring to pp. 52 and 62.

Agreement of Adjectives.

Panjabi frequently uses adjectives where we should have adverbs, as in phrases like "he plays well," "he writes well." The question of their agreement causes some difficulty. The rules are—

(i) Intrans. verbs with no object. The adjective agrees with the nominative.

oh caṅgī khēḍdī e,	she plays well.

(ii) Trans. verbs with no object. The adjective is masc. governed by the verb.

oh baṛā caṅgā likhdī e,	she writes very well.

(iii) Trans. verbs with an object or intrans. verbs with a cognate object. The adjective agrees with the object.

oh kāpī caṅgī likhdā e,	he does his copy well.
oh kirkaṭ caṅgā khēḍdī e,	she plays cricket well.

Uses of *calṇā*.

(i) Accompany:	*mēre nāl cal,*	accompany me.
(ii) Start ..	*cal, āeā ā,*	start off, I am coming
	cal pher,	start off then.
	kadō cale sao,	when did you start?

(iii) With roots of verbs to express "almost" or "about to," see Grammar, p. 67.

mukk caleā e,	it is almost finished.
mērā hatth lagg caleā sī,	my hand was just about to touch it.

(iv) In negative sentences to express ability, Grammar, p. 112.

mēre kolō nehī puṭṭeā caleā,	I shall not be able to dig it.

(v) Like the English go or work (intrans.), go on, do its work, perform its functions, etc.

kamm caldā e,	the work is going on (well).
mashīn caldī e (nehī caldī),	the machine is working (won't work).
dārū nehī caldī,	the powder or medicine is not working, i.e. is not efficacious.
rupayyā caldā e,	the rupee passes or circulates (i.e. is not bad).
ohdā mukadmā nehī lagā calaṇ,	his case will not go on, he has no case.
paṭākhe or goḷe nehī calde,	the fire-works (special kinds) will not go off.

(vi) *Cal*, *cal whai*, *calo*, or *calo jī* often means "that's all right now", "there that's settled", etc.

Uses of *paiṇā* (see also G. 120, M. 124, 125).

It expresses—

(1) The idea of actually doing a thing at the moment spoken of, G. 67, 68: *oh gōḍḍā e peā*, *oh peā gōḍḍā e* (never *gōḍḍā peā e*), he is hoeing.

(2) Indifference (with the pres. subj.): *peī uḍīke*, let her wait (I do not mind). (1) and (2) only with past part. *peā*.

(3) Beginning or suddenness: *bhaḵḵ paiṇā*, blaze up: *akk paiṇā*, get tired of: *ḍigg paiṇā*, fall: *phull paiṇā*, blossom: *miḷ paiṇā*, meet: *raḷ paiṇā*, join oneself to, and many more.

(4) Necessity, to have to, must, G. 67 *otthe aṭakṇā pawīdā*. you will have to wait there.

(5) Fall, in a wide sense of the word: *raḷā paiṇā*, be adulterated: *peī hoeā*, fallen, lying (of ground), fallow: *lammā paiṇā*, lie down: *suttā peā*, asleep: hence also with words for rain, drops of water, etc., dew, shadow, reflection (in water, etc.), night, darkness, cold, famine: also of blows, abuse, and of instrument with which blows are administered as stick, cane, shoe.

(6) Worry, annoy, attack: *mārn paiṇā*, *ṭuṭṭke paiṇā*, *hatthī paiṇā*, all mean rush at or attack: *kuttā paindā e*, the dog attacks: *magar* or *picche paiṇā*, follow annoyingly, not to cease following: *gaḷ paiṇā*, harass, etc.

It expresses mental or physical feelings or conditions.

(7) Mental feelings: words for habit as *hiḷtar gējh* or *ādat paiṇī*: *sauṛ* or *kāhḷ paiṇī*, be in a hurry: hence also with *sāṛā*, envy: *jhass* or *caskā*, taste: *rohb*, influence: of a person, *bhaiṛā paiṇā*, become ashamed: *sauṛā*, *kāhḷā p.*, impatient, etc.

(8) Physical conditions: with words like *chāllā*, blister: *bakhōṛ*, cramp: *trāṭ*, *waṭṭ*, *pīṛ*, all meaning pain or kinds of pain: *phollā*, *cittā*, white ulcer in eye: *pāṇī*, water (in eyes): *laūs*, *lās*, weal: *jhurrī*, wrinkle: *pāk*, pus (in wound, etc.): *khurk*, itch: of person, *pīḷā paiṇā*, become pale.

(9) Happen, occur, with words for love, friendship, discord, noise, disturbance, loss, also hole, hollow, indentation, turn.

(10) Happen, occur, become, and meanings difficult to classify: *waḷā paiṇā*, long way round: *pherā paiṇā*, have to pay visit: *phaḷ* or *phull paiṇe*, fruit or flowers be formed: *dalīlī*

paiṇā, argue, hesitate : ***bhann paiṇī***, become creased : ***piṛ palle nā paiṇā***, not understand : ***kurāhe paiṇā***, go astray : ***warhā paiṇā***, get respite for year : ***jādū paiṇā***, be bewitched : ***pete paiṇā***, be responsible for : ***wāh paiṇā***, have to do with : ***kamm paiṇā***, work turn up : ***tarīk paiṇī***, date be appointed : ***nazrī paiṇā***, become visible : ***pīngh paiṇī***, rainbow be formed : ***āgat paiṇā***, name be struck off list of debtors : ***kāṇõ paiṇī***, get warped : ***wagāṛ (phuṭṭ) paiṇā (-ī)***, discord, dispute occur : ***moche paiṇe***, short logs be cut up : ***wagyār paiṇī***, forced labour.

Past Participle in *-eā* or *-ā*.

Past participles end in *-eā* or *-ā*, and occasionally in both. It is not possible to give such rules as will enable students to decide in every case which form to use, but the following will perhaps be of some use. (The presence or absence of *h* makes no difference to the rules).

(1) Irregular past participles, whether transitive or intransitive, end in *-ā*, not *-eā* : ***traihṇā***, be startled, ***traṭṭhā*** : ***sihāṇṇā***, recognise, ***sihāttā*** (but note ***sihāṇeā*** in *-eā*, a regular past part.). See Grammar, pp. 47, 48.

Exceptions : ***marnā***, die, ***moeā*** : ***jāṇā***, go, ***geā***.

Slight vowel changes are not here considered irregularities.

(2) The following intransitive verbs whose roots end in a consonant have past parts. in *-ā* :—

bujjhṇā, be extinguished (but note the transitive ***bujjhṇā***, guess, solve, ***bujjheā***) : ***ḍiggṇā***, fall : ***ḍubbṇā***, sink : ***juttṇā***, be yoked, harnessed : ***labbhṇā***, be found (cf. below ***labbhṇa***, find) : ***laggṇā***, be applied, begin : ***pāṭṇā***, be torn : ***ṭuṭṭṇā***, break : ***bhajjṇā***, break (cf. below ***bhajjṇā***, run) : ***ḍhukkṇā***, draw near.

The following intrans. verbs have either *-ā* or *-eā* :—

bhajjṇā, run : ***bhijjṇā***, get wet : ***bajjhṇā***, be fastened : ***dhuccṇā***, be washed : ***gijjhṇā***, become accustomed : ***rijjhṇā***, be cooked : ***rujjhṇā***, be busy : ***wajjṇā***, strike : ***wijjhṇā***, be pierced : ***chuṭṭṇā***, escape : ***khubbhṇā***, stick (in mud, etc.) : ***gijjhṇā*** and ***rujjhṇā*** have also irreg. past parts. which of course end in *-ā*, ***giddhā***, ***ruddhā*** : with ***bhijjṇā*** *-eā* is rare.

(3) All regular verbs with roots ending in a vowel, and all regular transitive verbs (whether the roots end in a vowel or not) have past parts. in *-eā*, not *-ā* : ***khṛāṇā***, lose, ***khṛāeā*** : ***dhrūhṇā***, drag, ***dhrūheā***.

Exceptions : ***cubbhṇā***, pierce, ***cubbhā***, and ***cubbheā*** : ***labbhṇā***, find, ***labbhā*** and ***labbheā***.

Verbal Roots ending in *g*, *kh*.

Confusion is sometimes caused by the change of *g* into *g*, and *kh* into *k͟h*. The following general rules will be a guide:—

(1) Verbs with roots ending in a single *g* or *kh* change *g* to *g* and *kh* to *k͟h* in the simple imperative sing. (not in the -ī form), and when *d*, *k* and *n* (but not *ṇ*) follow: thus—

wēkhṇā, *wēkhaṇ*, *wekhãgā*, *wekheā*. but *wēk͟h*, *wēk͟hdā*, *wek͟hke*, *wek͟hnā*.

wagṇā, *wagaṇ*, *wagegā*, *wagī*, but *wag jā*, *wagdā*, *wagke*, *wagnā*.

So also *ākhṇā*, say.

Some people use *g* throughout in *wagṇā*: others say *wagke*, not *wagke*.

(2) Verbs with double *g* or *kkh* tend to keep *gg* or *kkh* throughout: so *ḍiggṇā*, fall; *rakkhṇā*, place; *sikkhṇā*, learn. It is, however, not uncommon to say *rak͟hdā*, *rak͟h*, *sik͟hdā*. *laggṇā*, begin, generally has past part. *lagā*. *lik͟hṇā*, write, *bhak͟hṇā*, blaze, do not come under either rule. They have *k͟h* in every part.

(3) The causal forms have *g* and *k͟h*: *wak͟hāṇā*, show; *ak͟hwāṇā*, be called, cause to be said; *sik͟hāṇā*, teach; *rak͟hāṇā*, have placed; *wagāṇā*, cause to flow.

Exception: *ḍēgṇā*, make fall.

The causal of *laggṇā* drops the *g* altogether, *lāṇā*, attach.

These rules are not strictly adhered to.

Formation of Causal Verbs: G. pp. 41–43.

Some difficulties are removed if one observes the following vowel changes which frequently occur in forming causal or transitive verbs. A double consonant becomes single.

a and *ai* become *ā*: *balṇā*, burn, *bālṇā*: *traihṇā*, be startled, *trāhṇā*: so also *saṛnā*, be burnt, *caṛhnā*, ascend; *marnā*, die; *waṛnā*, enter; *ḍhalṇā*, be poured in mould; *uddhalṇā*, elope; *ubbalṇā*, boil; *paiṇā*, fall; *ḍhaiṇā*, fall; *laihṇā*, descend; *gaihṇā*, be threshed; *ḍaihṇā*, be placed (bed. etc.).

a in second unaccented syllable of root sometimes becomes *ē*: *ukhaṛnā*, be loosened, *ukhēṛnā*; so also *nikkhaṛnā*, be separated, *nikhēṛnā*; *uggharnā*, open (eyes, etc.), *ughēṛnā*; *uddhaṛnā*, be ripped, *udhēṛnā*: *nibbaṛnā*, be settled, *nabēṛnā*: the double consonant of course becomes single.

i becomes *ē*: *riṛknā*, roll, *rēṛhnā*: so also *chiṛnā*, go to pasture; *giṛnā*, be turned (wheel, etc.); *ḍiggṇā*, fall, *ḍegṇā*: note too *wikṇā*, be sold, *wĕcṇā*.

u becomes *o*: *ghuḷṇā*, melt, *ghōḷṇā*: so also *ḍubbṇā*, sink, *ḍōbṇā*; *muṛnā*, turn: *ruṛhnā*, flow away; *cubbhṇā*. pierce; *khubbhṇā*, sink (in mud, etc.): *juṛnā*, be joined; *khurnā*, melt; note also with change of consonant, *tuṭṭṇā*, break. *tōṛnā*, *trōṛnā*; *ḍhukkṇā*, draw near, *ḍhoṇā*; *khussṇā*, be seized, *khohṇā*; *dhuccṇā* or *dhuppṇā*, be washed, *dhōṇā*; *juppṇā*, be yoked, *joṇā* (sometimes *juttṇā*, be yoked, *jōtṇā*).

A FEW HINTS.

(i) Translate ideas not words. See Manual, p. vi. where this is insisted upon. In parts II and III of the Manual the translation is free, not literal. This is deliberate. We should note the necessity of avoiding the literal translation of epigrammatic phrases such as "Look up, not in"; "if you're right with God you will not be wrong with man." As an illustration we may take the word "personal.". The coined word *shakhsī* means "possessing the attributes of personality": hence *mērā shakhsī Najāt-dēṇwālā* means a personal Saviour as opposed to an impersonal one, it does not suggest one personal to me. Again *shakhsī kamm* is devoid of meaning, for work cannot possess personality. In all these expressions the best rule is: Express the idea in other and simpler English words and then translate the explanation. Thus one would explain "personal work" as if one were talking to an educated non-Christian who did not understand the use of the word "personal," and then translate.

(ii) It is always wrong to omit the words for am, is, are, etc., except in negative sentences. The error is very common with Europeans, who constantly say *muṇḍā kitthe?* for *kitthe we* (where is the boy?): *oh kī ākhdā* for *kī ākhdā e*, (what is he saying?): *kihdīā citthīā* for *kihdīā citthīā ne* (whose letters are they?): *māshkī teār* for *teār e* (is the water-carrier ready?).

(iii) In English we use "do" to avoid some other verb already used. Thus: put them away. I have done so. In Panjabi this can never be *maĩ kītā e*. The two sentences would be *ohnā nū̃ sāhmke rakkh*. *maĩ rakkh chaḍḍe ne*. The same verb must be used again In this case it is *rakkhṇā*.

(iv) Similarly we are fond of an unnecessary "like that." We say:—don't cry like that: don't shout like that. If we translate by *es tarhā̃* it means: do not cry or shout in that particular way, do it in some other way. The words should simply be omitted.

(v) We are addicted to a great use of possessive pronouns. We say: "we read in our Bibles." In parts of the British Isles people say "he's having his tea," "I'm going to my bed." All these must be omitted.

Baibal wicc likheā hoeā e, we read in our Bibles.
maĩ saun caleā wā, I am going to (my) bed.

(v) The future is not much used in negative sentences. The following will show the common usage.

maĩ bawhā̃dā, I shall sit down: *maĩ nehī baihndā* or *nehī baihṇ lagā*, I will not sit down.

Yet sometimes we do hear the future with the negative, especially in promises, as—

adā̃ agge maĩ nehī karā̃ karā̃dā, in future I will not do so.

(vi) Interrogative words: the position of interrogative words should be noted.

The nominative of the sentence must never come between the interrogative word and the verb. Europeans accustomed to the English order "where are you going?", "what have you done?" are apt to say *kitthe tā̃ calea ẽ, kī tā̃ kītā e*. This is quite wrong. The following show the order:—

oh kāhde jogā kūndā e? why is he speaking?
bhrā kadõ āwīdā? when will your brother come?

Sometimes conversationally the nominative is brought to the end as: *kūndā kāhde jogā e oh, kadõ āwīdā bhrā*, but this does not violate the rule given above.

(vii) Excessive use of Compound Verbs: see p. 150.

APPENDIX II.

ADDITIONS TO VOCABULARY.

absolutely, add ***ukkā mukkā***: *see* altogether, thoroughly.

adulterate, add ***khōṭ pāṇā*** (*wicc*): *see* mix.

allow, add *see* permit, liberty.

angry, ***lūsṇā*** suggests inward, not outward anger.

anklet, add ***bā̃k*** f., ***lacchā***, m., ***sā̃ṭ***, f., ***saglā***, m.

annul, *see* cancel, abolish, repeal.

apologise, add ***koḷō*** of person a.-ed to, and ***dā*** of thing a.-ed for.

appease, add ***ṭhaṇḍā-k.***: a.-hunger. ***lāhṇī***, int. ***laihṇī***: *see* satisfy: quench thirst, *see* slake.

arm, of chair, ***bā̃h***, f.: of coat, ***bā̃h***, f: *see* next word.

armlet, ***ṭāḍḍ***, f., ***ṭaḍḍ***, f.

back (1), (lying) on back, ***utāṇā***: (carry) on shoulders or high up on b., ***kandhāṛe***, ***dhangāṛe***: lower down, also pick-aback, ***magar picche***.

bracelet, add ***kaṛā***, m.: *see* armlet in A.

bride, add ***wauhṭī***. wife.

butterfly, add ***titrī***. ***tittrī***, f.

buttermilk, milk and water, ***kaccī lassī***: boiled and curdled, ***pakkī lassī***.

cajole, *see* coax, wheedle.

cantankerous, *see* irritable.

card(1), ***piññā*** is softening before spinning, ***jhambṇā*** softening before seeding: to seed cotton is ***wēlṇā***.

cargo, ***māl asbāb***, m., ***asbāb***, m.

carniverous, ***māskhōr***, ***mās*** or ***gōsht khānwāḷā***.

cash, v., add ***tṛōṛnā***. ***bhannṇā***.

cataract in eye, add ***motīābind***, m.

catch, ***phaṛā dēṇā***, *see* explanation on pp. 143-4.

chaff, fr. rice, ***parāḷī***, f.

chain, on door, ***kuṇḍī***, f.

(1) **chink**, opening, split, ***trēṛ***, f.

(2) **chink**, sound, *see* tinkle.

compensation, *see* damage A.

cook (2), ***rōṭī lāṇī*** (int. ***laggṇī***), means to slap the "*chupattee*" on to side of oven.

cud, chew, *see* ruminate A.

cut teeth, ***dandīā kaḍḍhṇīā*** (int. ***nikḷṇīā***), of children; but back teeth, ***hanū*** (***kaḍḍhṇīā***, ***nikḷṇīā***): animals, ***dand*** (***kaḍḍhṇe***, ***nikḷṇe***).

damage, legal, ***harjā***, m., ***harj***, m.: damages, ***harjānnā***, m.: ordinary compensation, ***iwzānnā***, m.

dark, *see* Errata.

dentist, ***dand banāṇwāḷā***.

dismiss, add ***chuṭṭī dēṇī*** (***nū̃***), discharge, also give leave: ***makūf-k.***, dismiss.

disqualify, add ***nā̃wā lāhṇā*** (***dā***, int., ***laihṇā***).

divine, *Rabb dā*, *Khudā dā*, *Parmeshwar dā*, etc., *see* God: also *ilāhī* (U.).
divinity, godhead, *khudāī*, f.: *see* theology A.

feed, dogs, cats, etc., *ṭukkar pāṇā* (*nū*): cattle, *paṭṭhe pāṇe*, *ghāh pāṇā*, *gutāwā pāṇā* (all *nū*): horses, *ghāh pāṇā*, *nihārī dēṇī* (both *nū*).
fellow, *see* pair.
fever, *see* also quartan, tertian
fire (2), *see* shoot.
forget, add *menū ohdā thauh nehī rehā*, I forgot it.
free, adj., add *marzī dā mālak*.

gallop, v. tr., *poīā* or *sarpaṭṭ ṭōrnā*: *cakhuṛīā* or *caukhuṛīā saṭiṇā* (*nū*).

hereabouts, *etthe jaie*: thereabouts, *otthe jaie*: whereabouts (inter.), *kitthe jaie*, (rel.) *jitthe jaie*: (*jaie* for *jaihe* fr. *jehā*).

immoral, *see* blackguard.
inborn, add from birth, *jamāhndrū*: deaf from birth, *jamāhndrū ḍōrā*.

lie down, for woman use *leṭṇā*, not *lammā paiṇā*: lying down, *leṭī hoī e*.
luckily, *abihāre*.

permanent (resident, servant, service, work), *naṭhāhū*, *nāṭhehū*.
pip, of orange, apple, etc., *see* stone.
place (2), *ḍaihṇā* not used for water.
purgative, take effect, *laggṇā*.

reddish, *see* somewhat.
reliable, add *atbār wāḷā*.
renounce, add *hakk chaḍḍṇā* (*dā*, *apṇā*).
ruminate, chew cud, *ugāḷī karnī*: see meditate, think.

safe, add *rāzī bāzī*.
serv-ant, -ice, *see* permanent A.
sharpen, pencil, *ghaṛnā*.
snare, add *phāhī*, f.
stars; Bear, the Great, *palhang pīhṛā*, m.
Canopus, *agath*, m.
Orion's Belt, *trangaṛ*, m.
Pleiades, *khittīā*, f. pl.
Procyon and Sirius, *lohnde*, m. pl.
Pole Star, *kutub tārā*, m.
Venus (evening star), *shām dā tārā*, m.: (morning star), *waihṛ tārā*, m.

tainted, be, of meat, add *humh jāṇā*.
theology, *Khudā* or *dīn dā ilm*, *fikā*, m. (U.): *see* divinity in A, God
thereabouts, *see* hereabouts A.
threshing-floor, add *khalāṛā*, m.

whereabouts, *see* hereabouts A.
white and black, piebald, *ḍabbā*, *ḍabb khṛabbā*: small spots, lines, *tetrā metrā*.
work, *see* permanent A.

Weights and Measures.

Measures of Length.

inch, *incī*, f.
about 3 inches, *cappā*, m. (hand-breadth).
about 8 inches, *giṭṭh*, f. (span).

Cloth.

2¼ inches one *girhā*, f.
16 *girha's* one yard.

Distance.

12 inches one *fut*, *fit*, m. (foot).
3 feet one *gaz*, m. (yard).
220 yards one *farlāng*. m. (furlong).
8 furlongs one *mīl*, m. (mile):
1¼ miles one *koh*, m. (*kuhāṭrā*. m., approximately, or less than, a *koh*).

Land Measure.

5½ feet one *karū*, m.
22 feet one *jarīb*, f. (chain).

Square Measure (*land*).

one sq. *karū* is one *sarsāhī*, f.
9 sarsahi's one *marlā*, m.
20 marla's one *kanāl*, f.
4 kanals one *wighā*, m. (half acre).
8 kanals one *ghumā*, m. (acre) or *killā*. a killa is 40 karu's long by 36 broad.
25 acres one *murabbā*, m.

Weight (*precious metals or stones*).

1/240 oz. (nearly) one *rattī*, f.
8 ratti's one *māssā*, m.
12 massas one *tolā*, m.
5 tolas one *chaṭākī*.
16 chataki's or 80 tolas one *sēr*, m. (2 lbs. 0·914 oz.).

Food and general.

about 2 oz. one *chaṭākī*, f.
16 chatakis one *sēr* as above).
2 chatakis *addh pā*.
4 chatakis one *pā*, m. (quarter ser): 8 chatakis *addh sēr*.
6, 10, 12, 14 chatakis *ḍeḍh* or *ḍūḍh*, *ḍhāī*. *trai*. *sāḍhe trai pā*.
40 ser one *maṇ*, m. (maund).

Grain, etc., actually measured by toppas (*see below*).

20 ser one *maṇ*, m.
3 man one *paṇḍ*, f.
4 pands one *māṇī*, f. (12 *maṇ* of grain),
also the following:—

Capacity (*chiefly grain, etc.*).

4 cuha's one *paṛōppī*, f. (*cuhā*, m.: accent on second syllable).
2 paroppis one *ṭōppā*.
2 toppas one *daṛōppā*, m.
The weight of a toppa of grain varies from village to village. A 1¼ ser toppa is called *suāeā ṭōppā* (from *sawā sēr*): a 1½ ser toppa is *ḍeḍh serā ṭōppā*: a 1¾ ser toppa is *sat pāeā ṭōppā*: a 1⅞ ser toppa is *sāṛhsatpāeā ṭōppā* (from *sāḍhe satt pā*), while a 2 ser toppa is called *dusērā ṭōppā*.